FIRE FORCE

ATSUSHI
OHKUBO

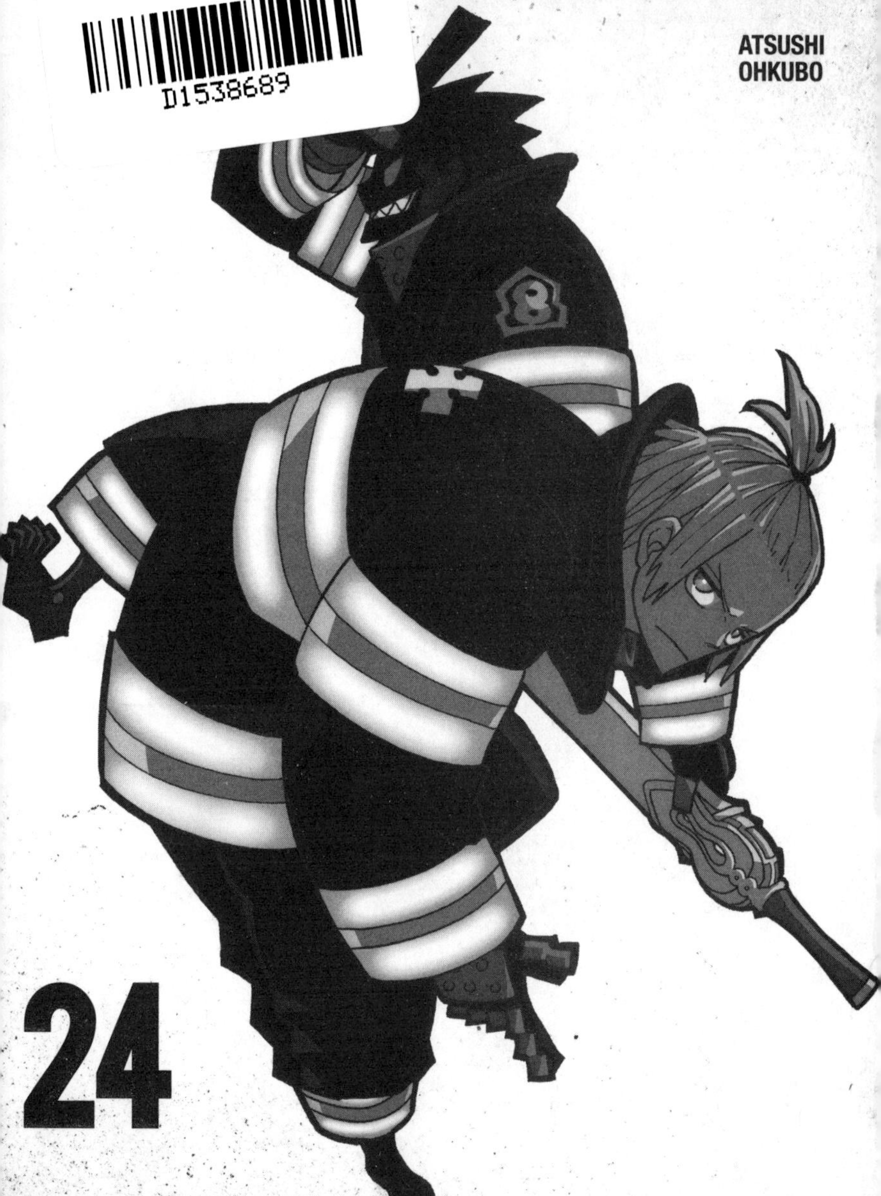

24

the disaster

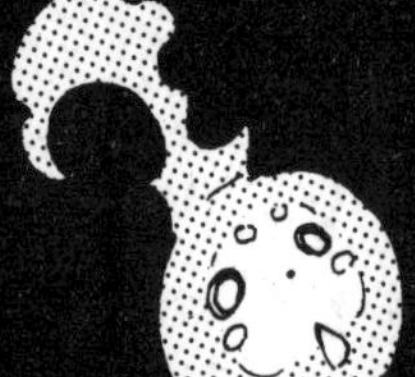

VOL. 24

ATSUSHI OHKUBO

Prepare for great

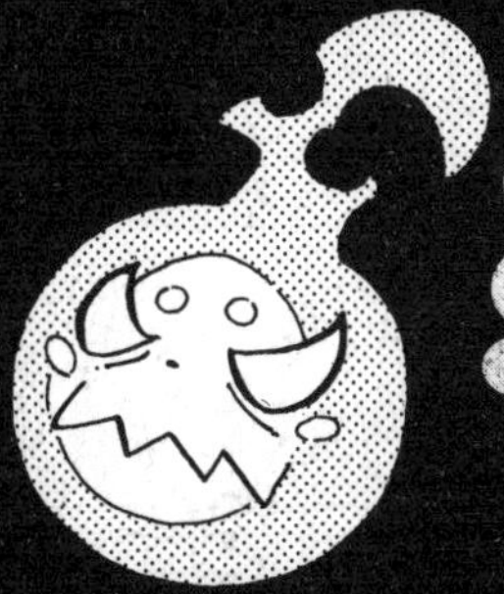

FIRE FORCE

FIRE FORCE: SPECIAL FIRE FORCE ROSTER OF FIRE SOLDIERS

SPECIAL FIRE FORCE COMPANY 8

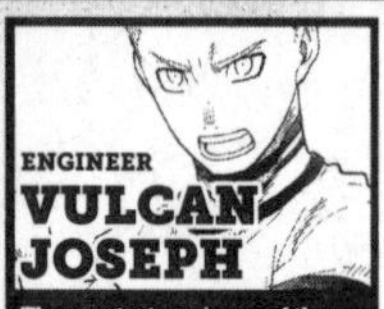

ENGINEER
VULCAN JOSEPH

The greatest engineer of the day, renowned as the God of Fire and the Forge. Has promised to reforge Excalibur for Arthur.

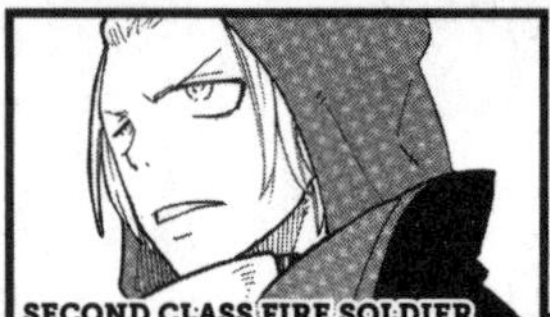

SECOND CLASS FIRE SOLDIER (THIRD GENERATION PYROKINETIC)
ARTHUR BOYLE

Trained at the academy with Shinra. He follows his own personal code of chivalry as the self-proclaimed Knight King. He's a blockhead who is bad at mental exercise. He's a weirdo who grows stronger the more delusional he gets. When he becomes depressed over the loss of Excalibur in Fuchū, Vulcan invites him on a quest to find orichalcum!

WATCHES OUT FOR

TRUSTS

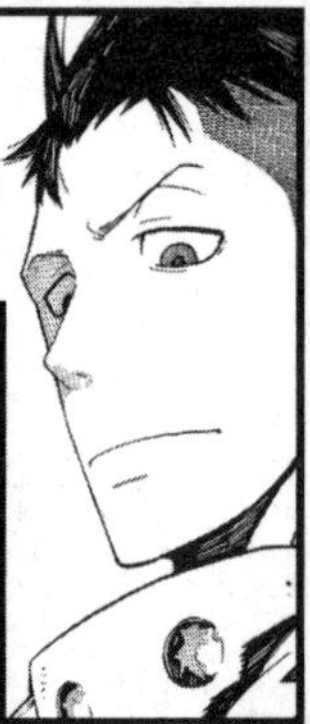

CAPTAIN (NON-POWERED)
AKITARU ŌBI

The caring leader of the newly established Company 8. Has no powers, but uses his finely honed muscles as a weapon in a battle style that makes him worthy of the Captain title. He is taking action to prepare for the Great Cataclysm that is to come.

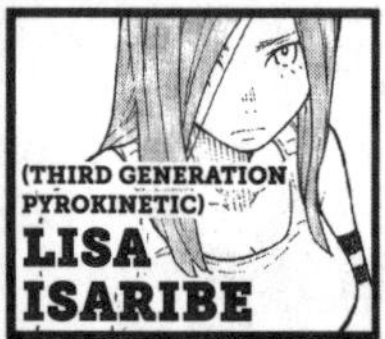

(THIRD GENERATION PYROKINETIC)
LISA ISARIBE

Formerly a spy sent by Dr. Giovanni, she is now a member of Company 8. She controls tentacles of flame.

IDIOT!!

WATCHES OUT FOR

TRUSTS

STRONG BOND

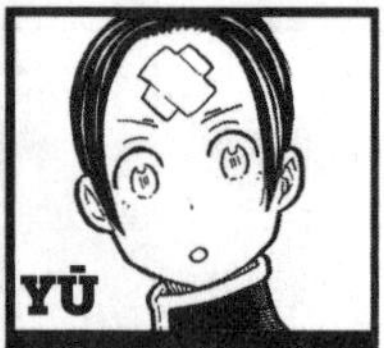

YŪ

A self-proclaimed apprentice of Vulcan's. Has now recovered from the injuries inflicted by Dr. Giovanni.

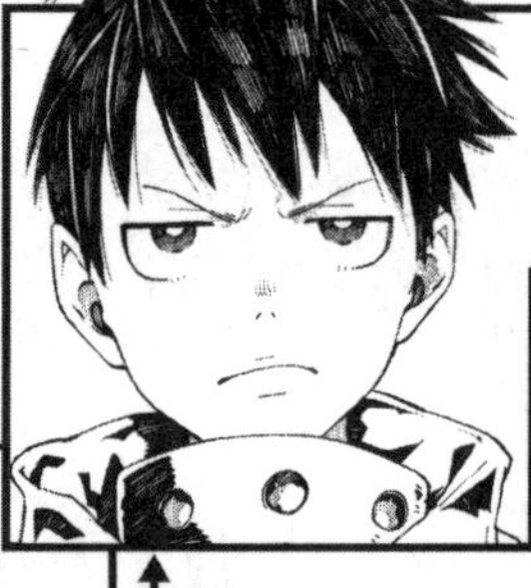

SECOND CLASS FIRE SOLDIER (THIRD GENERATION PYROKINETIC)
SHINRA KUSAKABE

Dreams of becoming a hero who saves people from spontaneous combustion! His weapon is a fiery kick. He wields a special flame called the Adolla Burst. In Fuchū, he fights an intense battle against Burns to save Captain Ōbi. What he sees at its end is...

A NICE GIRL

LOOKS AWESOME ON THE JOB

A TOUGH BUT WEIRD LADY

HANG IN THERE, ROOKIE!

TERRIFIED

STRICT DISCIPLINARIAN

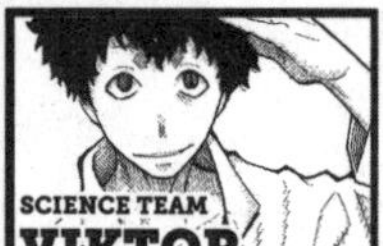

SCIENCE TEAM
VIKTOR LICHT

A genius deployed to Company 8 from Haijima Industries. Has confessed to being a Haijima spy.

HAS HIM ON HER MIND

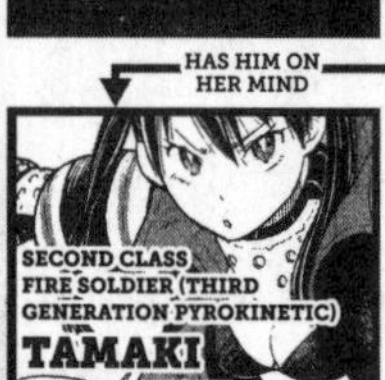

SECOND CLASS FIRE SOLDIER (THIRD GENERATION PYROKINETIC)
TAMAKI KOTATSU

A rookie from Company 1 currently in Company 8's care. She controls nekomata-like flames.

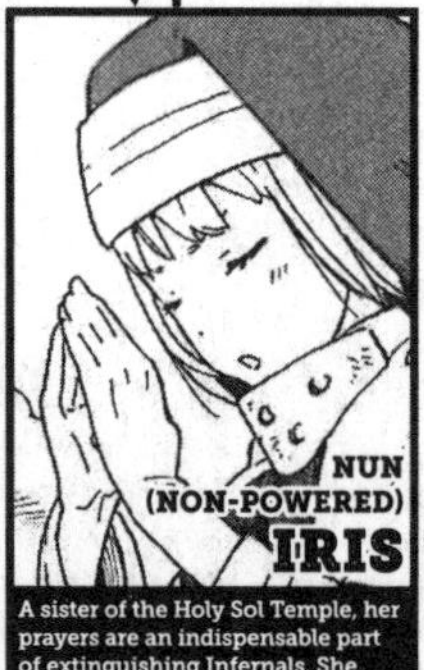

NUN (NON-POWERED)
IRIS

A sister of the Holy Sol Temple, her prayers are an indispensable part of extinguishing Infernals. She demonstrated incredible resilience in facing the Infernal hordes.

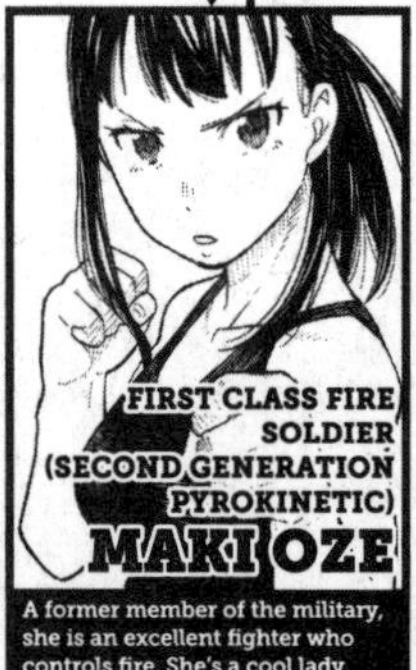

FIRST CLASS FIRE SOLDIER (SECOND GENERATION PYROKINETIC)
MAKI OZE

A former member of the military, she is an excellent fighter who controls fire. She's a cool lady, but is mad about love stories, and her beauty is overshadowed by her "head full of flowers and wedding bells."

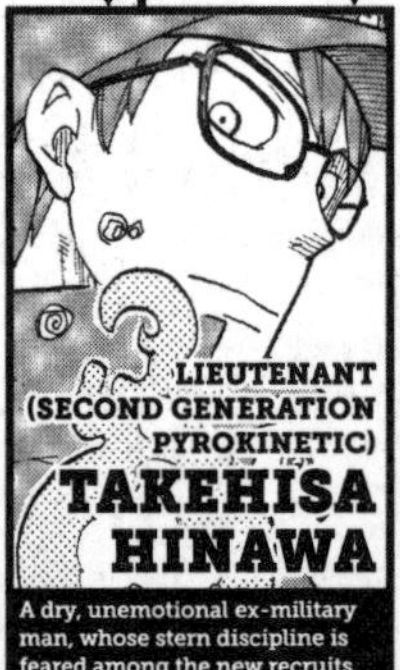

LIEUTENANT (SECOND GENERATION PYROKINETIC)
TAKEHISA HINAWA

A dry, unemotional ex-military man, whose stern discipline is feared among the new recruits. The gun he uses is a cherished memento from his friend who became an Infernal.

THE GIRLS' CLUB

RESPECTS

HOLY SOL TEMPLE + "EVANGELIST"

AFTER 250 YEARS, ANOTHER GREAT CATACLYSM IS AT HAND!

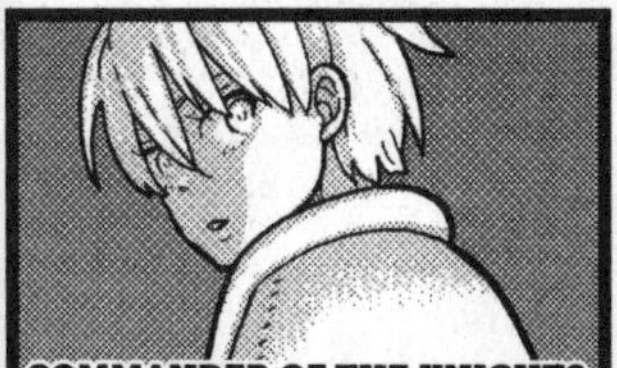

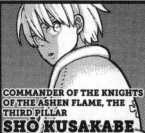

COMMANDER OF THE KNIGHTS OF THE ASHEN FLAME, THE THIRD PILLAR

SHŌ KUSAKABE

Shinra's long-lost brother, and the commander of an order of knights that works for the Evangelist. Has the power to stop time for everything and everyone around him. Though under Haumea's control, does he feel his brother's warmth through an Adolla Link?

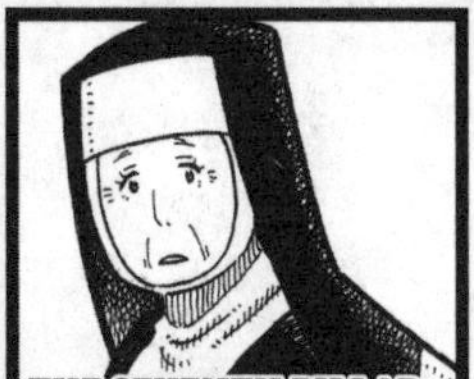

THE SEVENTH PILLAR

SISTER SŪMIRE

Had been performing human experiments on children like Hibana at St. Raffles Convent. She uses a power called Shivering, in which she makes all the muscles in her body vibrate to produce heat.

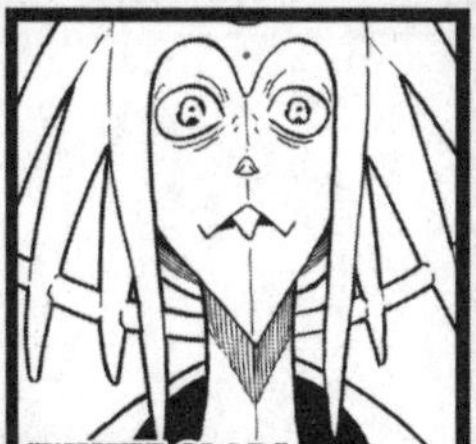

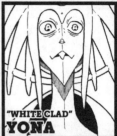

"WHITE CLAD"

YONA

An inhuman-looking member of the "White Clad" cult. Has the power to reconstruct the appearances of others.

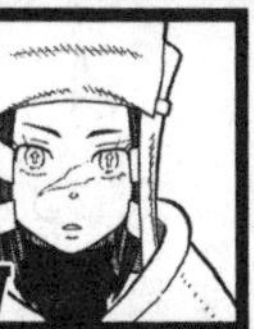

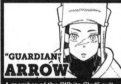

"GUARDIAN"

ARROW

A member of the "White Clad" cult, and Shō's Guardian. Has the power to attack with arrows made of flame.

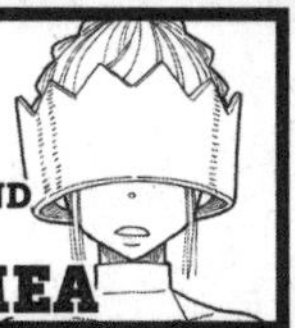

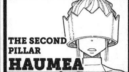

THE SECOND PILLAR

HAUMEA

A member of the "White Clad" cult. Has the power to control others through mind-jacking. Also has a sharp tongue.

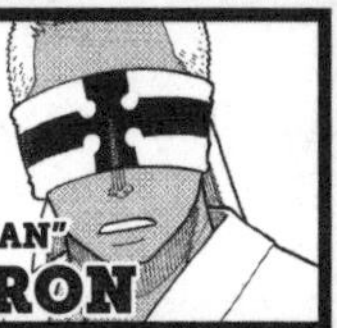

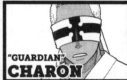

"GUARDIAN"

CHARON

A member of the "White Clad" cult. A talkative man who specializes in barraging people with questions. He boasts explosive offensive power and overwhelming endurance.

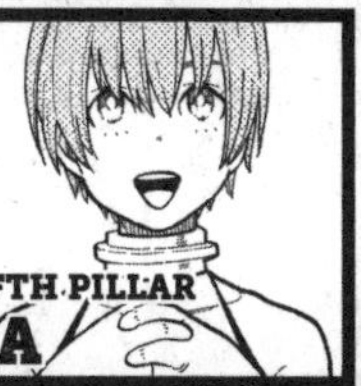

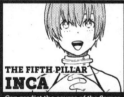

THE FIFTH PILLAR

INCA

Can predict the course of the flames. She joined the Evangelist out of her hatred of boredom.

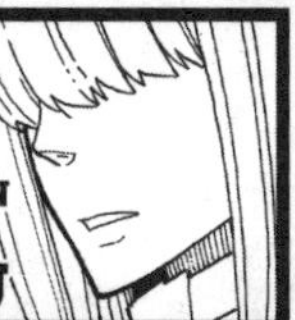

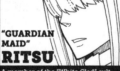

"GUARDIAN MAID"

RITSU

A member of the "White Clad" cult, and Inca's Guardian Maid. Has the power to control corpses and create the Great Fiery Infernal.

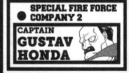

SPECIAL FIRE FORCE COMPANY 2

CAPTAIN

GUSTAV HONDA

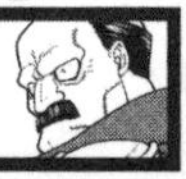

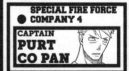

SPECIAL FIRE FORCE COMPANY 4

CAPTAIN

PURT CO PAN

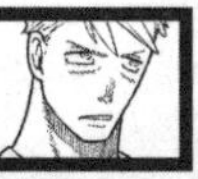

SUMMARY

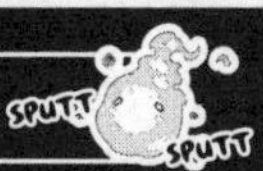
SPUTT
SPUTT

With the help of Moonlite Mask (actually Company 7's Captain Shinmon), Company 8 narrowly escaped the Fuchū Penitentiary. Although they have been branded as traitors to the Empire, some fellow fire soldiers still believe in Company 8, and take their return as a cue to jump into action themselves. Company 5's Captain Hibana goes to the ruins of the convent where she grew up, and learns that Sister Sumire was doing experiments on children to find Pillars for the next Great Cataclysm. Meanwhile, in an attempt to raise Arthur's spirits after the loss of Excalibur, Vulcan comes to him with a quest to find orichalcum, the material needed to make the holy sword. They go to the Nether, where they find pre-Cataclysm technology, and obtain a space rocket fairing... Is the holy sword's return at hand?!

FIRE FORCE 24

CONTENTS

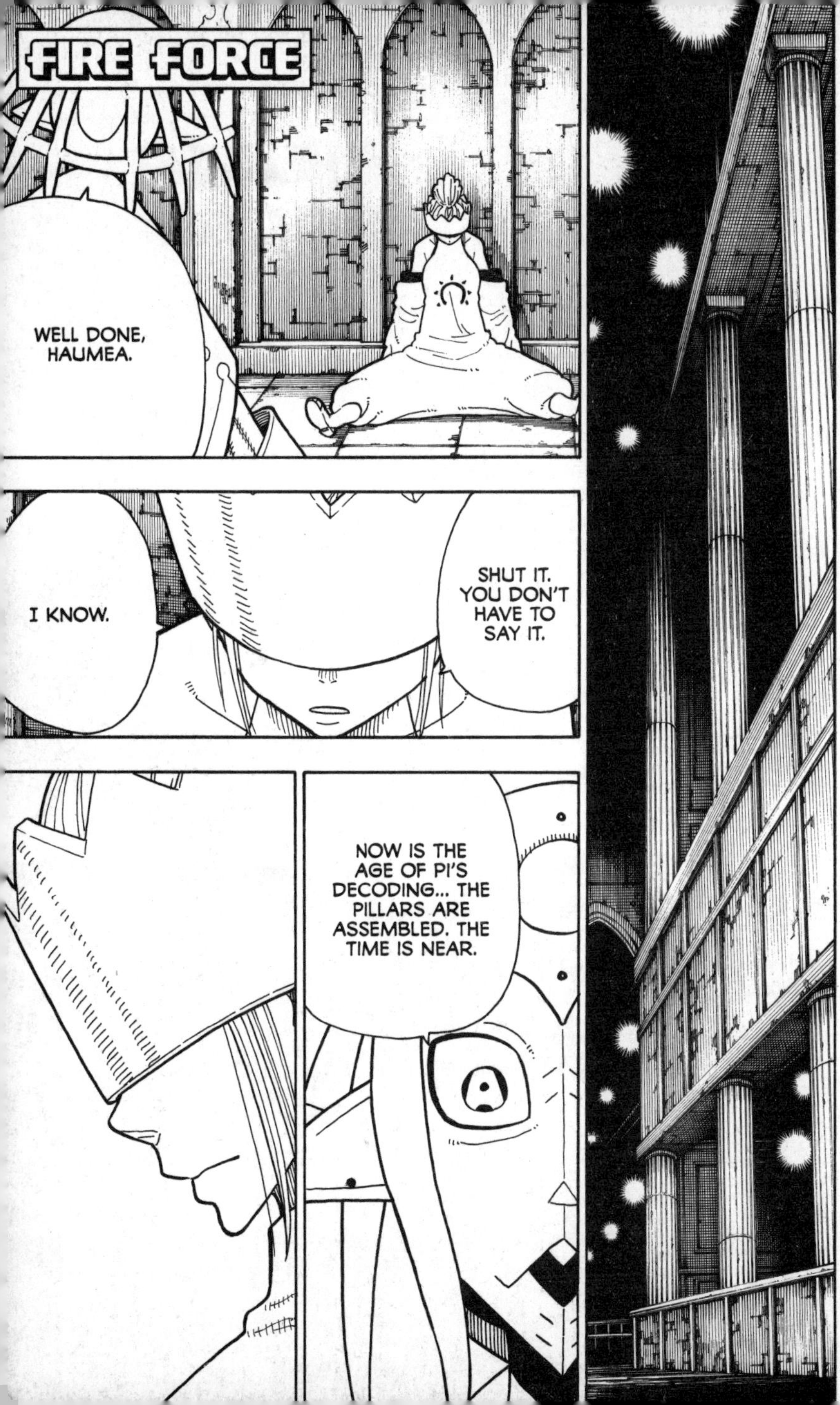
FIRE FORCE
WELL DONE, HAUMEA.
SHUT IT. YOU DON'T HAVE TO SAY IT.
I KNOW.
NOW IS THE AGE OF PI'S DECODING... THE PILLARS ARE ASSEMBLED. THE TIME IS NEAR.

"THE GREAT CATACLYSM"

THE HOLY SWORD REBORN

CHAPTER CCV:

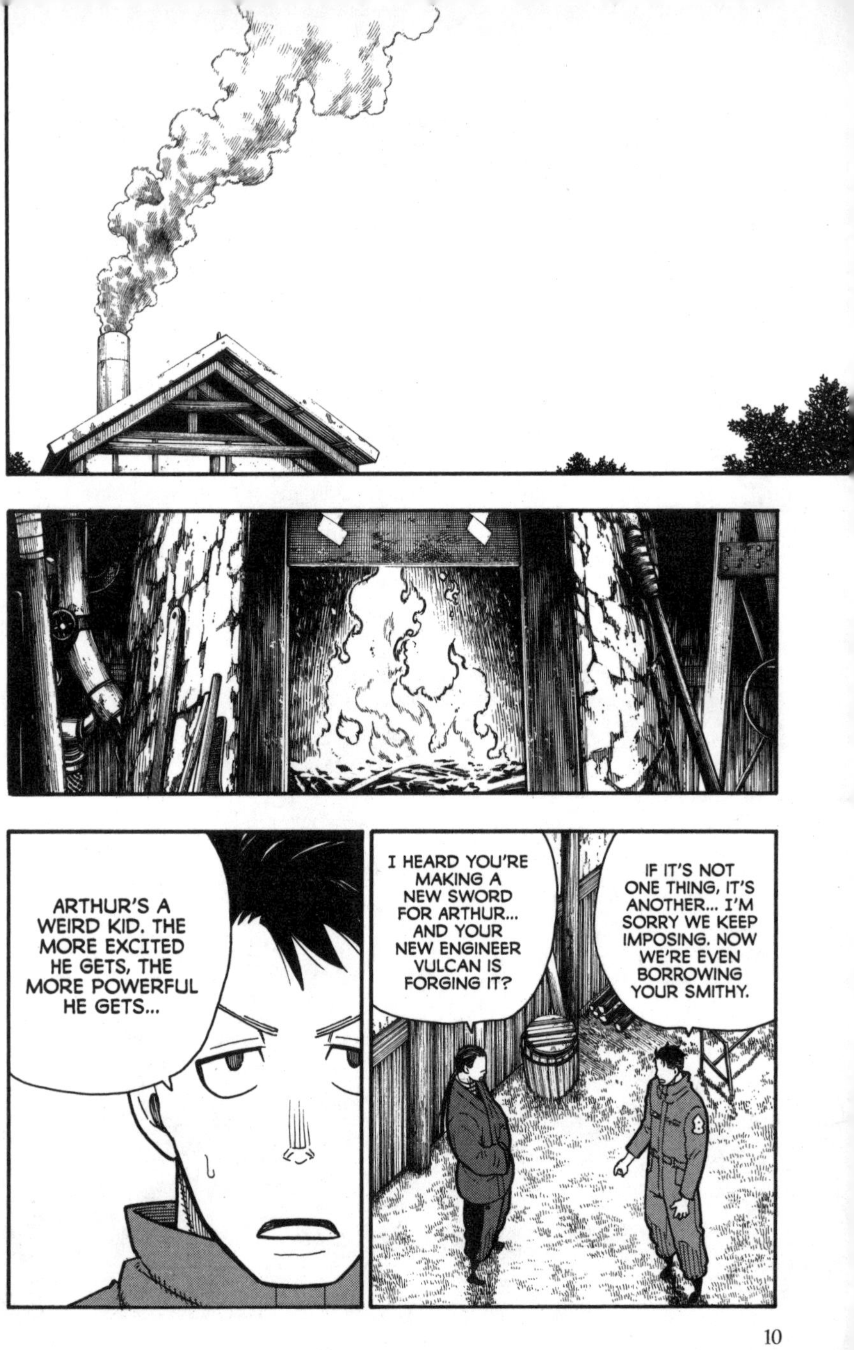
IF IT'S NOT ONE THING, IT'S ANOTHER... I'M SORRY WE KEEP IMPOSING. NOW WE'RE EVEN BORROWING YOUR SMITHY.
I HEARD YOU'RE MAKING A NEW SWORD FOR ARTHUR... AND YOUR NEW ENGINEER VULCAN IS FORGING IT?
ARTHUR'S A WEIRD KID. THE MORE EXCITED HE GETS, THE MORE POWERFUL HE GETS...

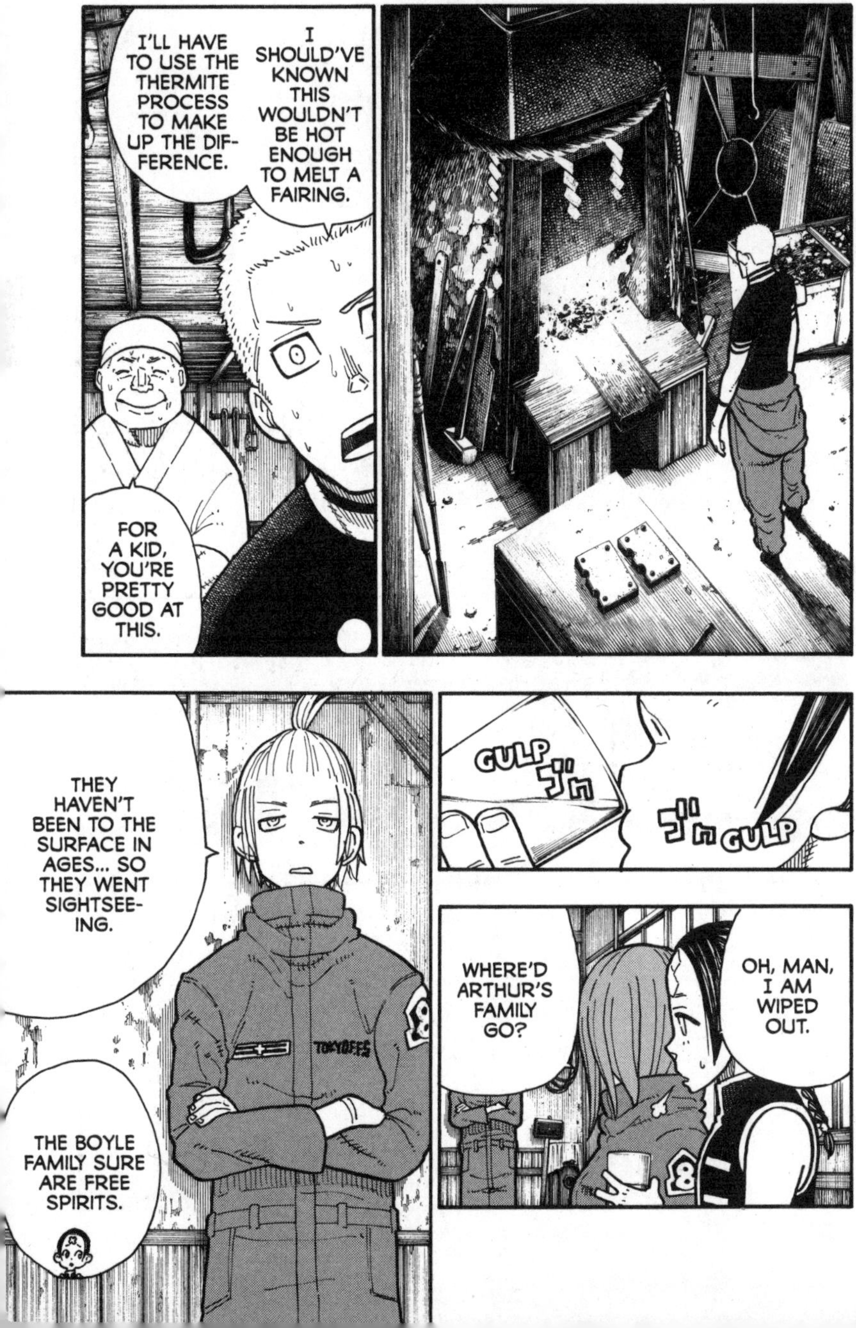
I SHOULD'VE KNOWN THIS WOULDN'T BE HOT ENOUGH TO MELT A FAIRING.
I'LL HAVE TO USE THE THERMITE PROCESS TO MAKE UP THE DIF-FERENCE.
FOR A KID, YOU'RE PRETTY GOOD AT THIS.
GULP
GULP
OH, MAN, I AM WIPED OUT.
WHERE'D ARTHUR'S FAMILY GO?
THEY HAVEN'T BEEN TO THE SURFACE IN AGES... SO THEY WENT SIGHTSEE-ING.
THE BOYLE FAMILY SURE ARE FREE SPIRITS.

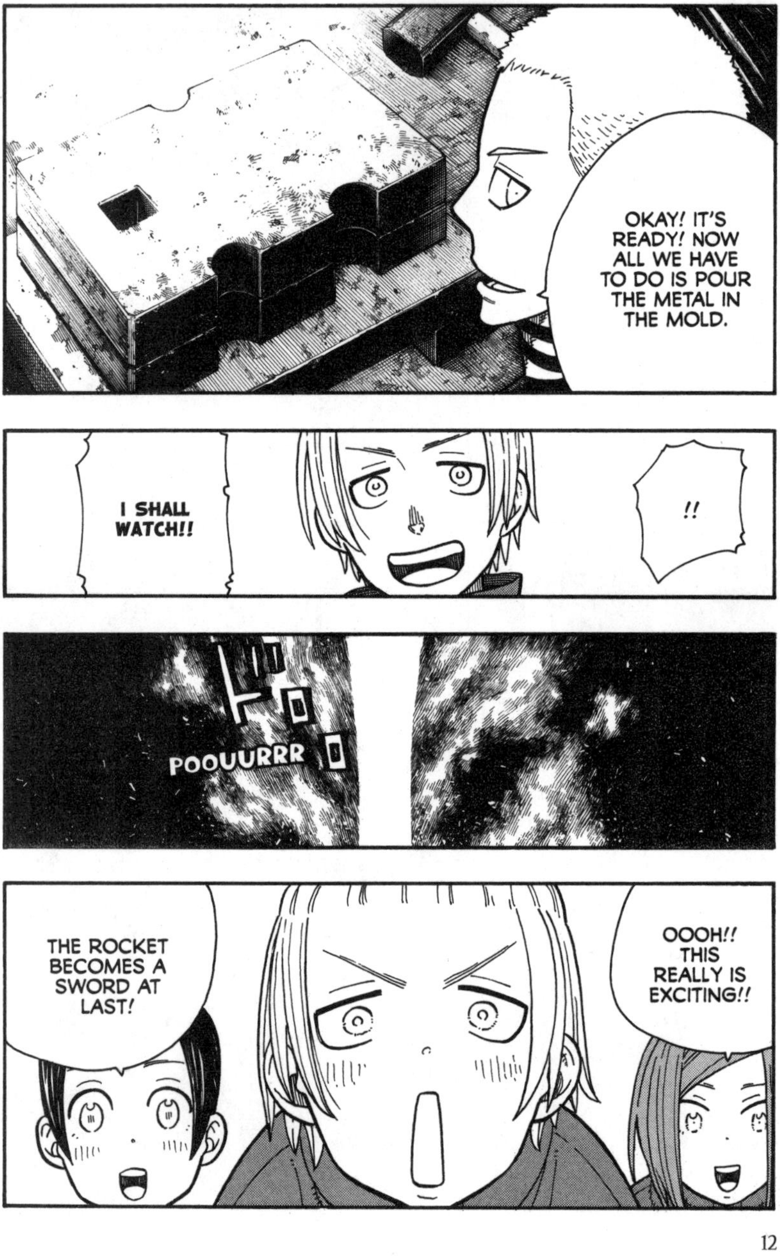
OKAY! IT'S READY! NOW ALL WE HAVE TO DO IS POUR THE METAL IN THE MOLD.
!!
I SHALL WATCH!!
POOUURRR
OOOH!! THIS REALLY IS EXCITING!!
THE ROCKET BECOMES A SWORD AT LAST!

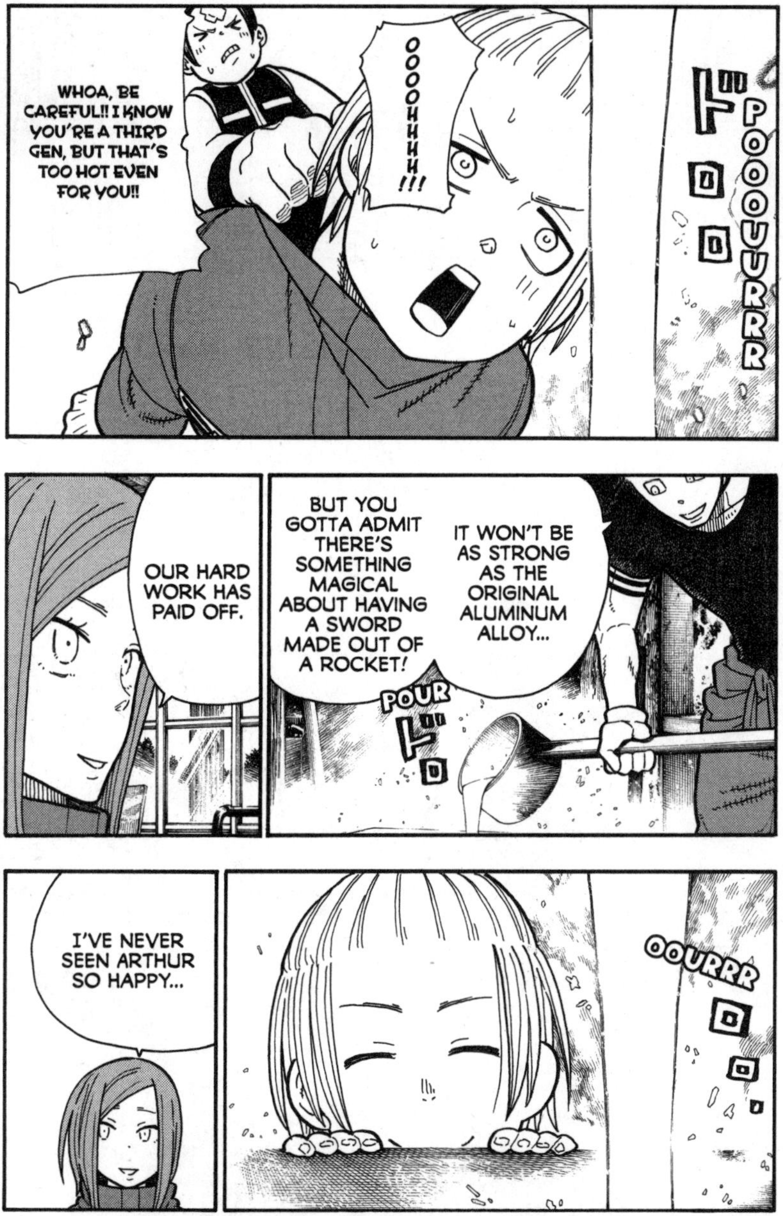
ドドド
POOOOUURRR
OOOOHHHH!!!
WHOA, BE CAREFUL!! I KNOW YOU'RE A THIRD GEN, BUT THAT'S TOO HOT EVEN FOR YOU!!
IT WON'T BE AS STRONG AS THE ORIGINAL ALUMINUM ALLOY...
BUT YOU GOTTA ADMIT THERE'S SOMETHING MAGICAL ABOUT HAVING A SWORD MADE OUT OF A ROCKET!
POUR
ドド
OUR HARD WORK HAS PAID OFF.
OOURRR
I'VE NEVER SEEN ARTHUR SO HAPPY...

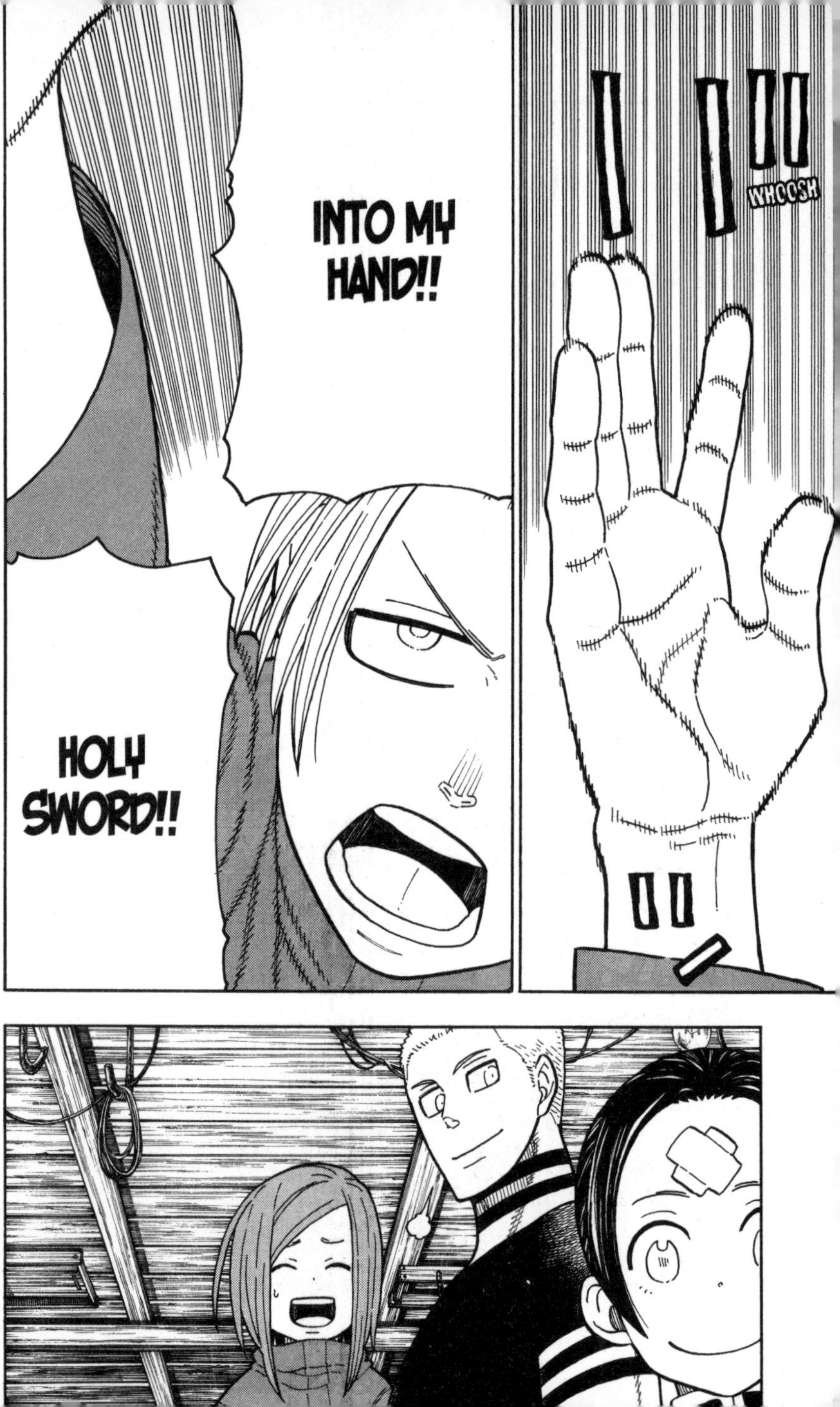
WHOOSH
INTO MY HAND!!
HOLY SWORD!!

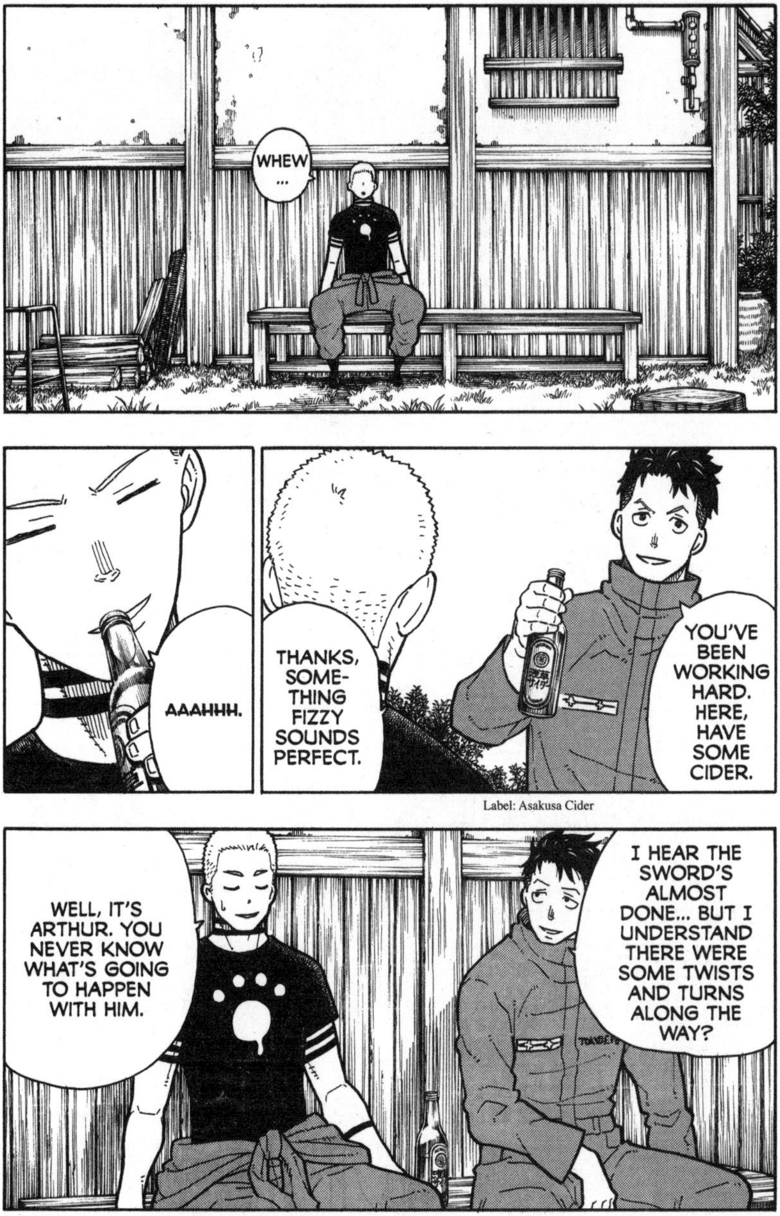
WHEW ...
YOU'VE BEEN WORKING HARD. HERE, HAVE SOME CIDER.
THANKS, SOME-THING FIZZY SOUNDS PERFECT.
AAAHHH.
I HEAR THE SWORD'S ALMOST DONE... BUT I UNDERSTAND THERE WERE SOME TWISTS AND TURNS ALONG THE WAY?
WELL, IT'S ARTHUR. YOU NEVER KNOW WHAT'S GOING TO HAPPEN WITH HIM.
Label: Asakusa Cider

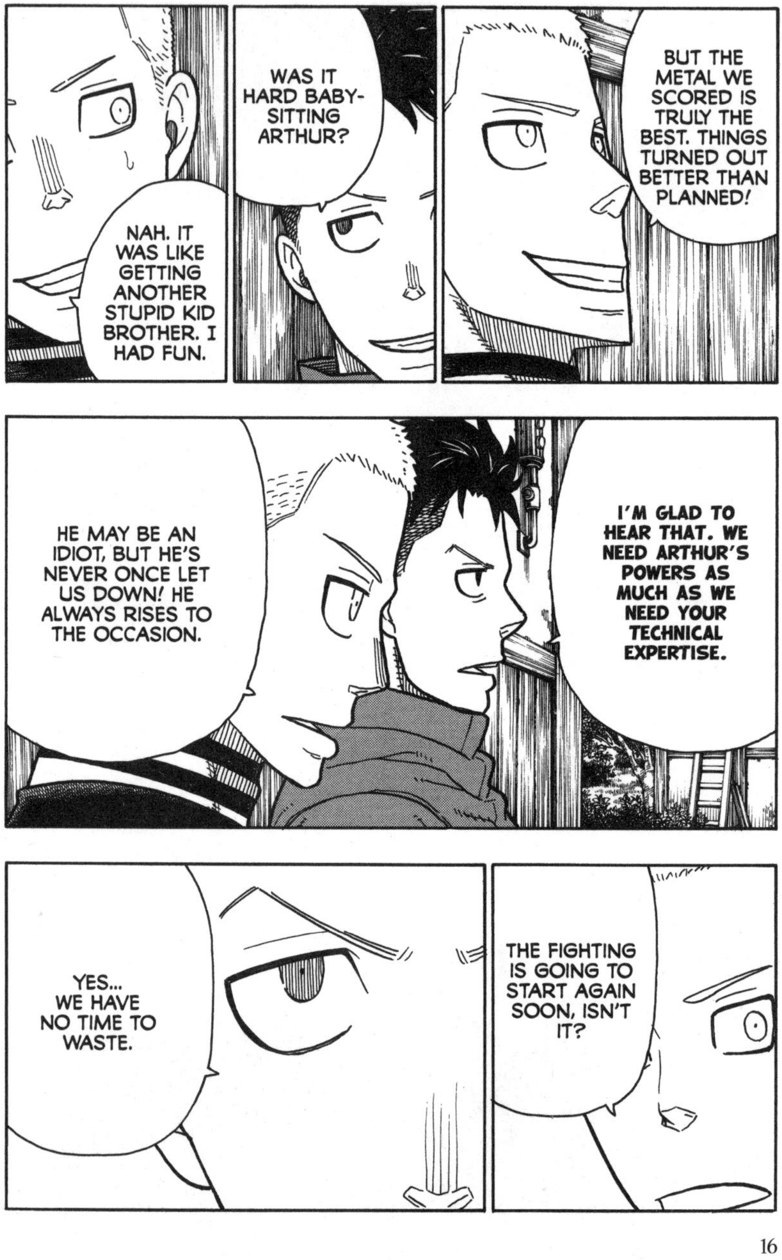
BUT THE METAL WE SCORED IS TRULY THE BEST. THINGS TURNED OUT BETTER THAN PLANNED!
WAS IT HARD BABY-SITTING ARTHUR?
NAH. IT WAS LIKE GETTING ANOTHER STUPID KID BROTHER. I HAD FUN.
I'M GLAD TO HEAR THAT. WE NEED ARTHUR'S POWERS AS MUCH AS WE NEED YOUR TECHNICAL EXPERTISE.
HE MAY BE AN IDIOT, BUT HE'S NEVER ONCE LET US DOWN! HE ALWAYS RISES TO THE OCCASION.
THE FIGHTING IS GOING TO START AGAIN SOON, ISN'T IT?
YES... WE HAVE NO TIME TO WASTE.

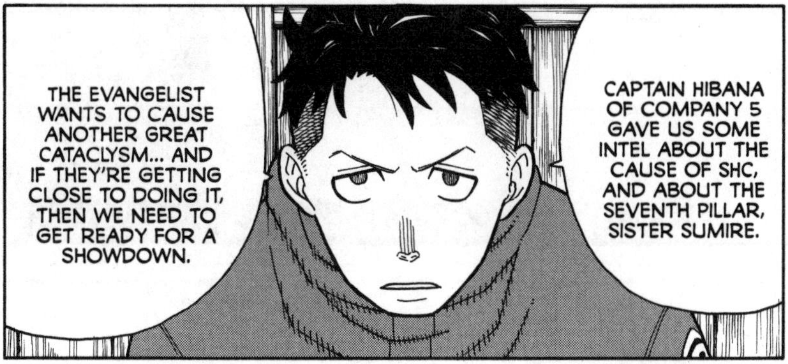
CAPTAIN HIBANA OF COMPANY 5 GAVE US SOME INTEL ABOUT THE CAUSE OF SHC, AND ABOUT THE SEVENTH PILLAR, SISTER SUMIRE.
THE EVANGELIST WANTS TO CAUSE ANOTHER GREAT CATACLYSM... AND IF THEY'RE GETTING CLOSE TO DOING IT, THEN WE NEED TO GET READY FOR A SHOWDOWN.

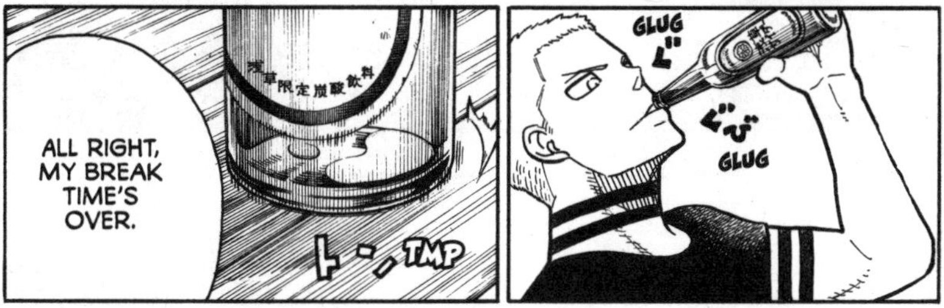
GLUG
GLUG
ALL RIGHT, MY BREAK TIME'S OVER.
TMP

Label: Asakusa Cider

Label: Asakusa Exclusive Carbonated Beverage

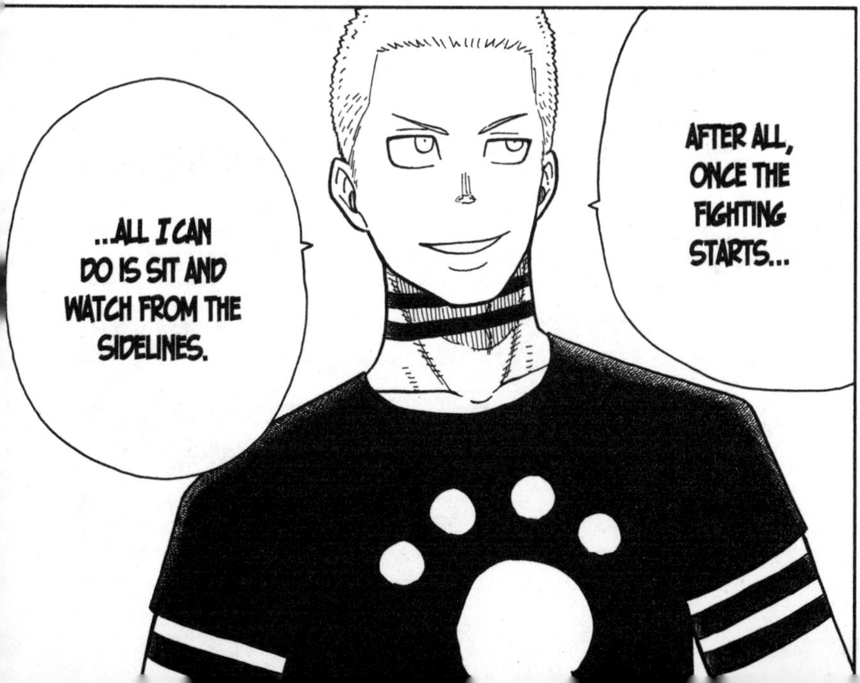
AFTER ALL, ONCE THE FIGHTING STARTS...
...ALL I CAN DO IS SIT AND WATCH FROM THE SIDELINES.

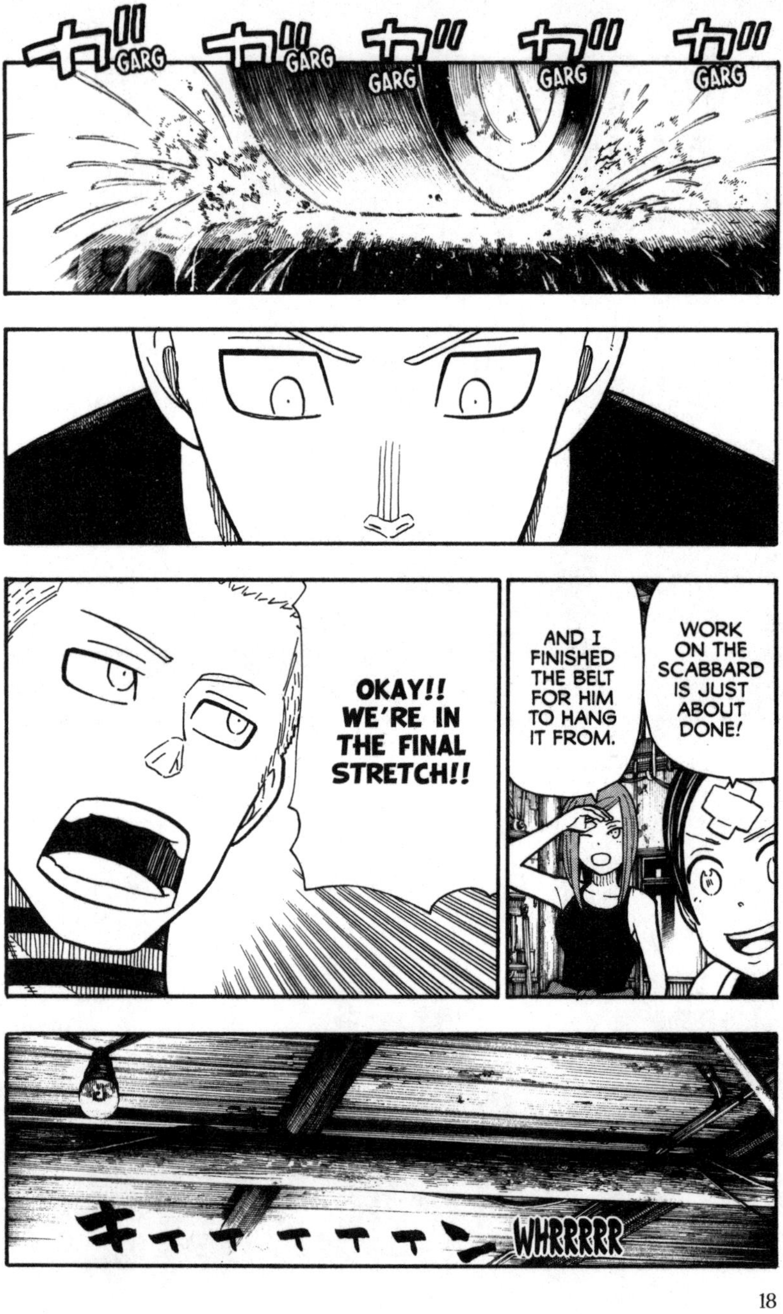
ガ GARG
ガ GARG
ガ GARG
ガ GARG
ガ GARG
WORK ON THE SCABBARD IS JUST ABOUT DONE!
AND I FINISHED THE BELT FOR HIM TO HANG IT FROM.
OKAY!! WE'RE IN THE FINAL STRETCH!!
キィィィィン WHRRRRR

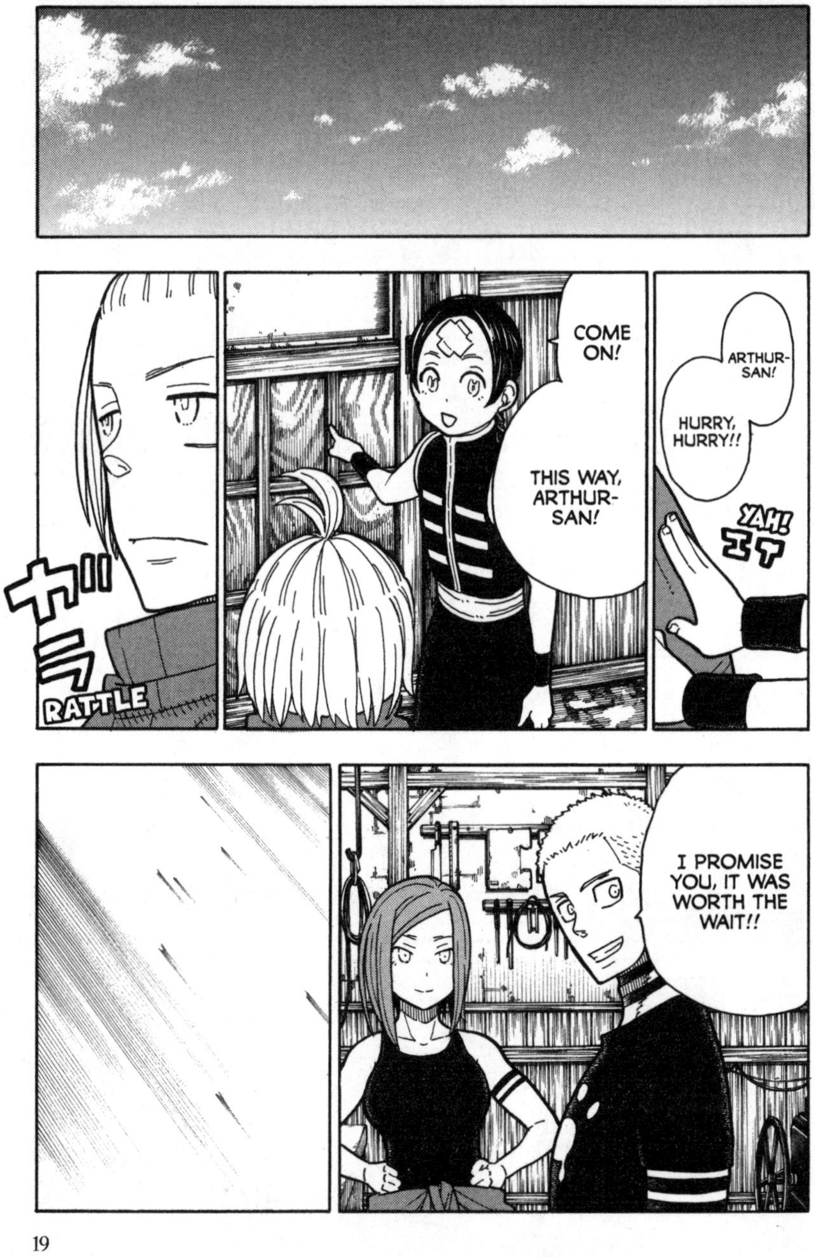
ARTHUR-SAN!
HURRY, HURRY!!
YAH!
COME ON!
THIS WAY, ARTHUR-SAN!
RATTLE
I PROMISE YOU, IT WAS WORTH THE WAIT!!

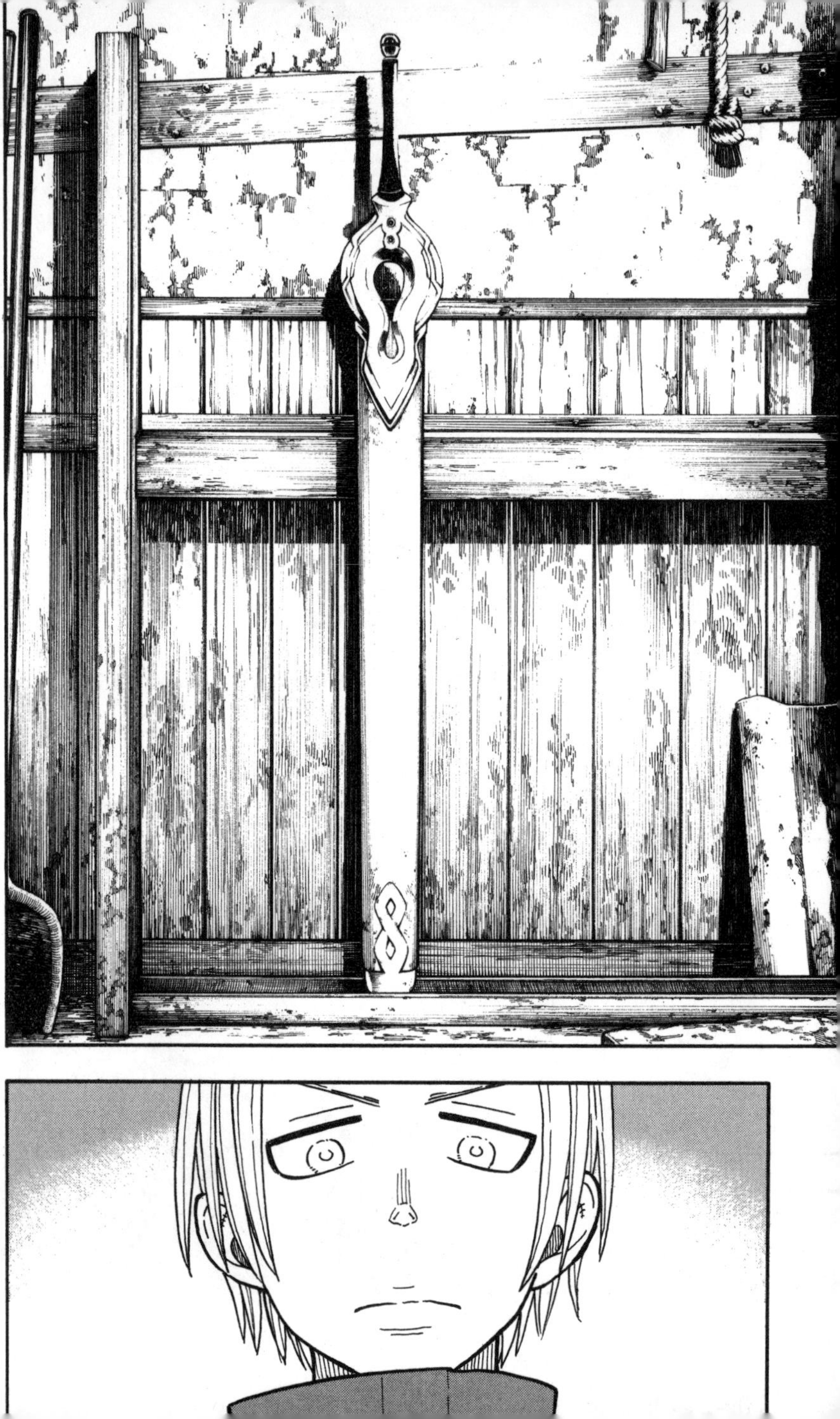

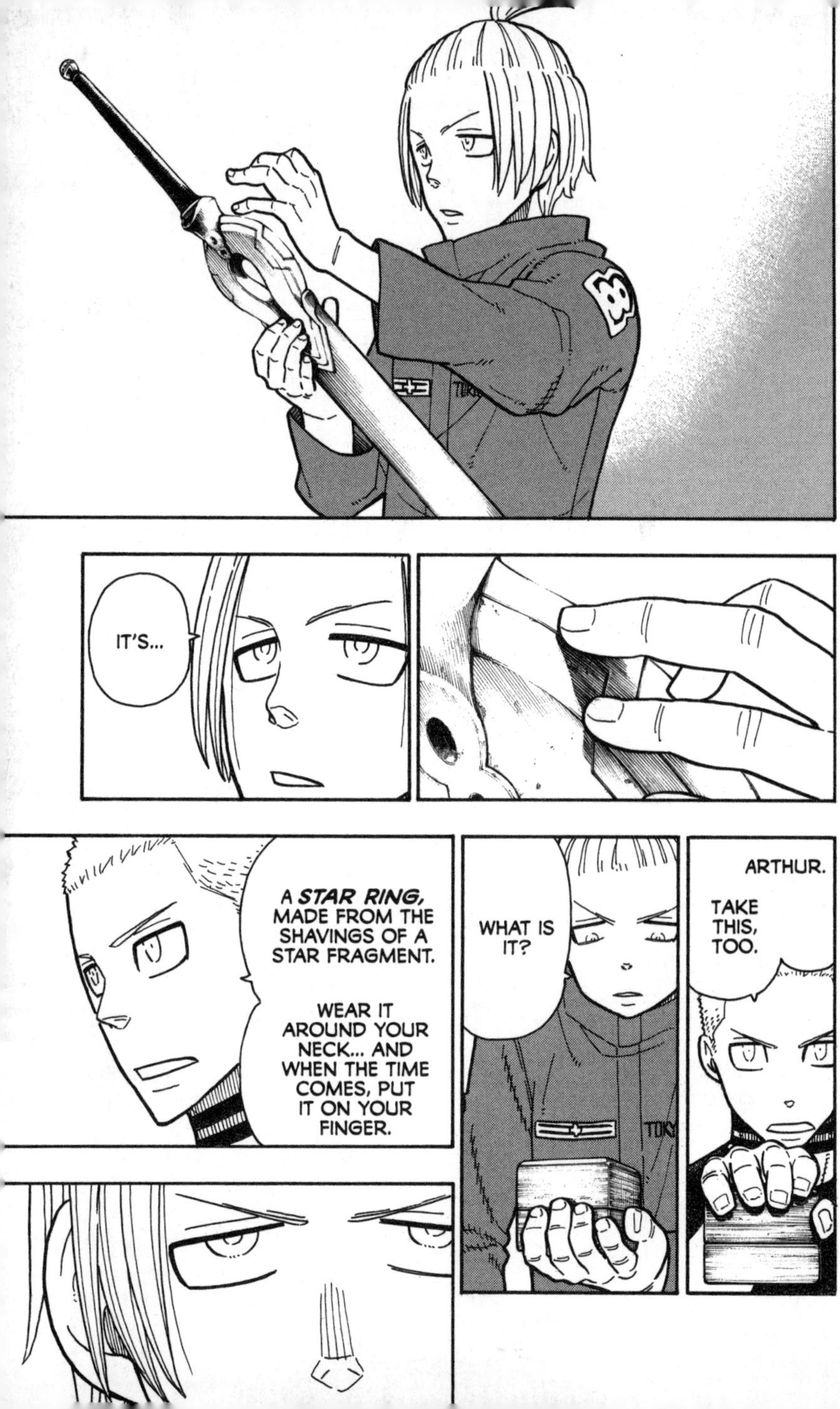
IT'S...
ARTHUR.
TAKE THIS, TOO.
WHAT IS IT?
A STAR RING, MADE FROM THE SHAVINGS OF A STAR FRAGMENT.
WEAR IT AROUND YOUR NECK... AND WHEN THE TIME COMES, PUT IT ON YOUR FINGER.

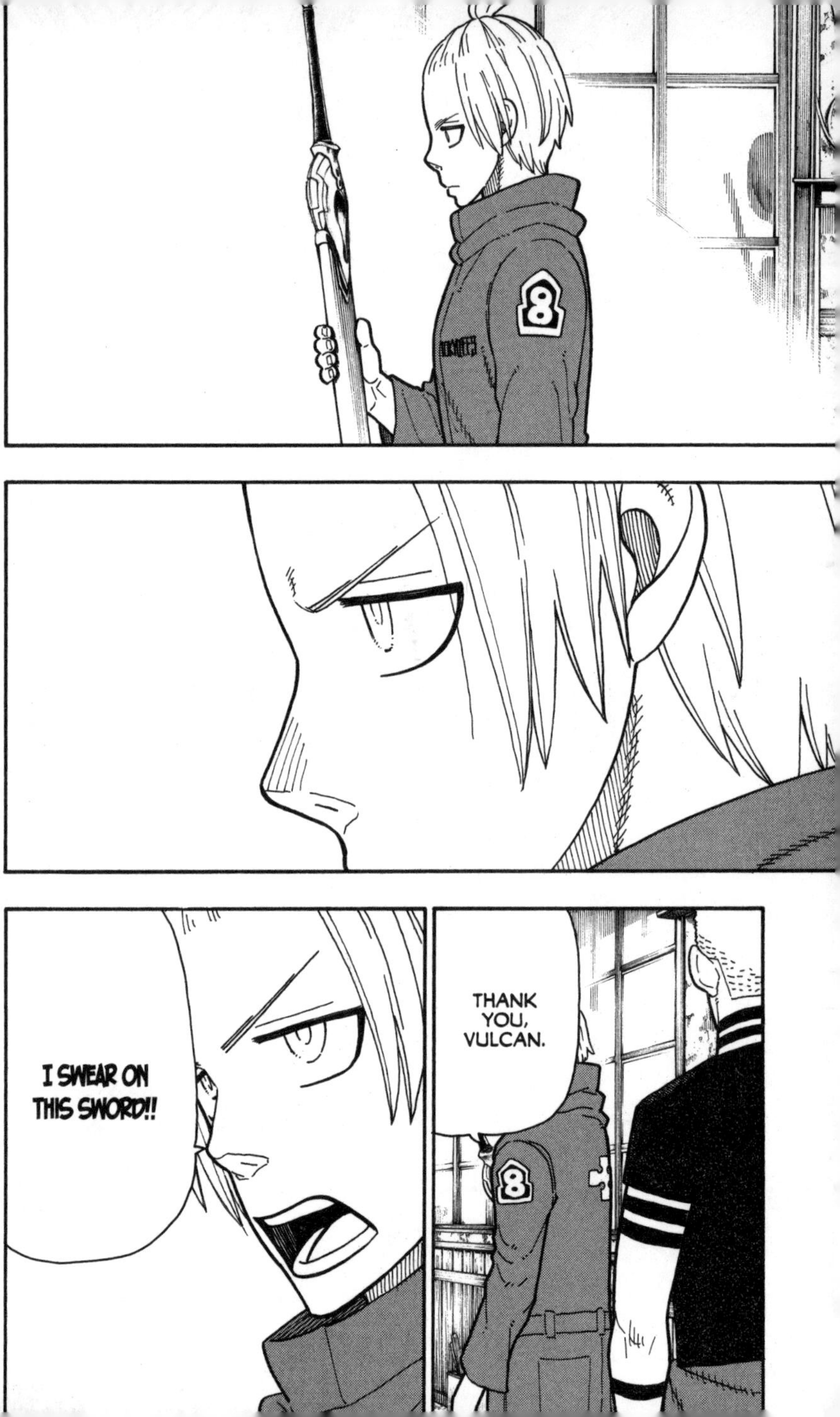
THANK YOU, VULCAN.
I SWEAR ON THIS SWORD!!

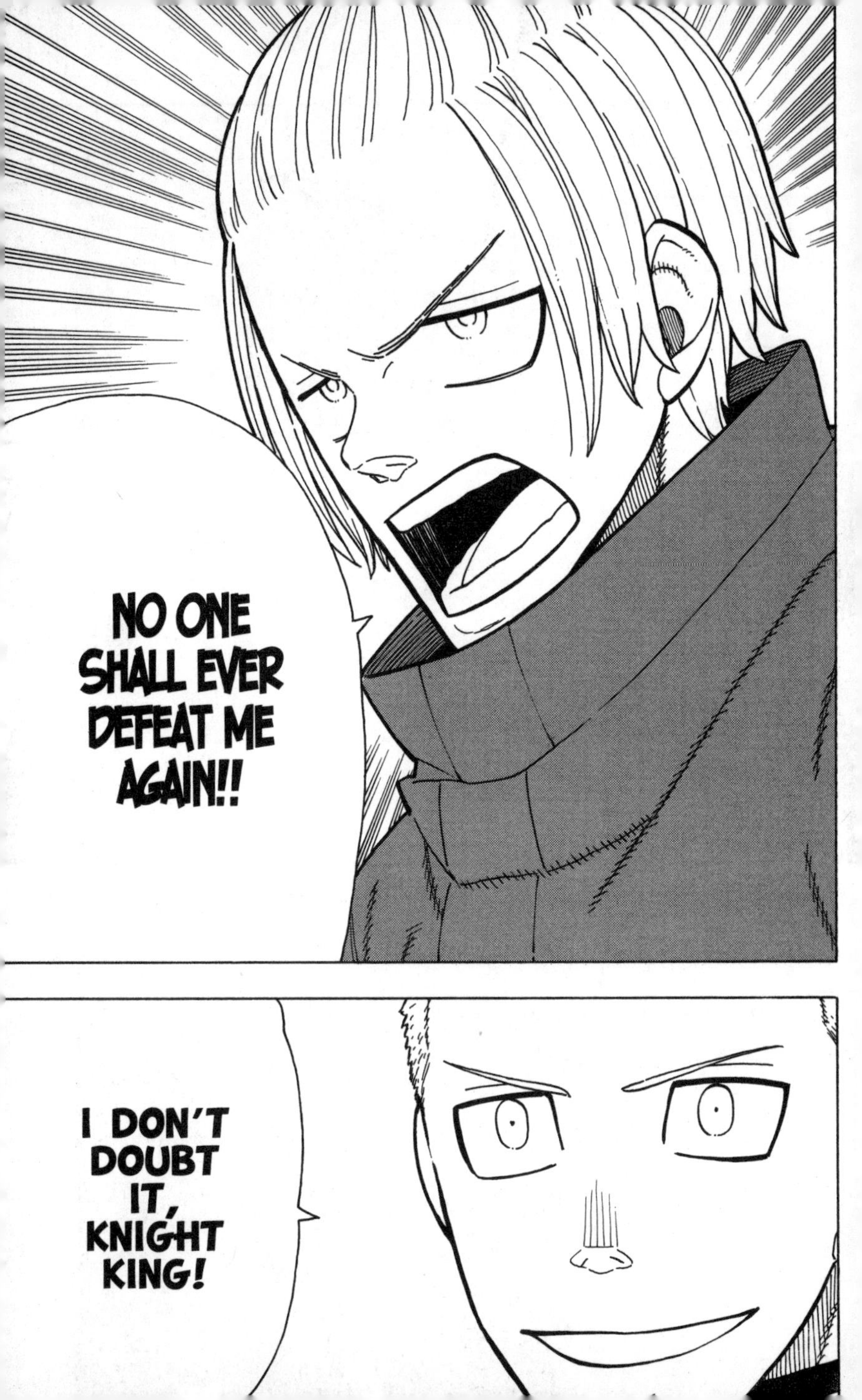
NO ONE SHALL EVER DEFEAT ME AGAIN!!
I DON'T DOUBT IT, KNIGHT KING!

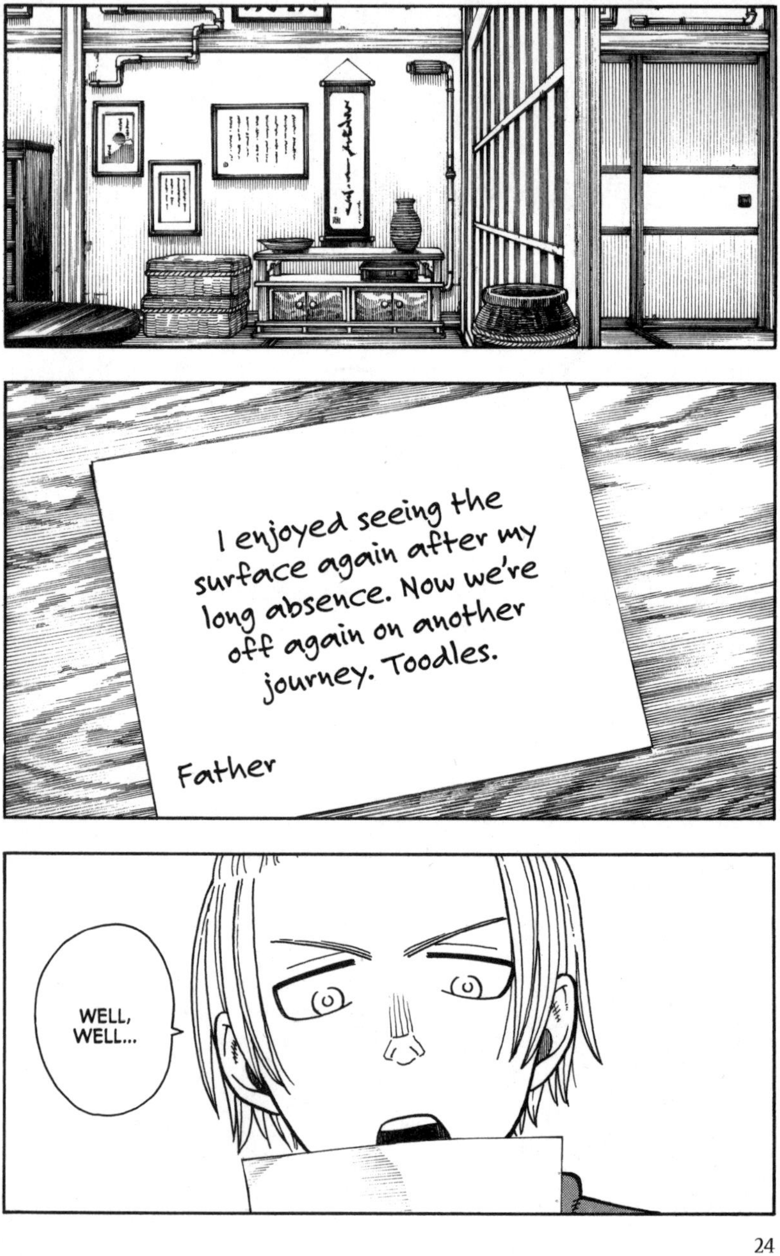
I enjoyed seeing the surface again after my long absence. Now we're off again on another journey. Toodles.
Father
WELL, WELL...

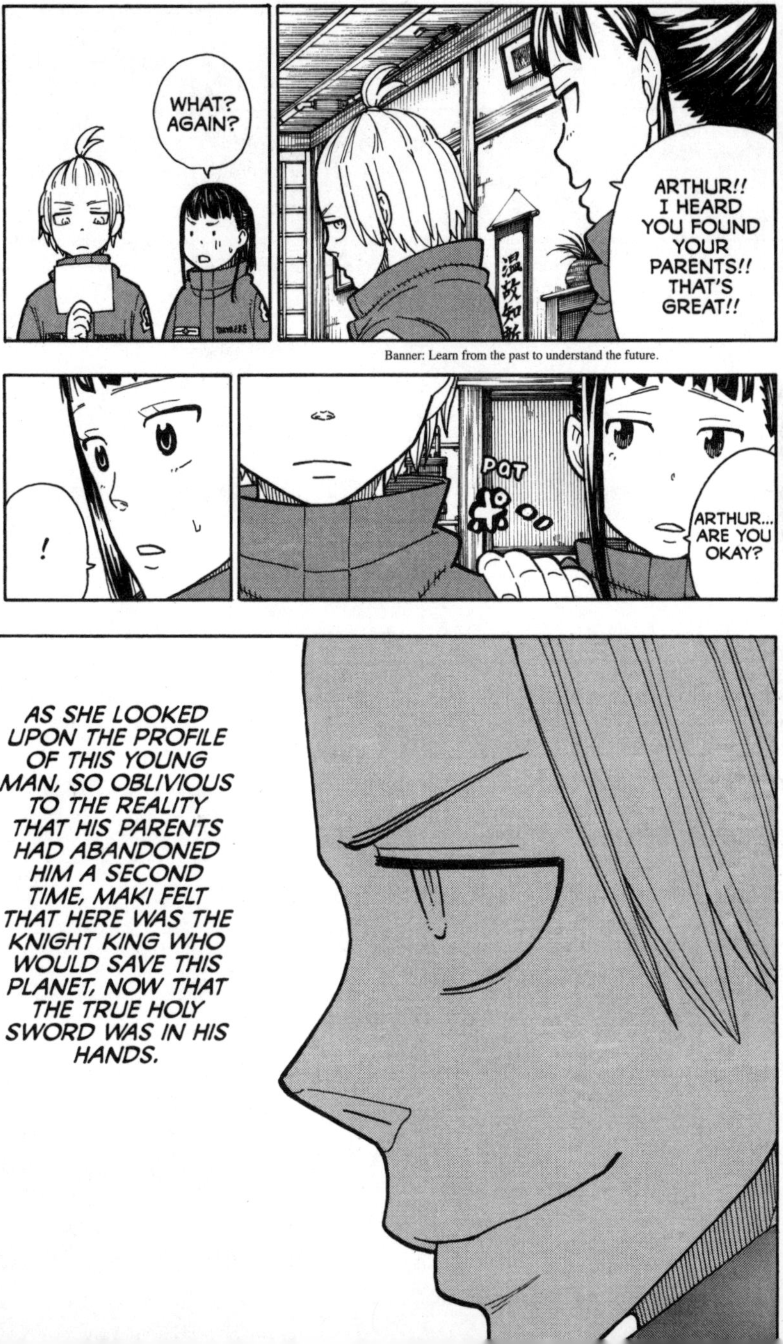
ARTHUR!! I HEARD YOU FOUND YOUR PARENTS!! THAT'S GREAT!!
WHAT? AGAIN?
PAT
ARTHUR... ARE YOU OKAY?
!
AS SHE LOOKED UPON THE PROFILE OF THIS YOUNG MAN, SO OBLIVIOUS TO THE REALITY THAT HIS PARENTS HAD ABANDONED HIM A SECOND TIME, MAKI FELT THAT HERE WAS THE KNIGHT KING WHO WOULD SAVE THIS PLANET, NOW THAT THE TRUE HOLY SWORD WAS IN HIS HANDS.
Banner: Learn from the past to understand the future.

FIRE FORCE

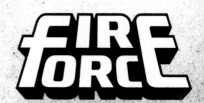

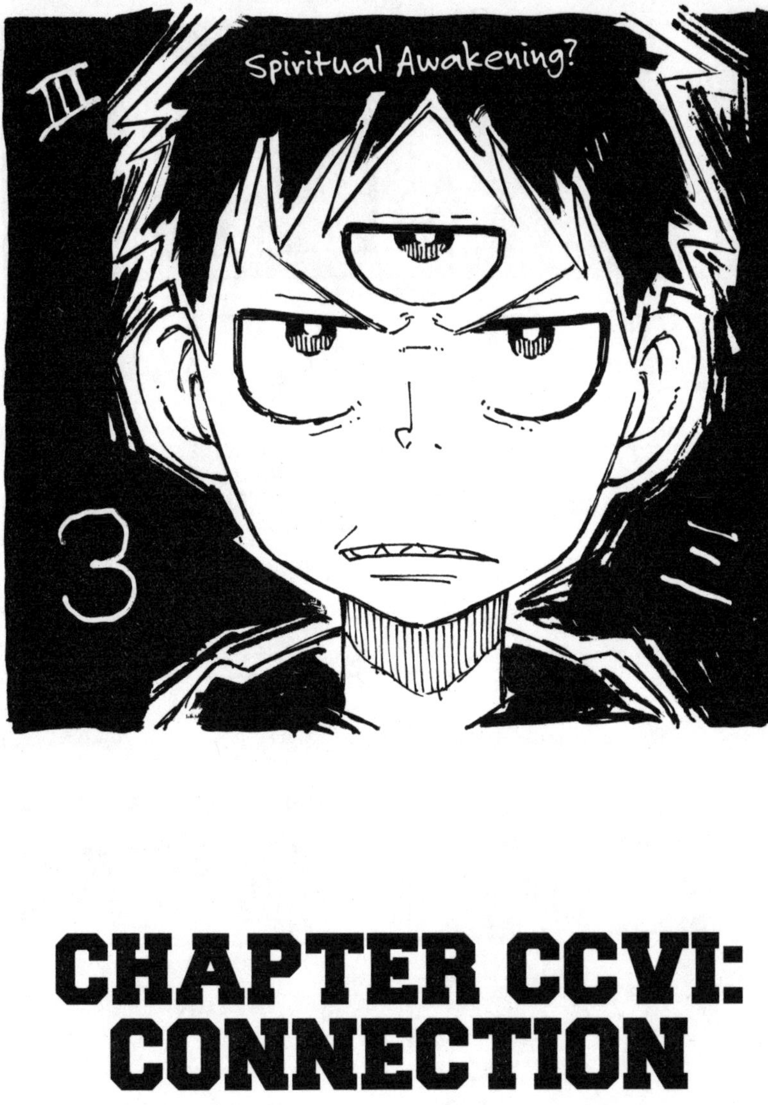
Spiritual Awakening?
III
3

CHAPTER CCVI: CONNECTION

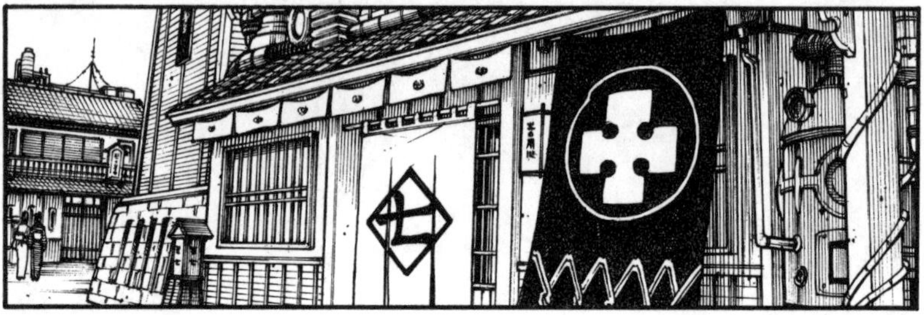

Sign: Fire Safety

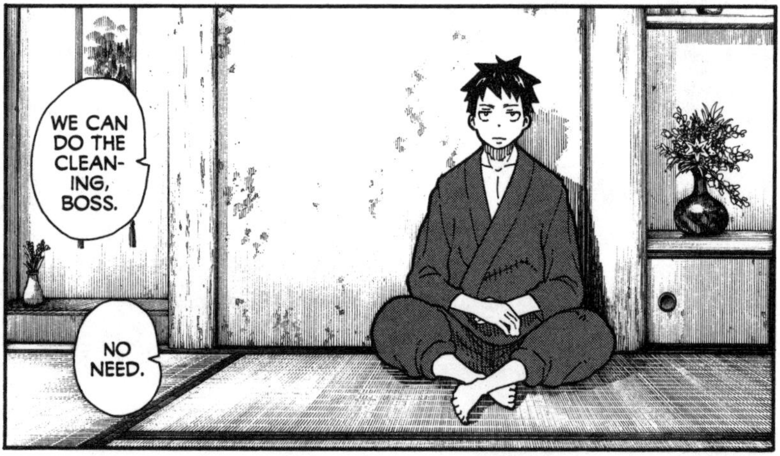
WE CAN DO THE CLEAN-ING, BOSS.
NO NEED.

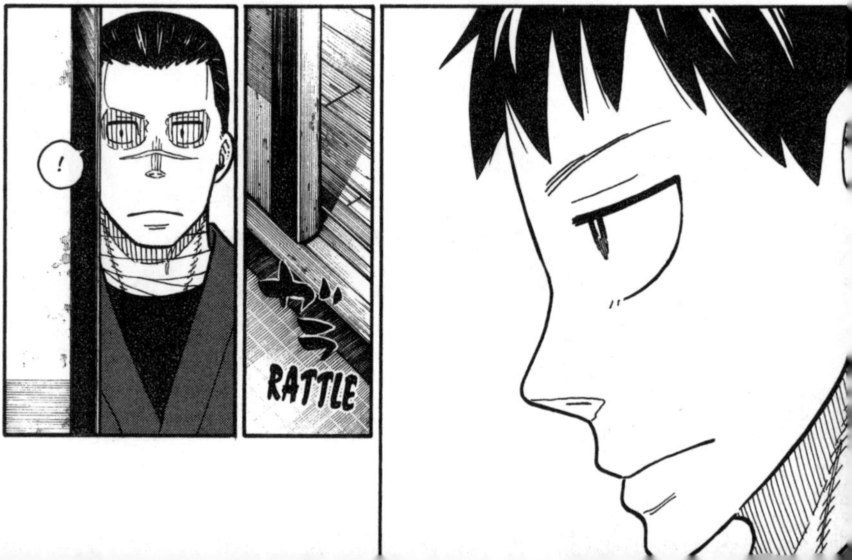
RATTLE
!

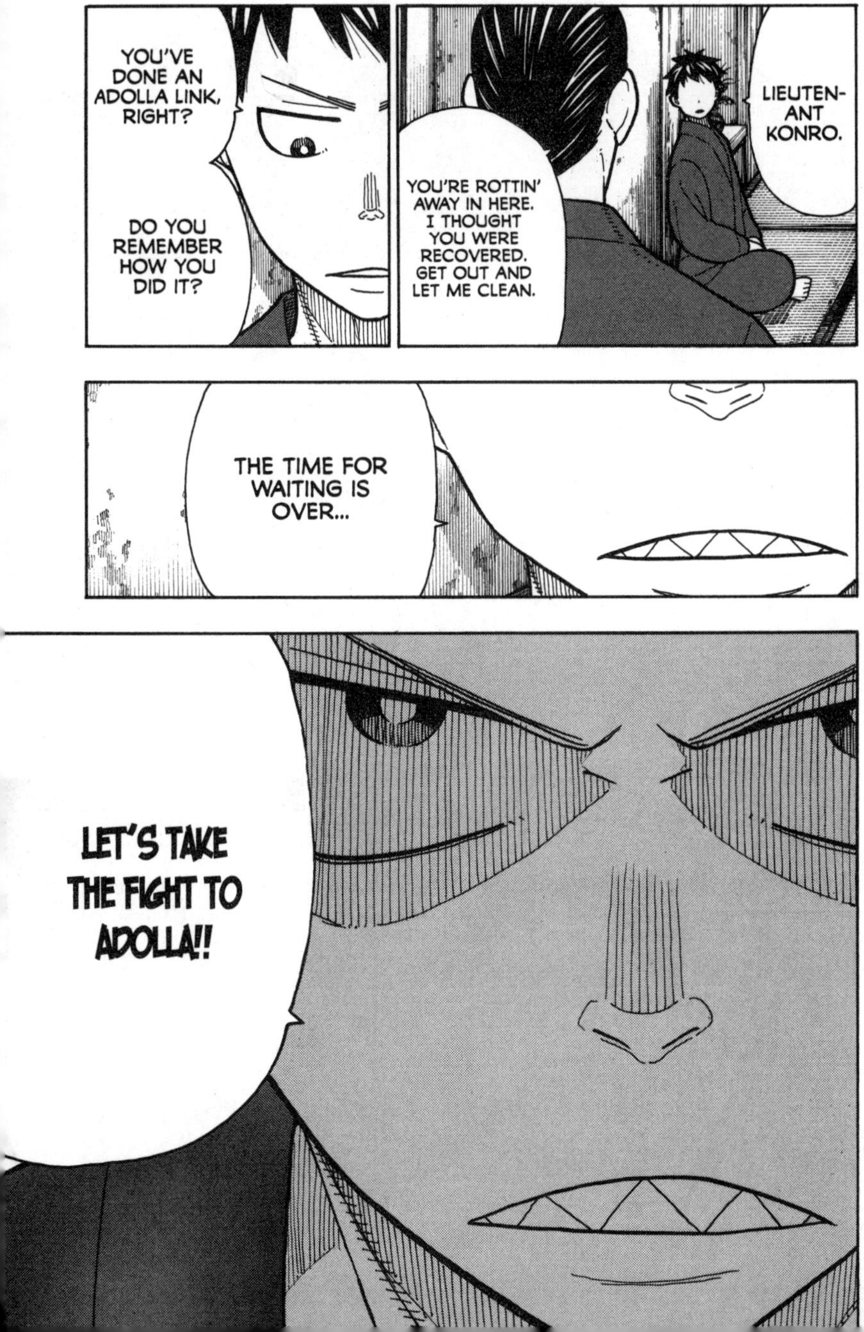
LIEUTEN-ANT KONRO.
YOU'RE ROTTIN' AWAY IN HERE. I THOUGHT YOU WERE RECOVERED. GET OUT AND LET ME CLEAN.
YOU'VE DONE AN ADOLLA LINK, RIGHT?
DO YOU REMEMBER HOW YOU DID IT?
THE TIME FOR WAITING IS OVER...
LET'S TAKE THE FIGHT TO ADOLLA!!

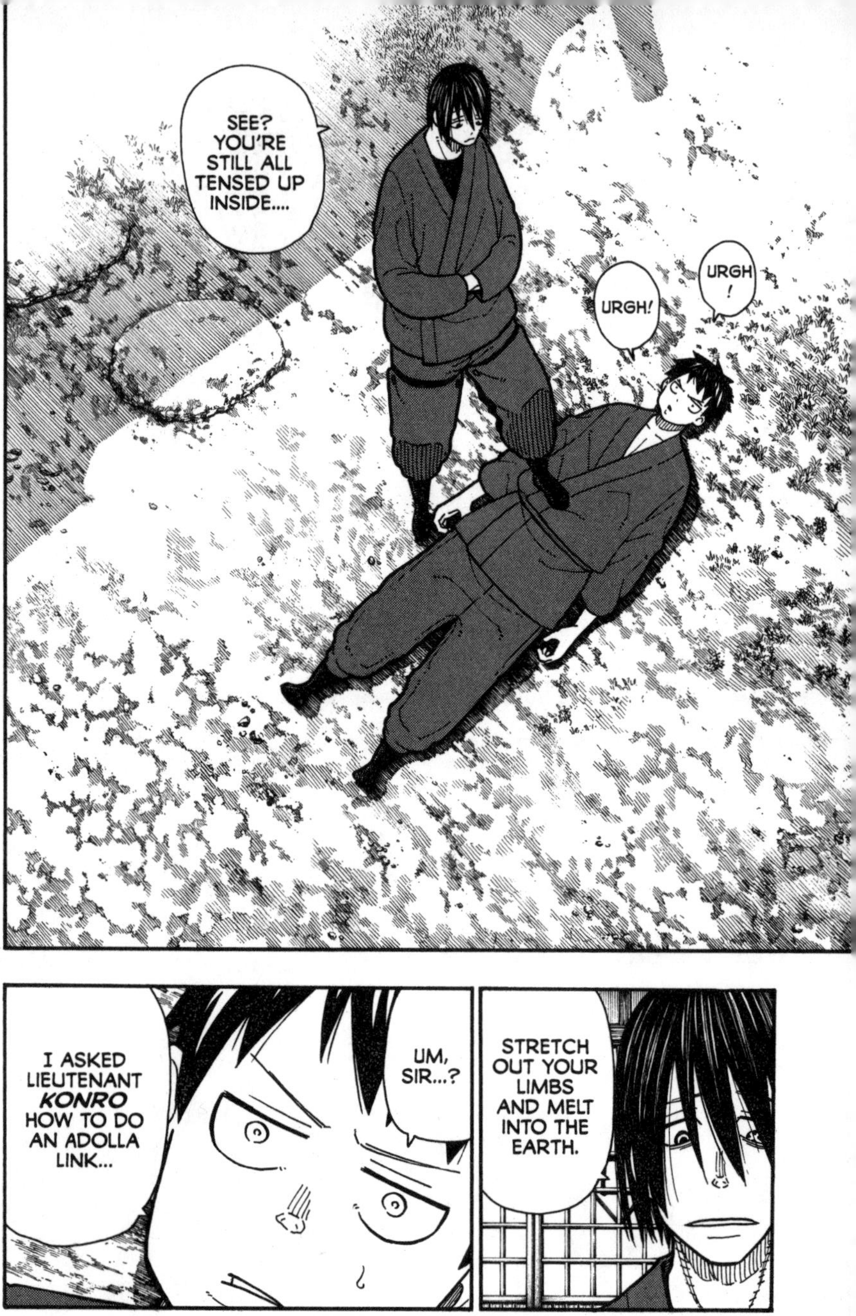
SEE? YOU'RE STILL ALL TENSED UP INSIDE....
URGH!
URGH!
STRETCH OUT YOUR LIMBS AND MELT INTO THE EARTH.
UM, SIR...?
I ASKED LIEUTENANT ***KONRO*** HOW TO DO AN ADOLLA LINK...

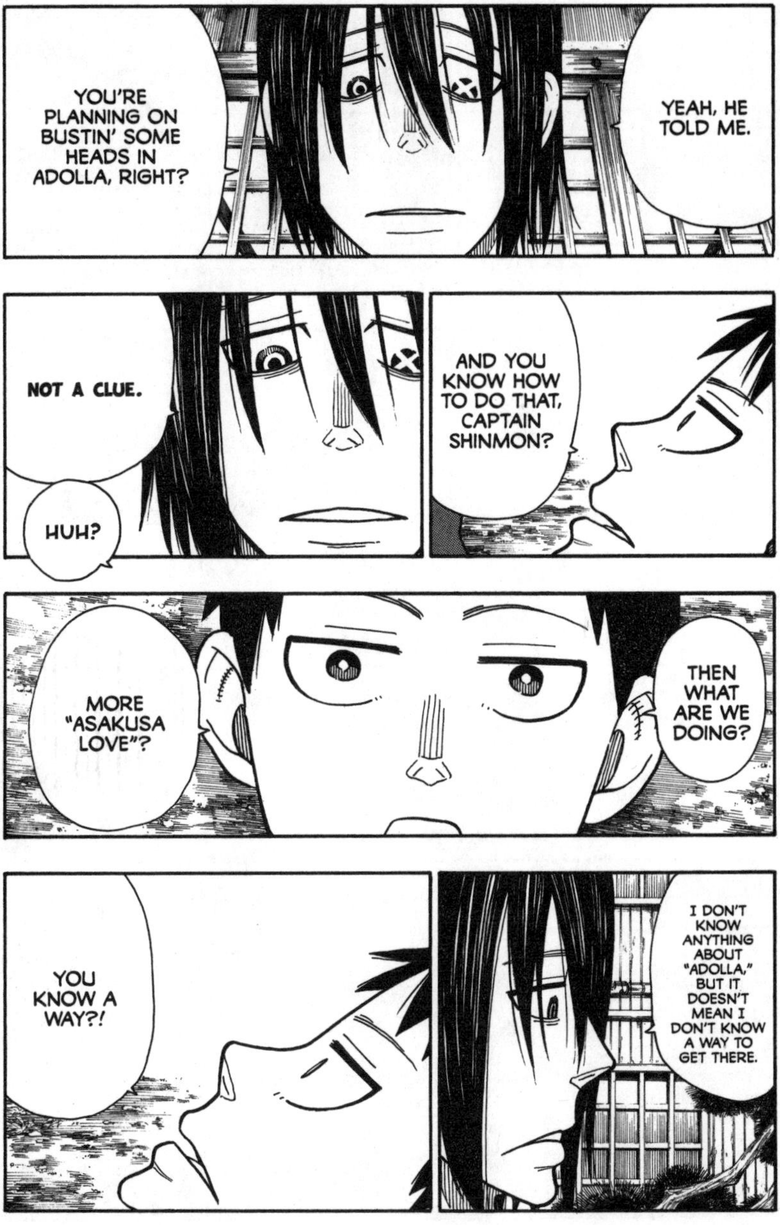
YEAH, HE TOLD ME.
YOU'RE PLANNING ON BUSTIN' SOME HEADS IN ADOLLA, RIGHT?
AND YOU KNOW HOW TO DO THAT, CAPTAIN SHINMON?
NOT A CLUE.
HUH?
THEN WHAT ARE WE DOING?
MORE "ASAKUSA LOVE"?
I DON'T KNOW ANYTHING ABOUT "ADOLLA," BUT IT DOESN'T MEAN I DON'T KNOW A WAY TO GET THERE.
YOU KNOW A WAY?!

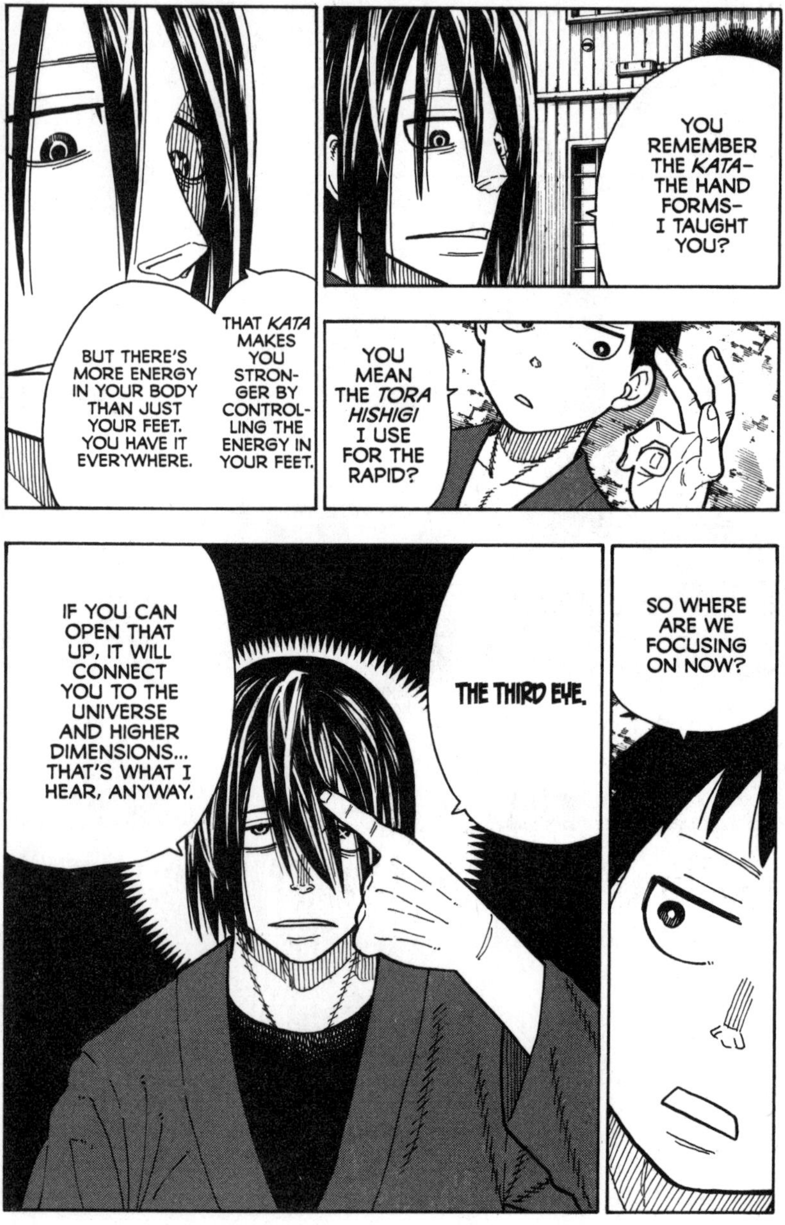
YOU REMEMBER THE *KATA*–THE HAND FORMS–I TAUGHT YOU?
YOU MEAN THE *TORA HISHIGI* I USE FOR THE RAPID?
THAT *KATA* MAKES YOU STRONGER BY CONTROLLING THE ENERGY IN YOUR FEET.
BUT THERE'S MORE ENERGY IN YOUR BODY THAN JUST YOUR FEET. YOU HAVE IT EVERYWHERE.
SO WHERE ARE WE FOCUSING ON NOW?
THE THIRD EYE.
IF YOU CAN OPEN THAT UP, IT WILL CONNECT YOU TO THE UNIVERSE AND HIGHER DIMENSIONS... THAT'S WHAT I HEAR, ANYWAY.

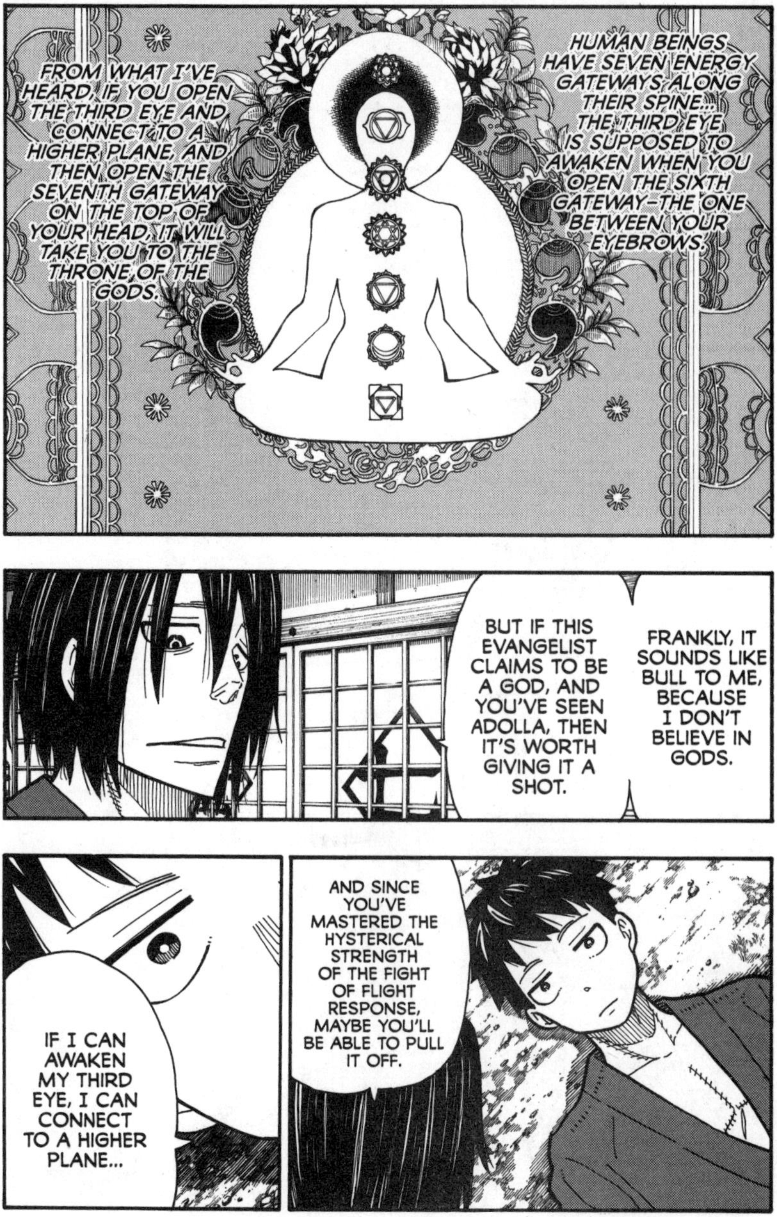
HUMAN BEINGS HAVE SEVEN ENERGY GATEWAYS ALONG THEIR SPINE... THE THIRD EYE IS SUPPOSED TO AWAKEN WHEN YOU OPEN THE SIXTH GATEWAY–THE ONE BETWEEN YOUR EYEBROWS.
FROM WHAT I'VE HEARD, IF YOU OPEN THE THIRD EYE AND CONNECT TO A HIGHER PLANE, AND THEN OPEN THE SEVENTH GATEWAY ON THE TOP OF YOUR HEAD, IT WILL TAKE YOU TO THE THRONE OF THE GODS.
FRANKLY, IT SOUNDS LIKE BULL TO ME, BECAUSE I DON'T BELIEVE IN GODS.
BUT IF THIS EVANGELIST CLAIMS TO BE A GOD, AND YOU'VE SEEN ADOLLA, THEN IT'S WORTH GIVING IT A SHOT.
AND SINCE YOU'VE MASTERED THE HYSTERICAL STRENGTH OF THE FIGHT OF FLIGHT RESPONSE, MAYBE YOU'LL BE ABLE TO PULL IT OFF.
IF I CAN AWAKEN MY THIRD EYE, I CAN CONNECT TO A HIGHER PLANE...

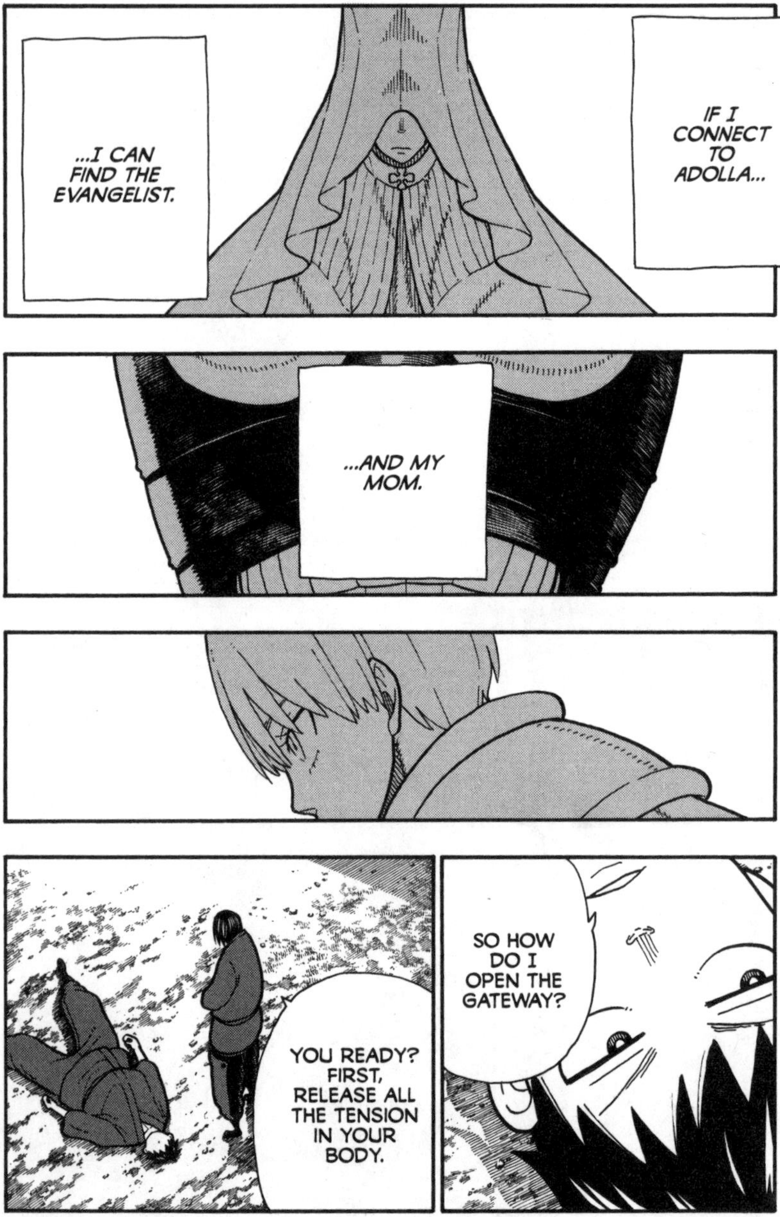
IF I CONNECT TO ADOLLA...
...I CAN FIND THE EVANGELIST.
...AND MY MOM.
SO HOW DO I OPEN THE GATEWAY?
YOU READY? FIRST, RELEASE ALL THE TENSION IN YOUR BODY.

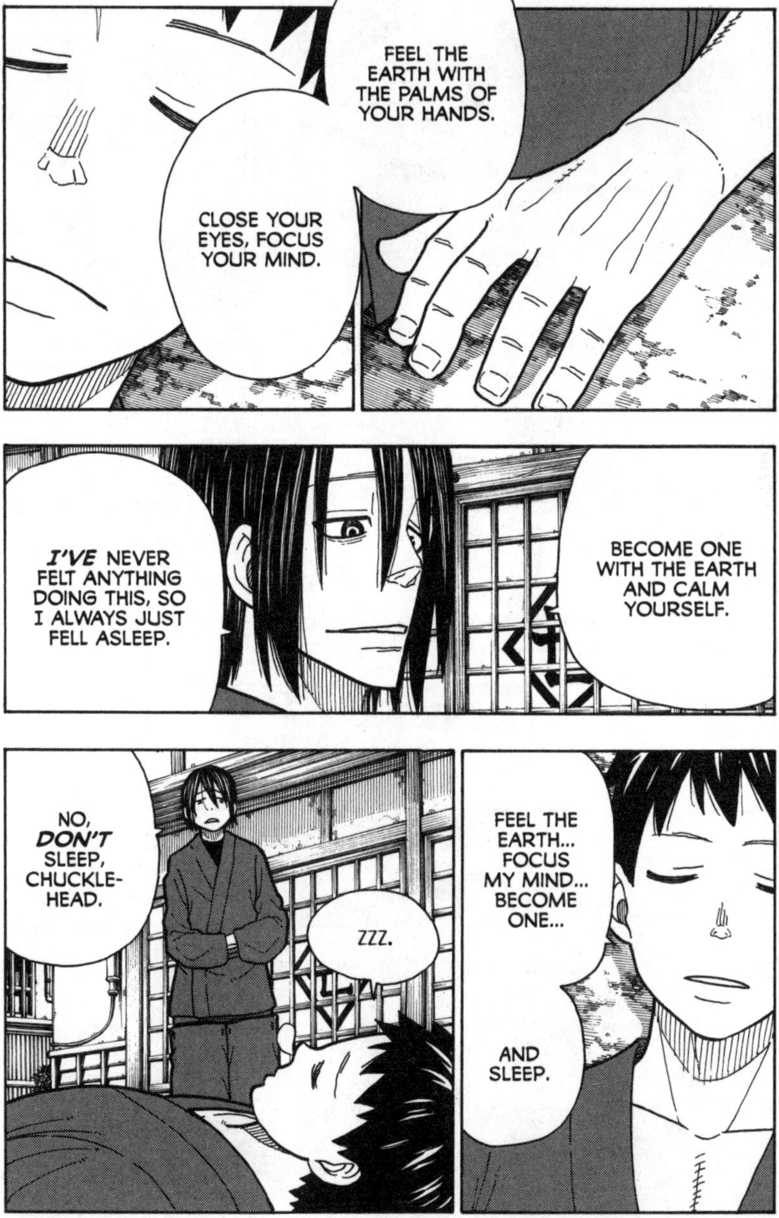
FEEL THE EARTH WITH THE PALMS OF YOUR HANDS.
CLOSE YOUR EYES, FOCUS YOUR MIND.
BECOME ONE WITH THE EARTH AND CALM YOURSELF.
I'VE NEVER FELT ANYTHING DOING THIS, SO I ALWAYS JUST FELL ASLEEP.
FEEL THE EARTH... FOCUS MY MIND... BECOME ONE...
AND SLEEP.
ZZZ.
NO, *DON'T* SLEEP, CHUCKLE-HEAD.

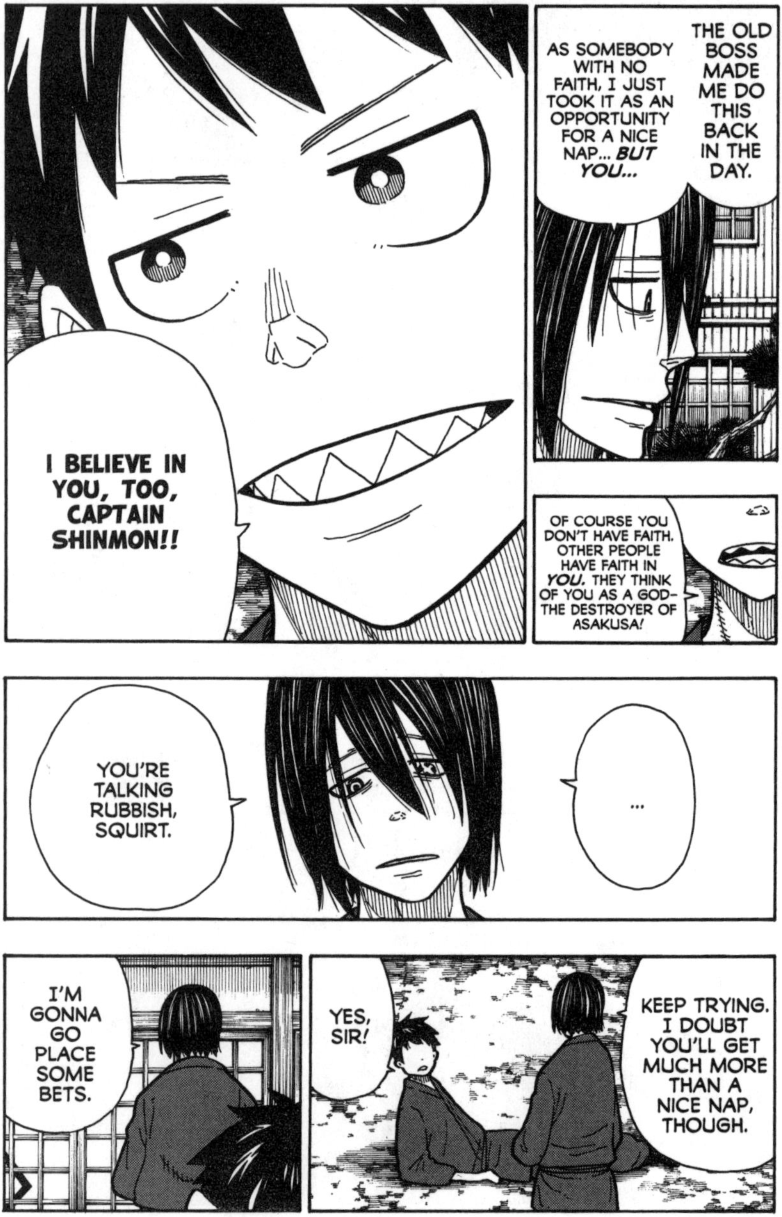
THE OLD BOSS MADE ME DO THIS BACK IN THE DAY.
AS SOMEBODY WITH NO FAITH, I JUST TOOK IT AS AN OPPORTUNITY FOR A NICE NAP... BUT YOU...
OF COURSE YOU DON'T HAVE FAITH. OTHER PEOPLE HAVE FAITH IN YOU. THEY THINK OF YOU AS A GOD—THE DESTROYER OF ASAKUSA!
I BELIEVE IN YOU, TOO, CAPTAIN SHINMON!!
...
YOU'RE TALKING RUBBISH, SQUIRT.
KEEP TRYING. I DOUBT YOU'LL GET MUCH MORE THAN A NICE NAP, THOUGH.
YES, SIR!
I'M GONNA GO PLACE SOME BETS.

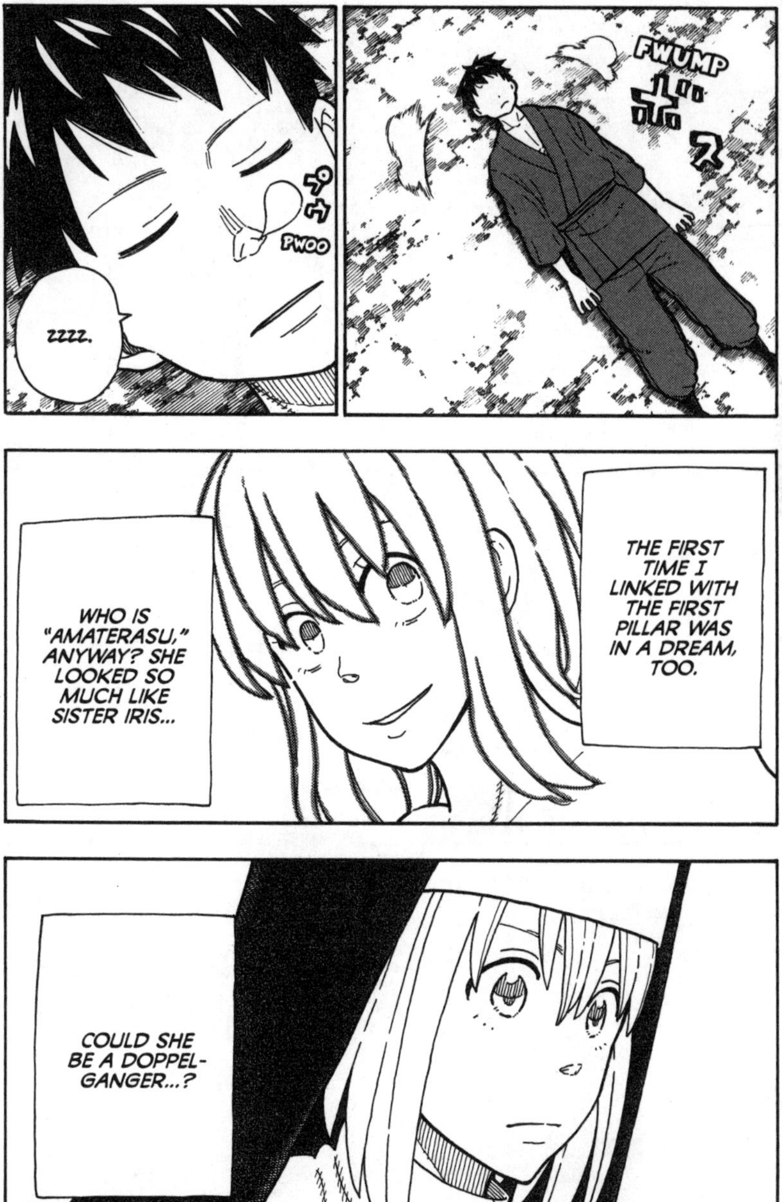
FWUMP
ボス
ぷう
PWOO
ZZZZ.
THE FIRST TIME I LINKED WITH THE FIRST PILLAR WAS IN A DREAM, TOO.
WHO IS "AMATERASU," ANYWAY? SHE LOOKED SO MUCH LIKE SISTER IRIS...
COULD SHE BE A DOPPEL-GANGER...?

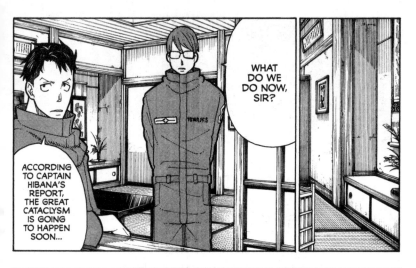

WHAT DO WE DO NOW, SIR?
ACCORDING TO CAPTAIN HIBANA'S REPORT, THE GREAT CATACLYSM IS GOING TO HAPPEN SOON...
VULCAN IS MAKING US SOME NEW WEAPONS.
I DON'T KNOW HOW MUCH HELP WE CAN GET FROM THE OTHER COMPANIES, BUT OUR JOB IS TO RALLY WHATEVER TROOPS WE CAN BEFORE THE ENEMY IS READY TO CARRY OUT THEIR PLANS.
THEN WE'D BETTER HURRY.
I HOPE SHINRA'S TRAINING GOES AS WELL AS ARTHUR'S POWER-UP...

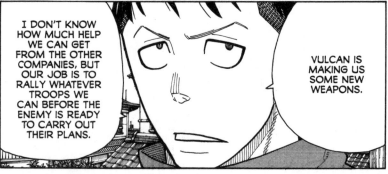

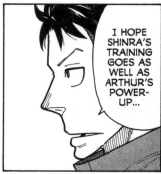

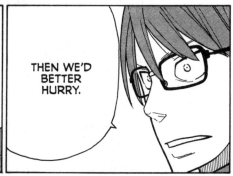

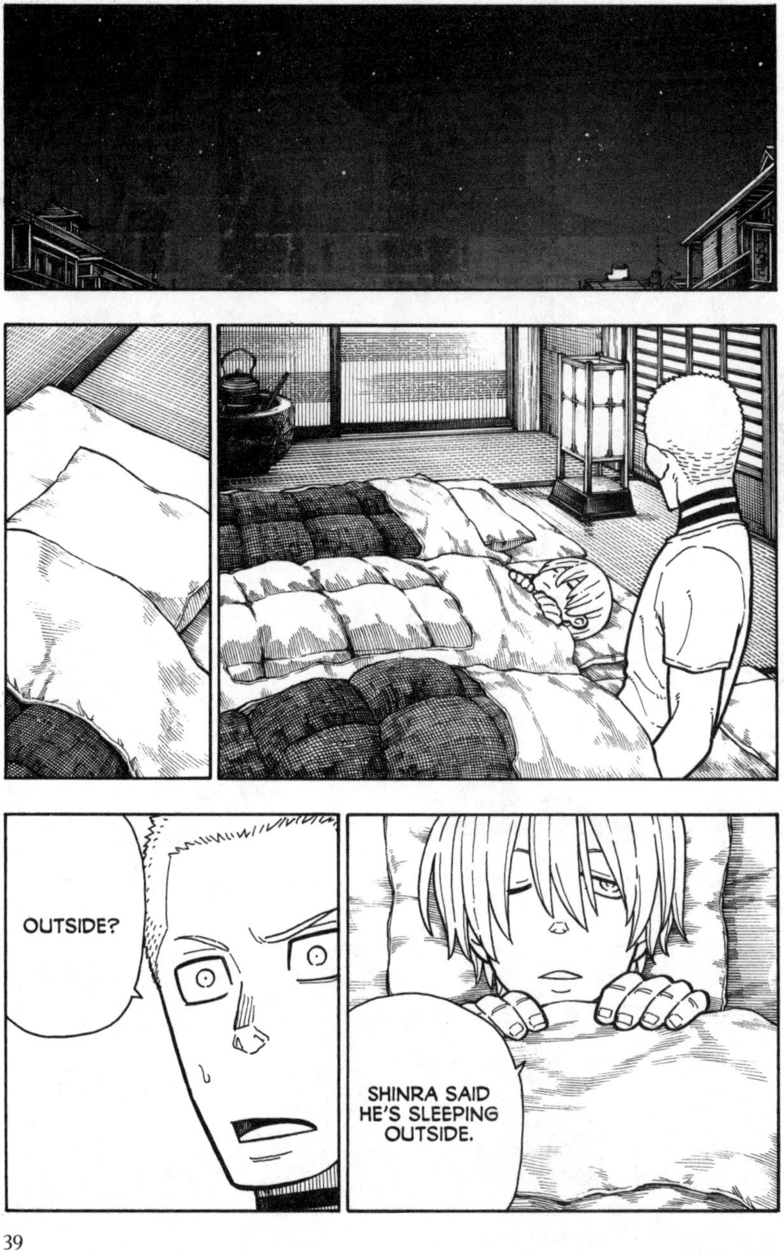
SHINRA SAID HE'S SLEEPING OUTSIDE.
OUTSIDE?

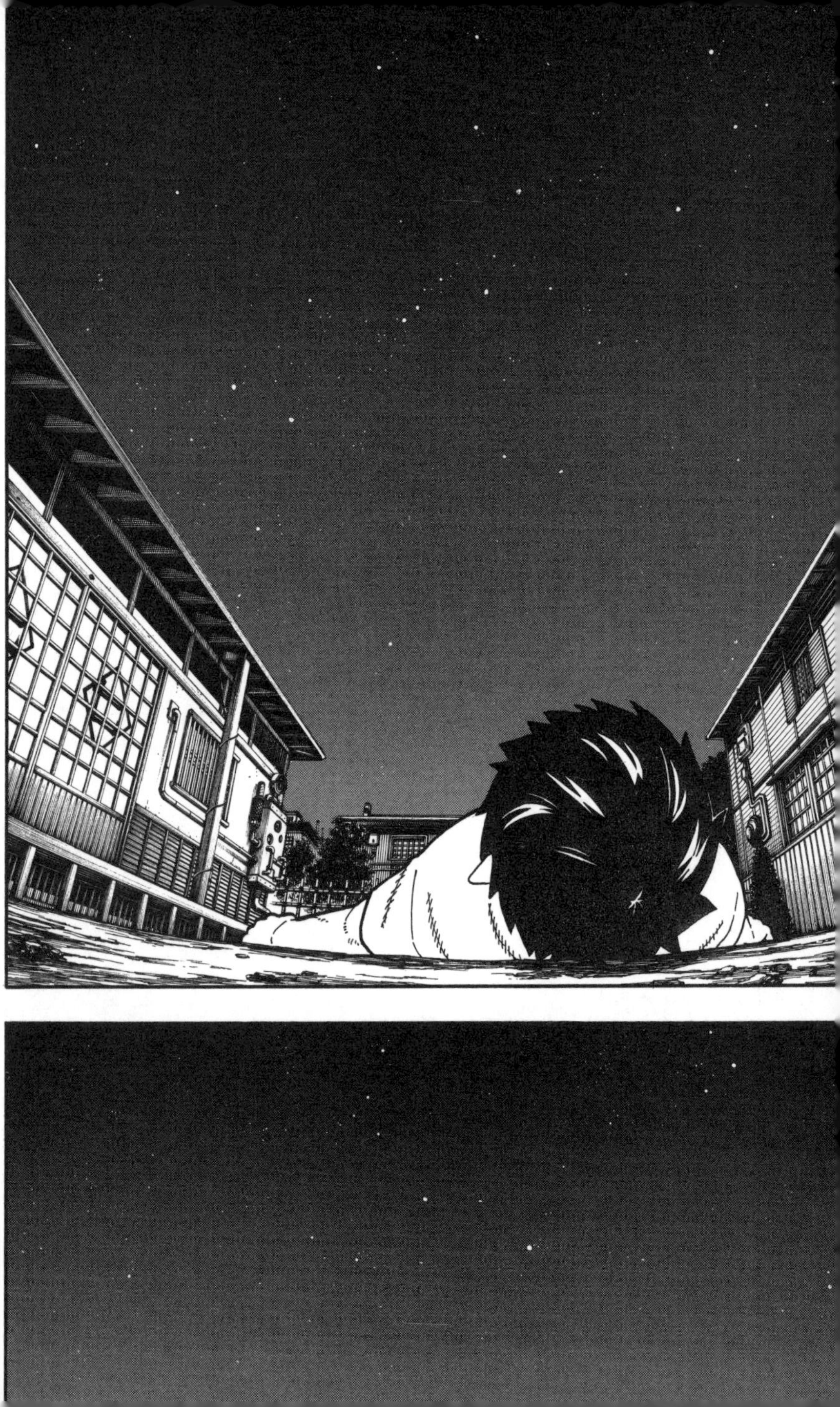

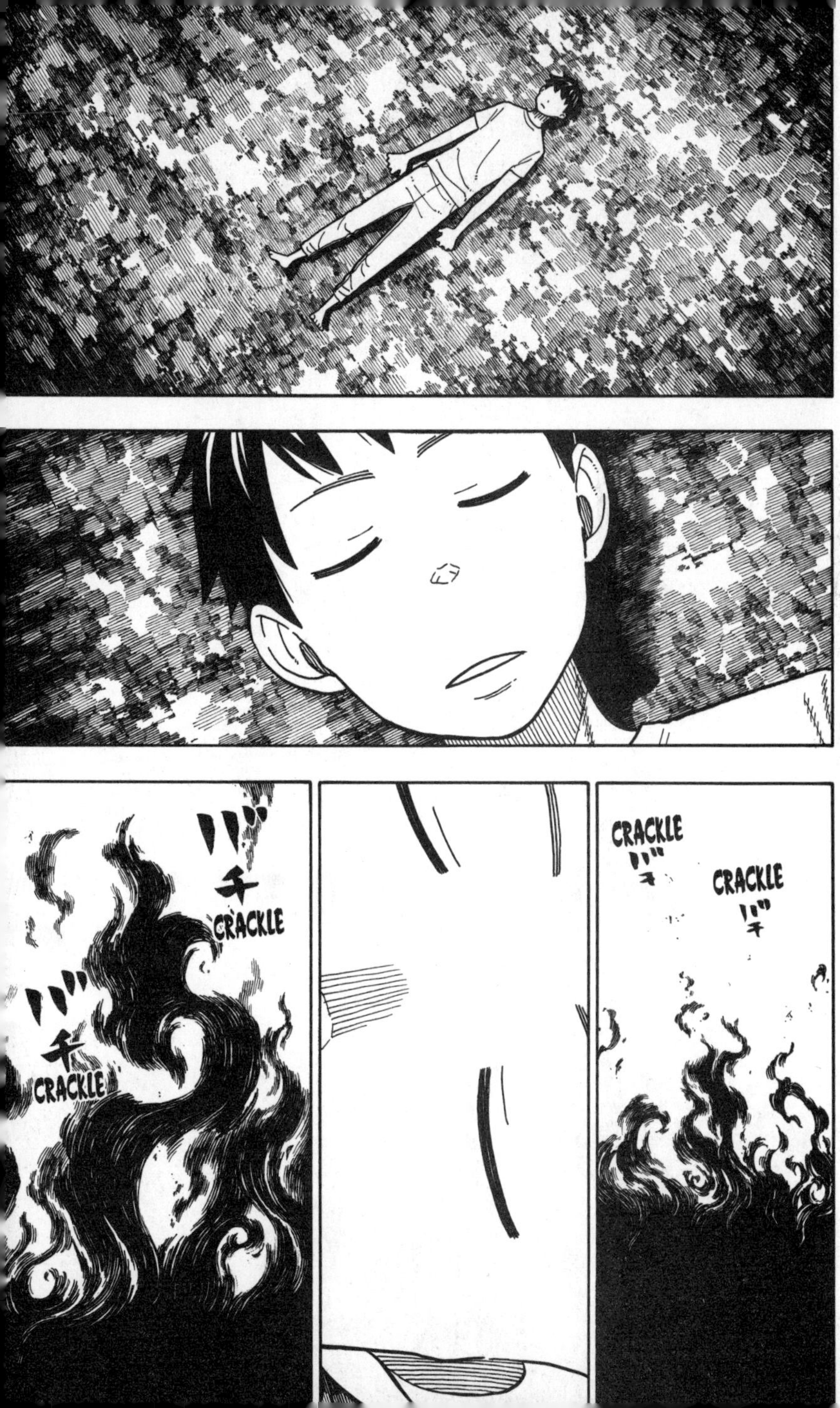
CRACKLE
バチ
CRACKLE
バチ
バチ
CRACKLE
バチ
CRACKLE

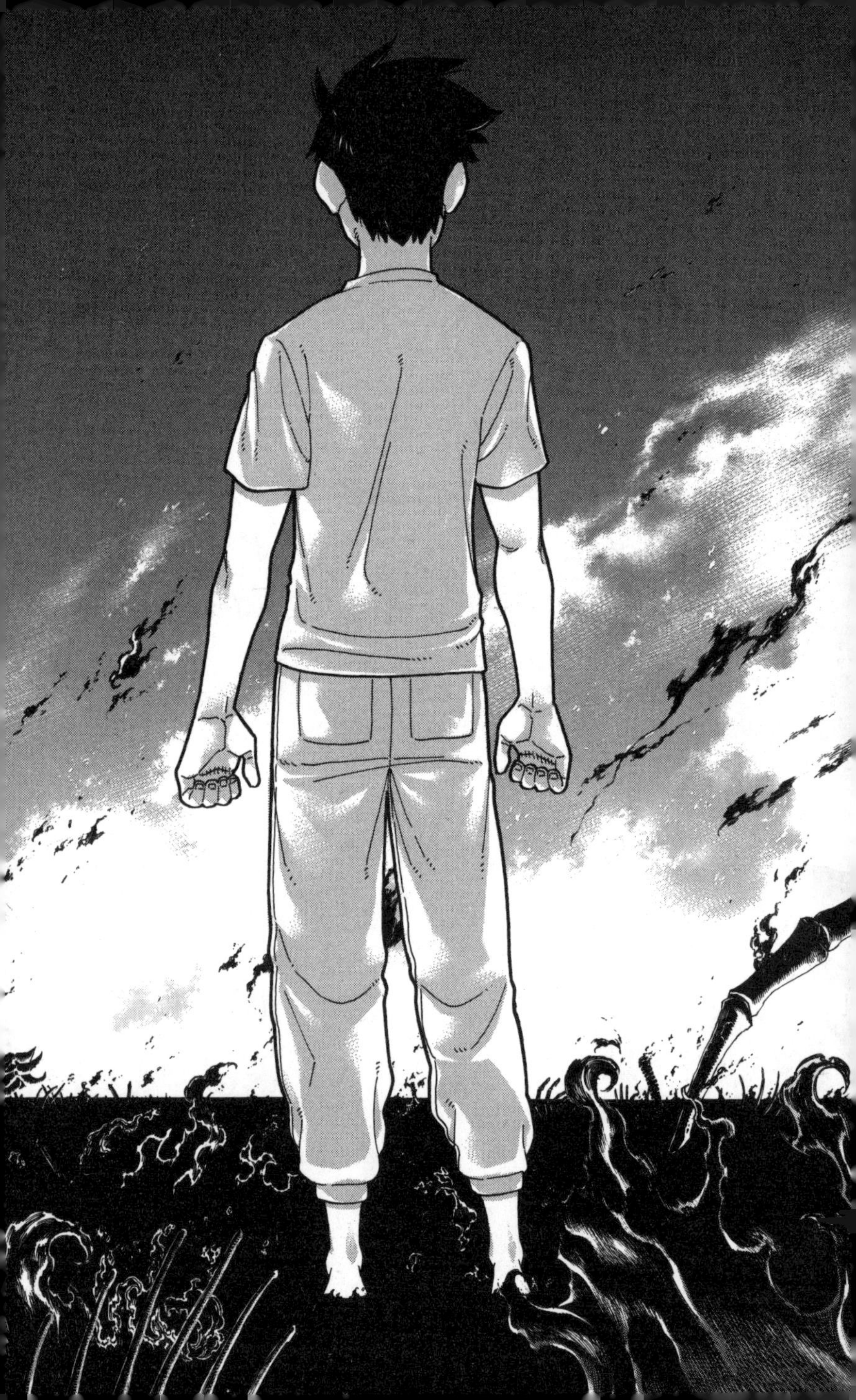

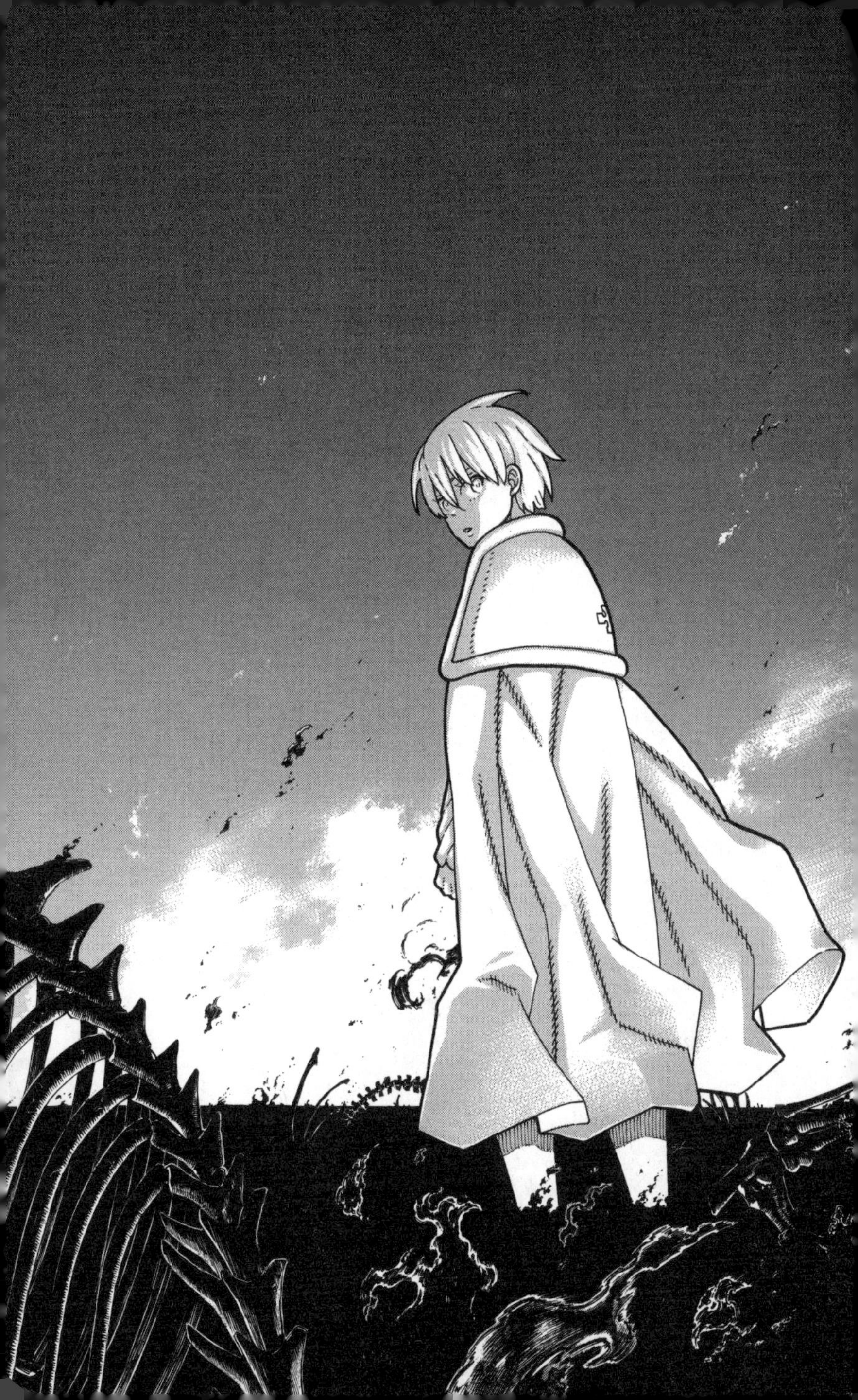

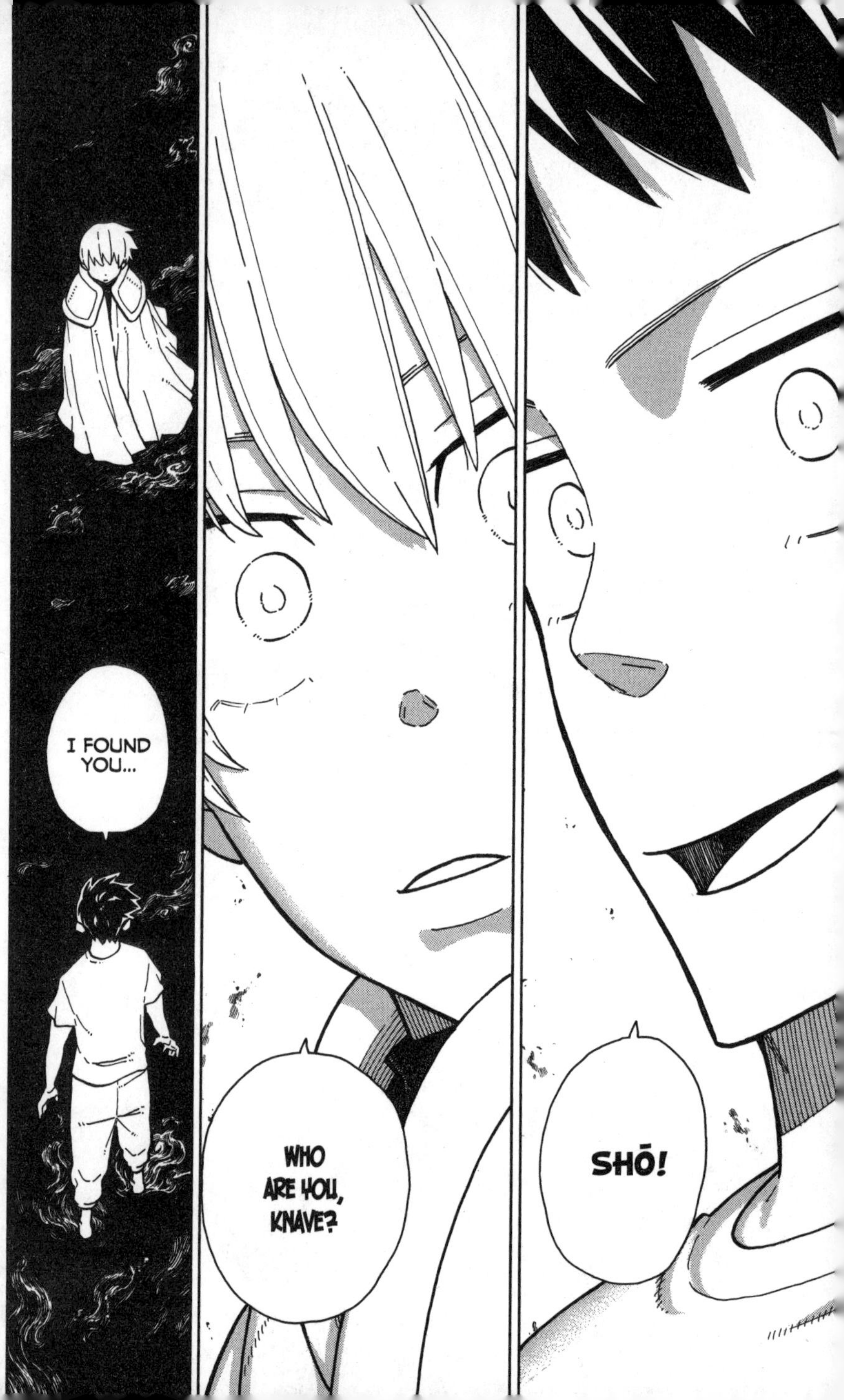
SHŌ!
WHO ARE YOU, KNAVE?
I FOUND YOU...

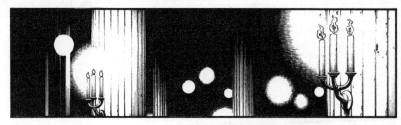

MY
BROTHER...

FIRE FORCE

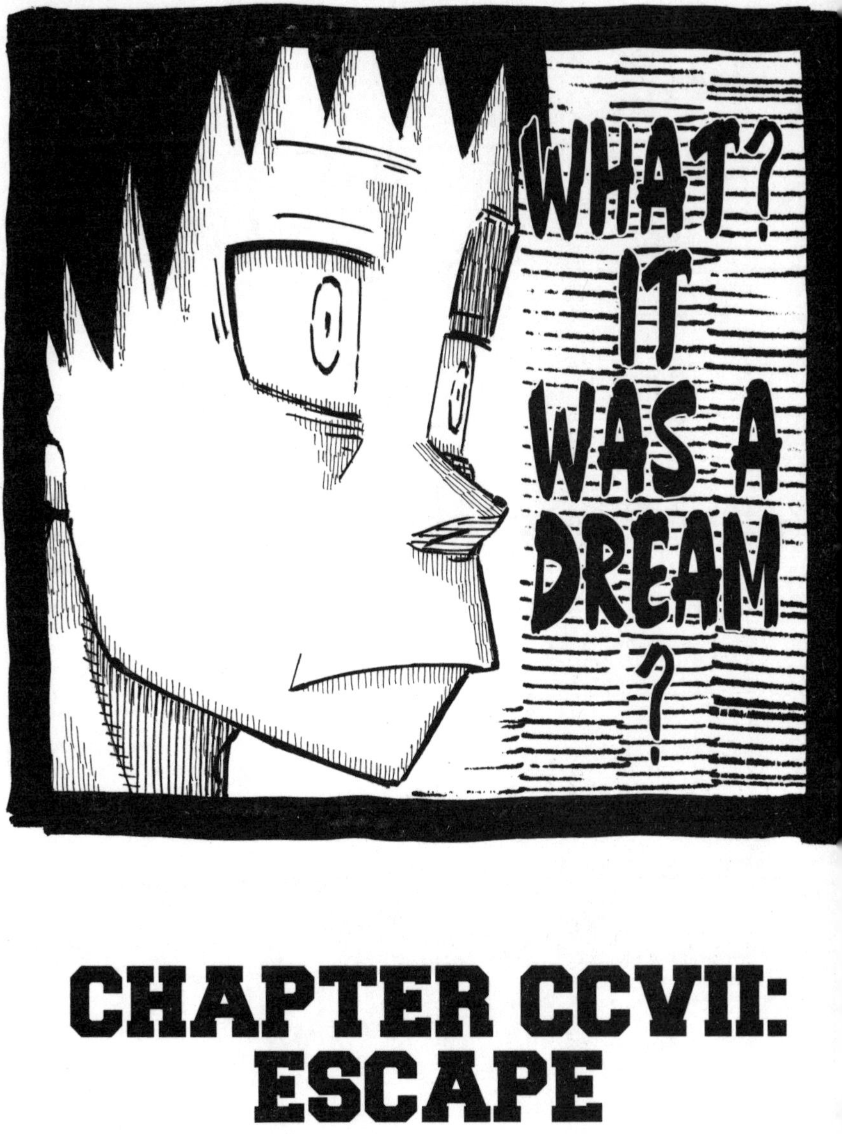
WHAT? IT WAS A DREAM??

CHAPTER CCVII: ESCAPE

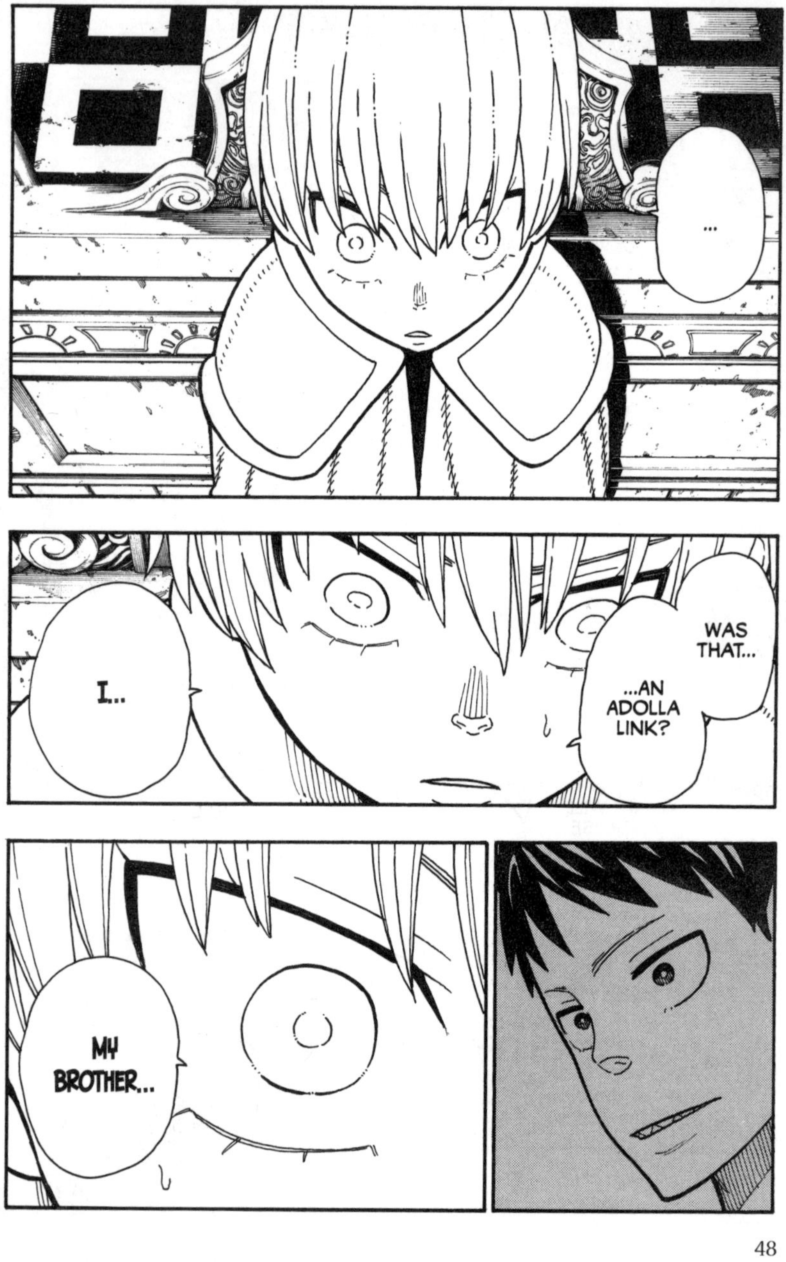
...
WAS THAT...
...AN ADOLLA LINK?
I...
MY BROTHER...

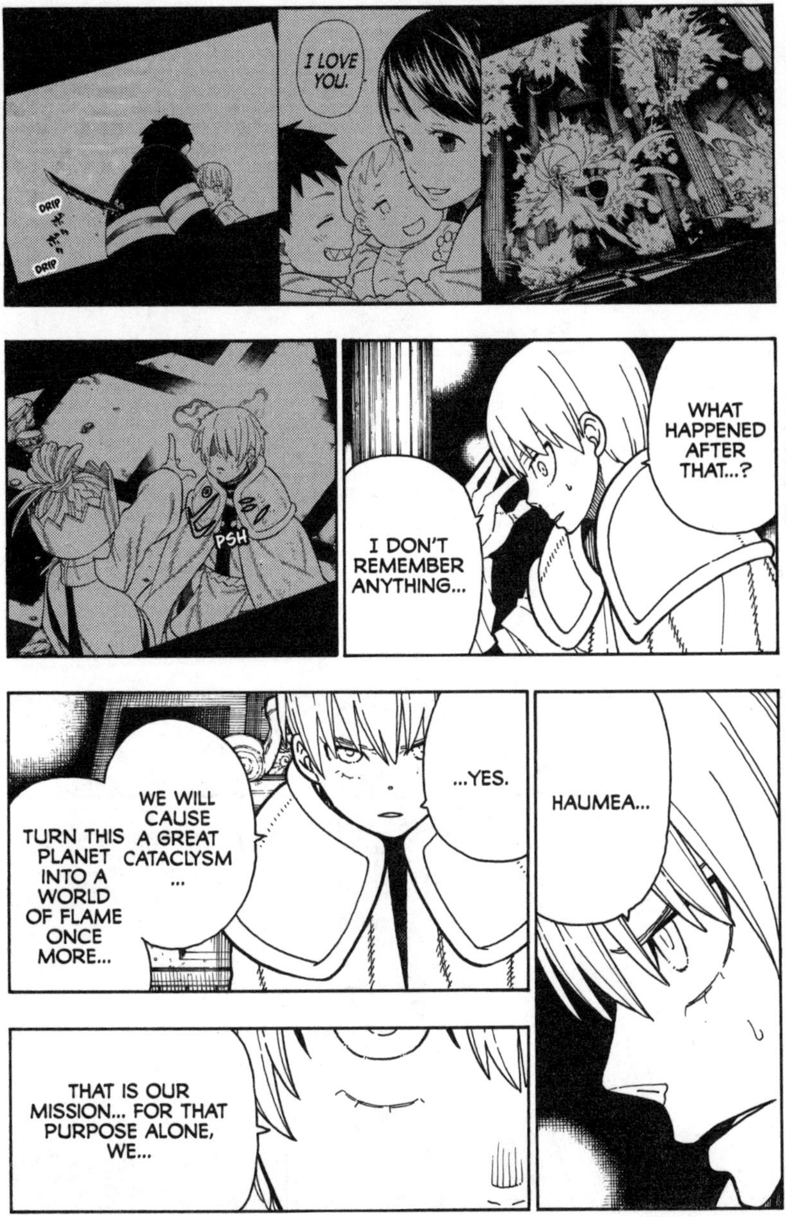
I LOVE YOU.
DRIP
DRIP
WHAT HAPPENED AFTER THAT...?
I DON'T REMEMBER ANYTHING...
PSH
HAUMEA...
...YES.
WE WILL CAUSE A GREAT CATACLYSM...
TURN THIS PLANET INTO A WORLD OF FLAME ONCE MORE...
THAT IS OUR MISSION... FOR THAT PURPOSE ALONE, WE...

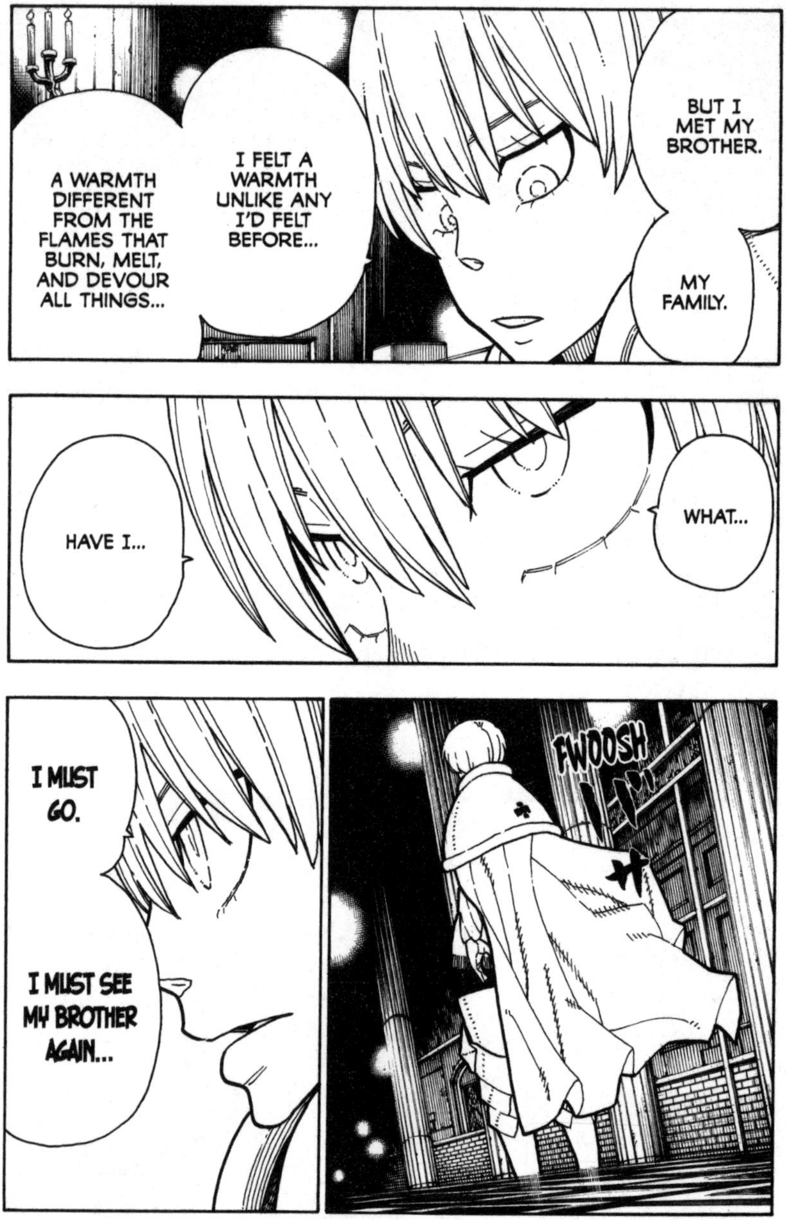
BUT I MET MY BROTHER.
MY FAMILY.
I FELT A WARMTH UNLIKE ANY I'D FELT BEFORE...
A WARMTH DIFFERENT FROM THE FLAMES THAT BURN, MELT, AND DEVOUR ALL THINGS...
WHAT...
HAVE I...
FWOOSH
I MUST GO.
I MUST SEE MY BROTHER AGAIN...

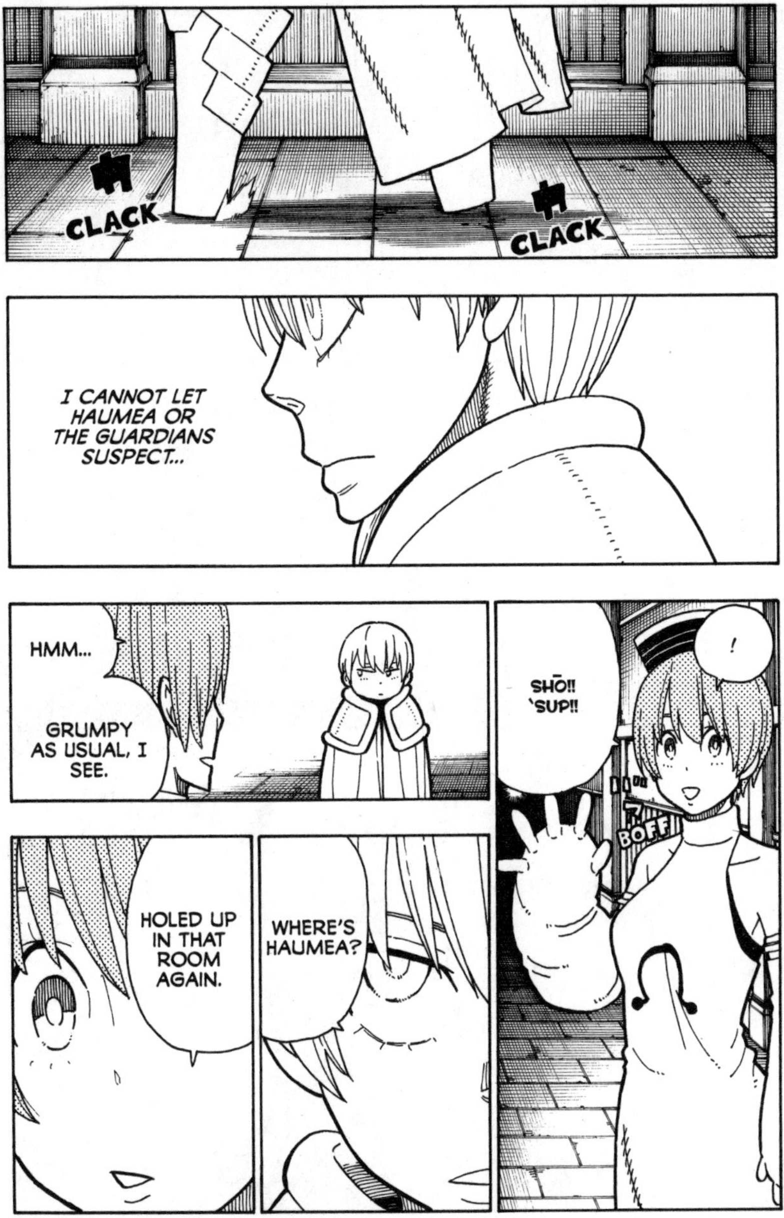
CLACK
CLACK
I CANNOT LET HAUMEA OR THE GUARDIANS SUSPECT...
!
SHŌ!! 'SUP!!
BOFF
HMM...
GRUMPY AS USUAL, I SEE.
WHERE'S HAUMEA?
HOLED UP IN THAT ROOM AGAIN.

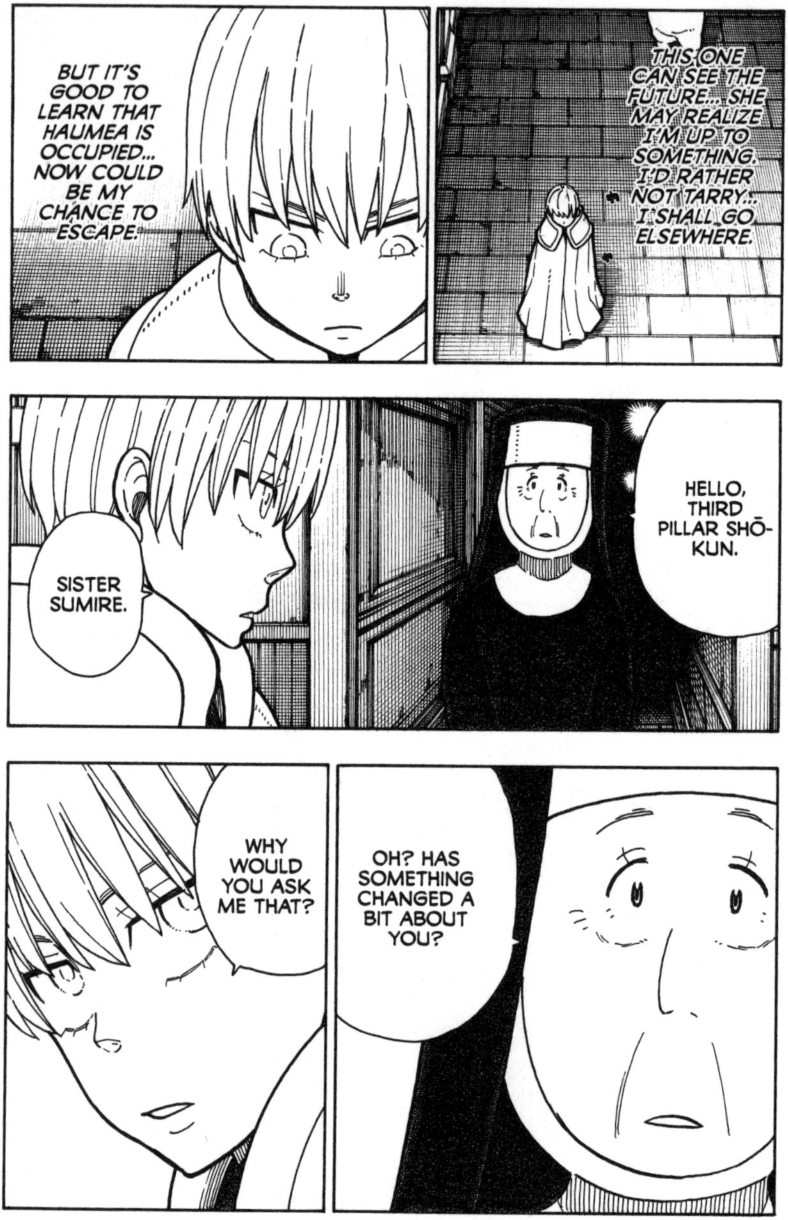
THIS ONE CAN SEE THE FUTURE... SHE MAY REALIZE I'M UP TO SOMETHING. I'D RATHER NOT TARRY... I SHALL GO ELSEWHERE.
BUT IT'S GOOD TO LEARN THAT HAUMEA IS OCCUPIED... NOW COULD BE MY CHANCE TO ESCAPE.
HELLO, THIRD PILLAR SHŌ-KUN.
SISTER SUMIRE.
OH? HAS SOMETHING CHANGED A BIT ABOUT YOU?
WHY WOULD YOU ASK ME THAT?

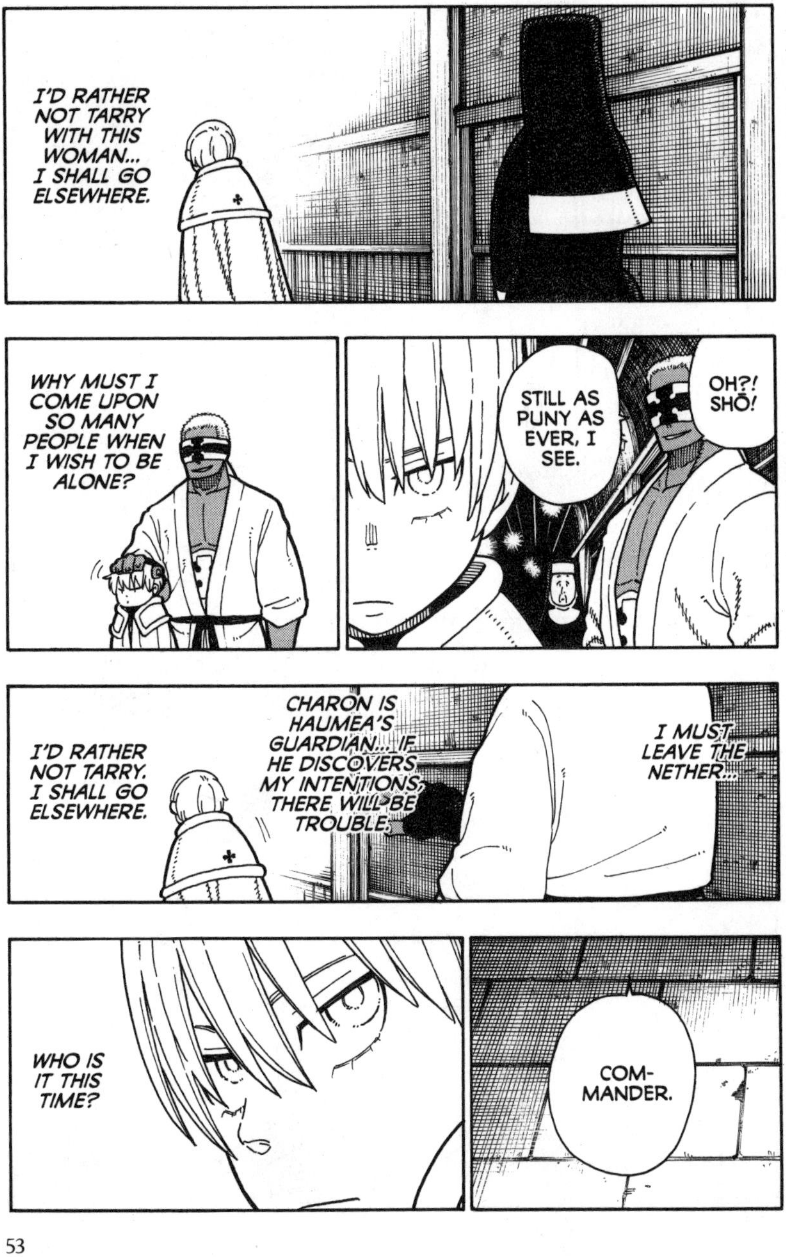
I'D RATHER NOT TARRY WITH THIS WOMAN... I SHALL GO ELSEWHERE.
OH?! SHŌ!
STILL AS PUNY AS EVER, I SEE.
WHY MUST I COME UPON SO MANY PEOPLE WHEN I WISH TO BE ALONE?
I MUST LEAVE THE NETHER...
CHARON IS HAUMEA'S GUARDIAN... IF HE DISCOVERS MY INTENTIONS, THERE WILL BE TROUBLE.
I'D RATHER NOT TARRY. I SHALL GO ELSEWHERE.
COM-MANDER.
WHO IS IT THIS TIME?

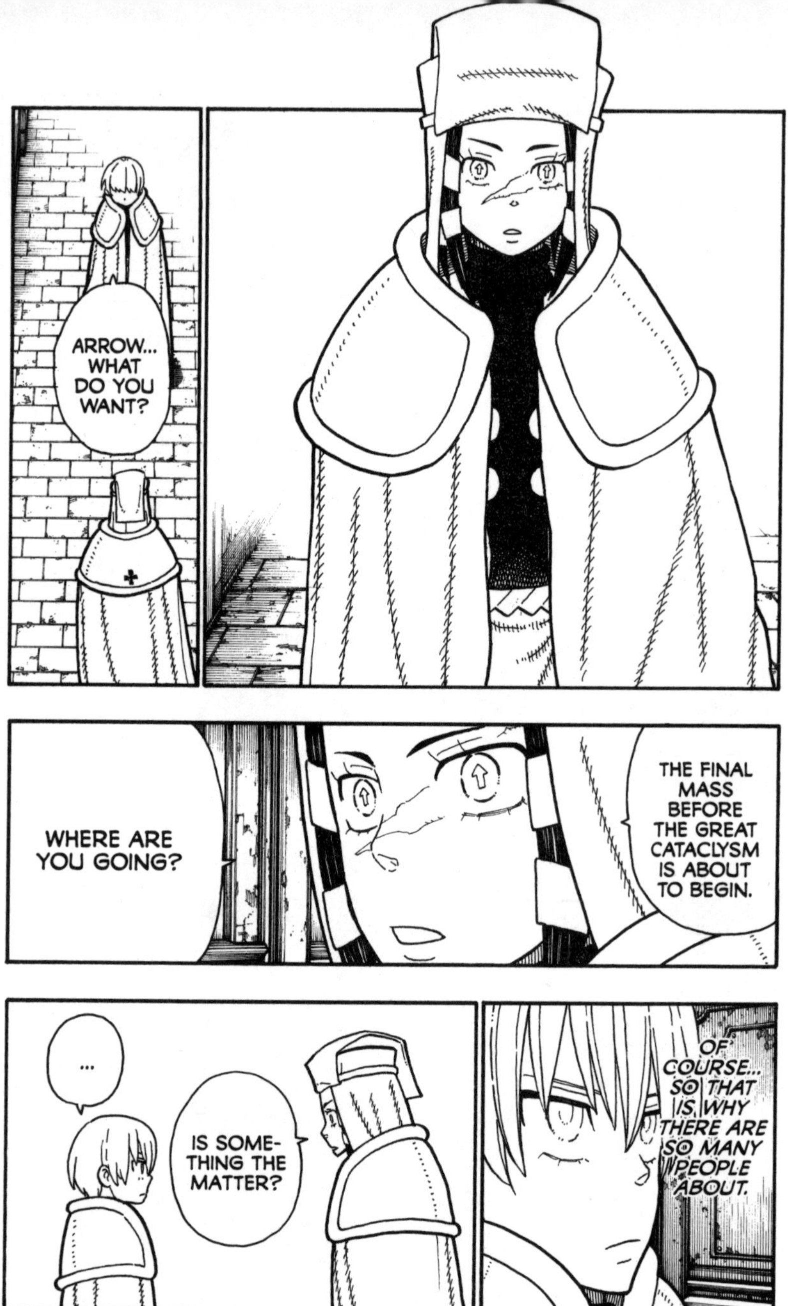
ARROW... WHAT DO YOU WANT?
THE FINAL MASS BEFORE THE GREAT CATACLYSM IS ABOUT TO BEGIN.
WHERE ARE YOU GOING?
OF COURSE... SO THAT IS WHY THERE ARE SO MANY PEOPLE ABOUT.
IS SOMETHING THE MATTER?
...

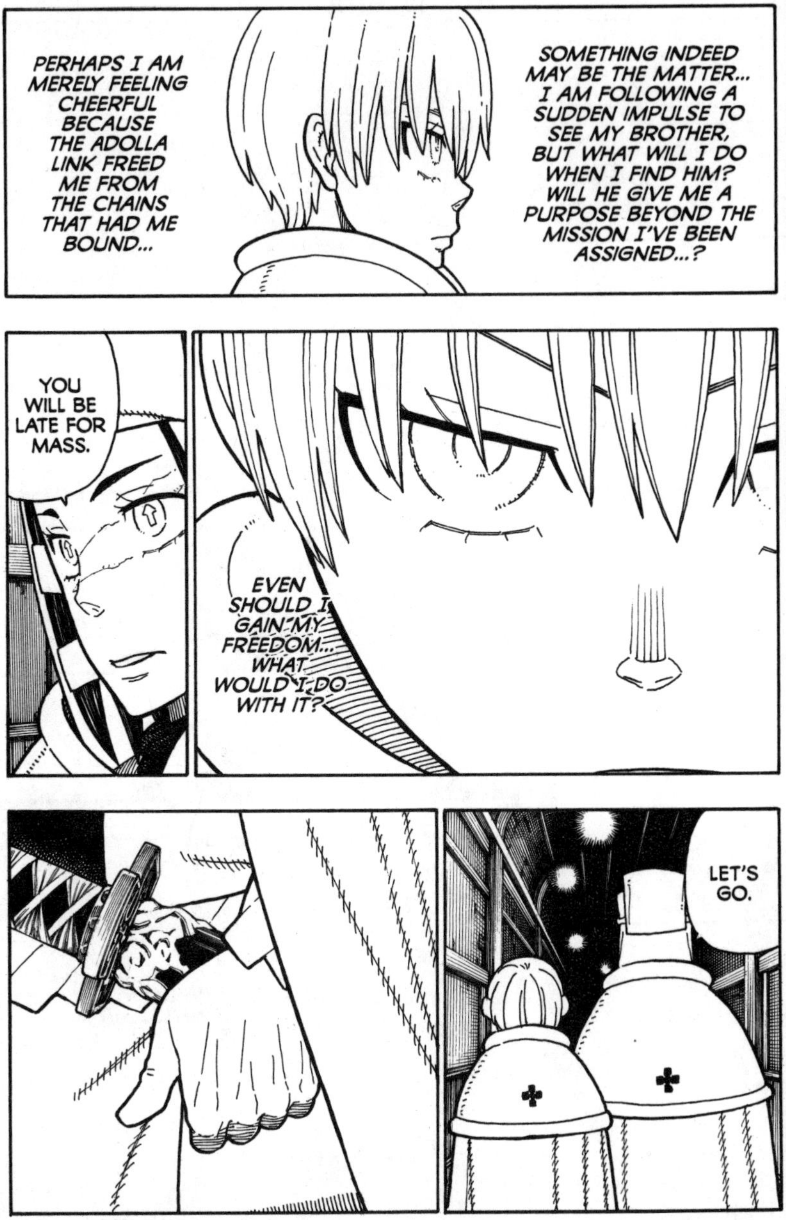
SOMETHING INDEED MAY BE THE MATTER... I AM FOLLOWING A SUDDEN IMPULSE TO SEE MY BROTHER, BUT WHAT WILL I DO WHEN I FIND HIM? WILL HE GIVE ME A PURPOSE BEYOND THE MISSION I'VE BEEN ASSIGNED...?
PERHAPS I AM MERELY FEELING CHEERFUL BECAUSE THE ADOLLA LINK FREED ME FROM THE CHAINS THAT HAD ME BOUND...
EVEN SHOULD I GAIN MY FREEDOM... WHAT WOULD I DO WITH IT?
YOU WILL BE LATE FOR MASS.
LET'S GO.

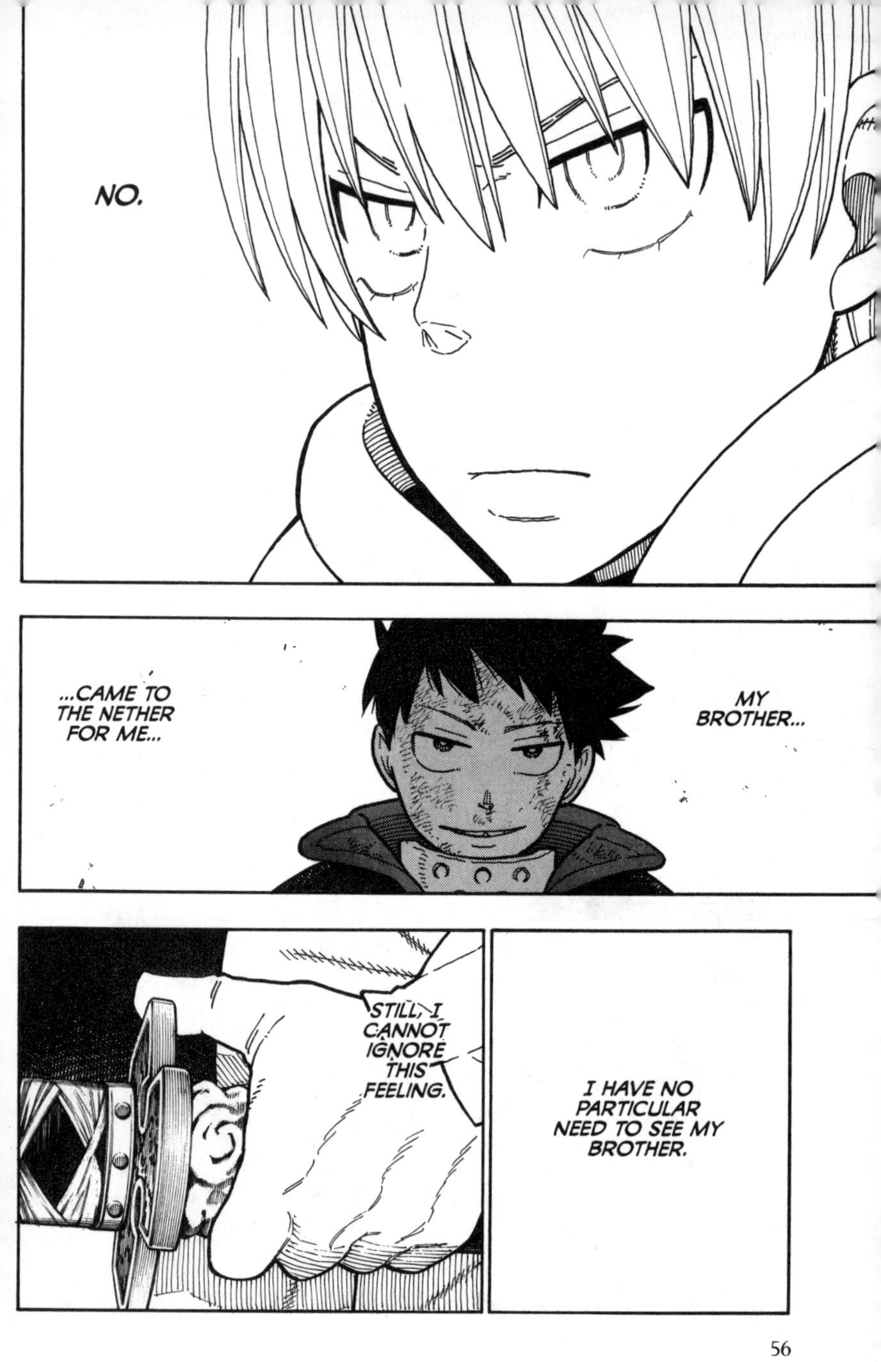
NO.
MY BROTHER...
...CAME TO THE NETHER FOR ME...
I HAVE NO PARTICULAR NEED TO SEE MY BROTHER.
STILL, I CANNOT IGNORE THIS FEELING.

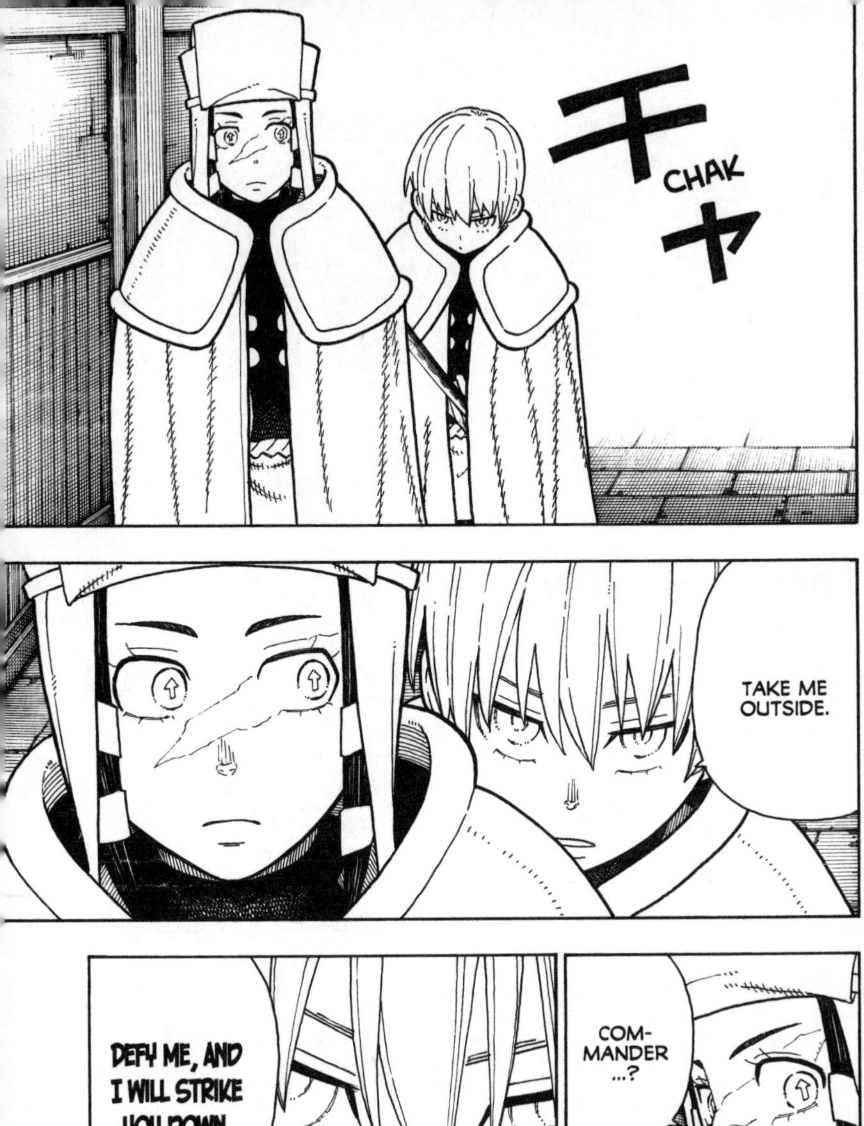
チャ
CHAK
TAKE ME OUTSIDE.
COM-MANDER ...?
DEFY ME, AND I WILL STRIKE YOU DOWN.

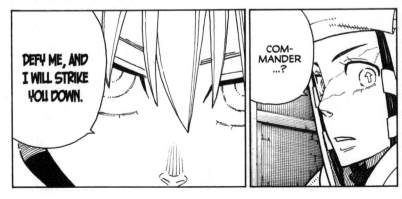

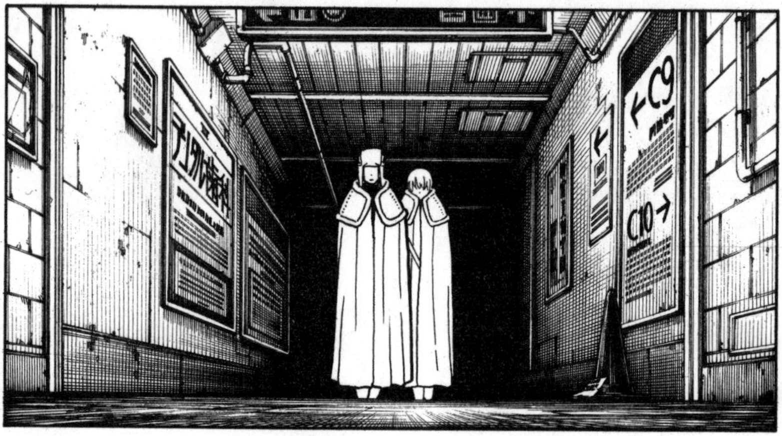
←C9
C10→

Sign: Dental Clinic

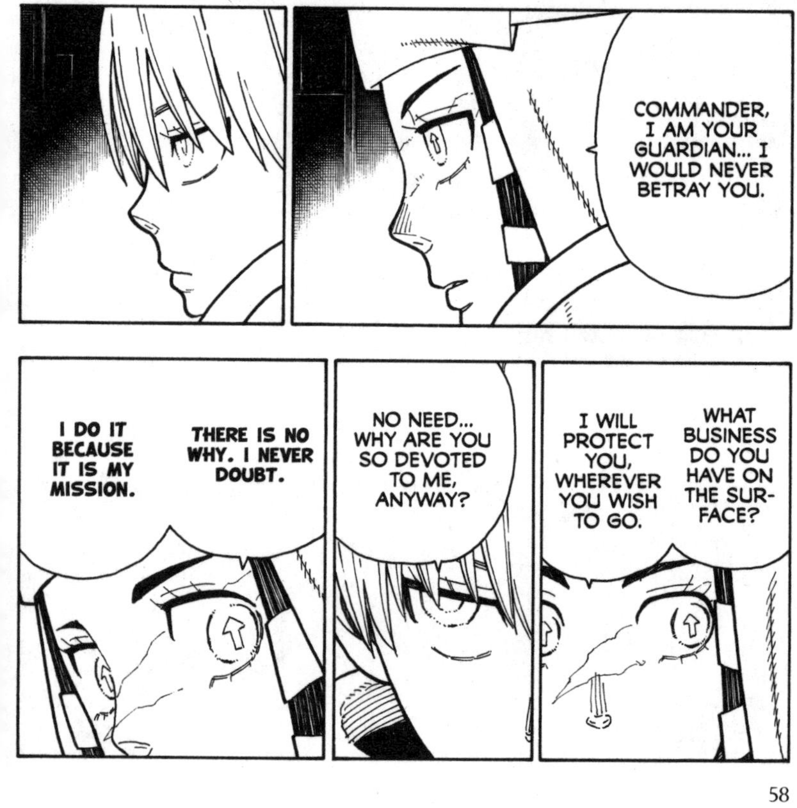
COMMANDER, I AM YOUR GUARDIAN... I WOULD NEVER BETRAY YOU.
WHAT BUSINESS DO YOU HAVE ON THE SURFACE?
I WILL PROTECT YOU, WHEREVER YOU WISH TO GO.
NO NEED... WHY ARE YOU SO DEVOTED TO ME, ANYWAY?
THERE IS NO WHY. I NEVER DOUBT.
I DO IT BECAUSE IT IS MY MISSION.

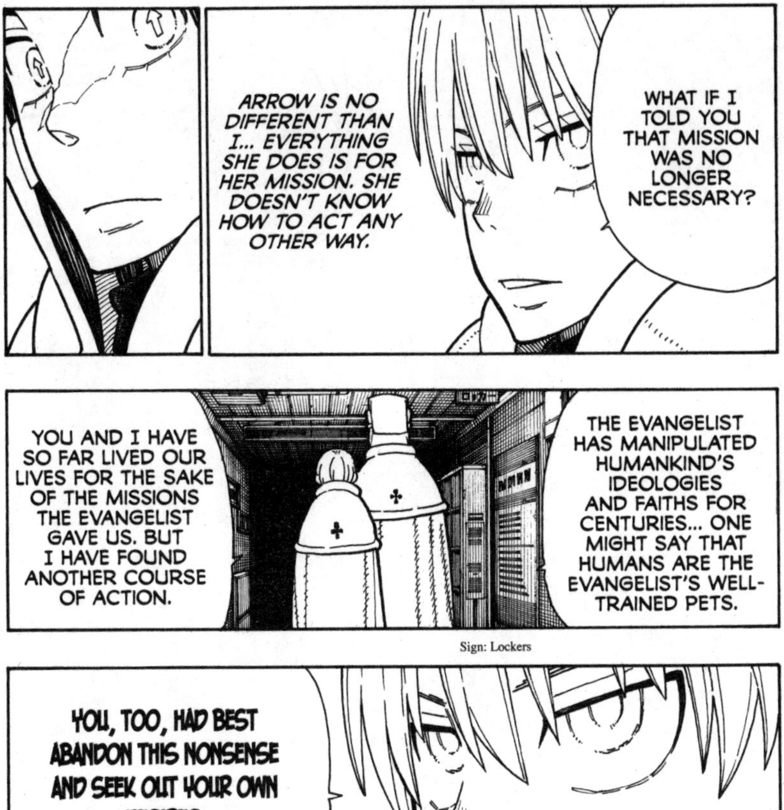

WHAT IF I TOLD YOU THAT MISSION WAS NO LONGER NECESSARY?
ARROW IS NO DIFFERENT THAN I... EVERYTHING SHE DOES IS FOR HER MISSION. SHE DOESN'T KNOW HOW TO ACT ANY OTHER WAY.
THE EVANGELIST HAS MANIPULATED HUMANKIND'S IDEOLOGIES AND FAITHS FOR CENTURIES... ONE MIGHT SAY THAT HUMANS ARE THE EVANGELIST'S WELL-TRAINED PETS.
YOU AND I HAVE SO FAR LIVED OUR LIVES FOR THE SAKE OF THE MISSIONS THE EVANGELIST GAVE US. BUT I HAVE FOUND ANOTHER COURSE OF ACTION.
YOU, TOO, HAD BEST ABANDON THIS NONSENSE AND SEEK OUT YOUR OWN DESIRES.
MY MISSION IS NOT "NONSENSE."
HOW IS IT NOT NONSENSE?

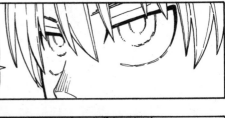

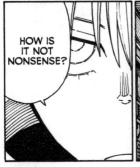

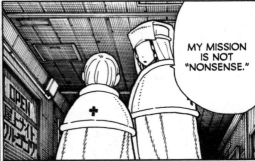

Sign: Lockers

Sign: Open
Night Cruising on the Roof

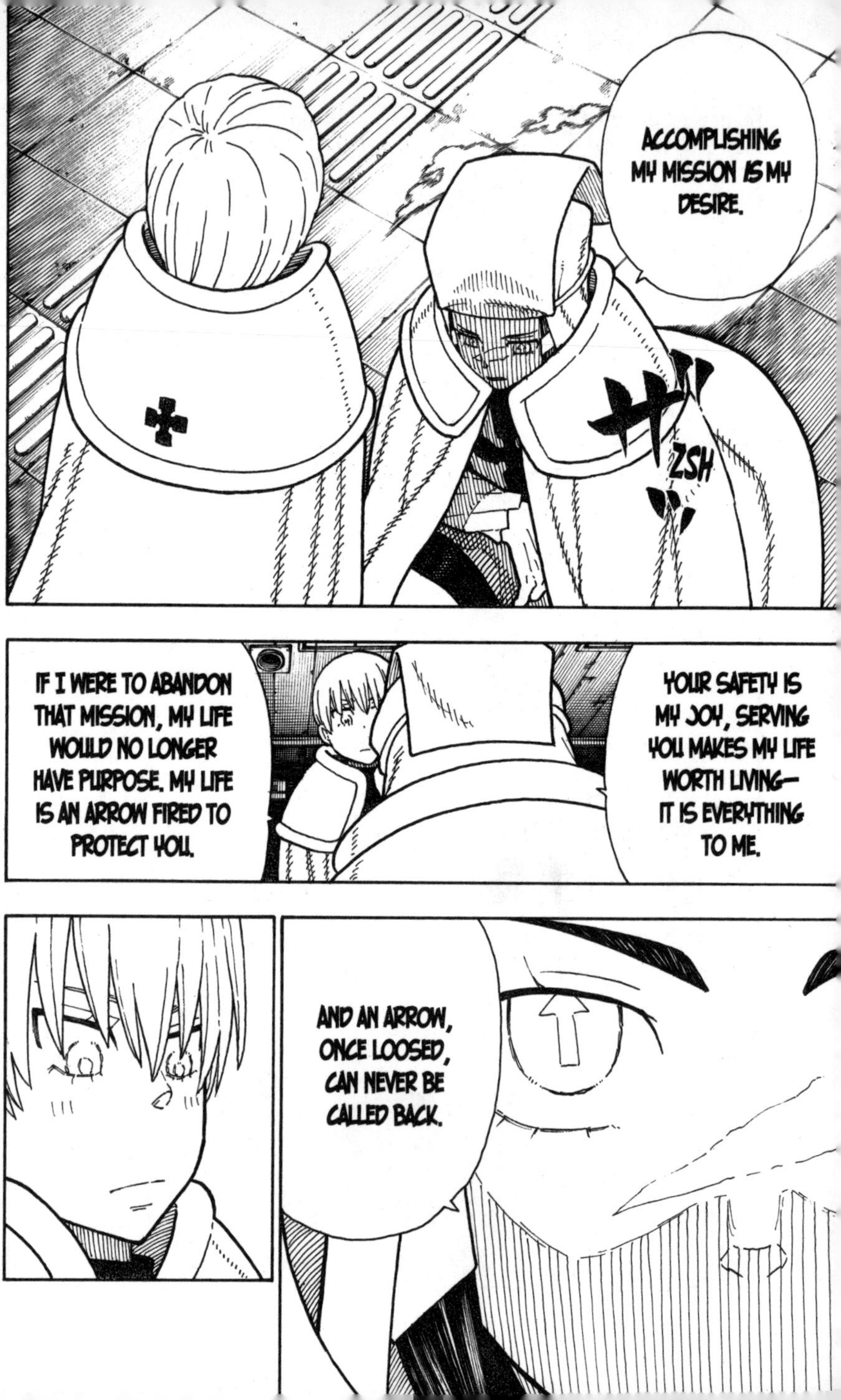
ACCOMPLISHING MY MISSION IS MY DESIRE.
ZSH
YOUR SAFETY IS MY JOY, SERVING YOU MAKES MY LIFE WORTH LIVING— IT IS EVERYTHING TO ME.
IF I WERE TO ABANDON THAT MISSION, MY LIFE WOULD NO LONGER HAVE PURPOSE. MY LIFE IS AN ARROW FIRED TO PROTECT YOU.
AND AN ARROW, ONCE LOOSED, CAN NEVER BE CALLED BACK.

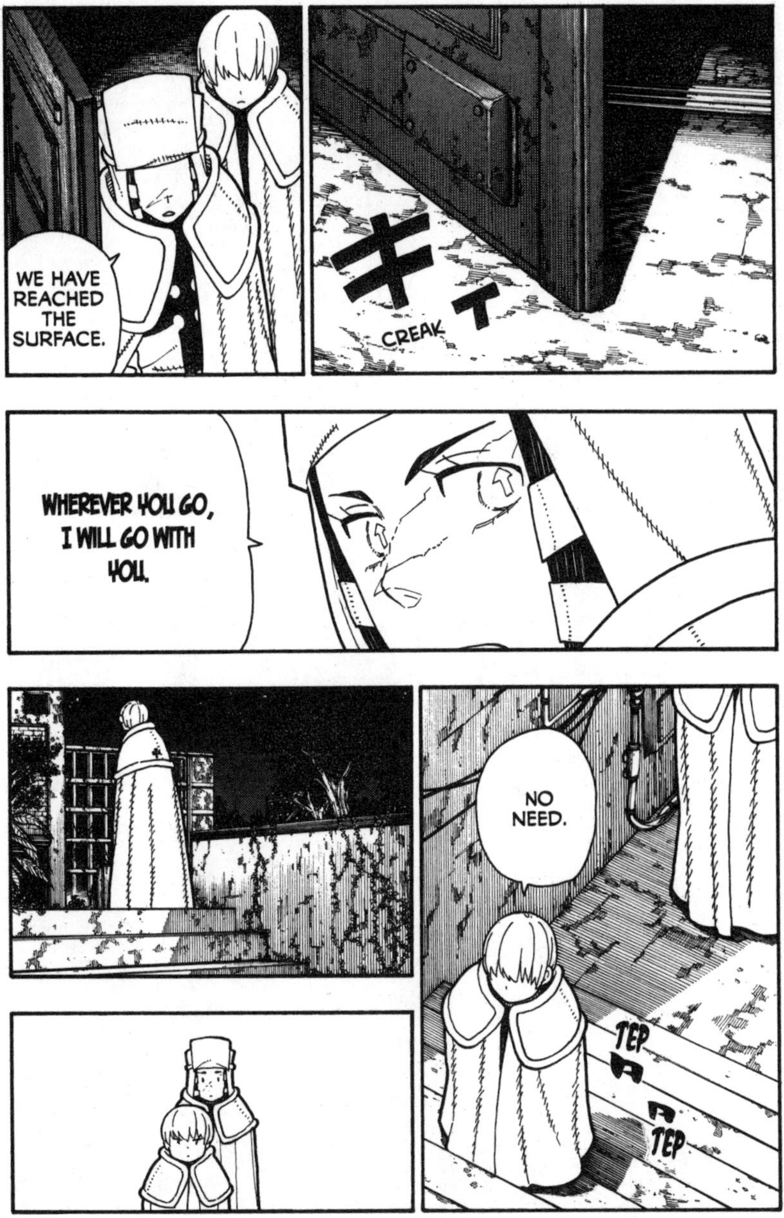
キィ
CREAK
WE HAVE REACHED THE SURFACE.
WHEREVER YOU GO, I WILL GO WITH YOU.
NO NEED.
TEP
TEP

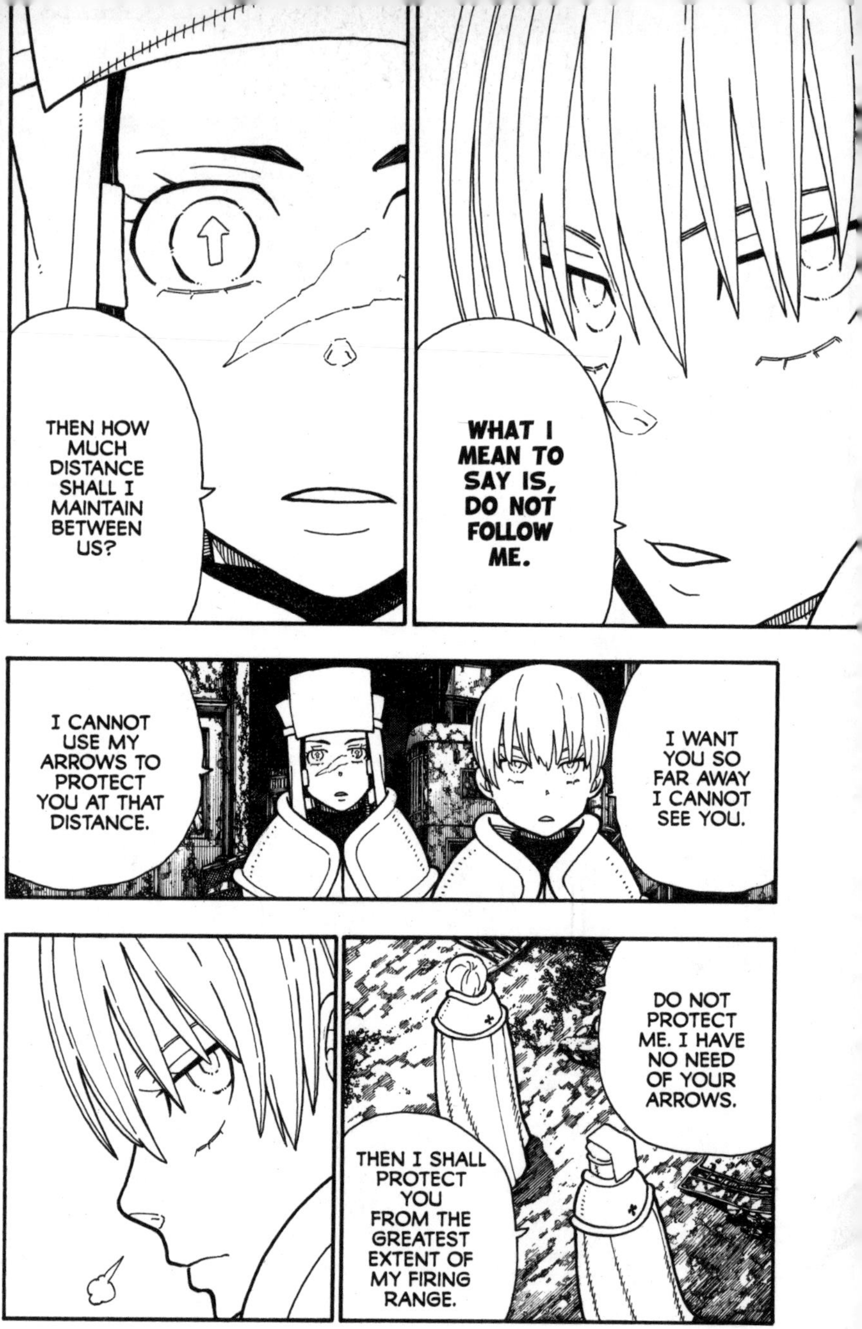
WHAT I MEAN TO SAY IS, DO NOT FOLLOW ME.
THEN HOW MUCH DISTANCE SHALL I MAINTAIN BETWEEN US?
I WANT YOU SO FAR AWAY I CANNOT SEE YOU.
I CANNOT USE MY ARROWS TO PROTECT YOU AT THAT DISTANCE.
DO NOT PROTECT ME. I HAVE NO NEED OF YOUR ARROWS.
THEN I SHALL PROTECT YOU FROM THE GREATEST EXTENT OF MY FIRING RANGE.

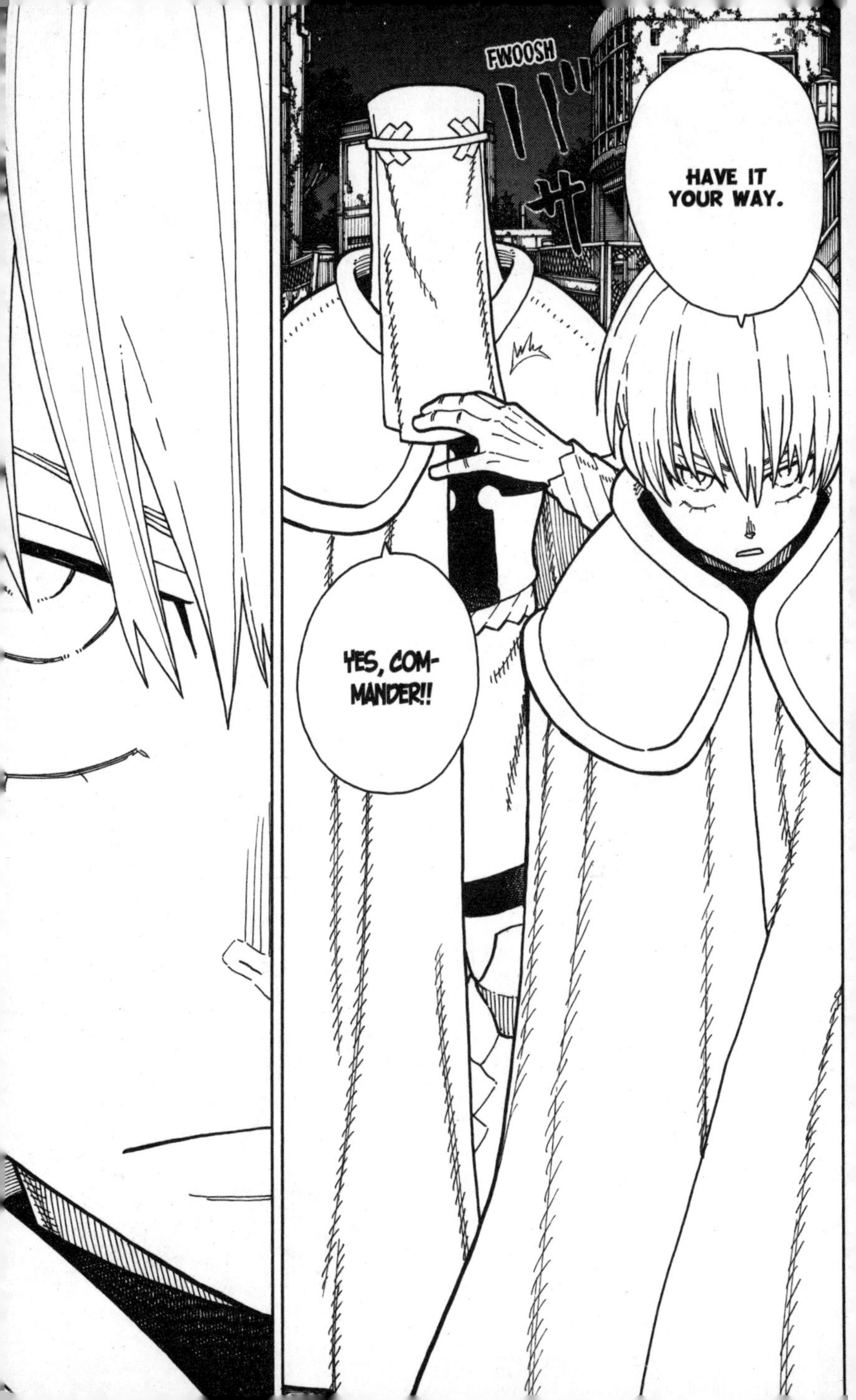
FWOOSH
HAVE IT YOUR WAY.
YES, COM-MANDER!!

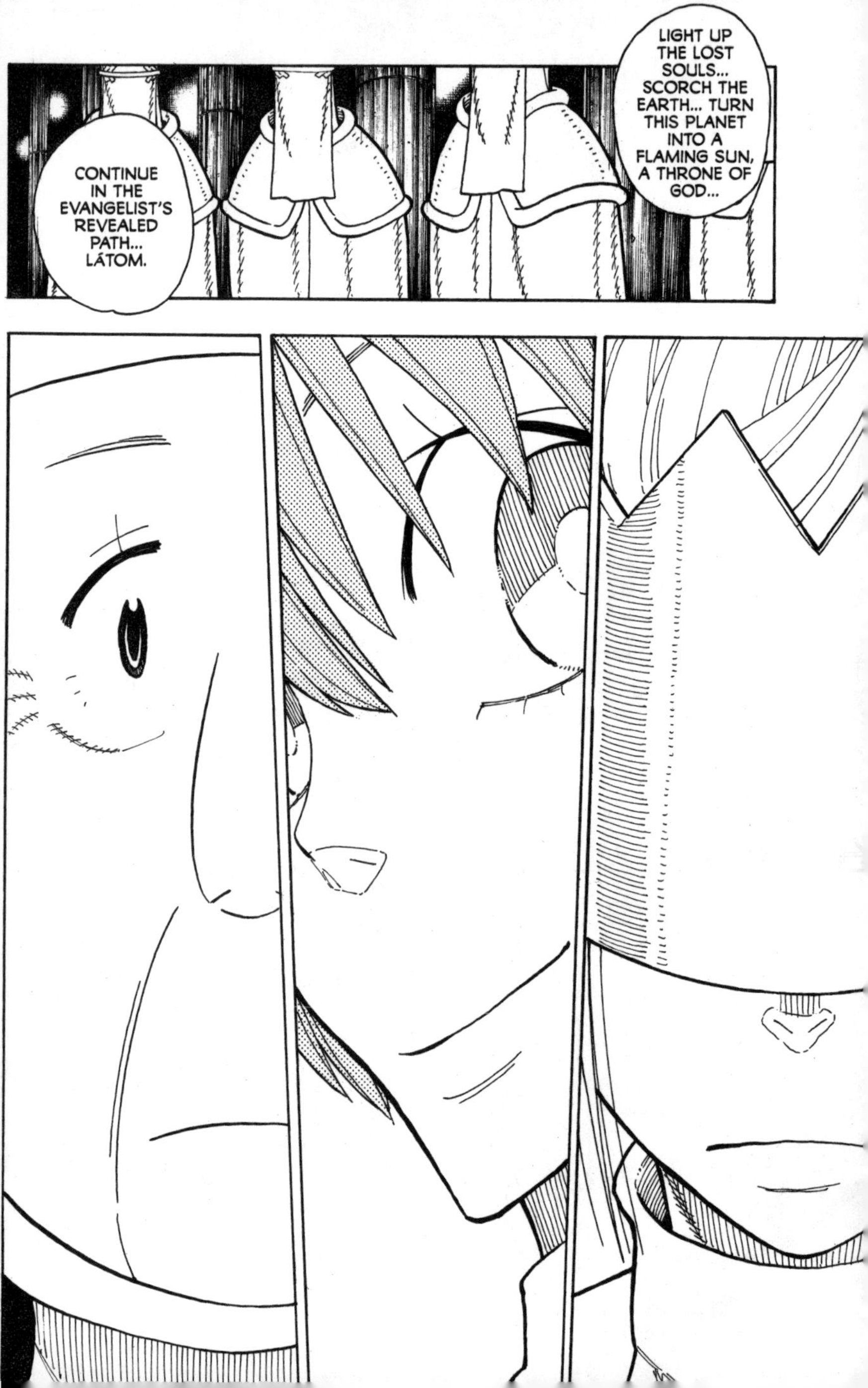
LIGHT UP THE LOST SOULS... SCORCH THE EARTH... TURN THIS PLANET INTO A FLAMING SUN, A THRONE OF GOD...
CONTINUE IN THE EVANGELIST'S REVEALED PATH... LÁTOM.

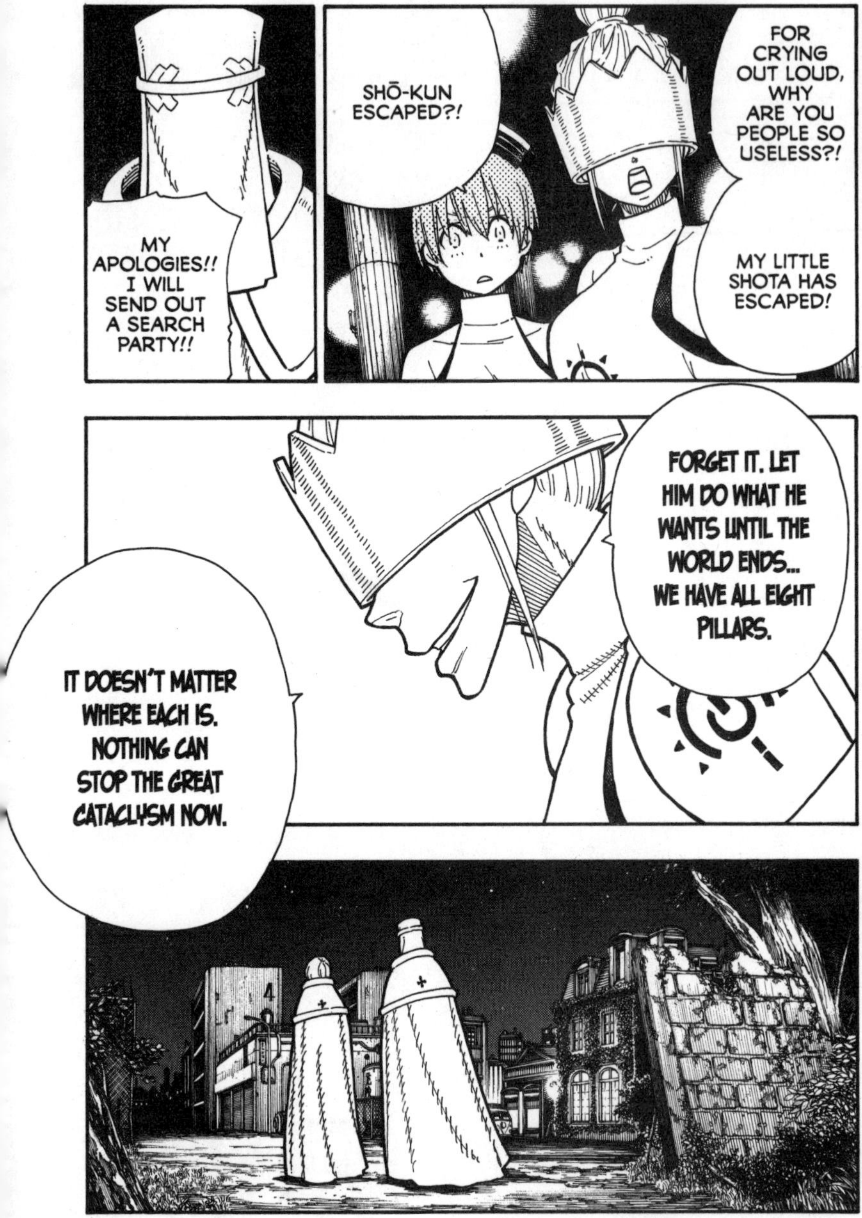
FOR CRYING OUT LOUD, WHY ARE YOU PEOPLE SO USELESS?!
SHŌ-KUN ESCAPED?!
MY LITTLE SHOTA HAS ESCAPED!
MY APOLOGIES!! I WILL SEND OUT A SEARCH PARTY!!
FORGET IT. LET HIM DO WHAT HE WANTS UNTIL THE WORLD ENDS... WE HAVE ALL EIGHT PILLARS.
IT DOESN'T MATTER WHERE EACH IS. NOTHING CAN STOP THE GREAT CATACLYSM NOW.

FIRE FORCE

Haumea

CHAPTER CCVIII: APOCALYPSE ASSEMBLY

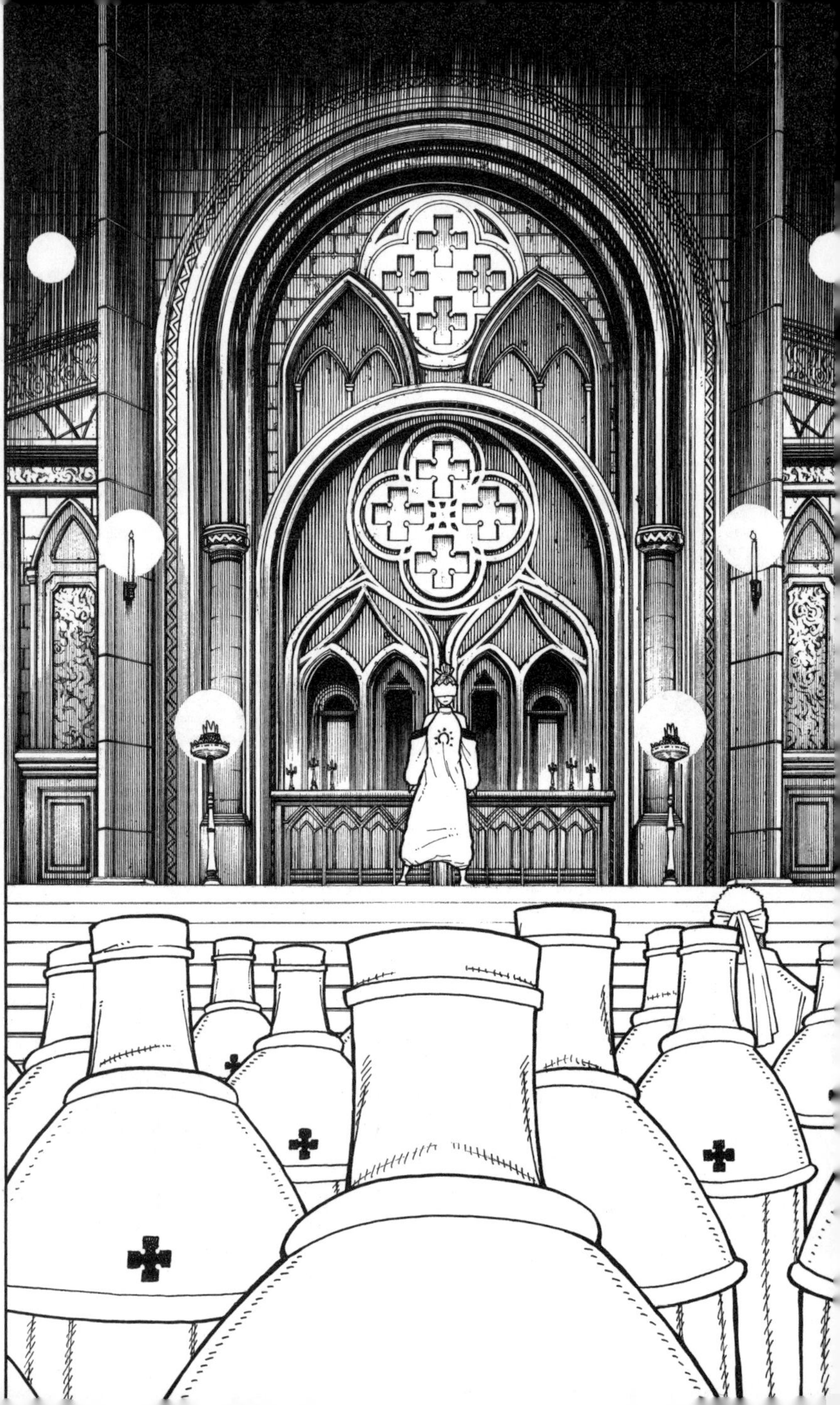

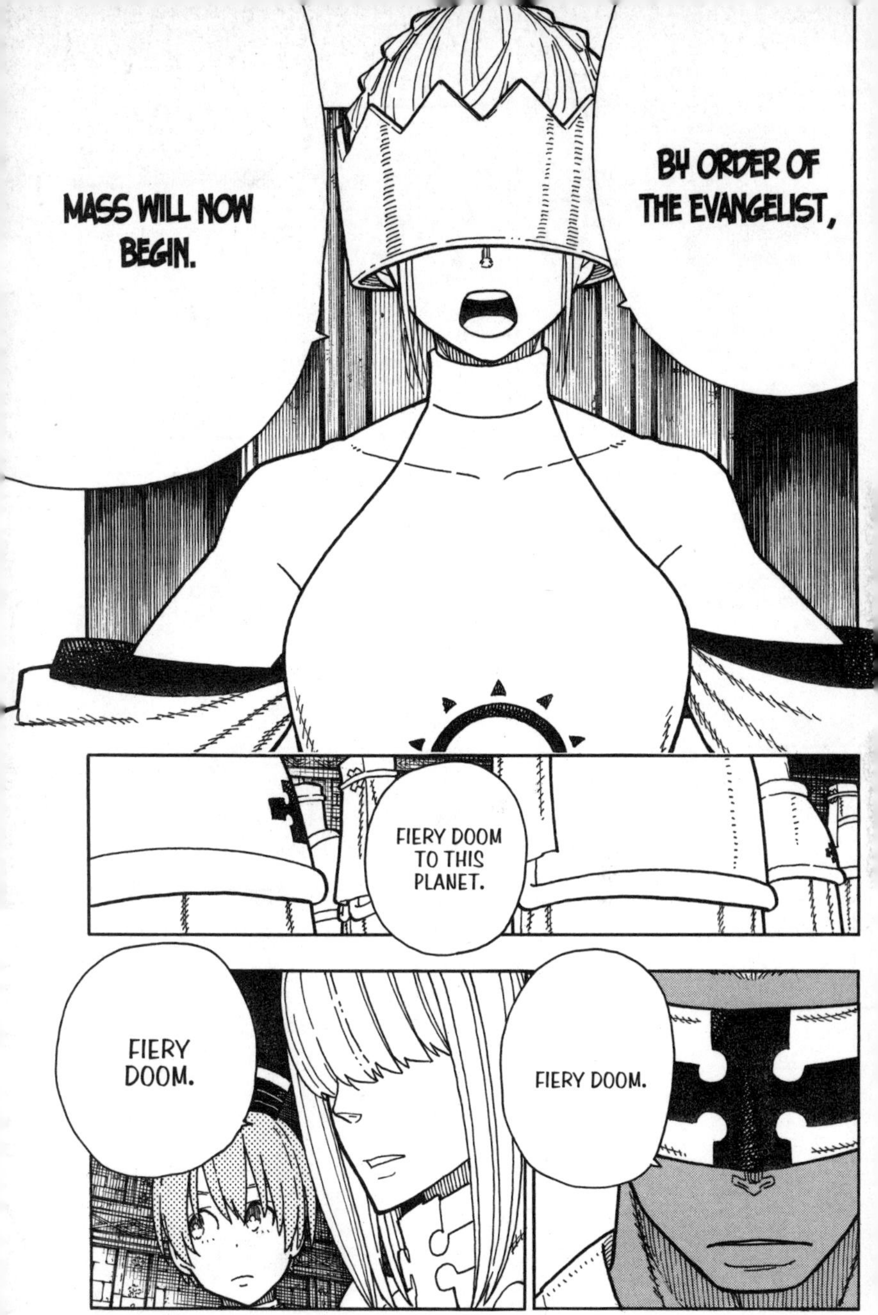
BY ORDER OF THE EVANGELIST,
MASS WILL NOW BEGIN.
FIERY DOOM TO THIS PLANET.
FIERY DOOM.
FIERY DOOM.

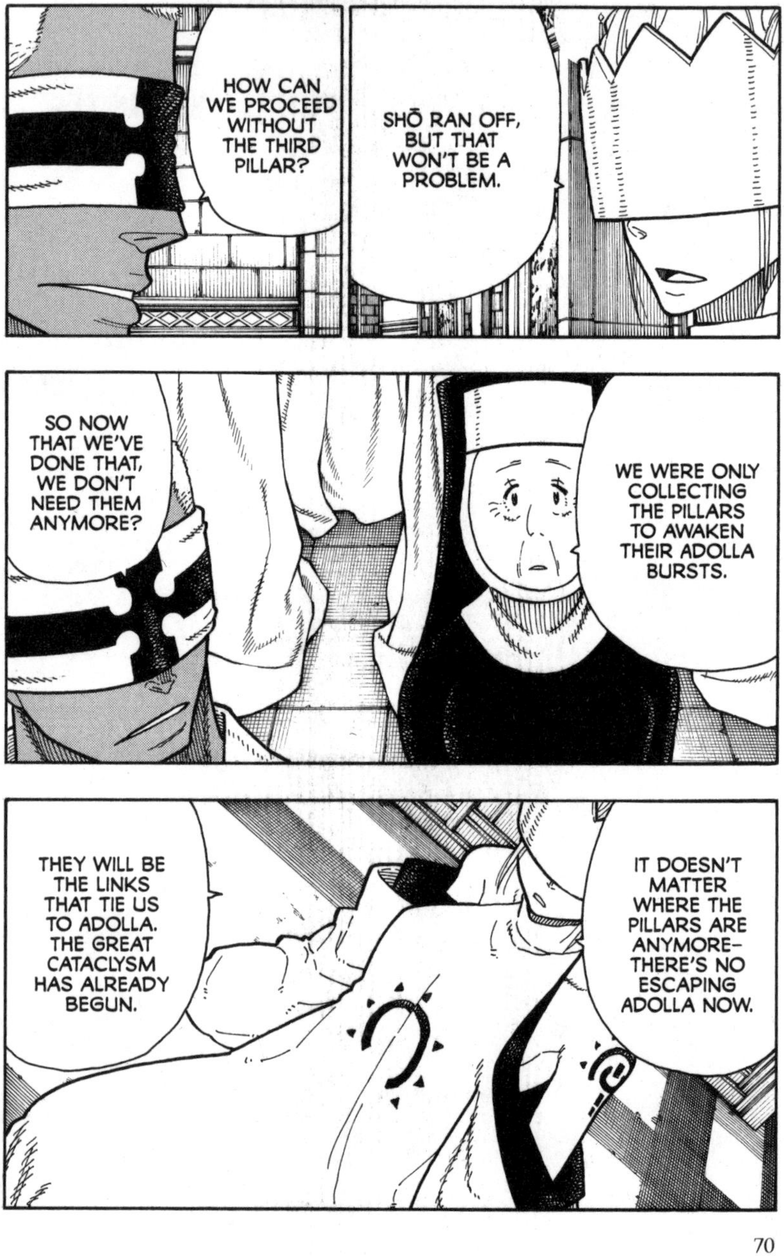
SHŌ RAN OFF, BUT THAT WON'T BE A PROBLEM.
HOW CAN WE PROCEED WITHOUT THE THIRD PILLAR?
WE WERE ONLY COLLECTING THE PILLARS TO AWAKEN THEIR ADOLLA BURSTS.
SO NOW THAT WE'VE DONE THAT, WE DON'T NEED THEM ANYMORE?
IT DOESN'T MATTER WHERE THE PILLARS ARE ANYMORE— THERE'S NO ESCAPING ADOLLA NOW.
THEY WILL BE THE LINKS THAT TIE US TO ADOLLA. THE GREAT CATACLYSM HAS ALREADY BEGUN.

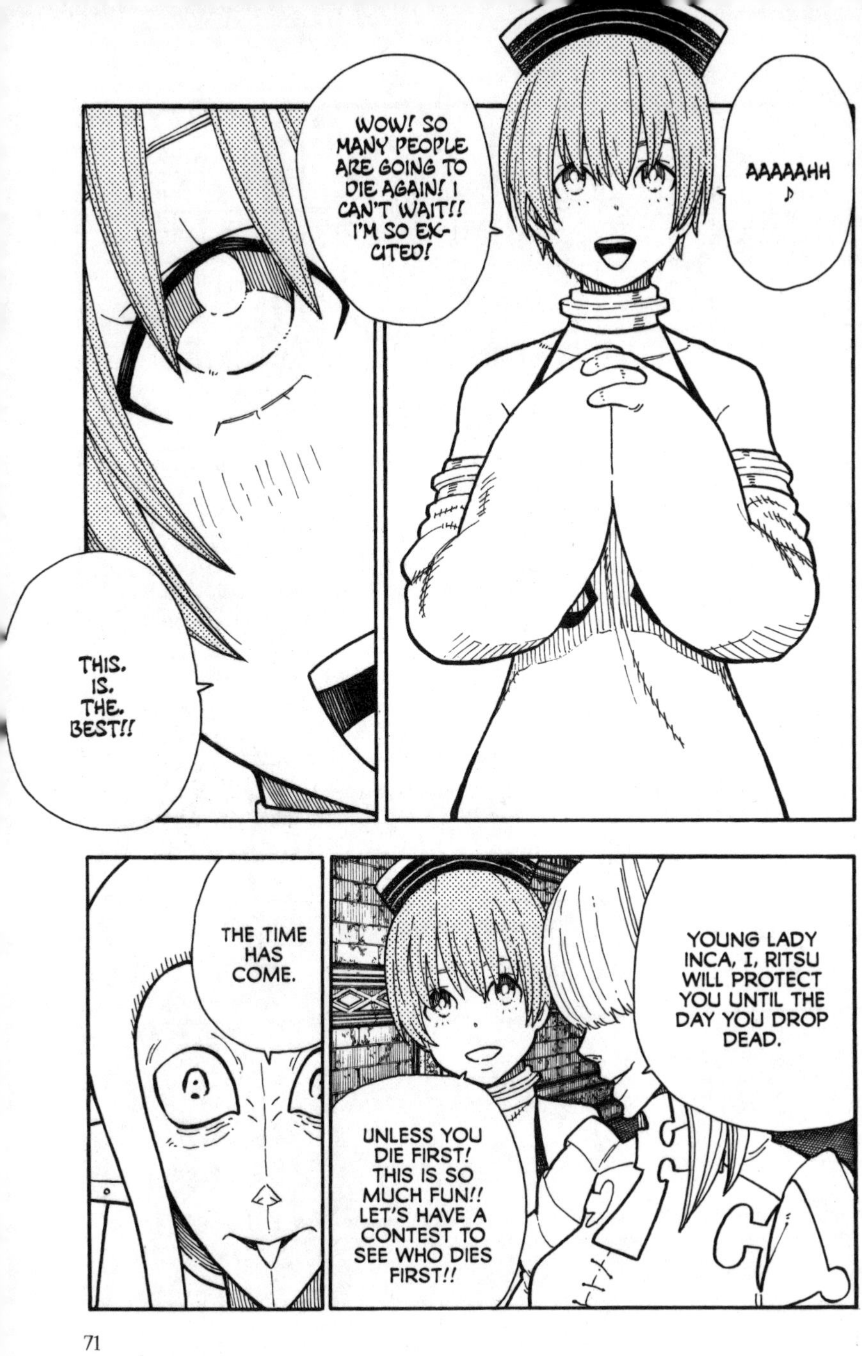
AAAAAHH ♪
WOW! SO MANY PEOPLE ARE GOING TO DIE AGAIN! I CAN'T WAIT!! I'M SO EX-CITED!
THIS. IS. THE. BEST!!
YOUNG LADY INCA, I, RITSU WILL PROTECT YOU UNTIL THE DAY YOU DROP DEAD.
UNLESS YOU DIE FIRST! THIS IS SO MUCH FUN!! LET'S HAVE A CONTEST TO SEE WHO DIES FIRST!!
THE TIME HAS COME.

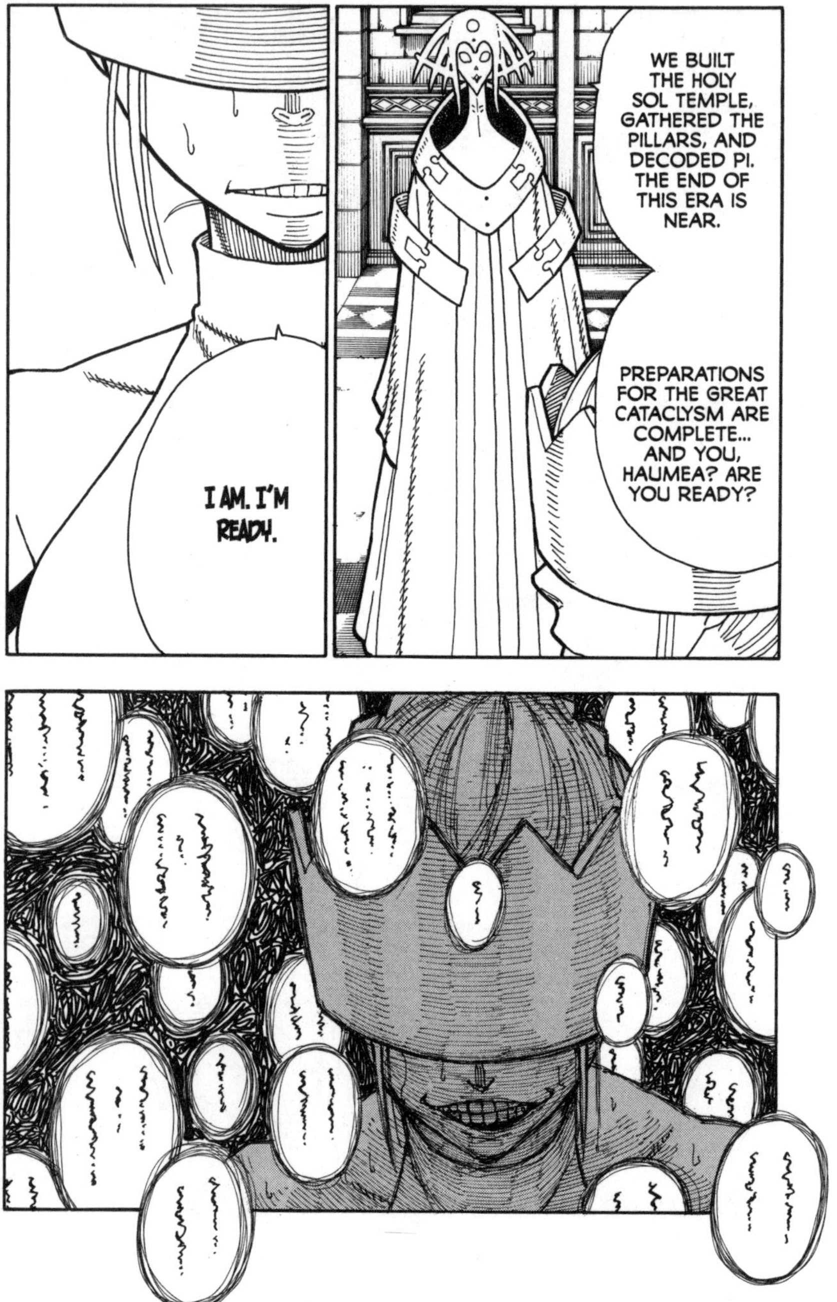
WE BUILT THE HOLY SOL TEMPLE, GATHERED THE PILLARS, AND DECODED PI. THE END OF THIS ERA IS NEAR.
PREPARATIONS FOR THE GREAT CATACLYSM ARE COMPLETE... AND YOU, HAUMEA? ARE YOU READY?
I AM. I'M READY.

THE EVANGELIST IS SATISFIED, TOO.

...

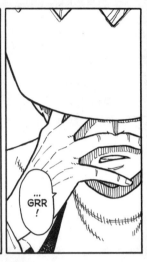
...
GRR!

YES.

THAT'S HOW LONG IT'S BEEN SINCE I CAME TO THIS WORLD.

IT'S BEEN 250 YEARS SINCE LAST TIME... SINCE WE FAILED.

THAT'S HOW LONG I'VE YEARNED FOR THIS DAY TO COME.

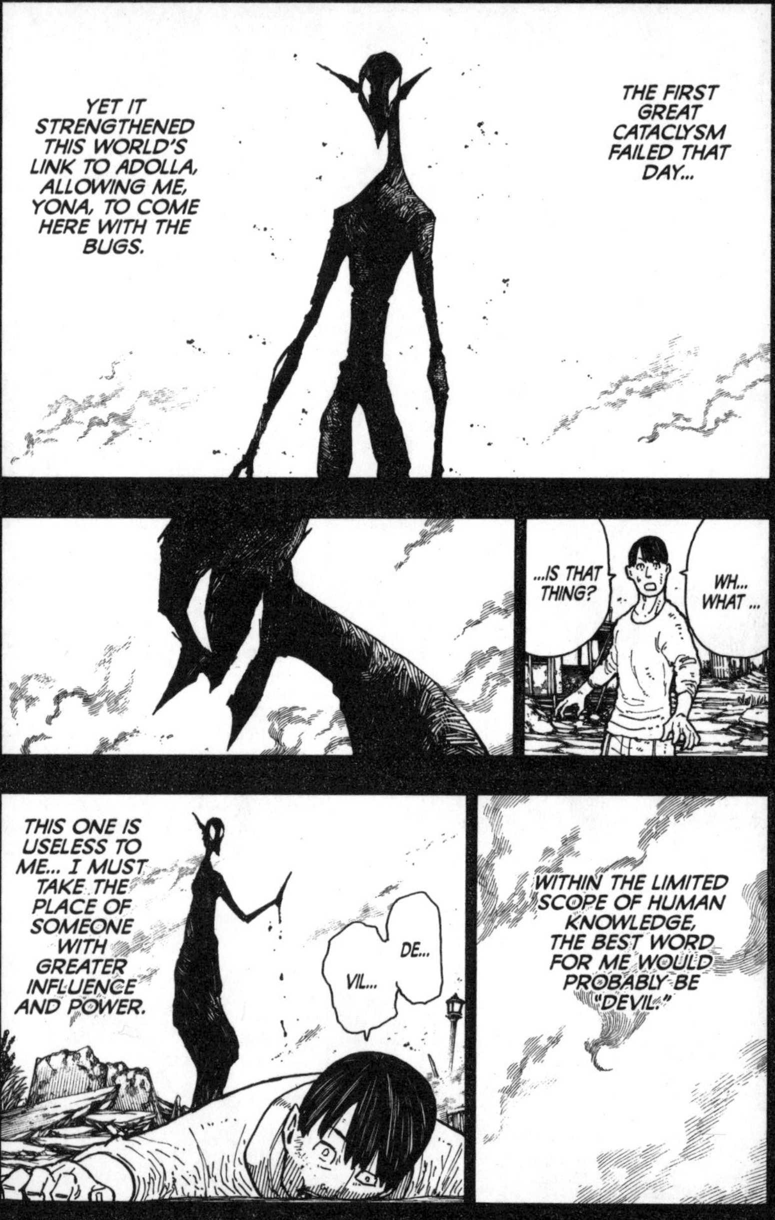
THE FIRST GREAT CATACLYSM FAILED THAT DAY...
YET IT STRENGTHENED THIS WORLD'S LINK TO ADOLLA, ALLOWING ME, YONA, TO COME HERE WITH THE BUGS.
WH... WHAT ...
...IS THAT THING?
WITHIN THE LIMITED SCOPE OF HUMAN KNOWLEDGE, THE BEST WORD FOR ME WOULD PROBABLY BE "DEVIL."
DE... VIL...
THIS ONE IS USELESS TO ME... I MUST TAKE THE PLACE OF SOMEONE WITH GREATER INFLUENCE AND POWER.

AND AS THAT PERSON...

...I WILL IMPART THIS GIRL TO HUMANKIND.

THIS GIRL WITH THE "ADOLLA BURST."

"AMATERASU."

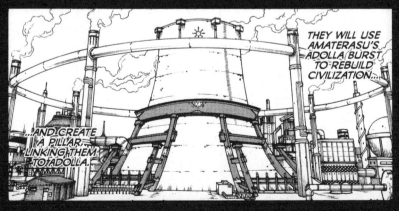

THEY WILL USE AMATERASU'S ADOLLA BURST TO REBUILD CIVILIZATION...

...AND CREATE A PILLAR, LINKING THEM TO ADOLLA.

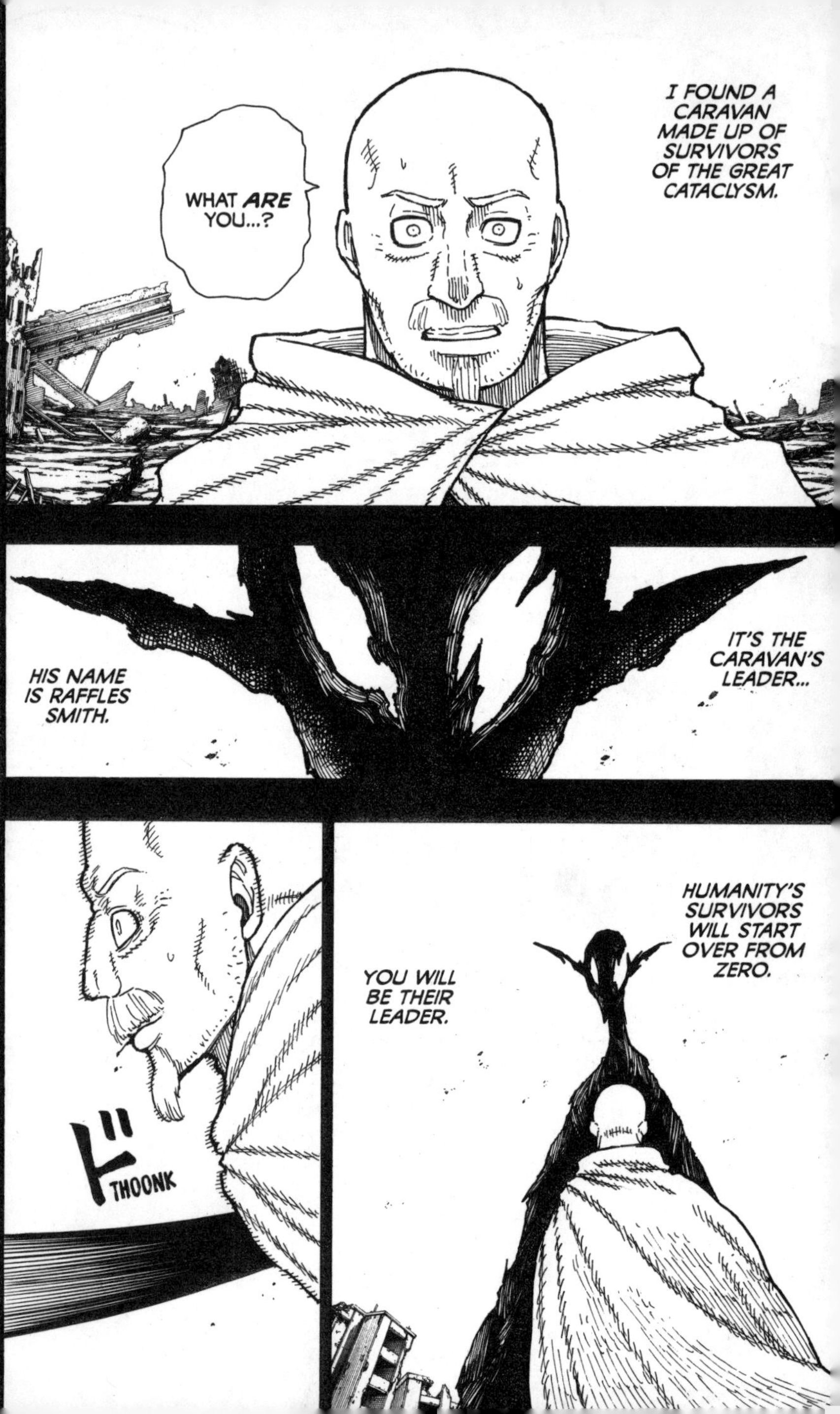
I FOUND A CARAVAN MADE UP OF SURVIVORS OF THE GREAT CATACLYSM.
WHAT ARE YOU...?
IT'S THE CARAVAN'S LEADER...
HIS NAME IS RAFFLES SMITH.
HUMANITY'S SURVIVORS WILL START OVER FROM ZERO.
YOU WILL BE THEIR LEADER.
ド
THOONK

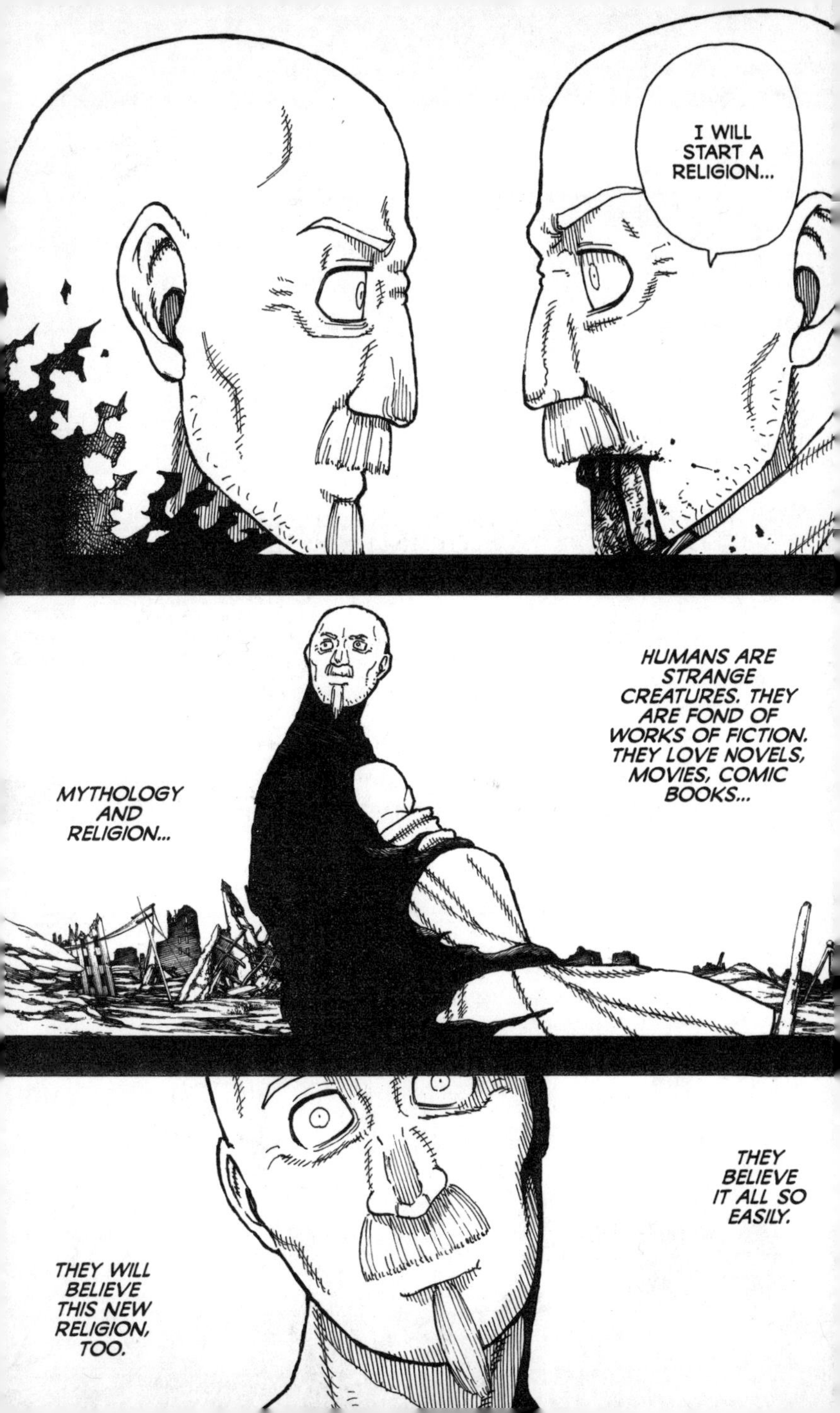
I WILL START A RELIGION...
HUMANS ARE STRANGE CREATURES. THEY ARE FOND OF WORKS OF FICTION. THEY LOVE NOVELS, MOVIES, COMIC BOOKS...
MYTHOLOGY AND RELIGION...
THEY BELIEVE IT ALL SO EASILY.
THEY WILL BELIEVE THIS NEW RELIGION, TOO.

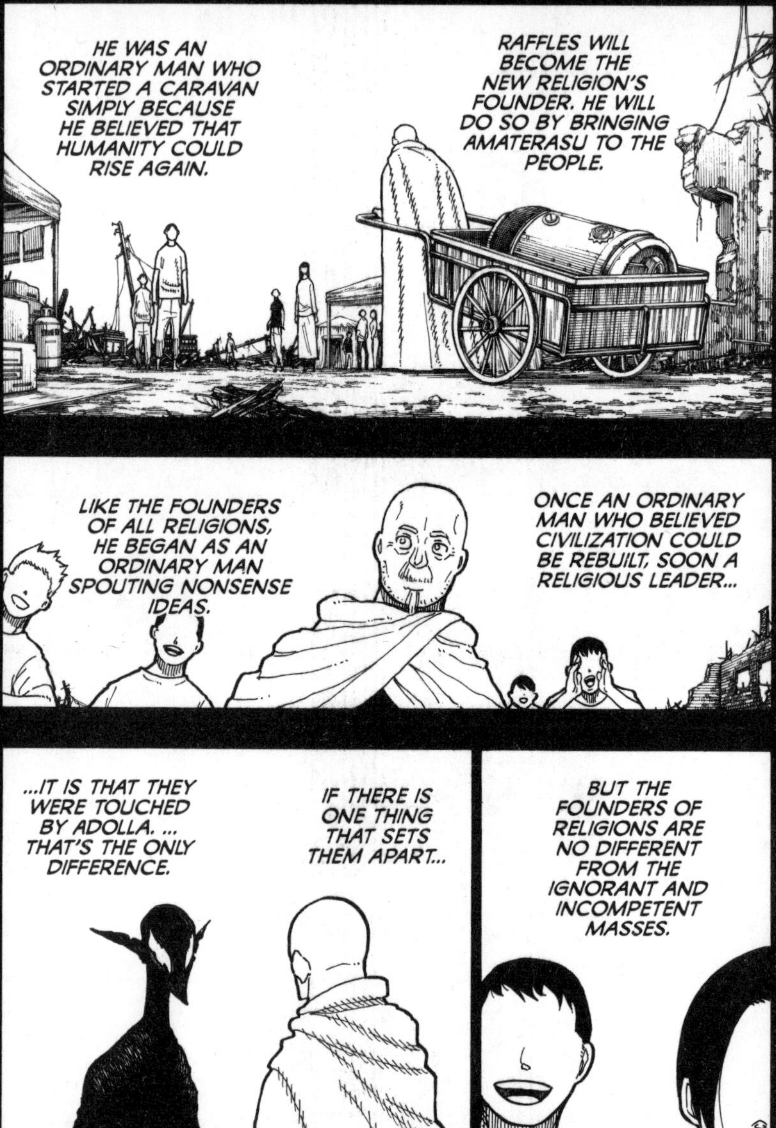
RAFFLES WILL BECOME THE NEW RELIGION'S FOUNDER. HE WILL DO SO BY BRINGING AMATERASU TO THE PEOPLE.
HE WAS AN ORDINARY MAN WHO STARTED A CARAVAN SIMPLY BECAUSE HE BELIEVED THAT HUMANITY COULD RISE AGAIN.
ONCE AN ORDINARY MAN WHO BELIEVED CIVILIZATION COULD BE REBUILT, SOON A RELIGIOUS LEADER...
LIKE THE FOUNDERS OF ALL RELIGIONS, HE BEGAN AS AN ORDINARY MAN SPOUTING NONSENSE IDEAS.
BUT THE FOUNDERS OF RELIGIONS ARE NO DIFFERENT FROM THE IGNORANT AND INCOMPETENT MASSES.
IF THERE IS ONE THING THAT SETS THEM APART...
...IT IS THAT THEY WERE TOUCHED BY ADOLLA. ... THAT'S THE ONLY DIFFERENCE.

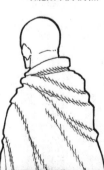

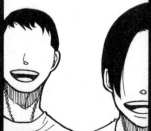

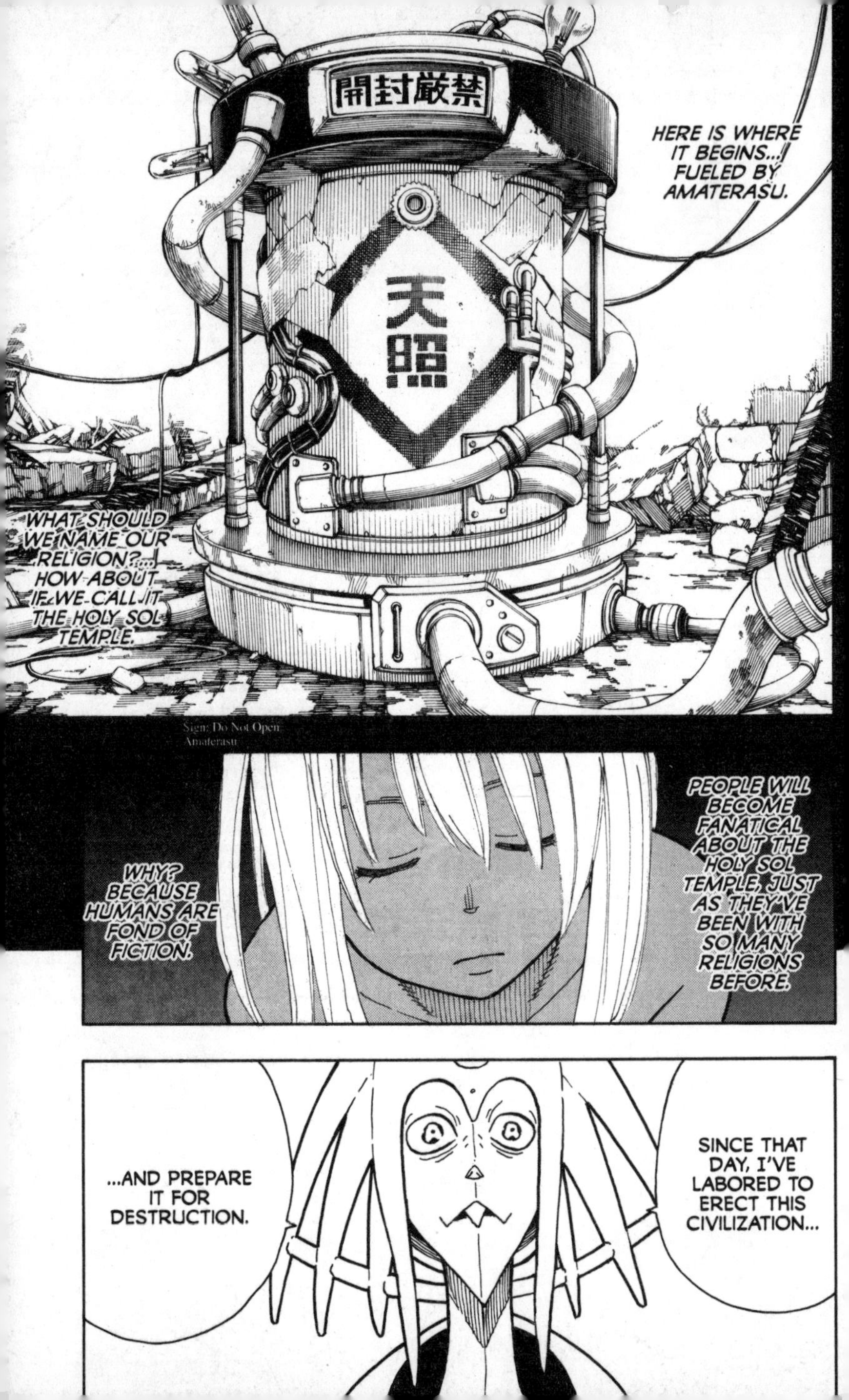
開封厳禁
天照
HERE IS WHERE IT BEGINS... FUELED BY AMATERASU.
WHAT SHOULD WE NAME OUR RELIGION?... HOW ABOUT IF WE CALL IT THE HOLY SOL TEMPLE.
Sign: Do Not Open
Amaterasu
PEOPLE WILL BECOME FANATICAL ABOUT THE HOLY SOL TEMPLE, JUST AS THEY'VE BEEN WITH SO MANY RELIGIONS BEFORE.
WHY? BECAUSE HUMANS ARE FOND OF FICTION.
SINCE THAT DAY, I'VE LABORED TO ERECT THIS CIVILIZATION...
...AND PREPARE IT FOR DESTRUCTION.

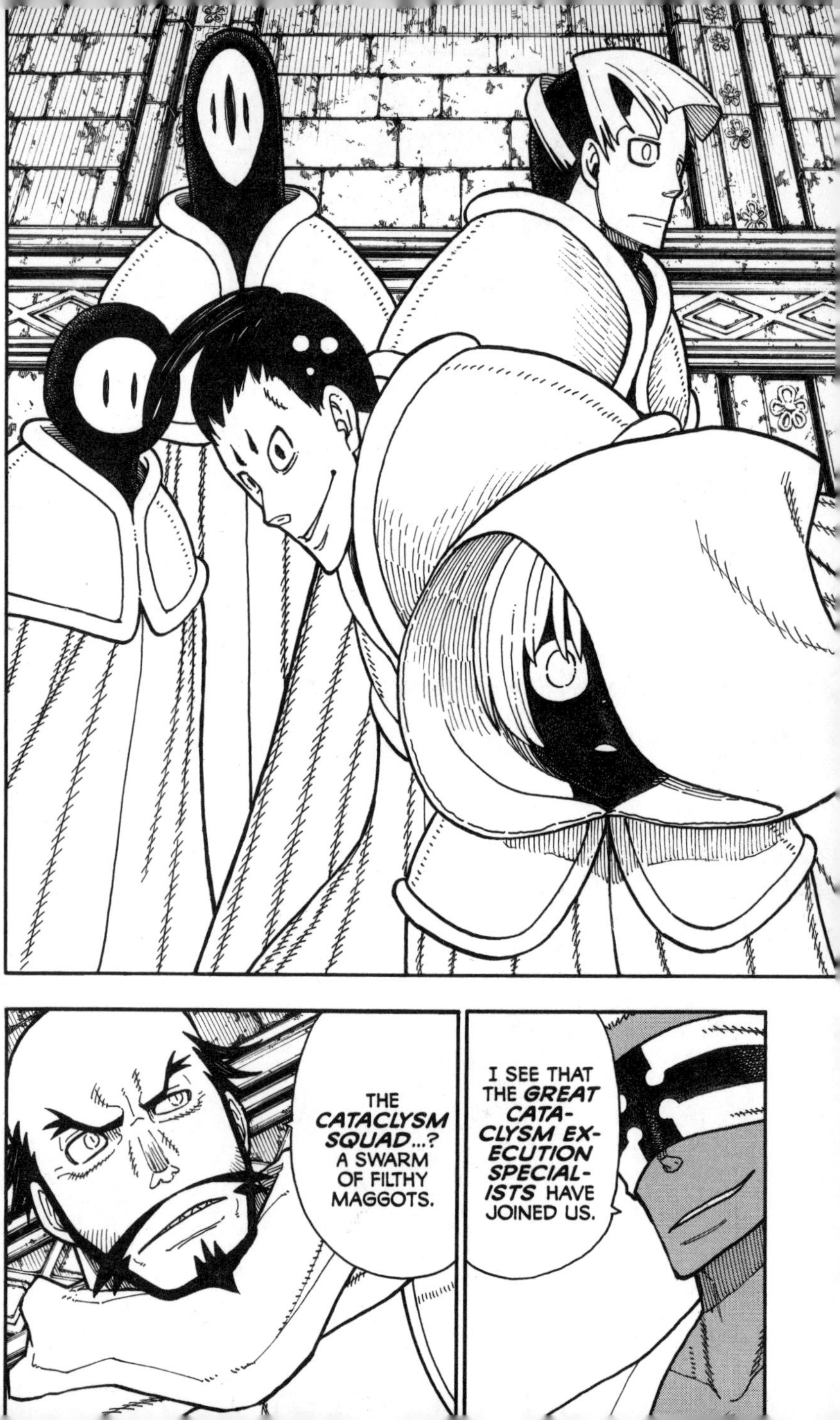
I SEE THAT THE ***GREAT CATACLYSM EXECUTION SPECIALISTS*** HAVE JOINED US.
THE ***CATACLYSM SQUAD***...? A SWARM OF FILTHY MAGGOTS.

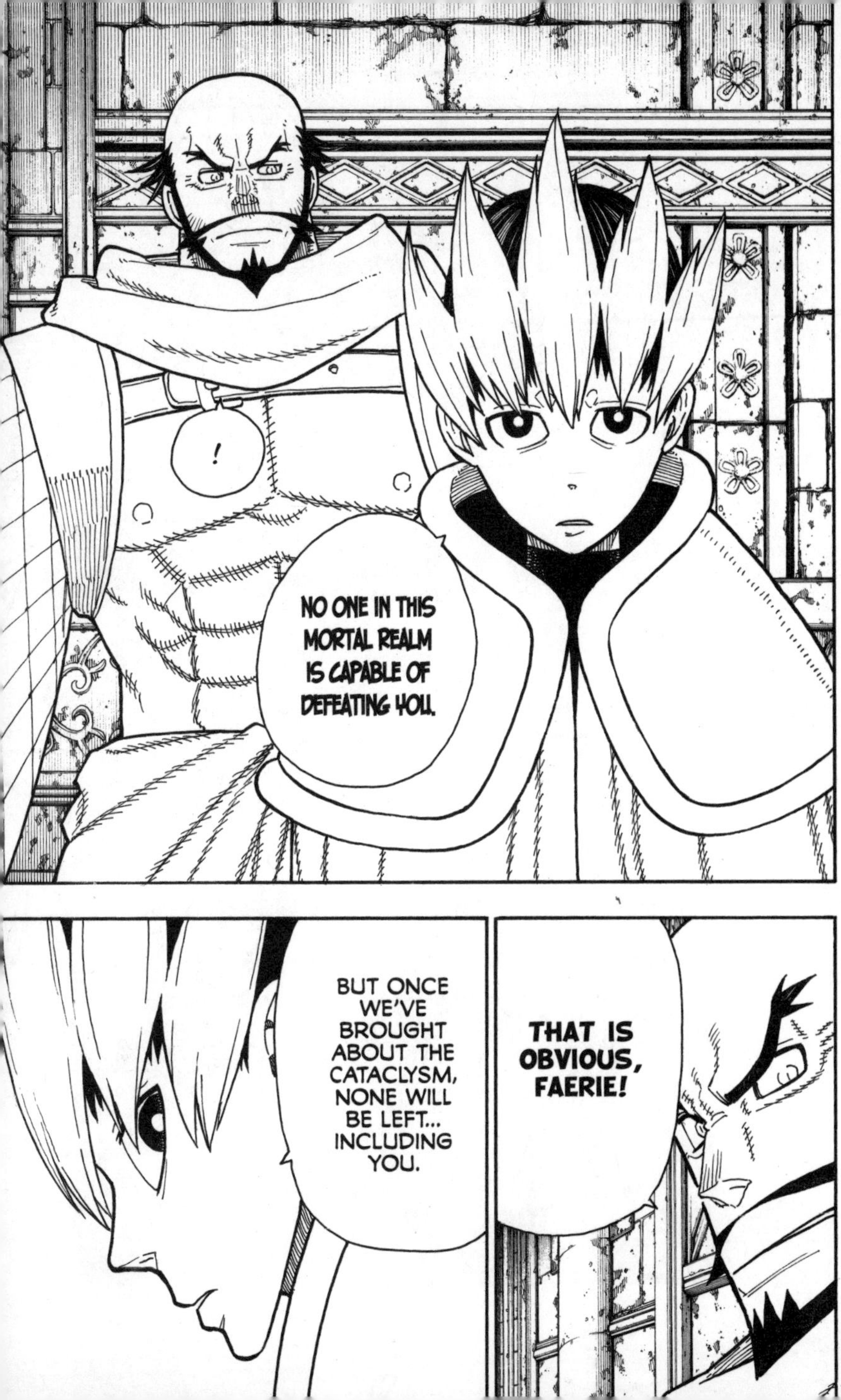
!
NO ONE IN THIS MORTAL REALM IS CAPABLE OF DEFEATING YOU.
THAT IS OBVIOUS, FAERIE!
BUT ONCE WE'VE BROUGHT ABOUT THE CATACLYSM, NONE WILL BE LEFT... INCLUDING YOU.

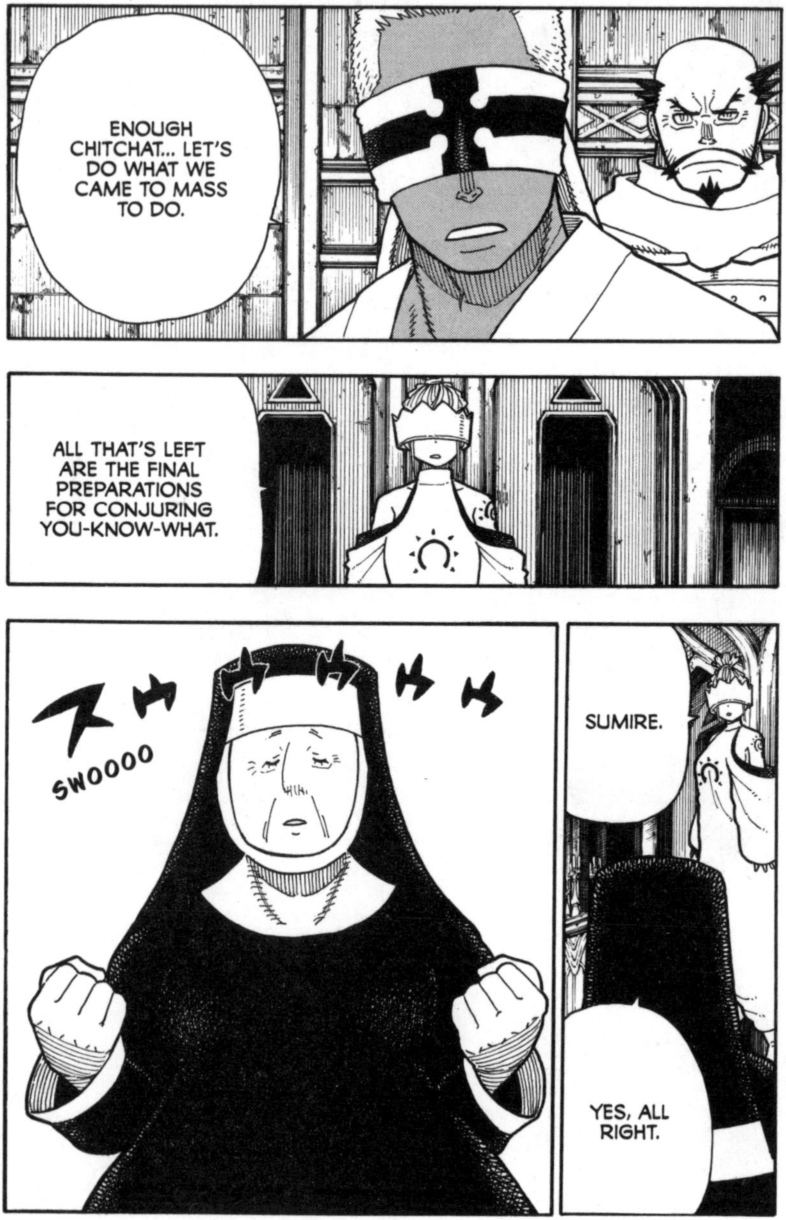
ENOUGH CHITCHAT... LET'S DO WHAT WE CAME TO MASS TO DO.
ALL THAT'S LEFT ARE THE FINAL PREPARATIONS FOR CONJURING YOU-KNOW-WHAT.
SUMIRE.
YES, ALL RIGHT.
SWOOOO

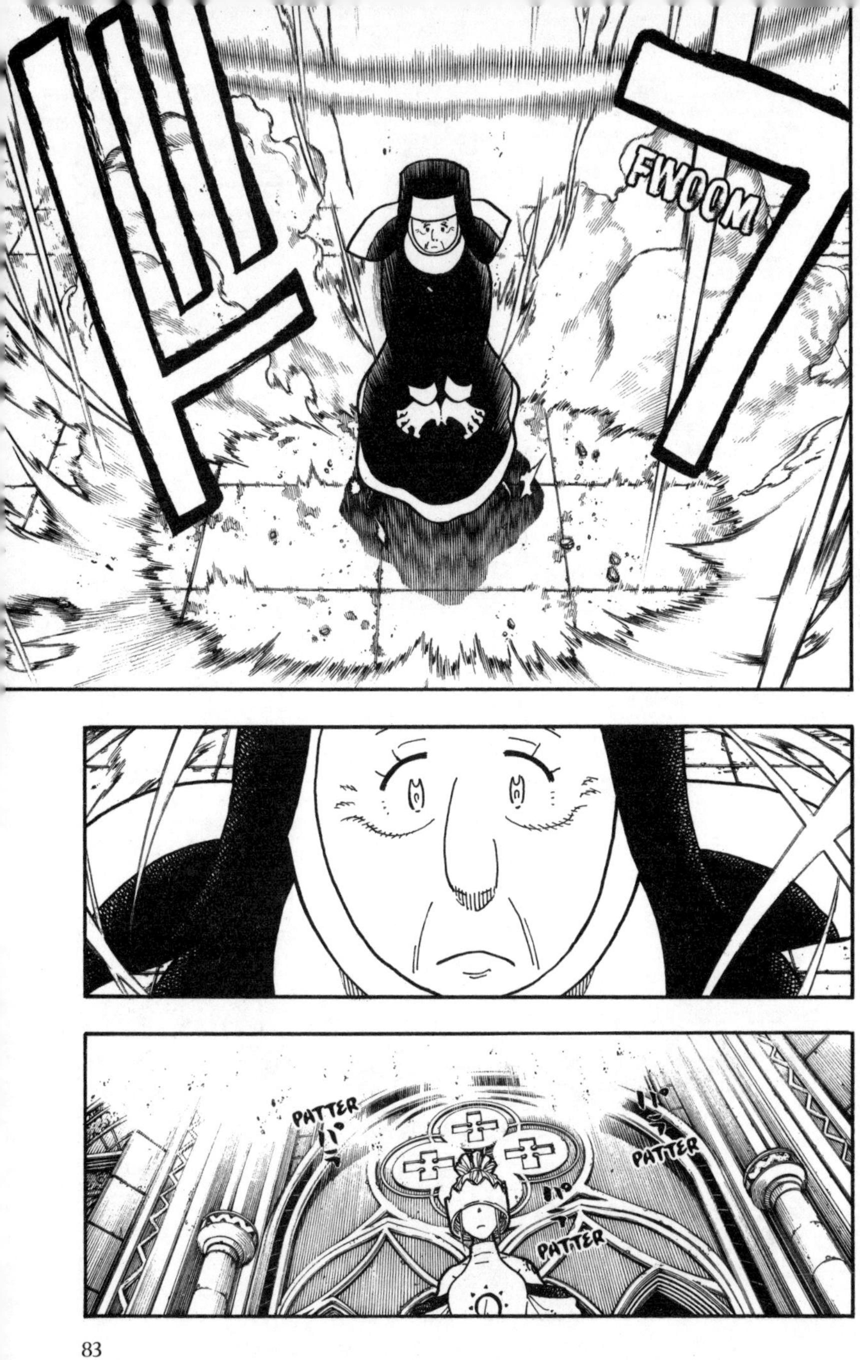
FWOOM
PATTER
PATTER
PATTER

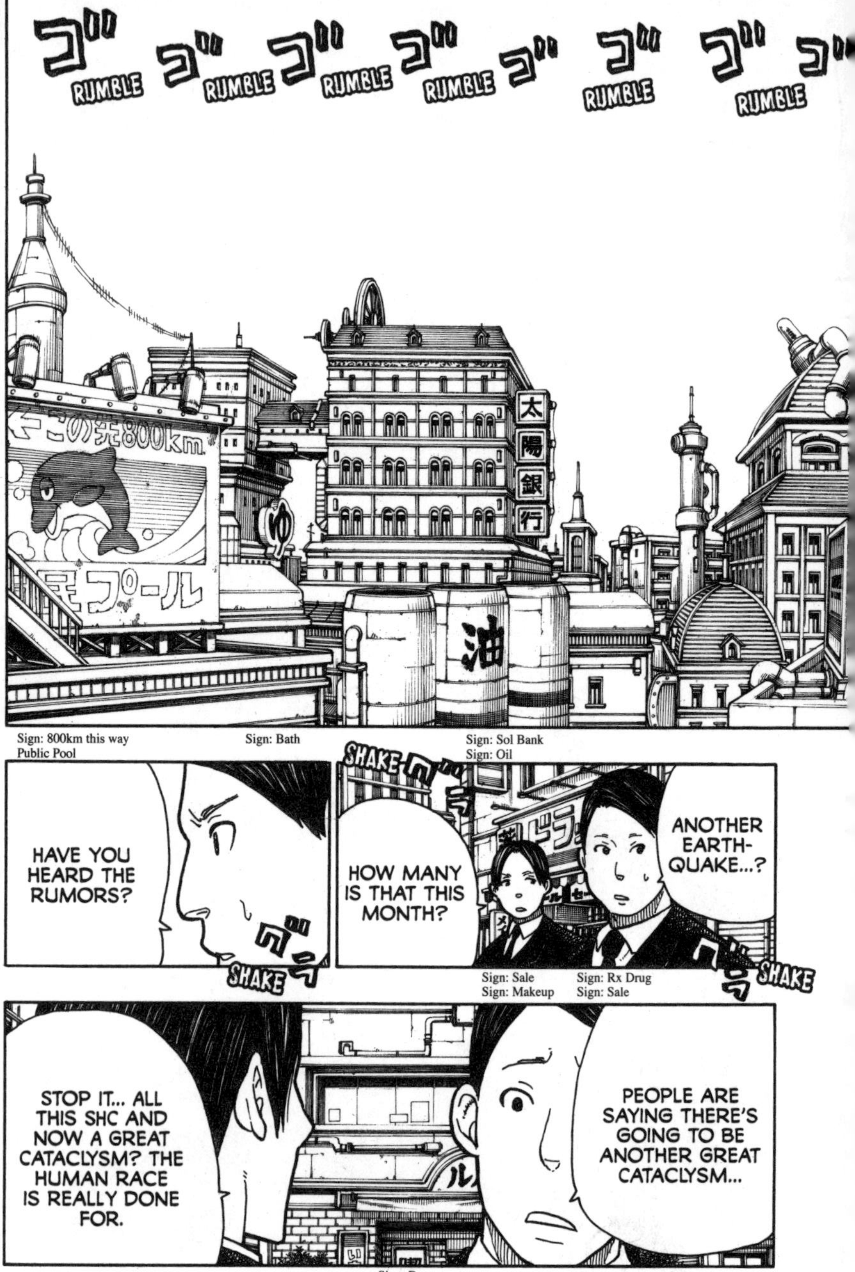
ゴ
RUMBLE
ゴ
RUMBLE
ゴ
RUMBLE
ゴ
RUMBLE
ゴ
RUMBLE
ゴ
RUMBLE
ゴ
RUMBLE
ゴ
太陽銀行
油
ANOTHER EARTH-QUAKE...?
HOW MANY IS THAT THIS MONTH?
SHAKE
SHAKE
HAVE YOU HEARD THE RUMORS?
SHAKE
PEOPLE ARE SAYING THERE'S GOING TO BE ANOTHER GREAT CATACLYSM...
STOP IT... ALL THIS SHC AND NOW A GREAT CATACLYSM? THE HUMAN RACE IS REALLY DONE FOR.

Sign: Sol Bank
Sign: Oil

Sign: Bath

Sign: 800km this way
Public Pool

Sign: Rx Drug
Sign: Sale

Sign: Sale
Sign: Makeup

Sign: Ru
Sign:Cafe

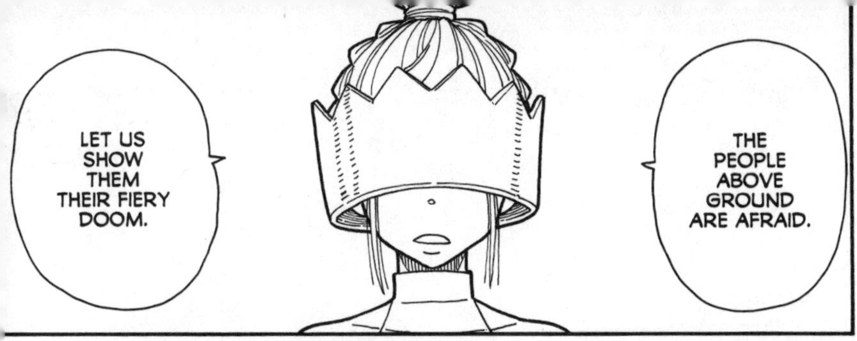
THE PEOPLE ABOVE GROUND ARE AFRAID.
LET US SHOW THEM THEIR FIERY DOOM.

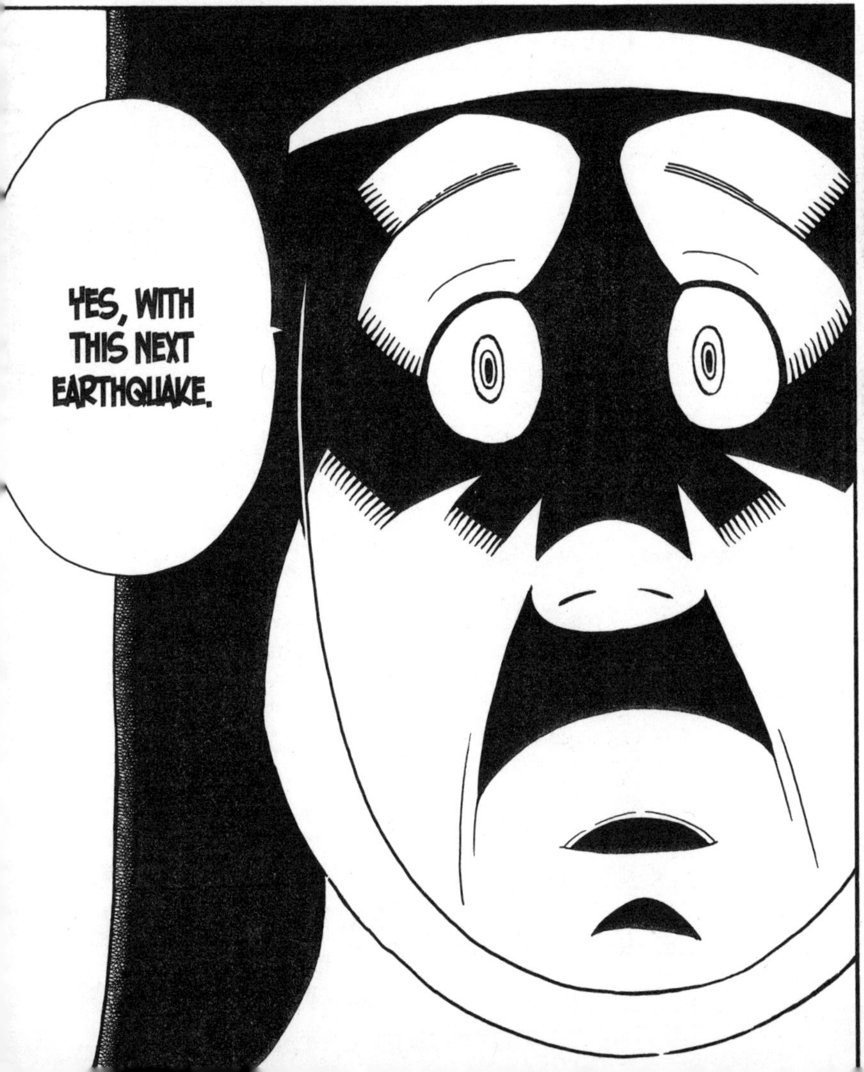
YES, WITH THIS NEXT EARTHQUAKE.

FIRE FORCE

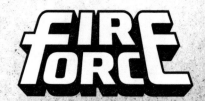

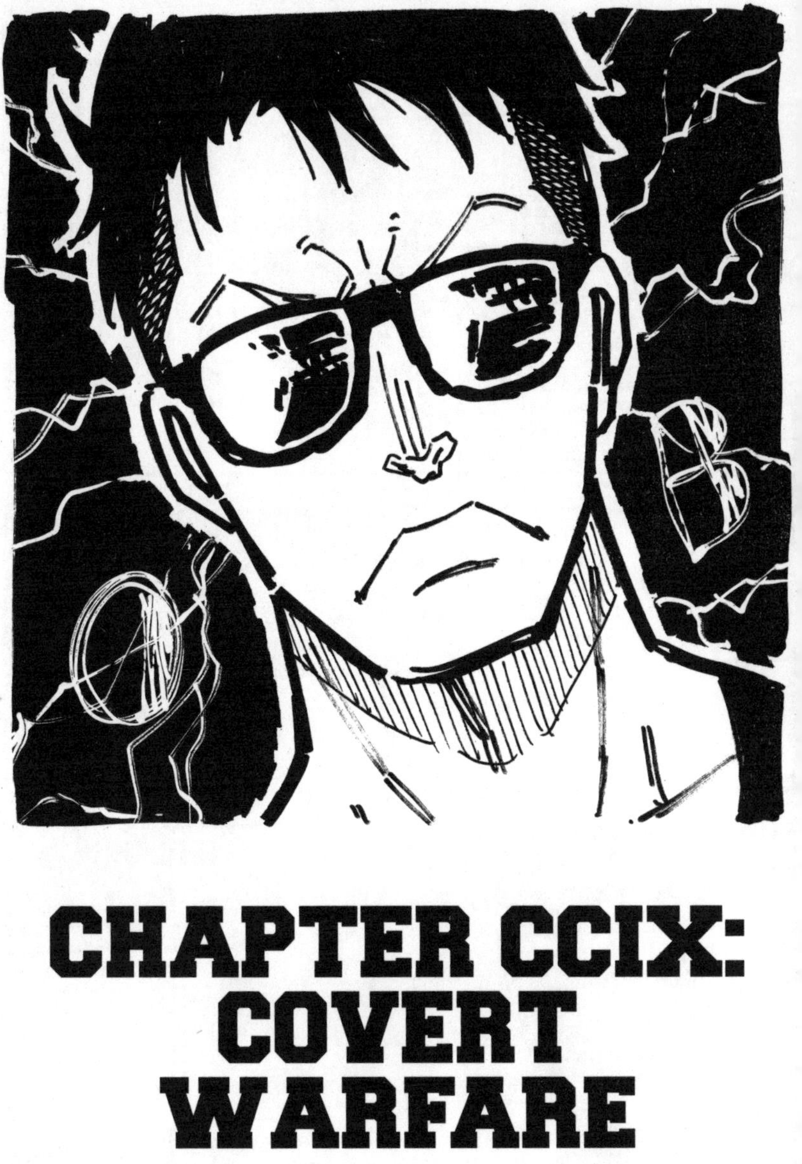

CHAPTER CCIX: COVERT WARFARE

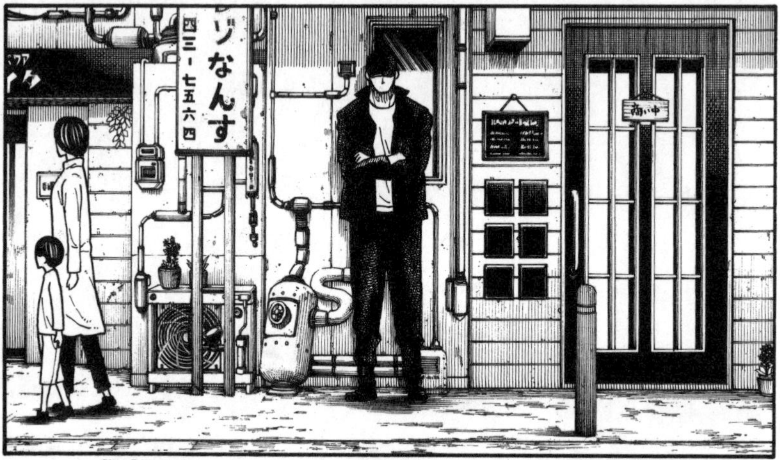
ゾなんす
四三-七五六四
商い中

Sign: Resonance
43-7564

Sign: Open

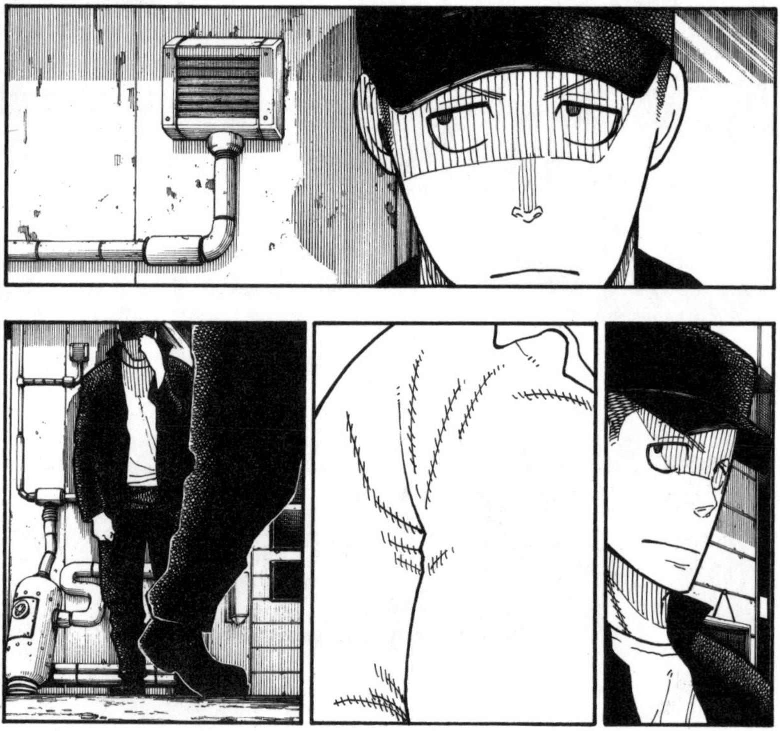

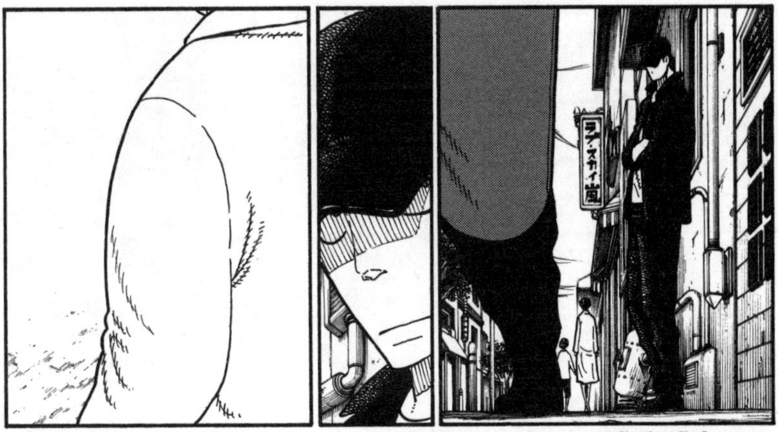
ラブ・スカイ嵐

Sign: Love Sky Storm

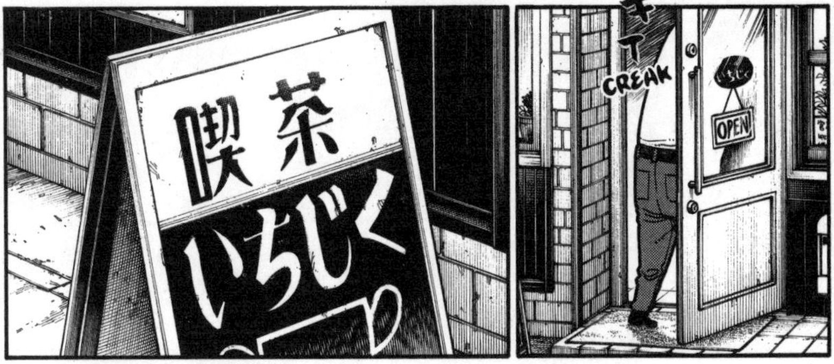
キイ
CREAK
OPEN
喫茶
いちじく

Sign: Cafe Ichijiku

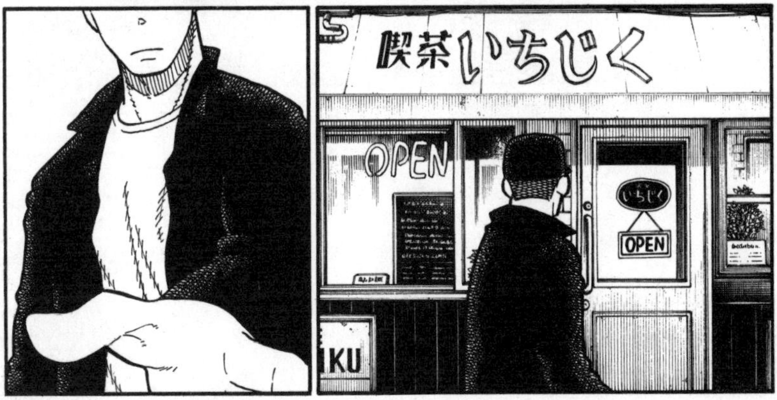
喫茶いちじく
OPEN
いちじく
OPEN
IKU

Sign: Cafe Ichijiku

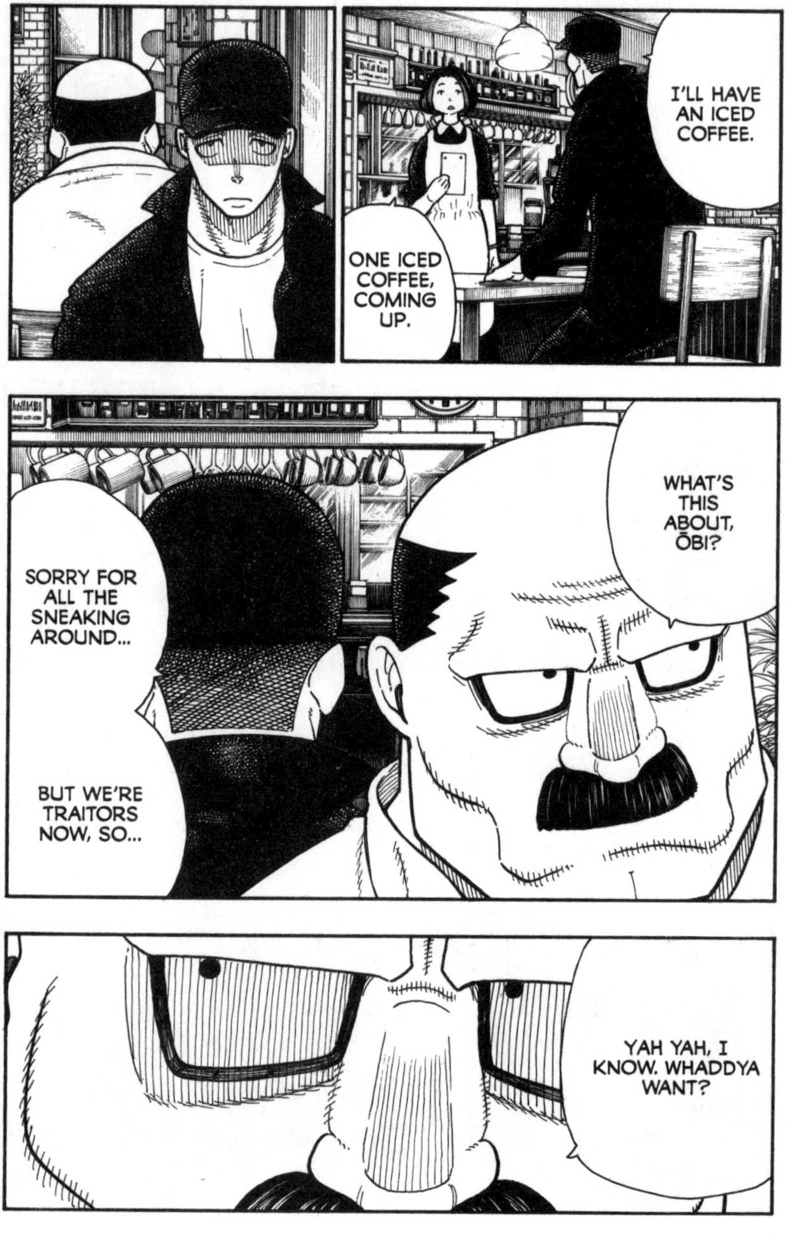
I'LL HAVE AN ICED COFFEE.
ONE ICED COFFEE, COMING UP.
WHAT'S THIS ABOUT, ŌBI?
SORRY FOR ALL THE SNEAKING AROUND...
BUT WE'RE TRAITORS NOW, SO...
YAH YAH, I KNOW. WHADDYA WANT?

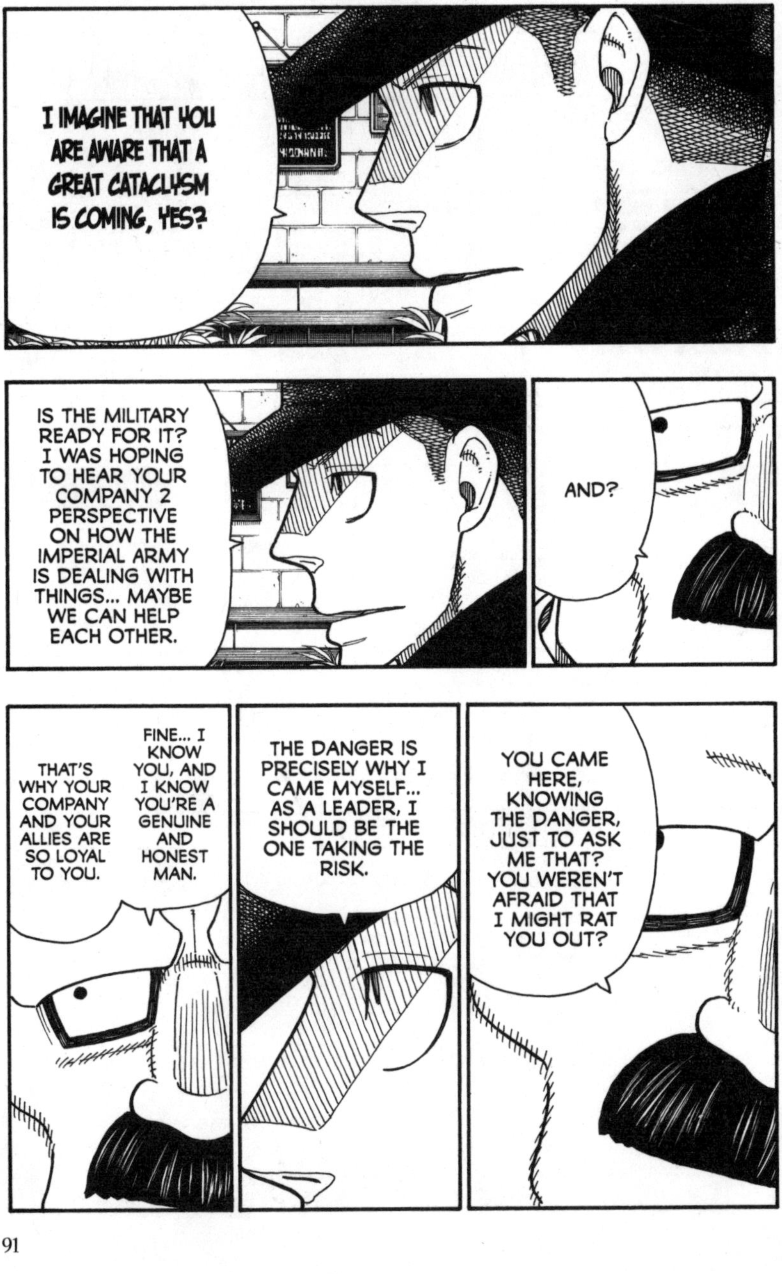
I IMAGINE THAT YOU ARE AWARE THAT A GREAT CATACLYSM IS COMING, YES?
AND?
IS THE MILITARY READY FOR IT? I WAS HOPING TO HEAR YOUR COMPANY 2 PERSPECTIVE ON HOW THE IMPERIAL ARMY IS DEALING WITH THINGS... MAYBE WE CAN HELP EACH OTHER.
YOU CAME HERE, KNOWING THE DANGER, JUST TO ASK ME THAT? YOU WEREN'T AFRAID THAT I MIGHT RAT YOU OUT?
THE DANGER IS PRECISELY WHY I CAME MYSELF... AS A LEADER, I SHOULD BE THE ONE TAKING THE RISK.
FINE... I KNOW YOU, AND I KNOW YOU'RE A GENUINE AND HONEST MAN.
THAT'S WHY YOUR COMPANY AND YOUR ALLIES ARE SO LOYAL TO YOU.

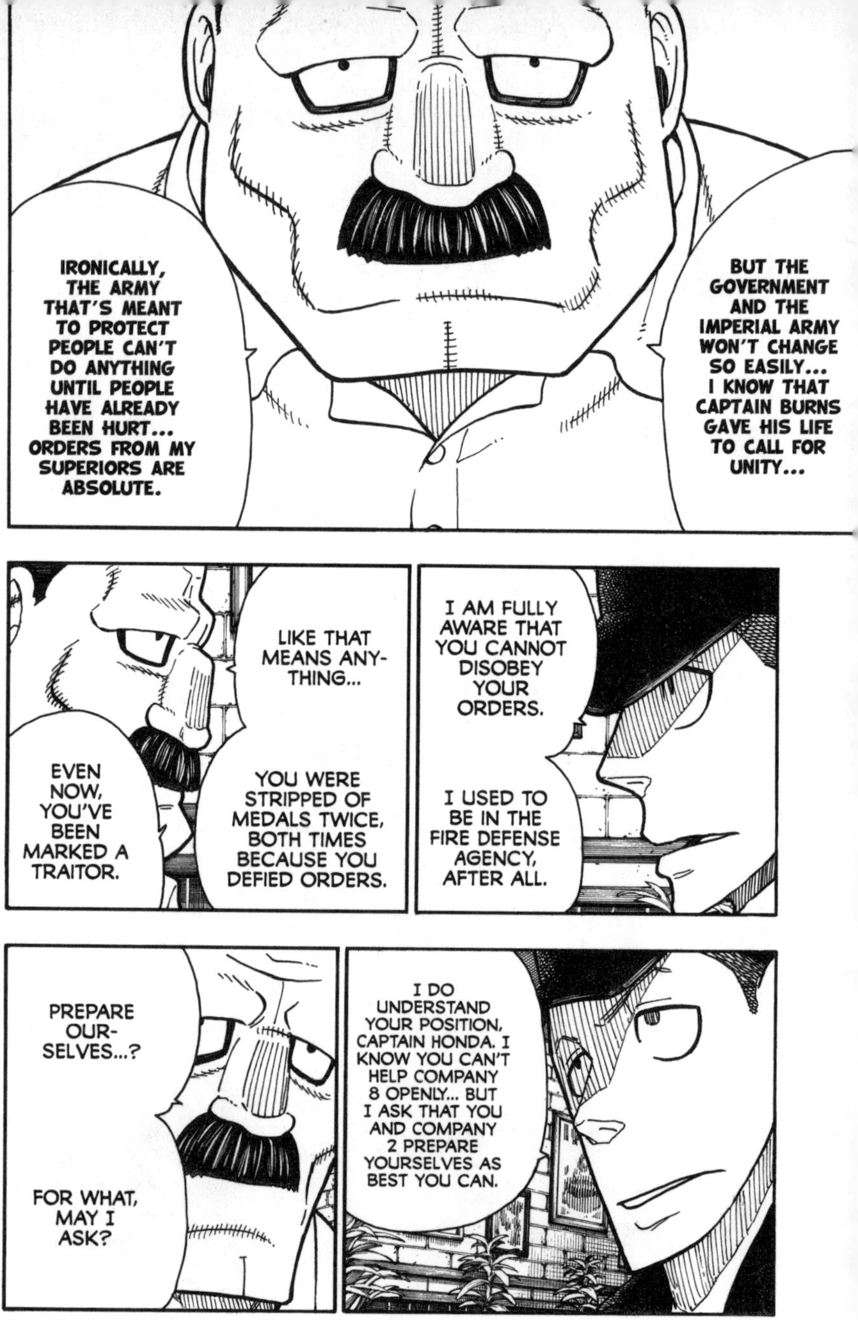
BUT THE GOVERNMENT AND THE IMPERIAL ARMY WON'T CHANGE SO EASILY... I KNOW THAT CAPTAIN BURNS GAVE HIS LIFE TO CALL FOR UNITY...
IRONICALLY, THE ARMY THAT'S MEANT TO PROTECT PEOPLE CAN'T DO ANYTHING UNTIL PEOPLE HAVE ALREADY BEEN HURT... ORDERS FROM MY SUPERIORS ARE ABSOLUTE.
I AM FULLY AWARE THAT YOU CANNOT DISOBEY YOUR ORDERS.
I USED TO BE IN THE FIRE DEFENSE AGENCY, AFTER ALL.
LIKE THAT MEANS ANY-THING...
YOU WERE STRIPPED OF MEDALS TWICE, BOTH TIMES BECAUSE YOU DEFIED ORDERS.
EVEN NOW, YOU'VE BEEN MARKED A TRAITOR.
I DO UNDERSTAND YOUR POSITION, CAPTAIN HONDA. I KNOW YOU CAN'T HELP COMPANY 8 OPENLY... BUT I ASK THAT YOU AND COMPANY 2 PREPARE YOURSELVES AS BEST YOU CAN.
PREPARE OUR-SELVES...?
FOR WHAT, MAY I ASK?

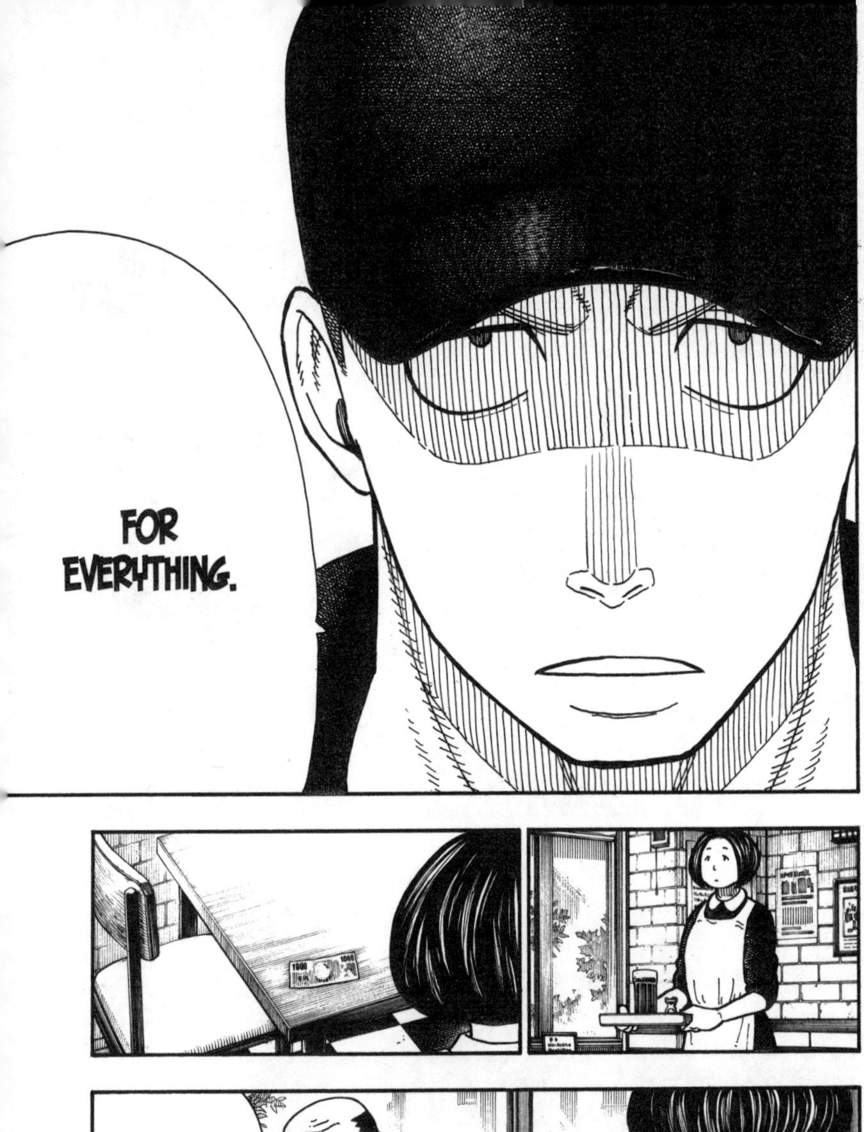
FOR EVERYTHING.
HE LEFT. HE SEEMED TO BE IN A HURRY.

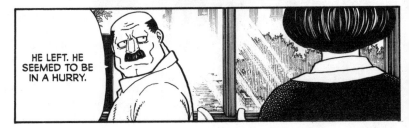

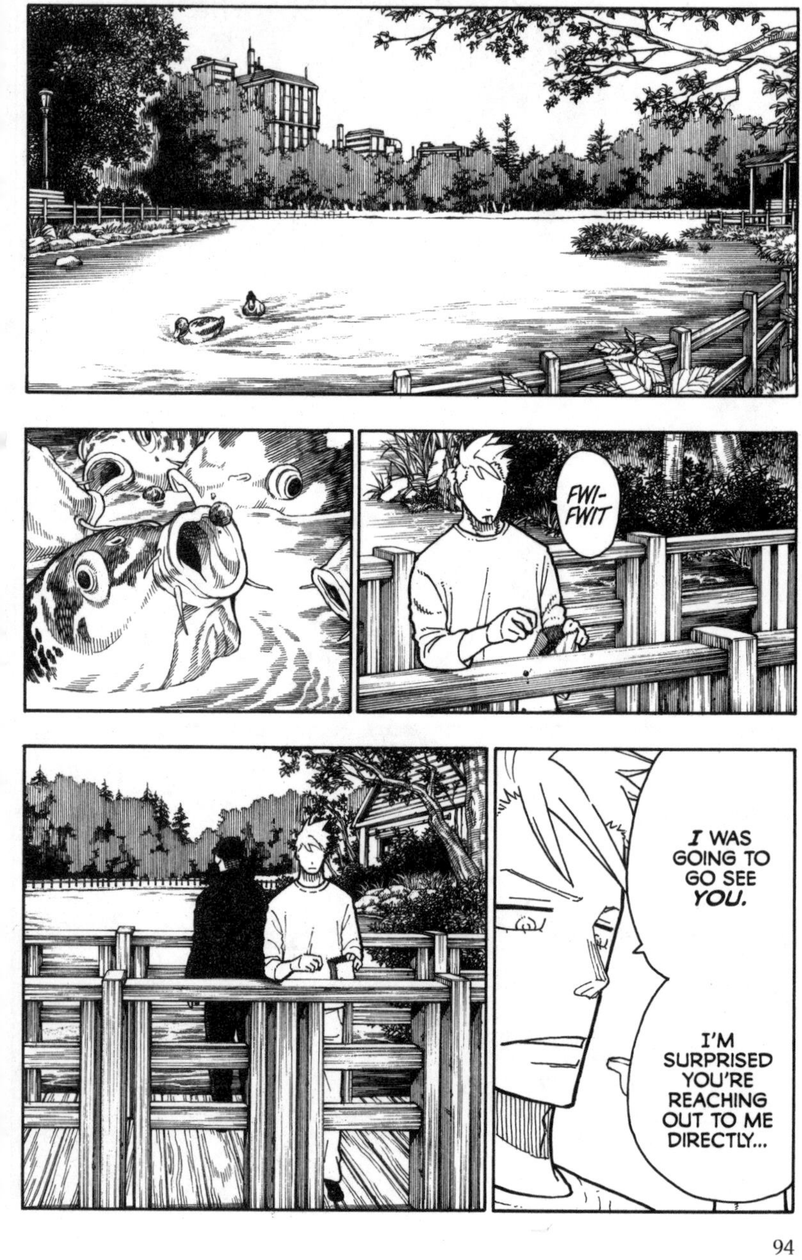
FWI-FWIT
I WAS GOING TO GO SEE *YOU.*
I'M SURPRISED YOU'RE REACHING OUT TO ME DIRECTLY...

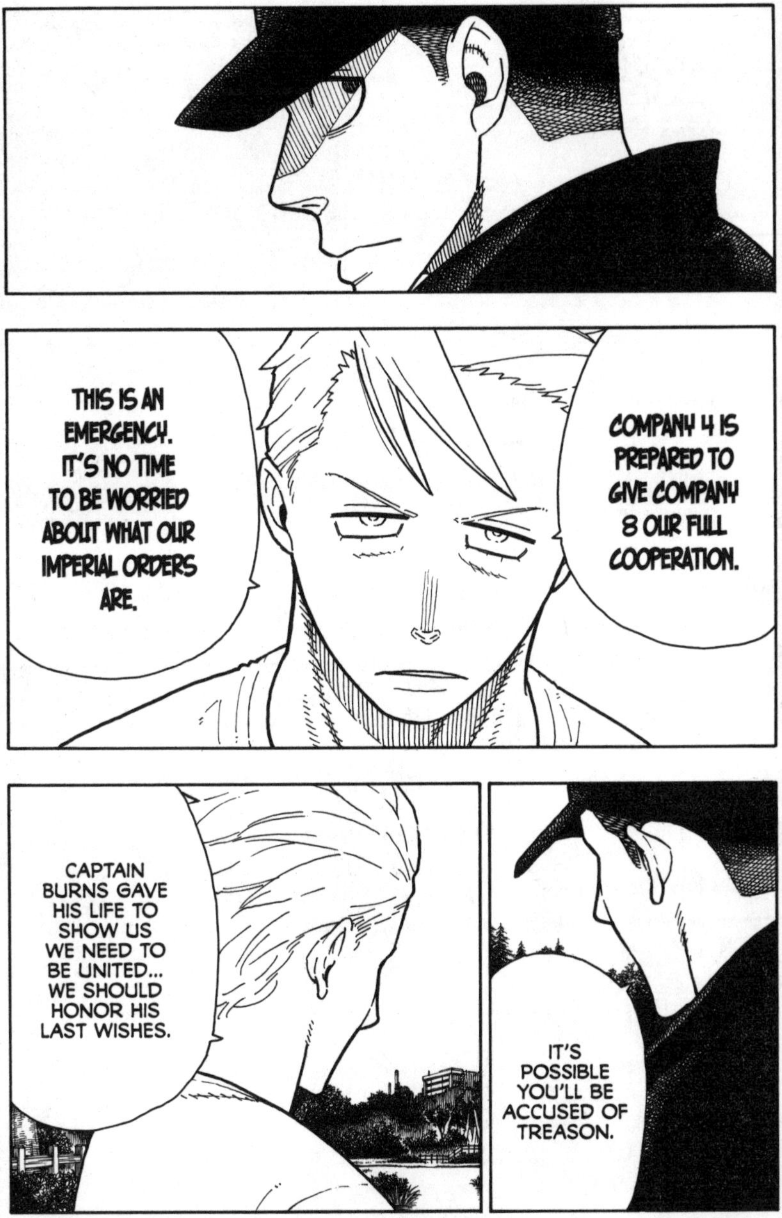
COMPANY 4 IS PREPARED TO GIVE COMPANY 8 OUR FULL COOPERATION.
THIS IS AN EMERGENCY. IT'S NO TIME TO BE WORRIED ABOUT WHAT OUR IMPERIAL ORDERS ARE.
IT'S POSSIBLE YOU'LL BE ACCUSED OF TREASON.
CAPTAIN BURNS GAVE HIS LIFE TO SHOW US WE NEED TO BE UNITED... WE SHOULD HONOR HIS LAST WISHES.

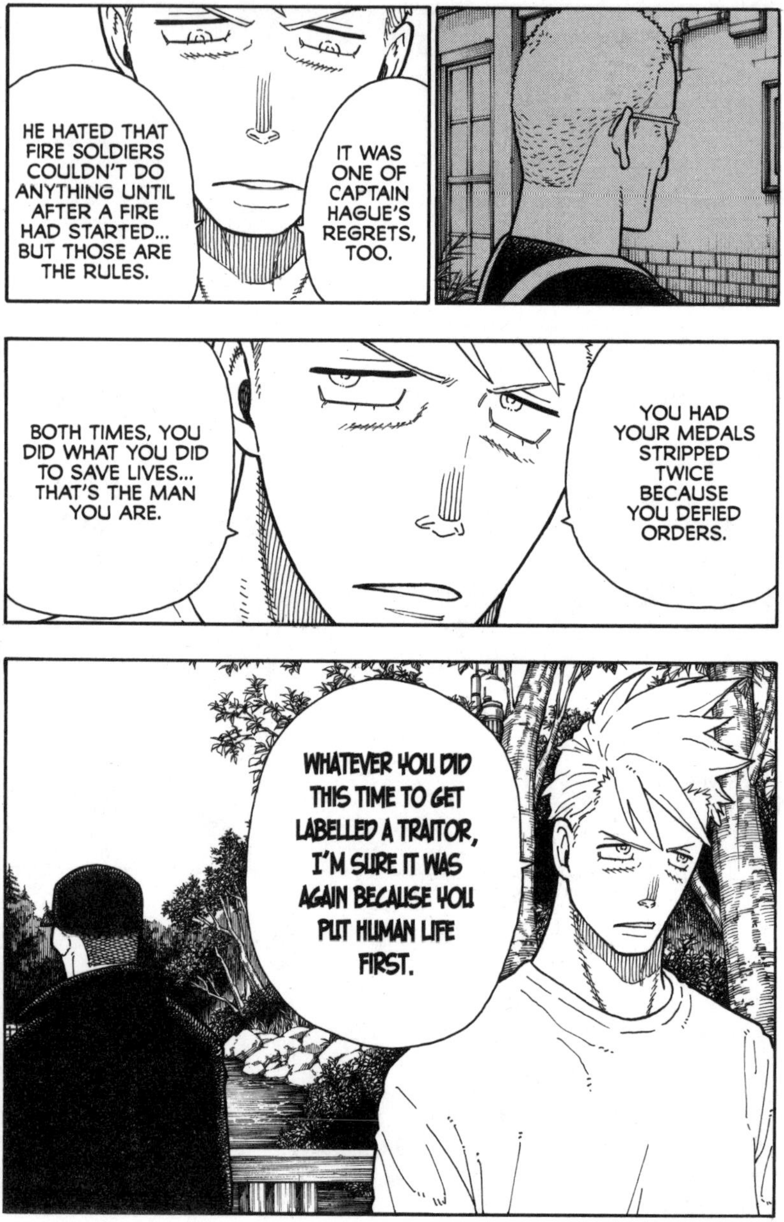
IT WAS ONE OF CAPTAIN HAGUE'S REGRETS, TOO.
HE HATED THAT FIRE SOLDIERS COULDN'T DO ANYTHING UNTIL AFTER A FIRE HAD STARTED... BUT THOSE ARE THE RULES.
YOU HAD YOUR MEDALS STRIPPED TWICE BECAUSE YOU DEFIED ORDERS.
BOTH TIMES, YOU DID WHAT YOU DID TO SAVE LIVES... THAT'S THE MAN YOU ARE.
WHATEVER YOU DID THIS TIME TO GET LABELLED A TRAITOR, I'M SURE IT WAS AGAIN BECAUSE YOU PUT HUMAN LIFE FIRST.

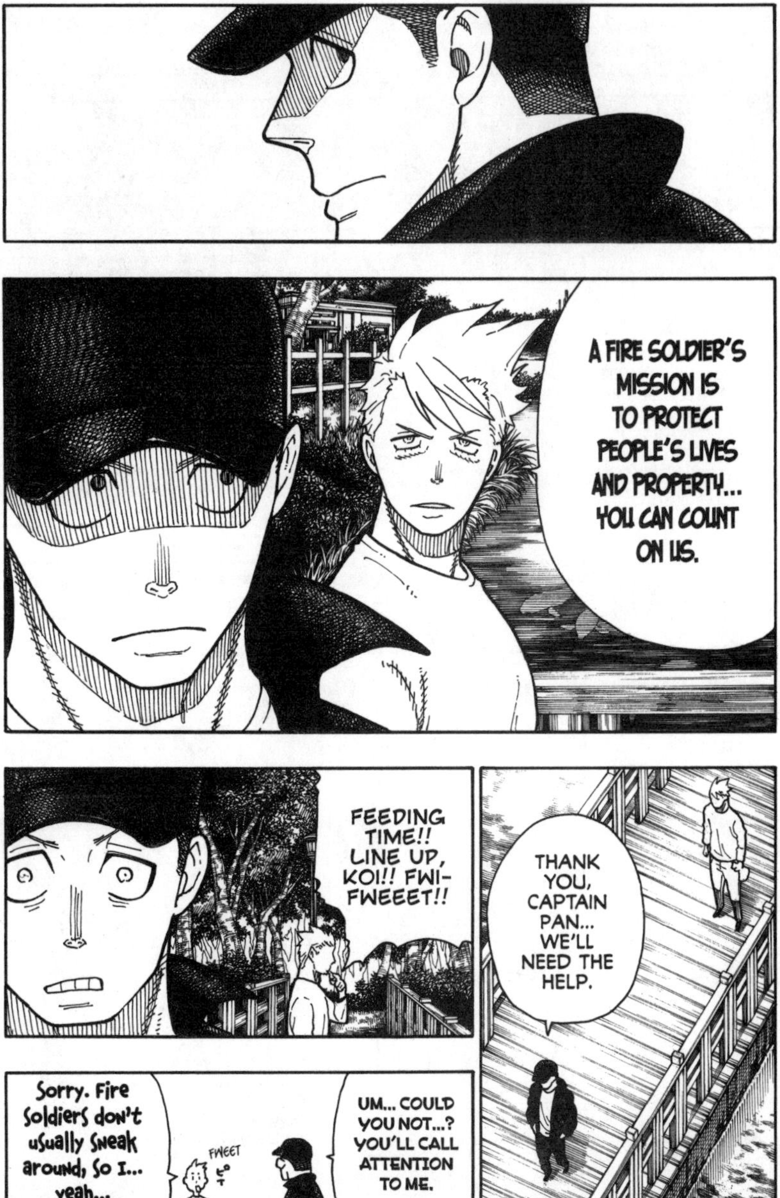
A FIRE SOLDIER'S MISSION IS TO PROTECT PEOPLE'S LIVES AND PROPERTY... YOU CAN COUNT ON US.
THANK YOU, CAPTAIN PAN... WE'LL NEED THE HELP.
FEEDING TIME!! LINE UP, KOI!! FWI-FWEEET!!
UM... COULD YOU NOT...? YOU'LL CALL ATTENTION TO ME.
FWEET
Sorry. Fire Soldiers don't usually sneak around, so I... yeah...

ASAKUSA

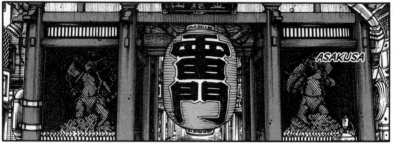

Lantern: Kaminarimon

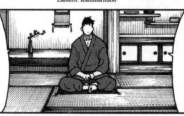

IT WON'T BE EASY TO GET HELP FROM THE HOLY SOL TEMPLE, INCLUDING COMPANY 1, OR FROM HAIJIMA.
NOR FROM THE ARMY, EITHER. THOUGH I'M SURE THERE'LL BE PEOPLE, LIKE CAPTAIN HONDA, WHO'LL HELP US OUT PRIVATELY.
I SPOKE WITH CAPTAIN HONDA PERSONALLY.
HE TOOK MY WARNINGS SERIOUSLY.
WERE YOU ABLE TO CONTACT COMPANY 4, SIR?
YES, AND THEY PROMISED TO HELP US!

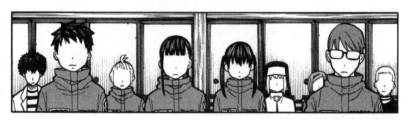

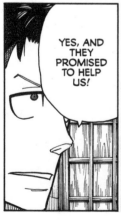

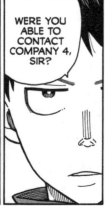

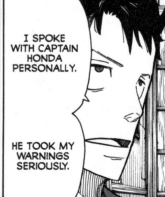

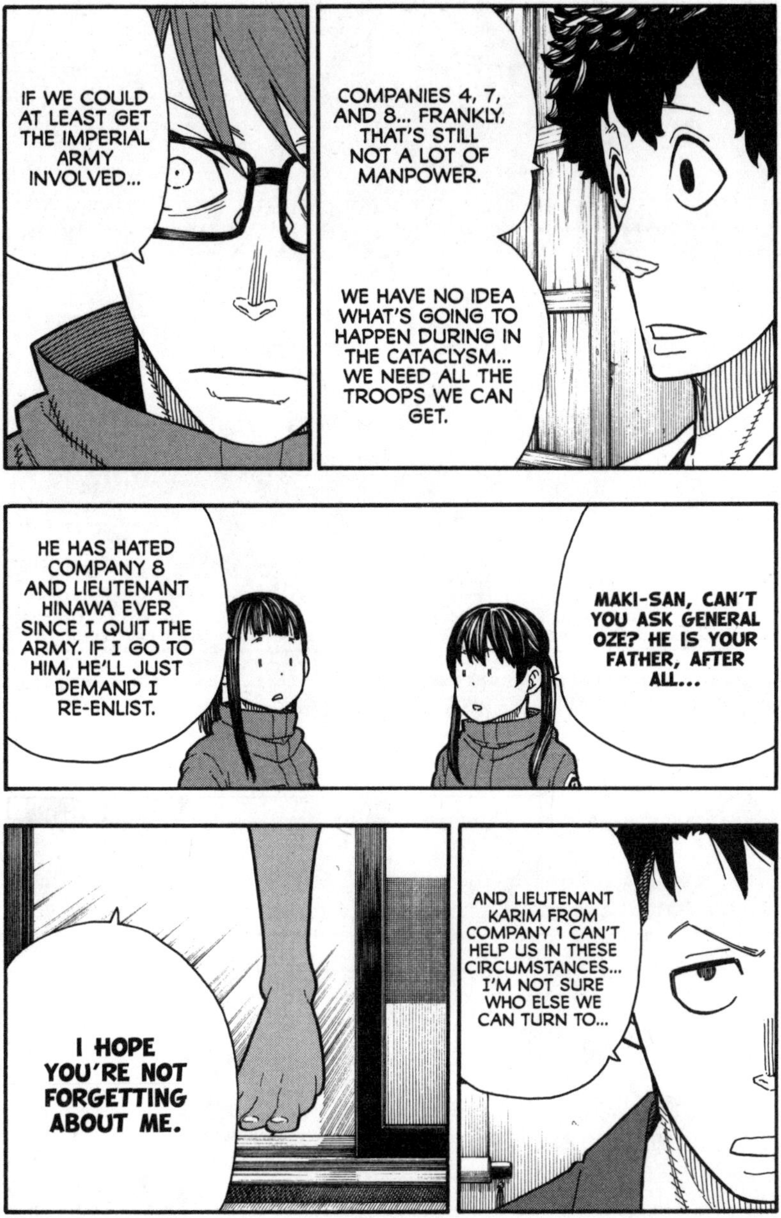
COMPANIES 4, 7, AND 8... FRANKLY, THAT'S STILL NOT A LOT OF MANPOWER.
WE HAVE NO IDEA WHAT'S GOING TO HAPPEN DURING IN THE CATACLYSM... WE NEED ALL THE TROOPS WE CAN GET.
IF WE COULD AT LEAST GET THE IMPERIAL ARMY INVOLVED...
MAKI-SAN, CAN'T YOU ASK GENERAL OZE? HE IS YOUR FATHER, AFTER ALL...
HE HAS HATED COMPANY 8 AND LIEUTENANT HINAWA EVER SINCE I QUIT THE ARMY. IF I GO TO HIM, HE'LL JUST DEMAND I RE-ENLIST.
AND LIEUTENANT KARIM FROM COMPANY 1 CAN'T HELP US IN THESE CIRCUMSTANCES... I'M NOT SURE WHO ELSE WE CAN TURN TO...
I HOPE YOU'RE NOT FORGETTING ABOUT ME.

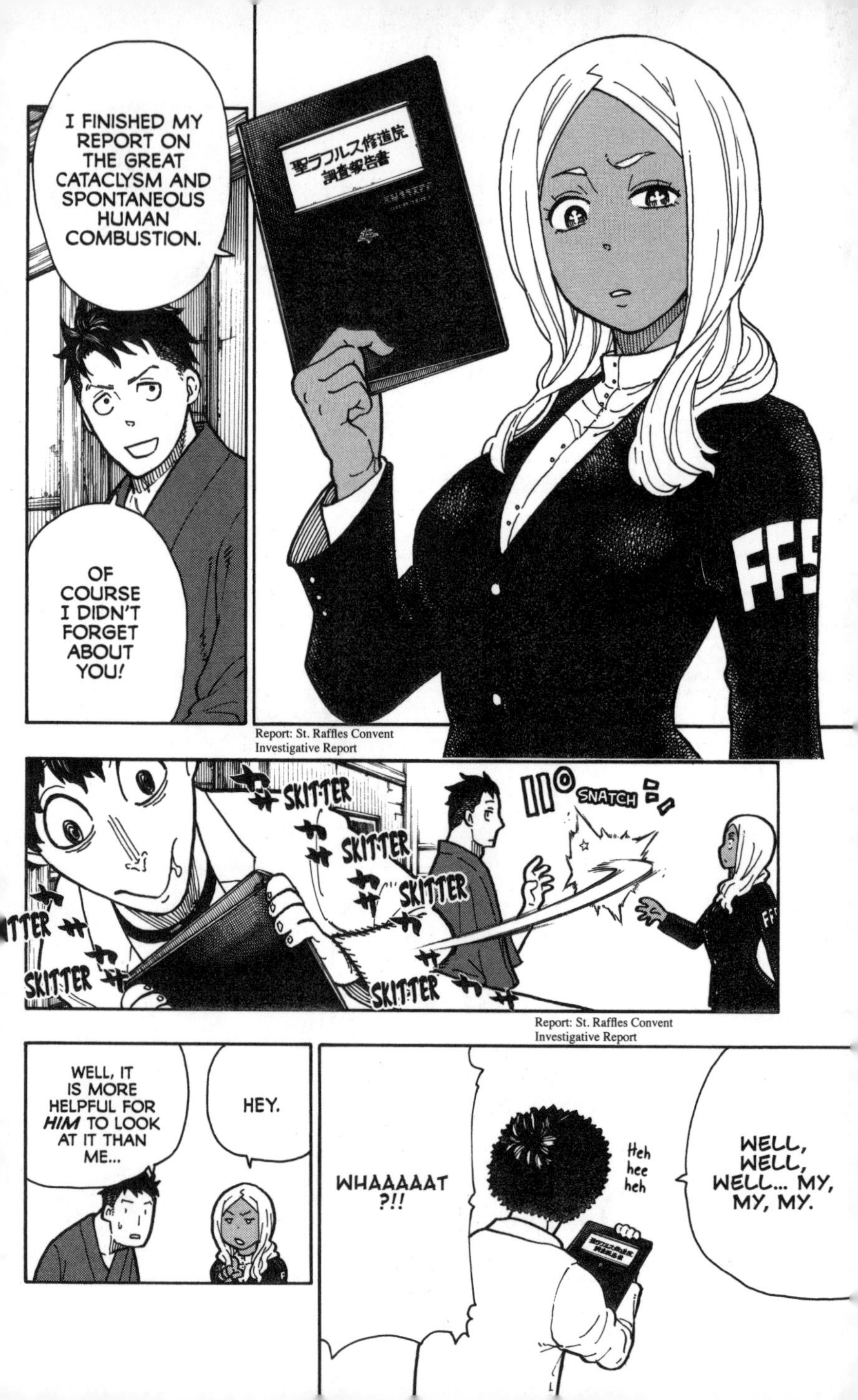
聖ラフルス修道院
調査報告書
FFS
Report: St. Raffles Convent Investigative Report
I FINISHED MY REPORT ON THE GREAT CATACLYSM AND SPONTANEOUS HUMAN COMBUSTION.
OF COURSE I DIDN'T FORGET ABOUT YOU!
SNATCH
SKIT·TER
SKIT·TER
SKITTER
SKIT·TER
SKITTER
SKITTER
Report: St. Raffles Convent Investigative Report
WELL, WELL, WELL... MY, MY, MY.
Heh hee heh
WHAAAAAT ?!!
HEY.
WELL, IT IS MORE HELPFUL FOR *HIM* TO LOOK AT IT THAN ME...

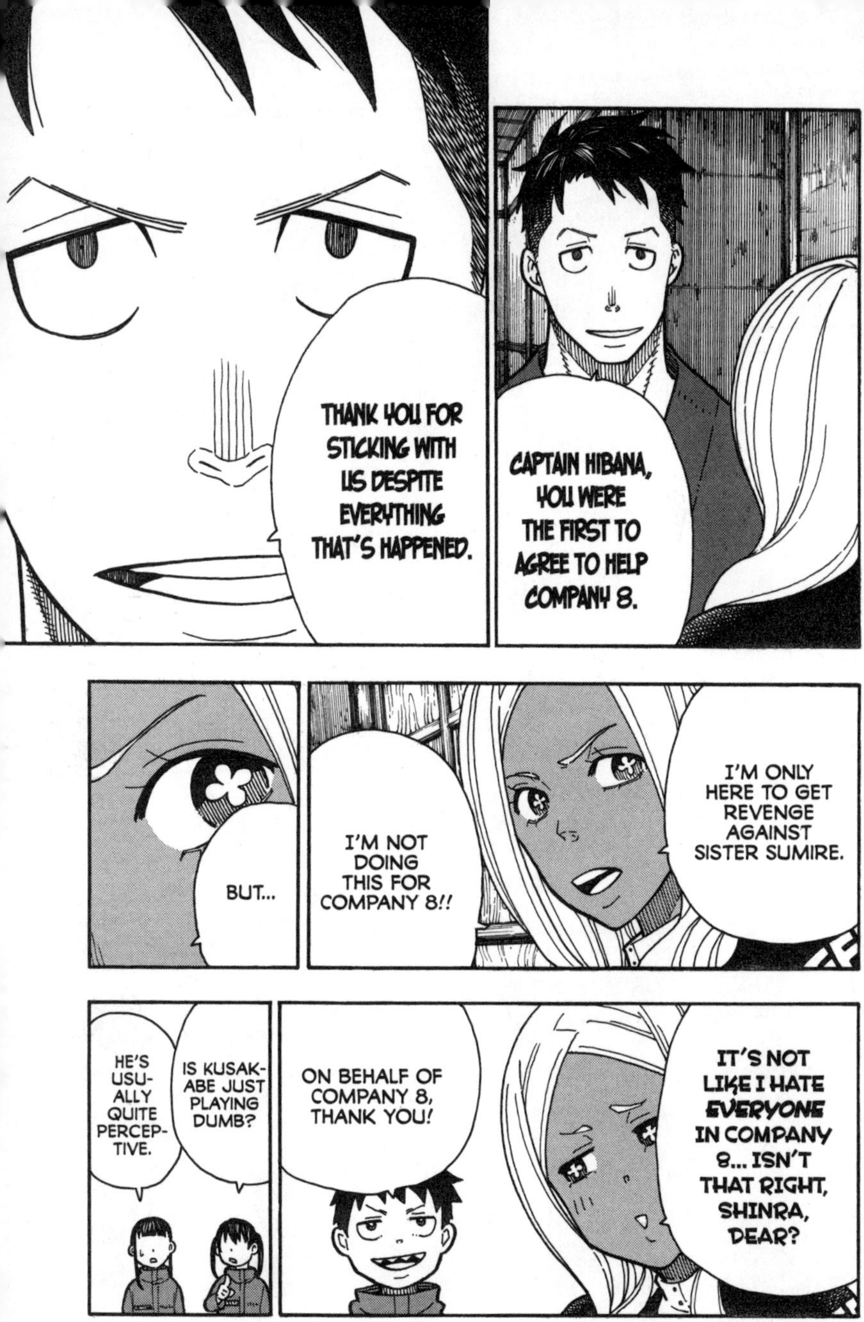
CAPTAIN HIBANA, YOU WERE THE FIRST TO AGREE TO HELP COMPANY 8.
THANK YOU FOR STICKING WITH US DESPITE EVERYTHING THAT'S HAPPENED.
I'M ONLY HERE TO GET REVENGE AGAINST SISTER SUMIRE.
I'M NOT DOING THIS FOR COMPANY 8!!
BUT...
IT'S NOT LIKE I HATE *EVERYONE* IN COMPANY 8... ISN'T THAT RIGHT, SHINRA, DEAR?
ON BEHALF OF COMPANY 8, THANK YOU!
IS KUSAK-ABE JUST PLAYING DUMB?
HE'S USU-ALLY QUITE PERCEP-TIVE.

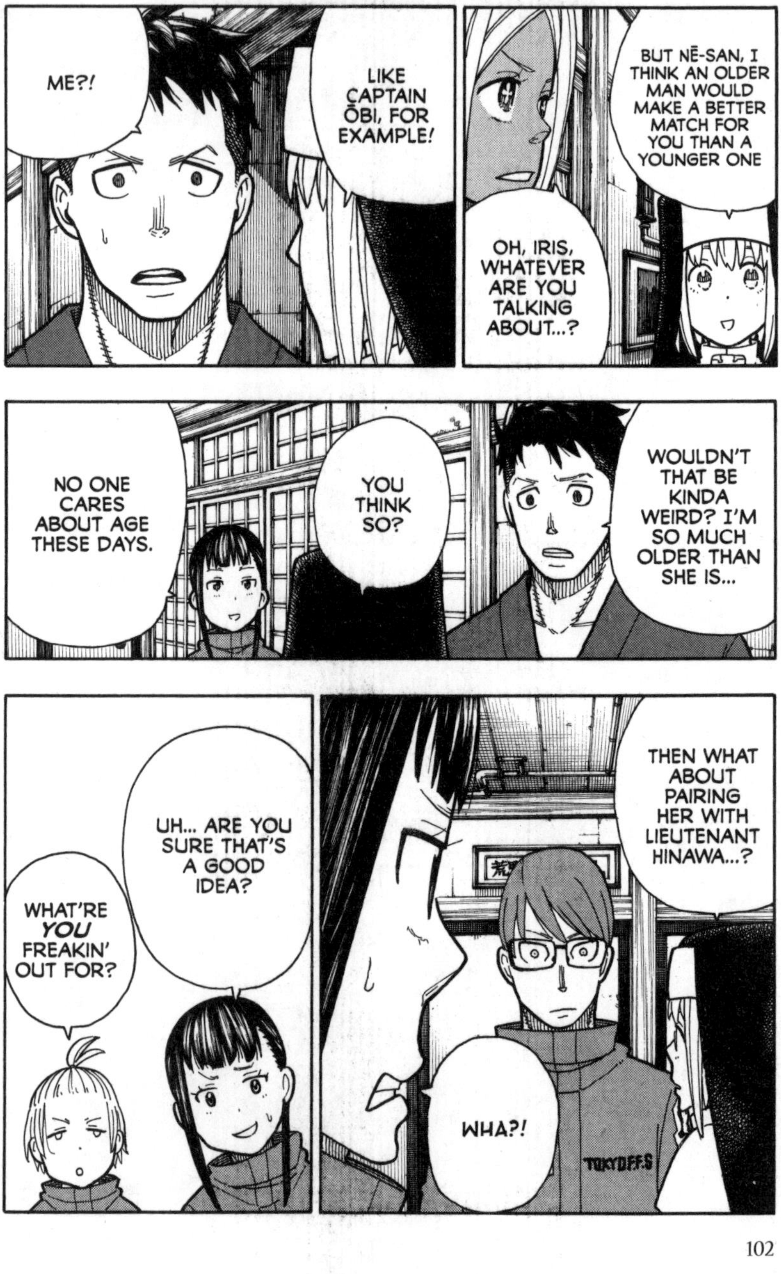
BUT NĒ-SAN, I THINK AN OLDER MAN WOULD MAKE A BETTER MATCH FOR YOU THAN A YOUNGER ONE
OH, IRIS, WHATEVER ARE YOU TALKING ABOUT...?
LIKE CAPTAIN ŌBI, FOR EXAMPLE!
ME?!
WOULDN'T THAT BE KINDA WEIRD? I'M SO MUCH OLDER THAN SHE IS...
YOU THINK SO?
NO ONE CARES ABOUT AGE THESE DAYS.
THEN WHAT ABOUT PAIRING HER WITH LIEUTENANT HINAWA...?
WHA?!
TOKYO F.F.S
UH... ARE YOU SURE THAT'S A GOOD IDEA?
WHAT'RE *YOU* FREAKIN' OUT FOR?

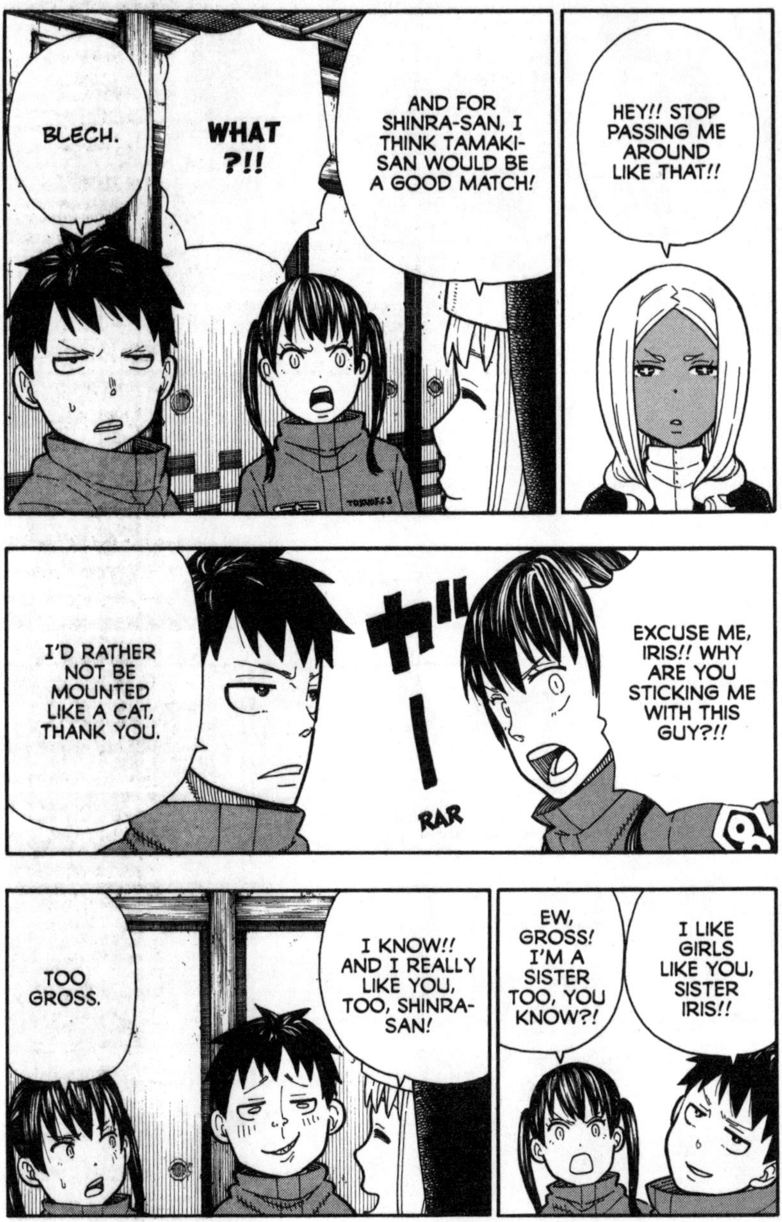
HEY!! STOP PASSING ME AROUND LIKE THAT!!
AND FOR SHINRA-SAN, I THINK TAMAKI-SAN WOULD BE A GOOD MATCH!
WHAT ?!!
BLECH.
EXCUSE ME, IRIS!! WHY ARE YOU STICKING ME WITH THIS GUY?!!
ガー
RAR
I'D RATHER NOT BE MOUNTED LIKE A CAT, THANK YOU.
I LIKE GIRLS LIKE YOU, SISTER IRIS!!
EW, GROSS! I'M A SISTER TOO, YOU KNOW?!
I KNOW!! AND I REALLY LIKE YOU, TOO, SHINRA-SAN!
TOO GROSS.

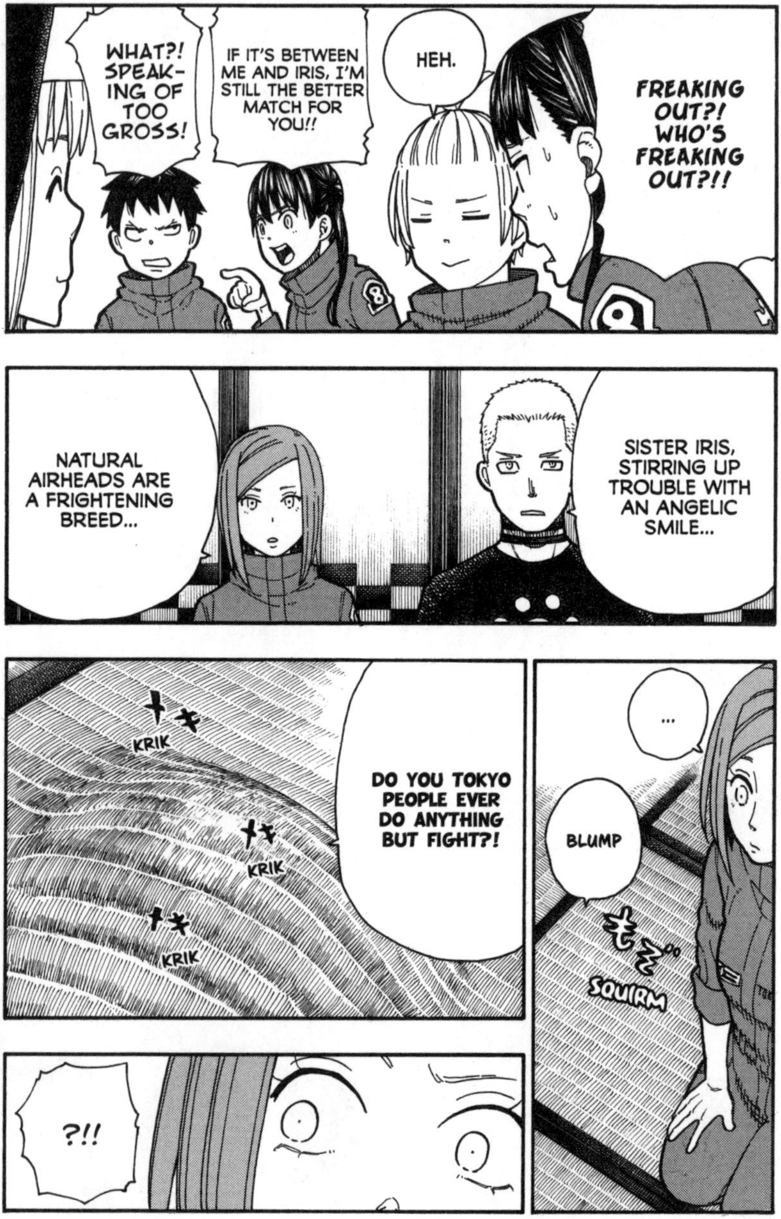
FREAKING OUT?! WHO'S FREAKING OUT?!!
HEH.
IF IT'S BETWEEN ME AND IRIS, I'M STILL THE BETTER MATCH FOR YOU!!
WHAT?! SPEAK-ING OF TOO GROSS!
SISTER IRIS, STIRRING UP TROUBLE WITH AN ANGELIC SMILE...
NATURAL AIRHEADS ARE A FRIGHTENING BREED...
...
BLUMP
SQUIRM
DO YOU TOKYO PEOPLE EVER DO ANYTHING BUT FIGHT?!
KRIK
KRIK
KRIK
?!!

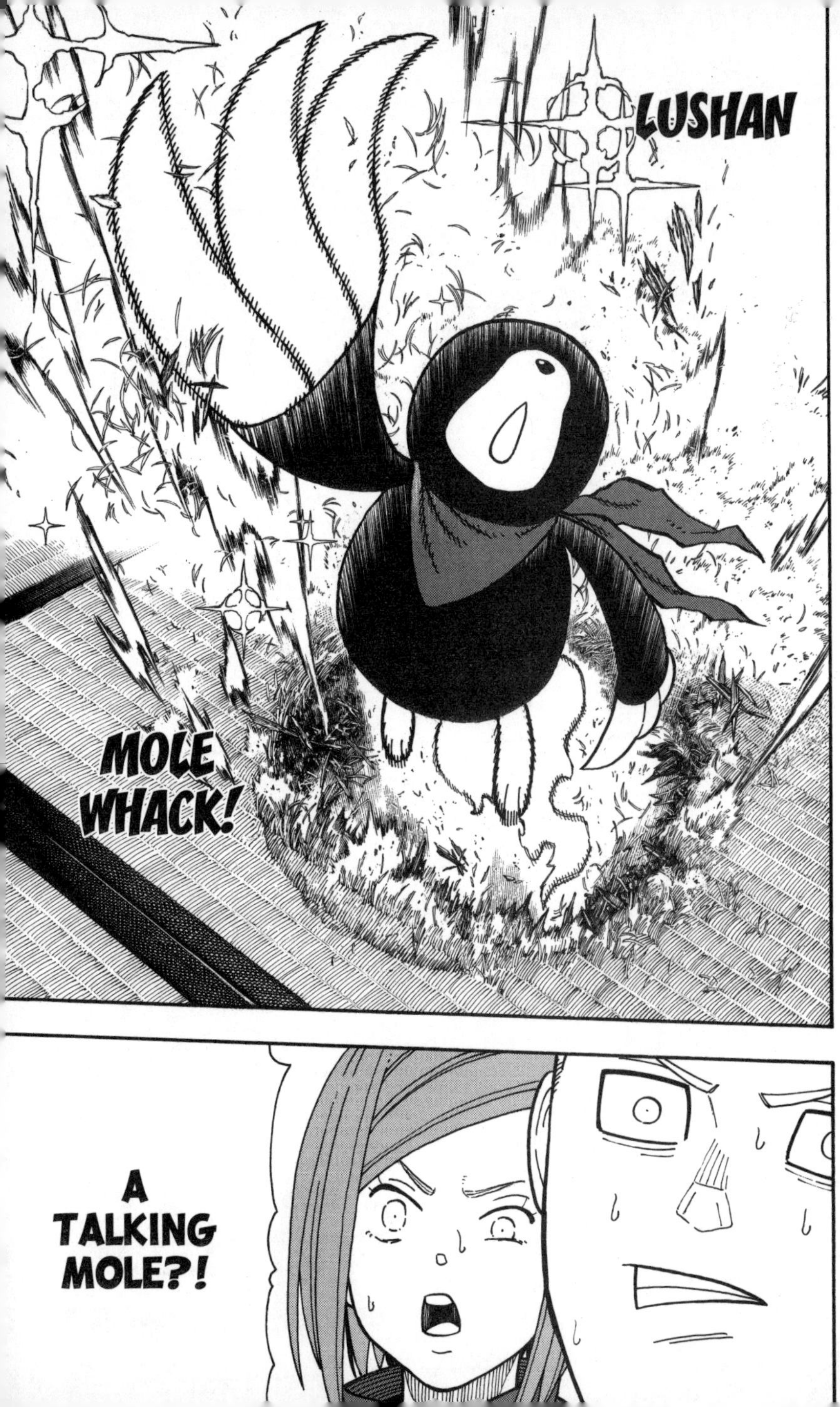
LUSHAN
MOLE WHACK!
A TALKING MOLE?!

FIRE FORCE

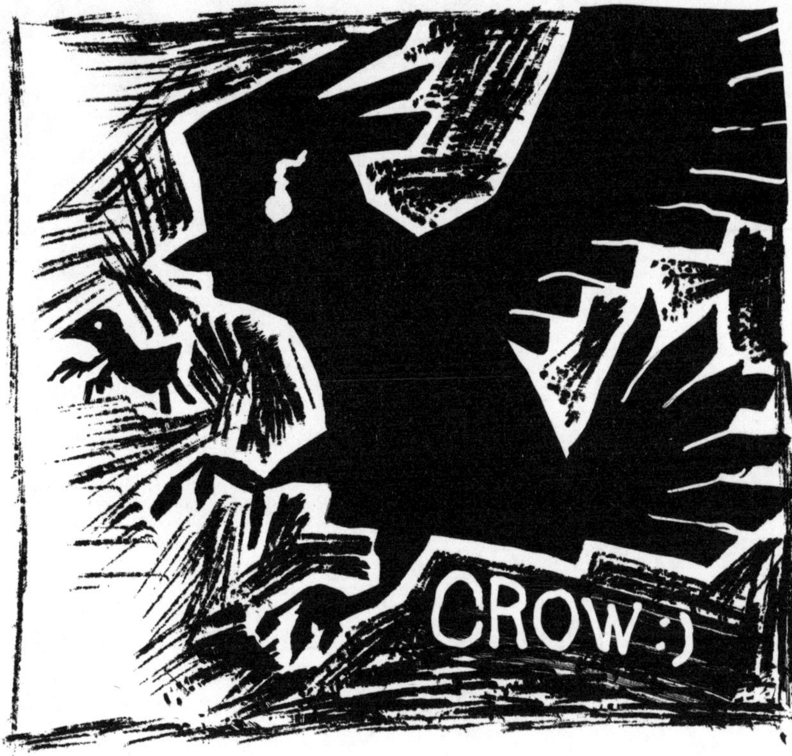
CROW :)

CHAPTER CCX: ADVENT

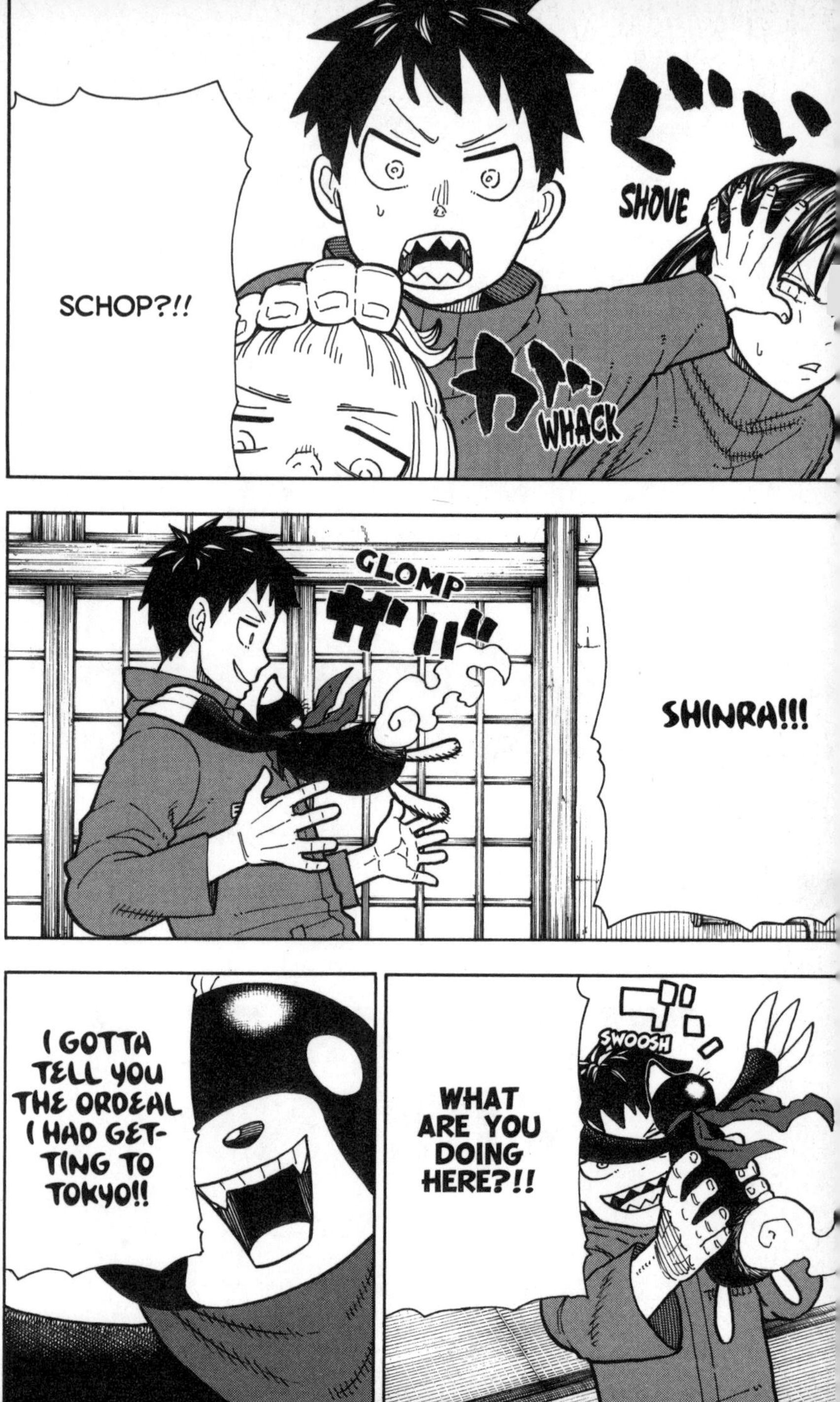
SHOVE
WHACK
SCHOP?!!
SHINRA!!!
GLOMP
SWOOSH
WHAT ARE YOU DOING HERE?!!
I GOTTA TELL YOU THE ORDEAL I HAD GET-TING TO TOKYO!!

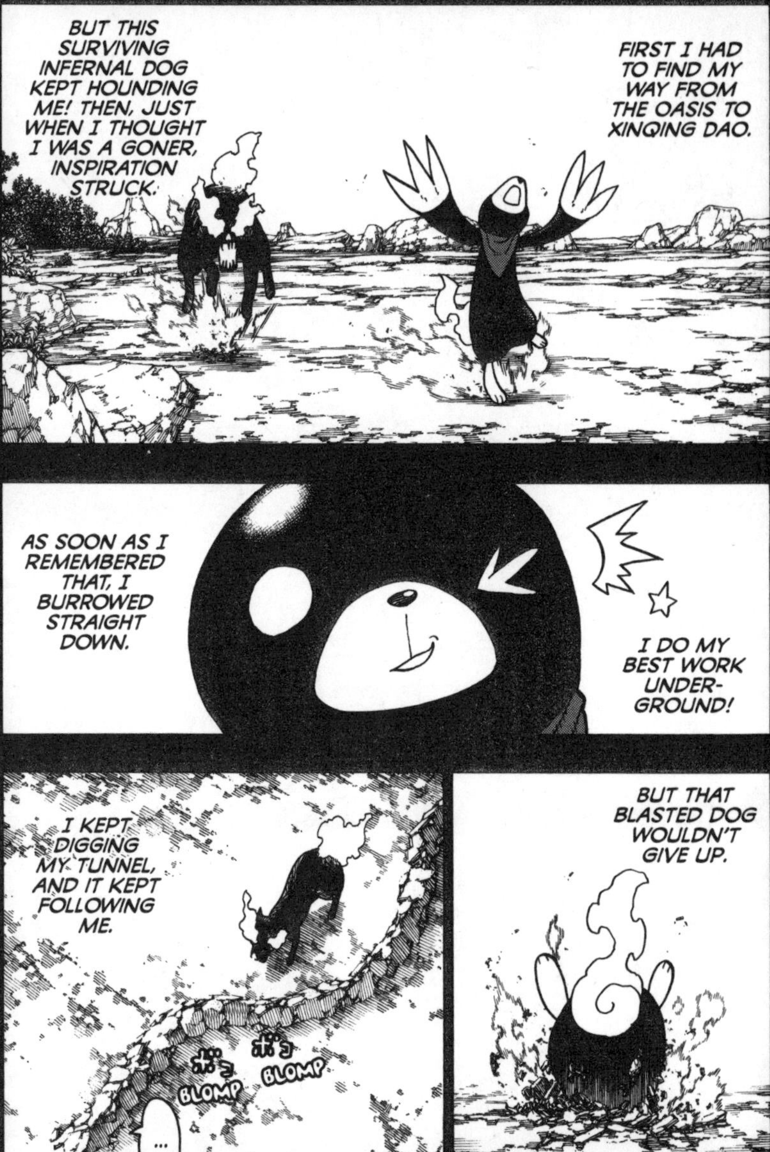
FIRST I HAD TO FIND MY WAY FROM THE OASIS TO XINQING DAO.
BUT THIS SURVIVING INFERNAL DOG KEPT HOUNDING ME! THEN, JUST WHEN I THOUGHT I WAS A GONER, INSPIRATION STRUCK.
I DO MY BEST WORK UNDER-GROUND!
AS SOON AS I REMEMBERED THAT, I BURROWED STRAIGHT DOWN.
BUT THAT BLASTED DOG WOULDN'T GIVE UP.
I KEPT DIGGING MY TUNNEL, AND IT KEPT FOLLOWING ME.
ボコ BLOMP
ボコ BLOMP
...

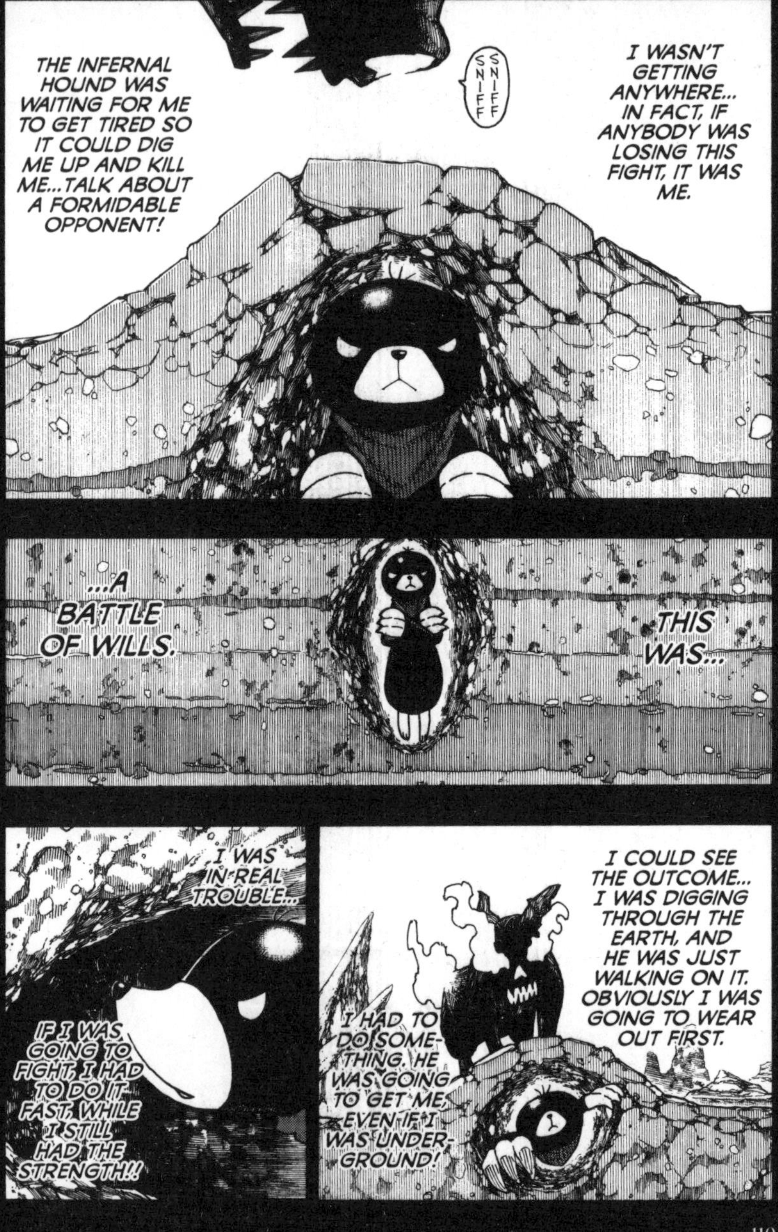

I WASN'T GETTING ANYWHERE... IN FACT, IF ANYBODY WAS LOSING THIS FIGHT, IT WAS ME.
SNIFF SNIFF
THE INFERNAL HOUND WAS WAITING FOR ME TO GET TIRED SO IT COULD DIG ME UP AND KILL ME...TALK ABOUT A FORMIDABLE OPPONENT!
THIS WAS...
...A BATTLE OF WILLS.
I COULD SEE THE OUTCOME... I WAS DIGGING THROUGH THE EARTH, AND HE WAS JUST WALKING ON IT. OBVIOUSLY I WAS GOING TO WEAR OUT FIRST.
I HAD TO DO SOME-THING. HE WAS GOING TO GET ME, EVEN IF I WAS UNDER-GROUND!
I WAS IN REAL TROUBLE...
IF I WAS GOING TO FIGHT, I HAD TO DO IT FAST, WHILE I STILL HAD THE STRENGTH!!

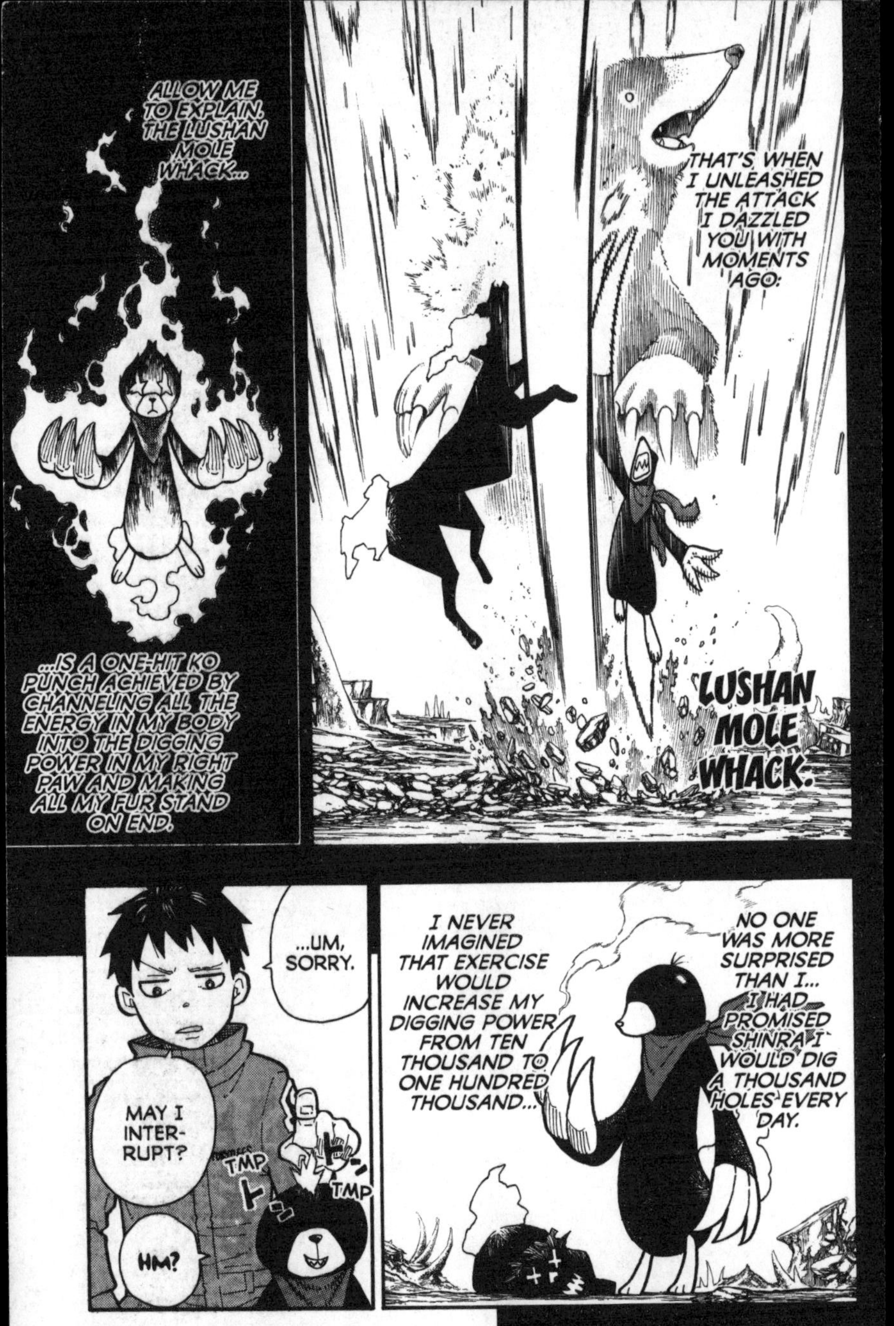
THAT'S WHEN I UNLEASHED THE ATTACK I DAZZLED YOU WITH MOMENTS AGO:
LUSHAN MOLE WHACK.
ALLOW ME TO EXPLAIN. THE LUSHAN MOLE WHACK...
...IS A ONE-HIT KO PUNCH ACHIEVED BY CHANNELING ALL THE ENERGY IN MY BODY INTO THE DIGGING POWER IN MY RIGHT PAW AND MAKING ALL MY FUR STAND ON END.
NO ONE WAS MORE SURPRISED THAN I... I HAD PROMISED SHINRA I WOULD DIG A THOUSAND HOLES EVERY DAY.
I NEVER IMAGINED THAT EXERCISE WOULD INCREASE MY DIGGING POWER FROM TEN THOUSAND TO ONE HUNDRED THOUSAND...
...UM, SORRY.
MAY I INTERRUPT?
TMP
TMP
HM?

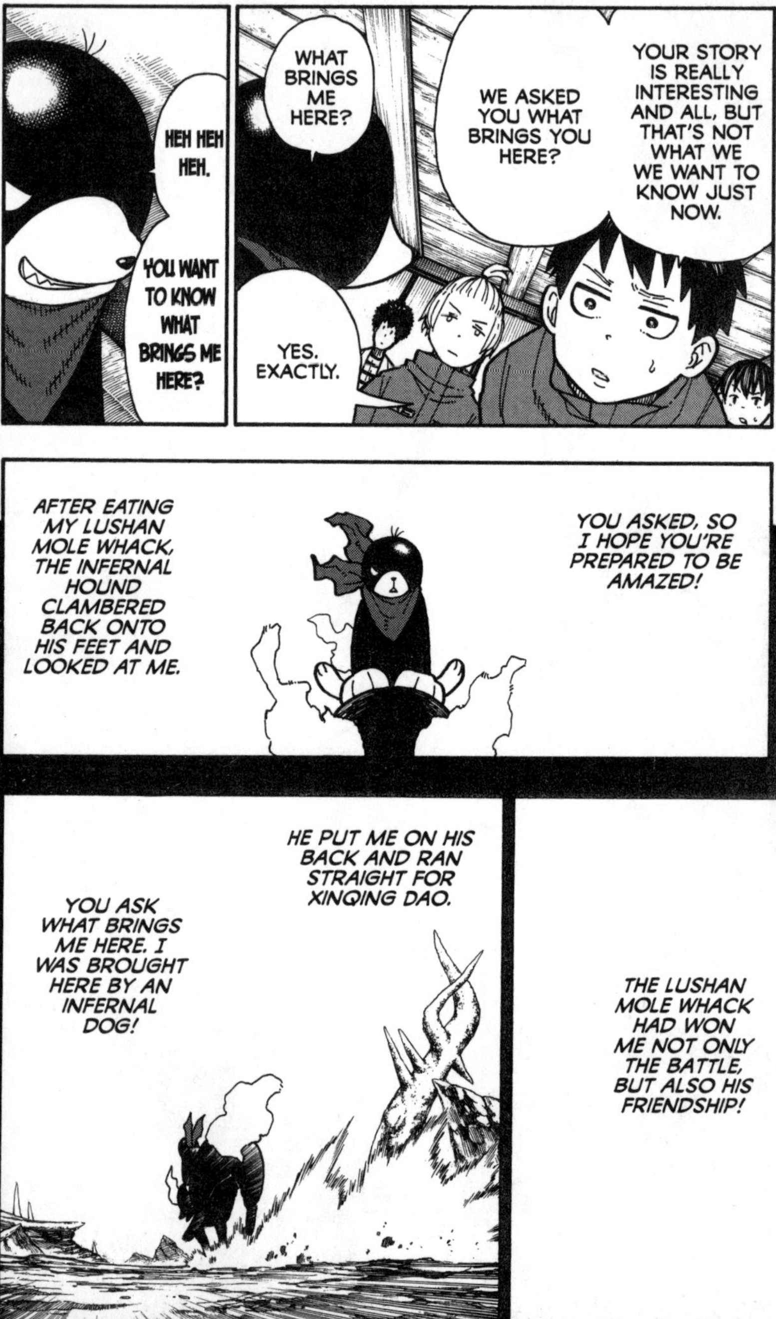
YOUR STORY IS REALLY INTERESTING AND ALL, BUT THAT'S NOT WHAT WE WE WANT TO KNOW JUST NOW.
WE ASKED YOU WHAT BRINGS YOU HERE?
WHAT BRINGS ME HERE?
YES. EXACTLY.
HEH HEH HEH.
YOU WANT TO KNOW WHAT BRINGS ME HERE?
YOU ASKED, SO I HOPE YOU'RE PREPARED TO BE AMAZED!
AFTER EATING MY LUSHAN MOLE WHACK, THE INFERNAL HOUND CLAMBERED BACK ONTO HIS FEET AND LOOKED AT ME.
THE LUSHAN MOLE WHACK HAD WON ME NOT ONLY THE BATTLE, BUT ALSO HIS FRIENDSHIP!
HE PUT ME ON HIS BACK AND RAN STRAIGHT FOR XINQING DAO.
YOU ASK WHAT BRINGS ME HERE. I WAS BROUGHT HERE BY AN INFERNAL DOG!

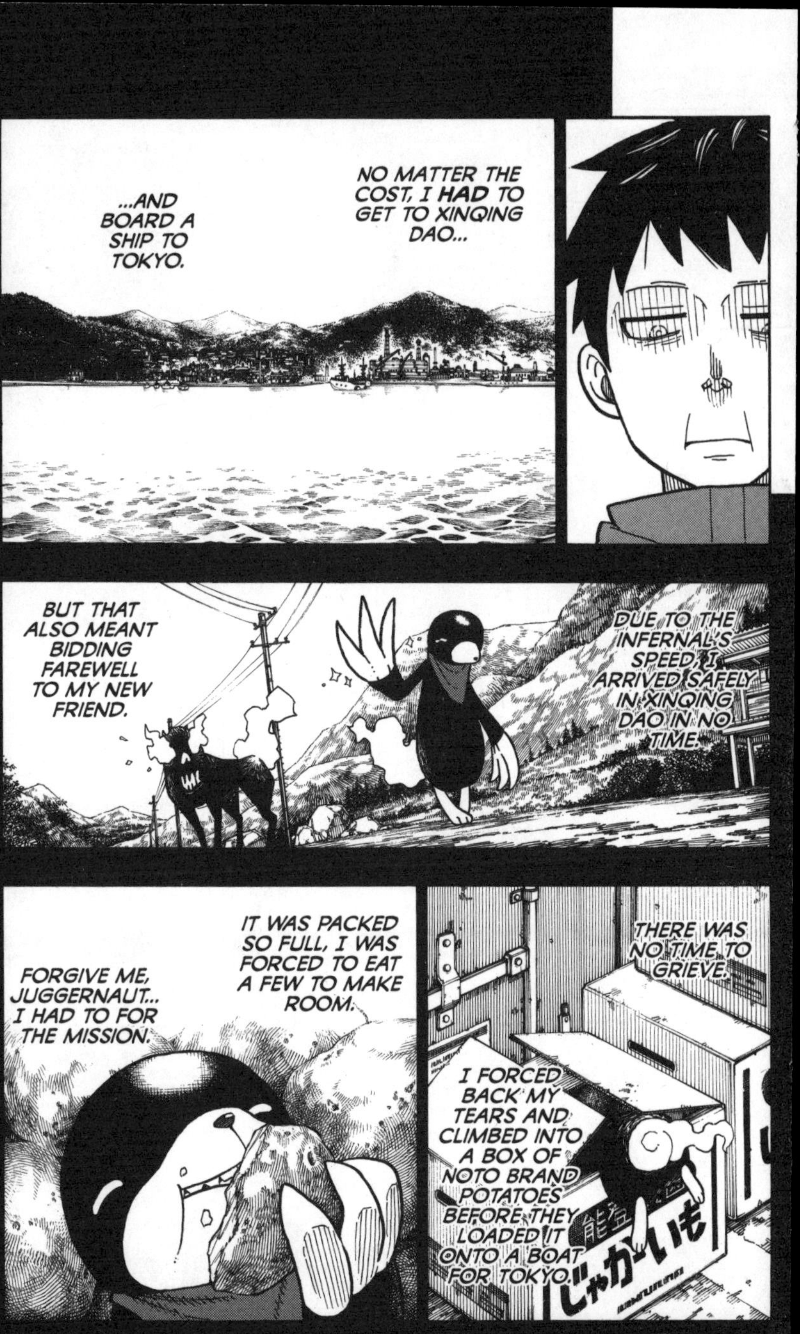
NO MATTER THE COST, I **HAD** TO GET TO XINQING DAO...
...AND BOARD A SHIP TO TOKYO.
DUE TO THE INFERNAL'S SPEED, I ARRIVED SAFELY IN XINQING DAO IN NO TIME.
BUT THAT ALSO MEANT BIDDING FAREWELL TO MY NEW FRIEND.
THERE WAS NO TIME TO GRIEVE.
I FORCED BACK MY TEARS AND CLIMBED INTO A BOX OF NOTO BRAND POTATOES BEFORE THEY LOADED IT ONTO A BOAT FOR TOKYO.
能登
じゃがいも
IT WAS PACKED SO FULL, I WAS FORCED TO EAT A FEW TO MAKE ROOM.
FORGIVE ME, JUGGERNAUT... I HAD TO FOR THE MISSION.

Box: Noto Farms Potatoes

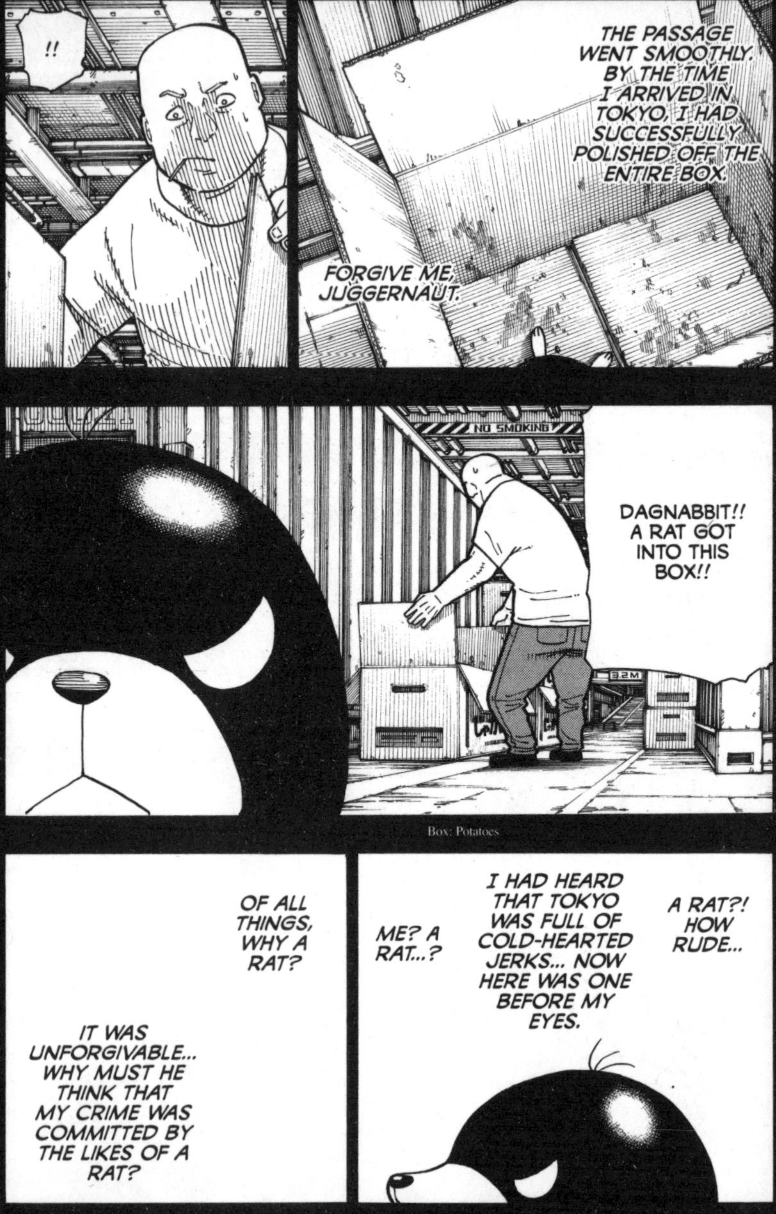
THE PASSAGE WENT SMOOTHLY. BY THE TIME I ARRIVED IN TOKYO, I HAD SUCCESSFULLY POLISHED OFF THE ENTIRE BOX.
FORGIVE ME, JUGGERNAUT.
!!
NO SMOKING
DAGNABBIT!! A RAT GOT INTO THIS BOX!!
3.2M
Box: Potatoes
A RAT?! HOW RUDE...
I HAD HEARD THAT TOKYO WAS FULL OF COLD-HEARTED JERKS... NOW HERE WAS ONE BEFORE MY EYES.
ME? A RAT...?
OF ALL THINGS, WHY A RAT?
IT WAS UNFORGIVABLE... WHY MUST HE THINK THAT MY CRIME WAS COMMITTED BY THE LIKES OF A RAT?

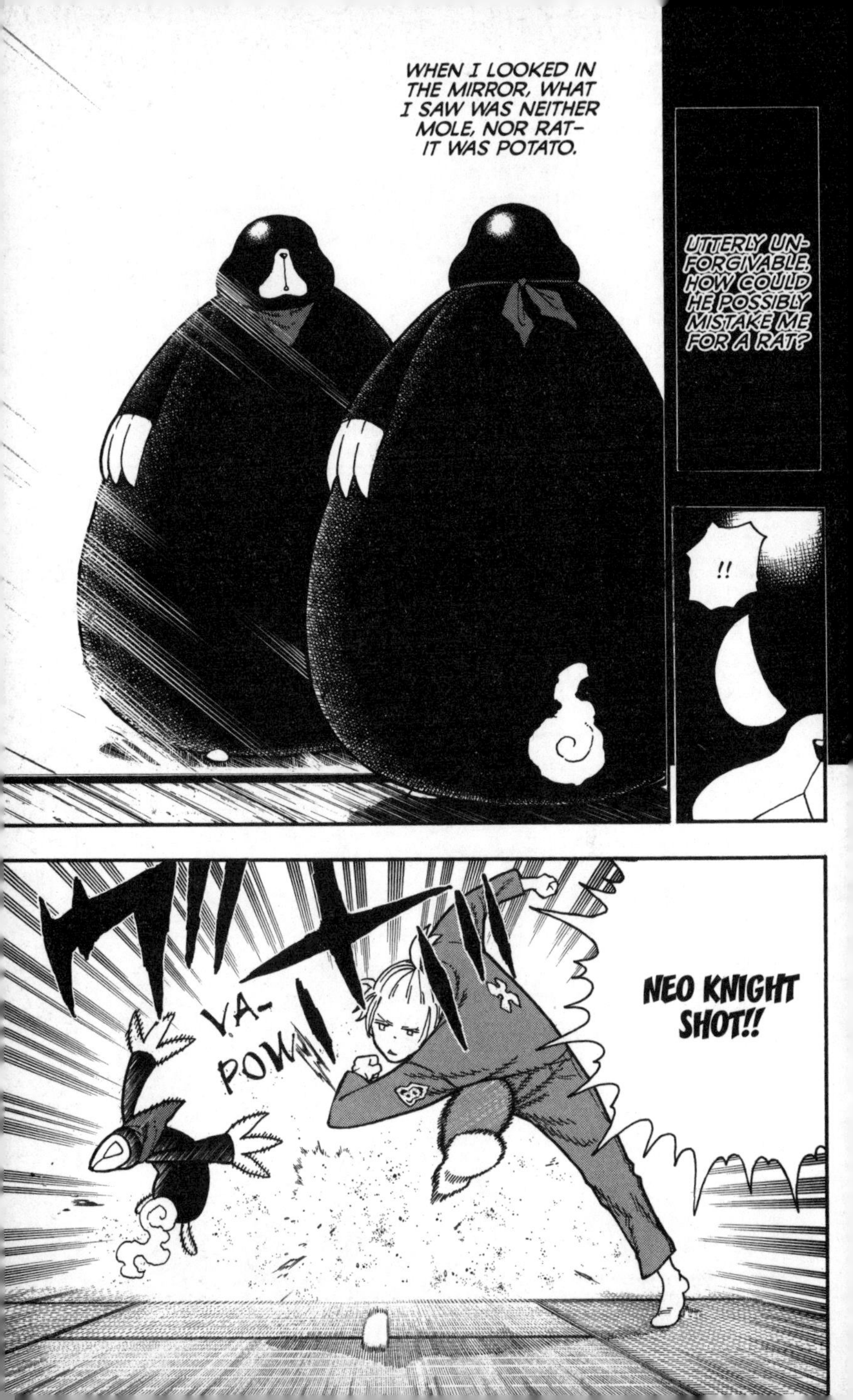
UTTERLY UNFORGIVABLE. HOW COULD HE POSSIBLY MISTAKE ME FOR A RAT?
!!
WHEN I LOOKED IN THE MIRROR, WHAT I SAW WAS NEITHER MOLE, NOR RAT– IT WAS POTATO.
NEO KNIGHT SHOT!!
VA-POW

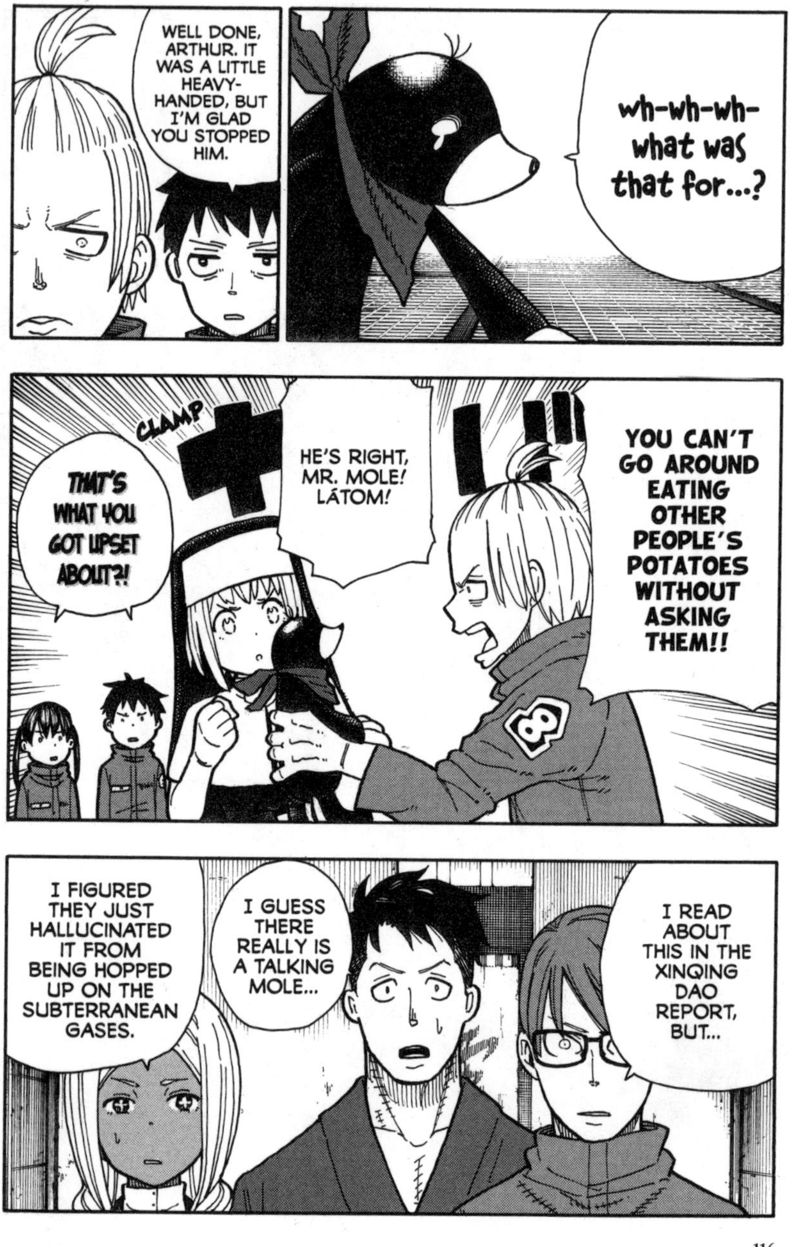
wh-wh-wh-what was that for...?
WELL DONE, ARTHUR. IT WAS A LITTLE HEAVY-HANDED, BUT I'M GLAD YOU STOPPED HIM.
YOU CAN'T GO AROUND EATING OTHER PEOPLE'S POTATOES WITHOUT ASKING THEM!!
HE'S RIGHT, MR. MOLE! LÁTOM!
CLAMP
THAT'S WHAT YOU GOT UPSET ABOUT?!
I READ ABOUT THIS IN THE XINQING DAO REPORT, BUT...
I GUESS THERE REALLY IS A TALKING MOLE...
I FIGURED THEY JUST HALLUCINATED IT FROM BEING HOPPED UP ON THE SUBTERRANEAN GASES.

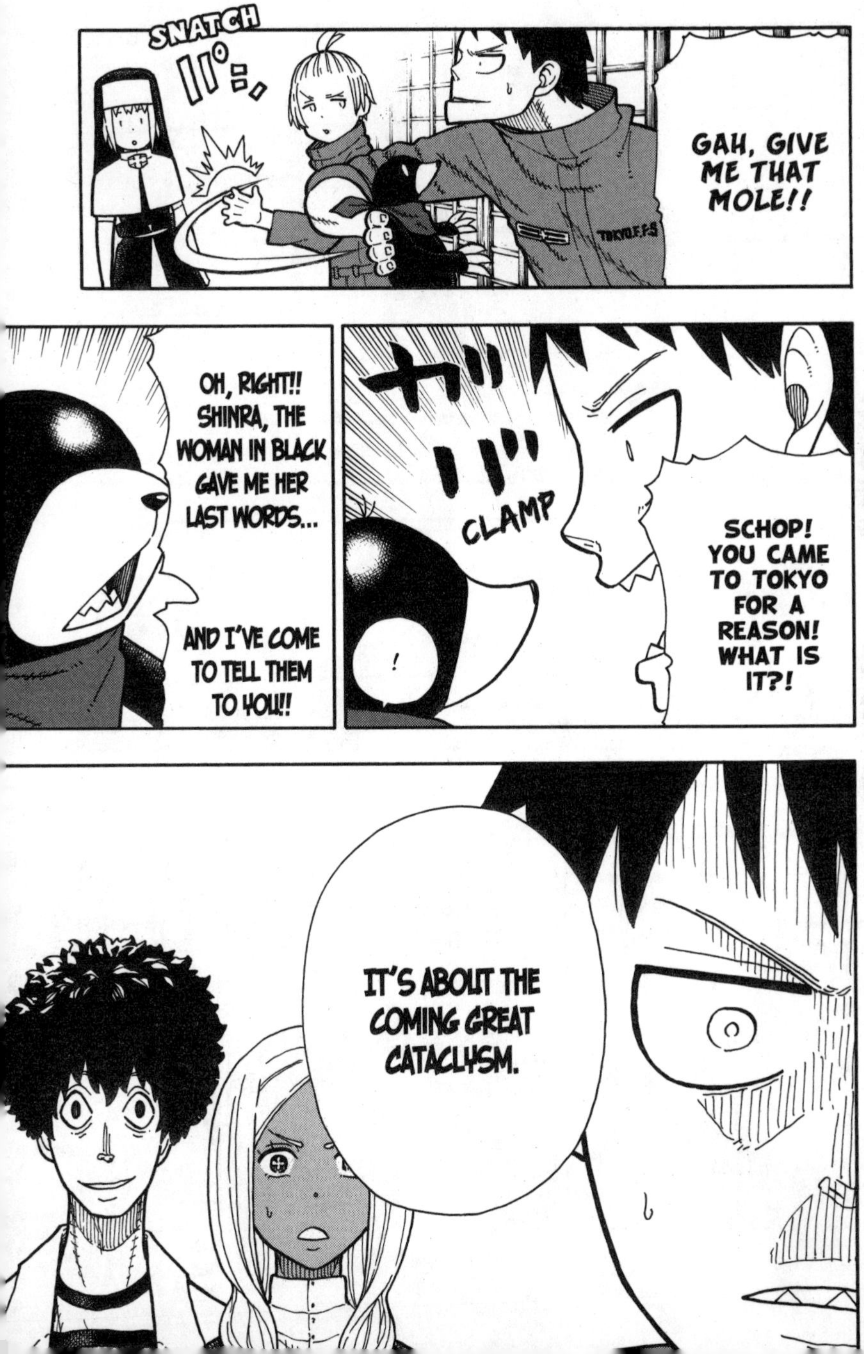
GAH, GIVE ME THAT MOLE!!
SNATCH
SCHOP! YOU CAME TO TOKYO FOR A REASON! WHAT IS IT?!
CLAMP
!
OH, RIGHT!! SHINRA, THE WOMAN IN BLACK GAVE ME HER LAST WORDS...
AND I'VE COME TO TELL THEM TO YOU!!
IT'S ABOUT THE COMING GREAT CATACLYSM.

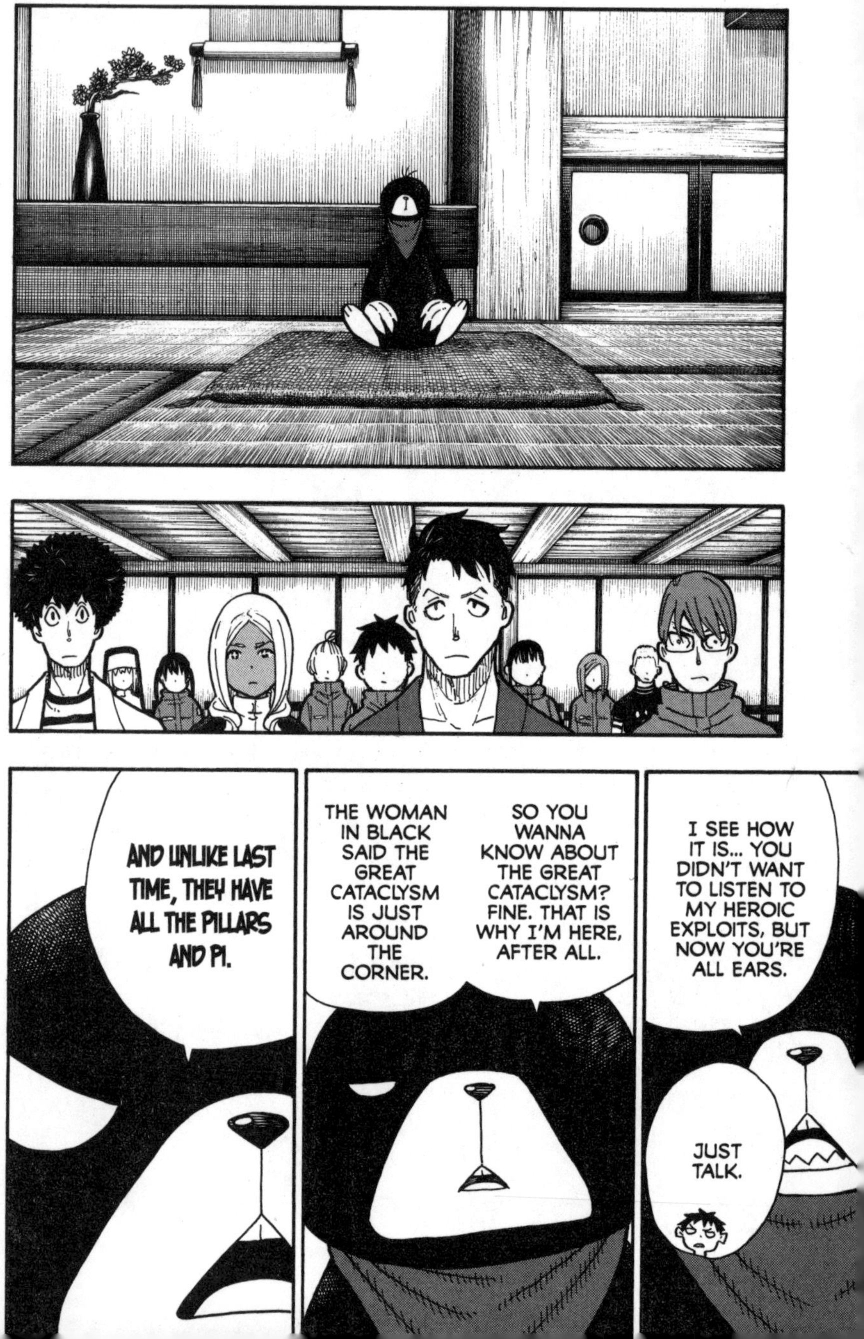
I SEE HOW IT IS... YOU DIDN'T WANT TO LISTEN TO MY HEROIC EXPLOITS, BUT NOW YOU'RE ALL EARS.
JUST TALK.
SO YOU WANNA KNOW ABOUT THE GREAT CATACLYSM? FINE. THAT IS WHY I'M HERE, AFTER ALL.
THE WOMAN IN BLACK SAID THE GREAT CATACLYSM IS JUST AROUND THE CORNER.
AND UNLIKE LAST TIME, THEY HAVE ALL THE PILLARS AND PI.

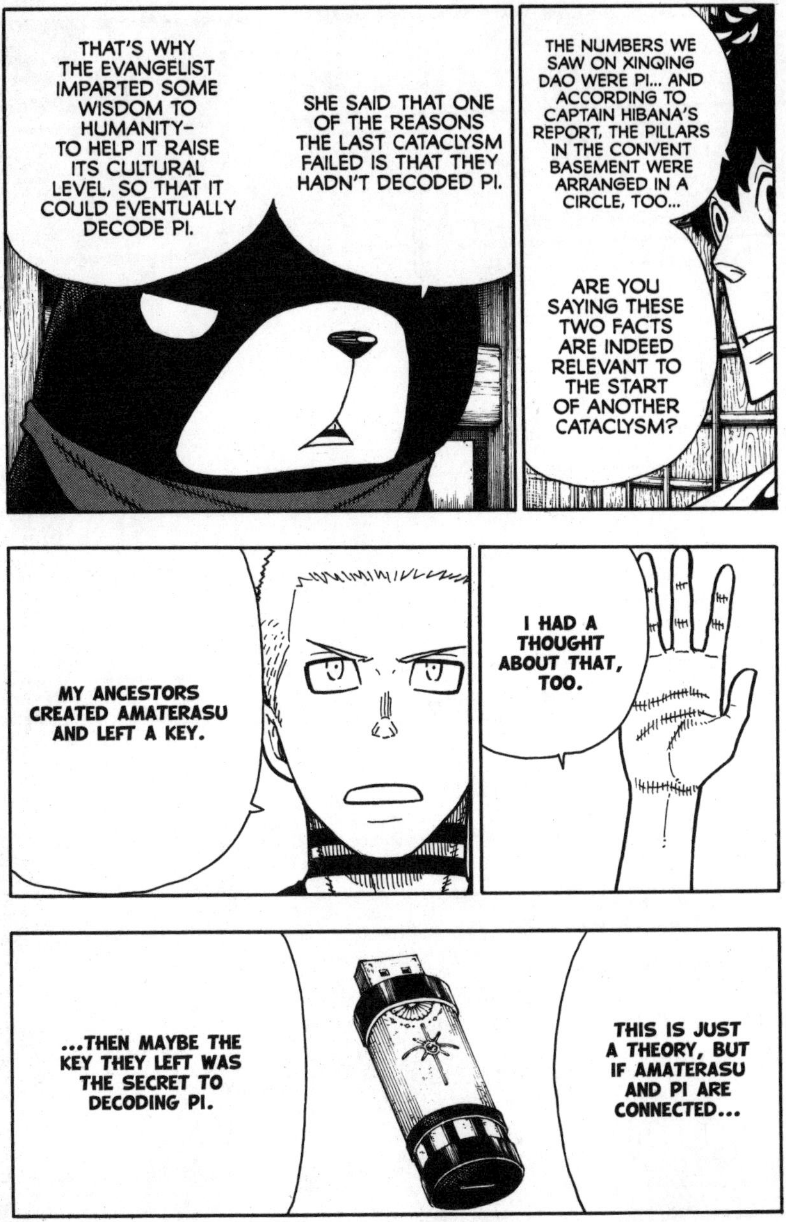
THE NUMBERS WE SAW ON XINQING DAO WERE PI... AND ACCORDING TO CAPTAIN HIBANA'S REPORT, THE PILLARS IN THE CONVENT BASEMENT WERE ARRANGED IN A CIRCLE, TOO...
ARE YOU SAYING THESE TWO FACTS ARE INDEED RELEVANT TO THE START OF ANOTHER CATACLYSM?
SHE SAID THAT ONE OF THE REASONS THE LAST CATACLYSM FAILED IS THAT THEY HADN'T DECODED PI.
THAT'S WHY THE EVANGELIST IMPARTED SOME WISDOM TO HUMANITY– TO HELP IT RAISE ITS CULTURAL LEVEL, SO THAT IT COULD EVENTUALLY DECODE PI.
I HAD A THOUGHT ABOUT THAT, TOO.
MY ANCESTORS CREATED AMATERASU AND LEFT A KEY.
THIS IS JUST A THEORY, BUT IF AMATERASU AND PI ARE CONNECTED...
...THEN MAYBE THE KEY THEY LEFT WAS THE SECRET TO DECODING PI.

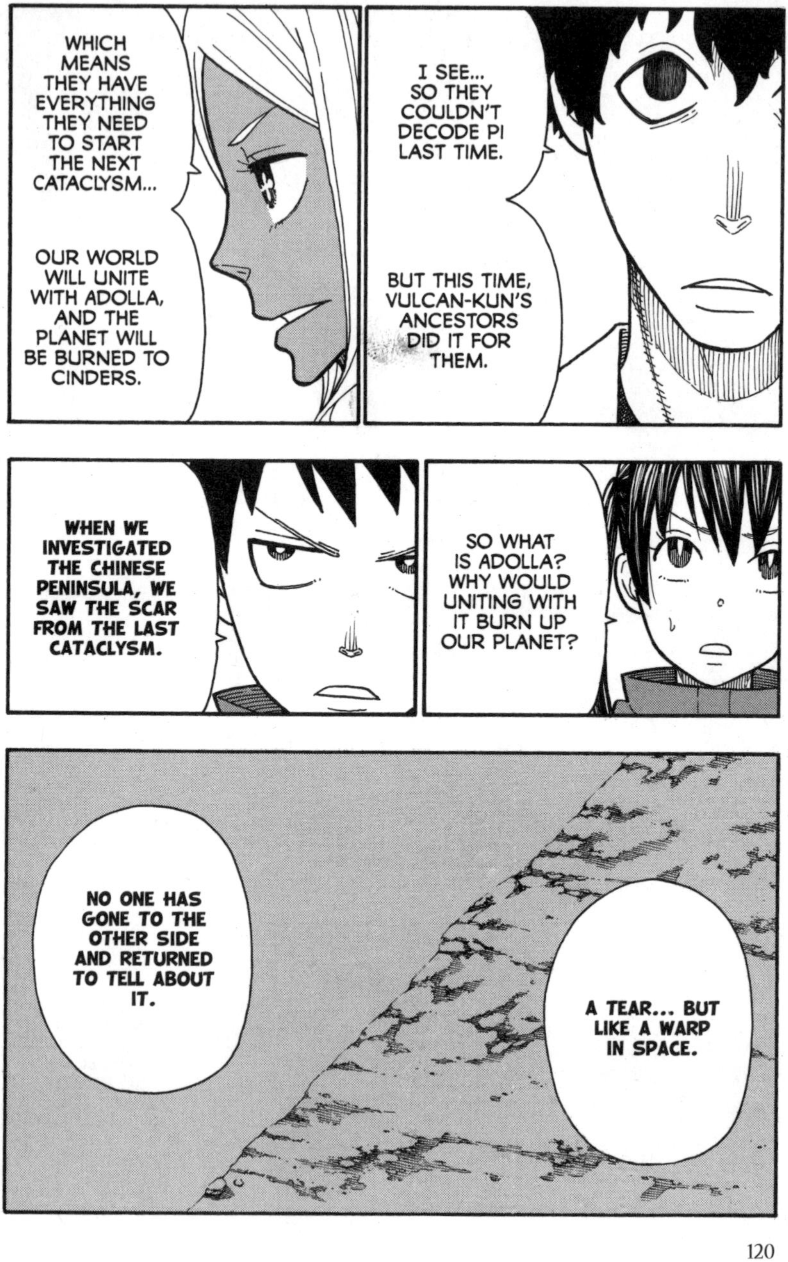
I SEE... SO THEY COULDN'T DECODE PI LAST TIME.
BUT THIS TIME, VULCAN-KUN'S ANCESTORS DID IT FOR THEM.
WHICH MEANS THEY HAVE EVERYTHING THEY NEED TO START THE NEXT CATACLYSM...
OUR WORLD WILL UNITE WITH ADOLLA, AND THE PLANET WILL BE BURNED TO CINDERS.
SO WHAT IS ADOLLA? WHY WOULD UNITING WITH IT BURN UP OUR PLANET?
WHEN WE INVESTIGATED THE CHINESE PENINSULA, WE SAW THE SCAR FROM THE LAST CATACLYSM.
A TEAR... BUT LIKE A WARP IN SPACE.
NO ONE HAS GONE TO THE OTHER SIDE AND RETURNED TO TELL ABOUT IT.

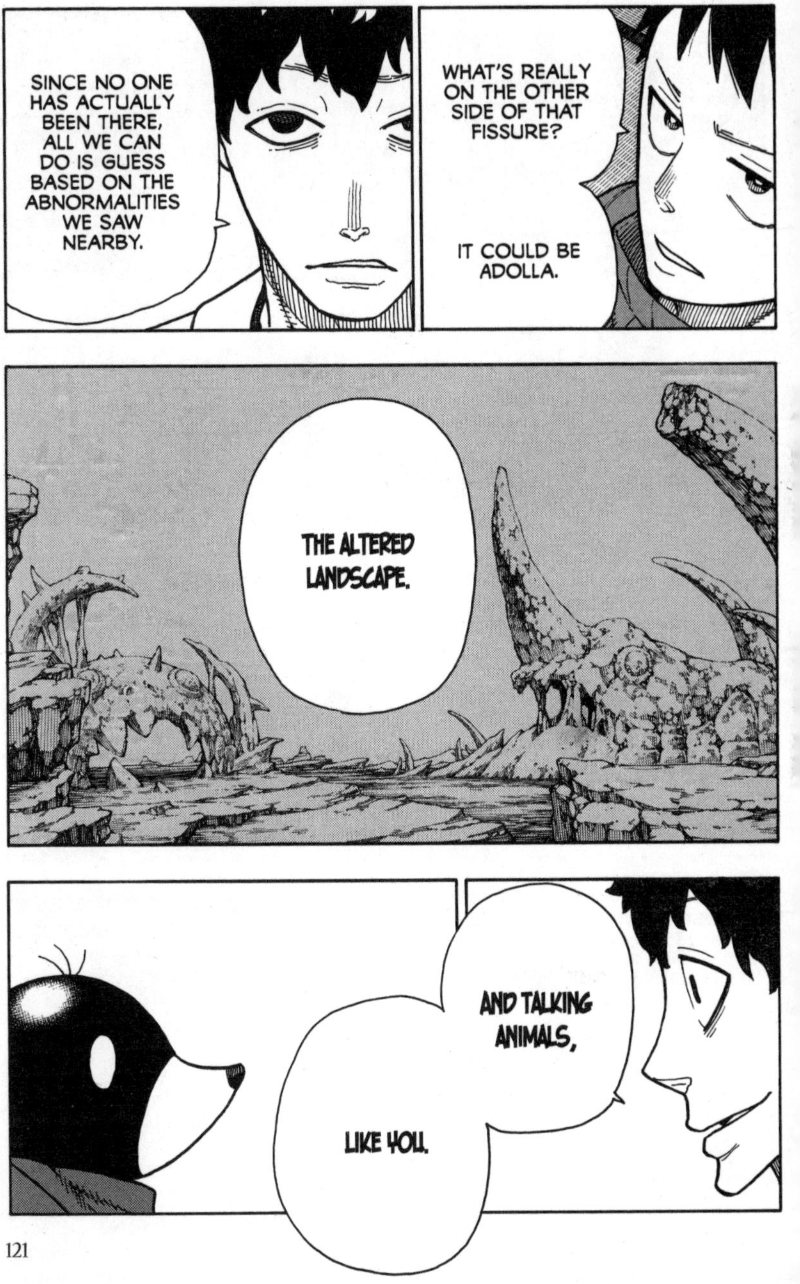
WHAT'S REALLY ON THE OTHER SIDE OF THAT FISSURE?
IT COULD BE ADOLLA.
SINCE NO ONE HAS ACTUALLY BEEN THERE, ALL WE CAN DO IS GUESS BASED ON THE ABNORMALITIES WE SAW NEARBY.
THE ALTERED LANDSCAPE.
AND TALKING ANIMALS,
LIKE YOU.

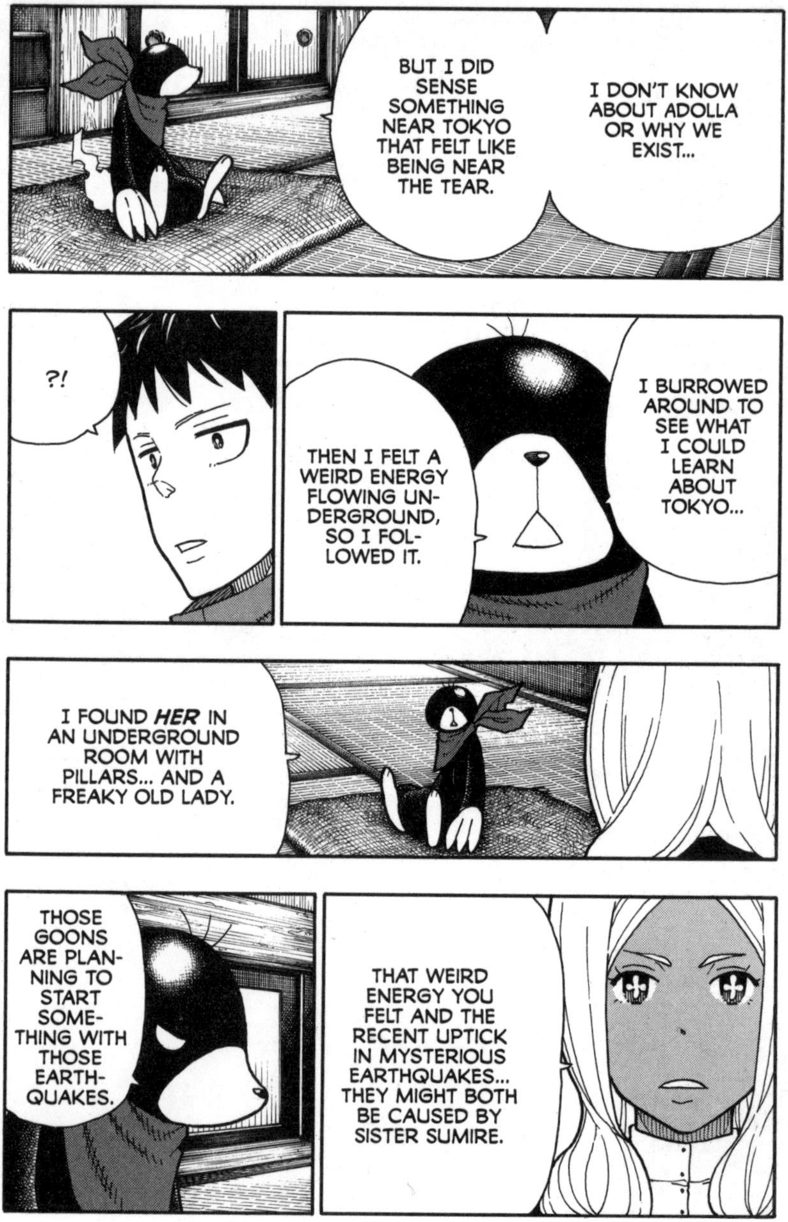
I DON'T KNOW ABOUT ADOLLA OR WHY WE EXIST...
BUT I DID SENSE SOMETHING NEAR TOKYO THAT FELT LIKE BEING NEAR THE TEAR.
I BURROWED AROUND TO SEE WHAT I COULD LEARN ABOUT TOKYO...
THEN I FELT A WEIRD ENERGY FLOWING UNDERGROUND, SO I FOLLOWED IT.
?!
I FOUND *HER* IN AN UNDERGROUND ROOM WITH PILLARS... AND A FREAKY OLD LADY.
THAT WEIRD ENERGY YOU FELT AND THE RECENT UPTICK IN MYSTERIOUS EARTHQUAKES... THEY MIGHT BOTH BE CAUSED BY SISTER SUMIRE.
THOSE GOONS ARE PLANNING TO START SOMETHING WITH THOSE EARTHQUAKES.

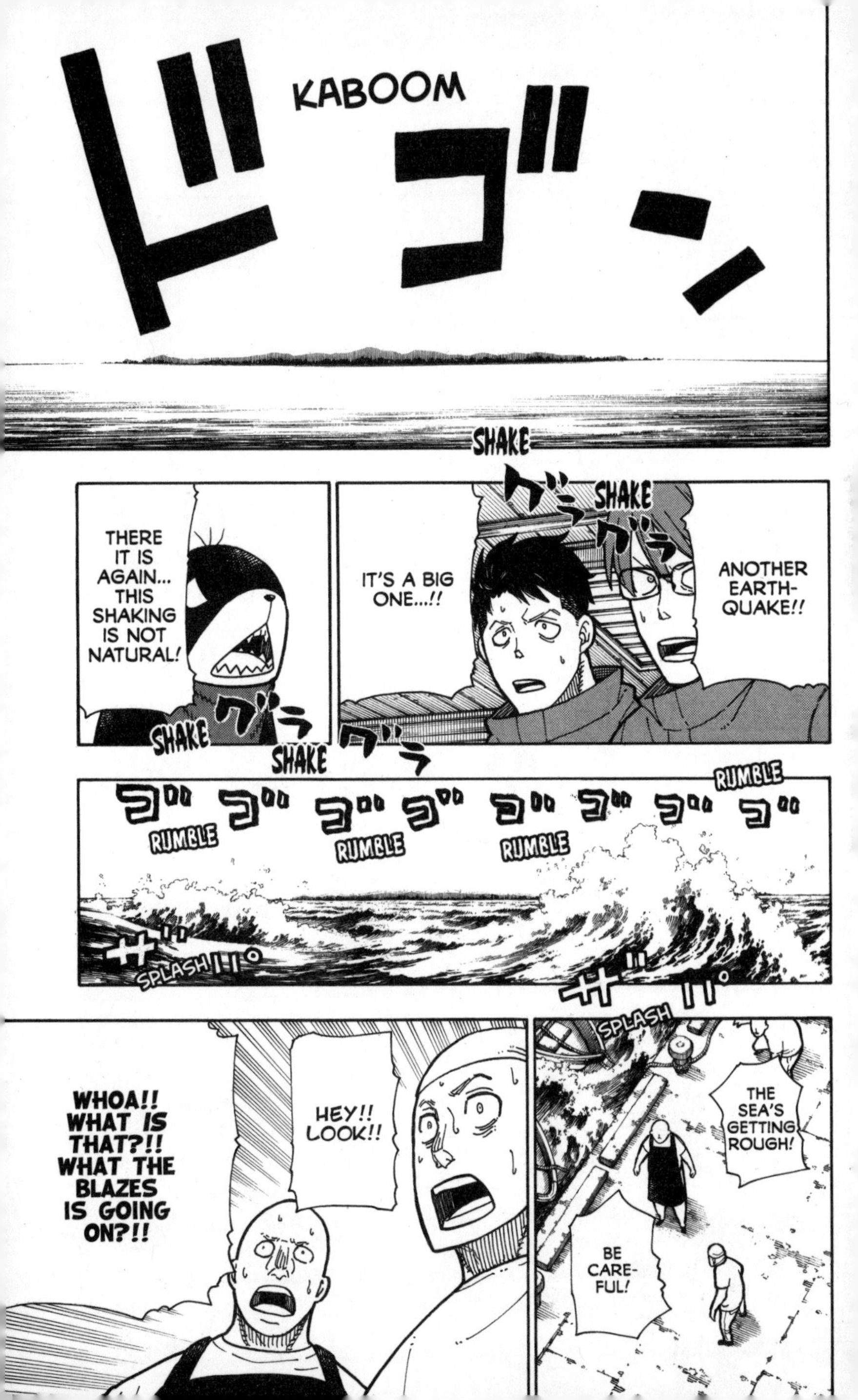

KABOOM
SHAKE
SHAKE
ANOTHER EARTH-QUAKE!!
IT'S A BIG ONE...!!
THERE IT IS AGAIN... THIS SHAKING IS NOT NATURAL!
SHAKE
SHAKE
RUMBLE
RUMBLE
RUMBLE
RUMBLE
SPLASH
SPLASH
THE SEA'S GETTING ROUGH!
BE CARE-FUL!
HEY!! LOOK!!
WHOA!! WHAT *IS* THAT?!! WHAT THE BLAZES IS GOING ON?!!

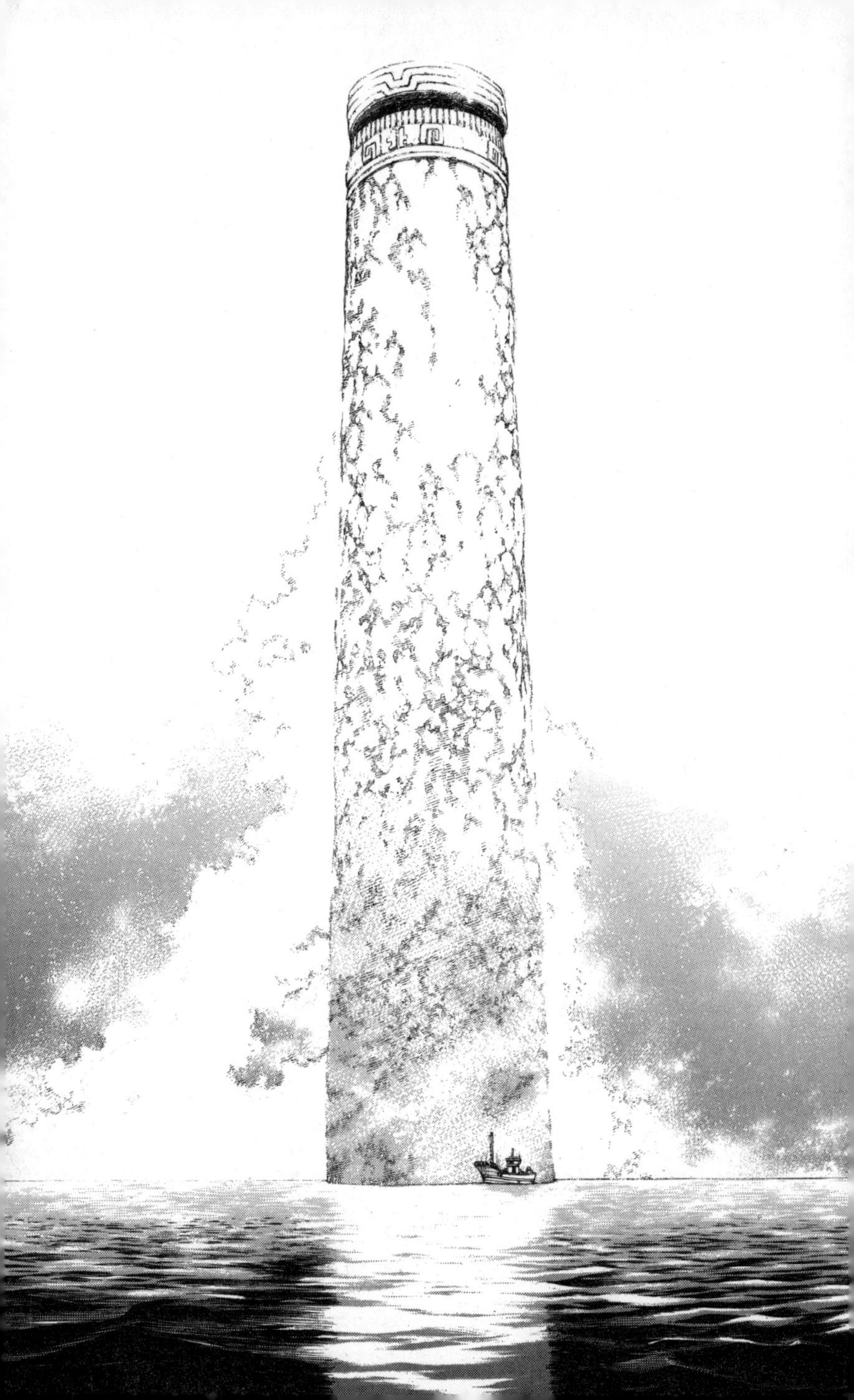

FIRE FORCE

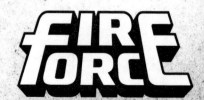

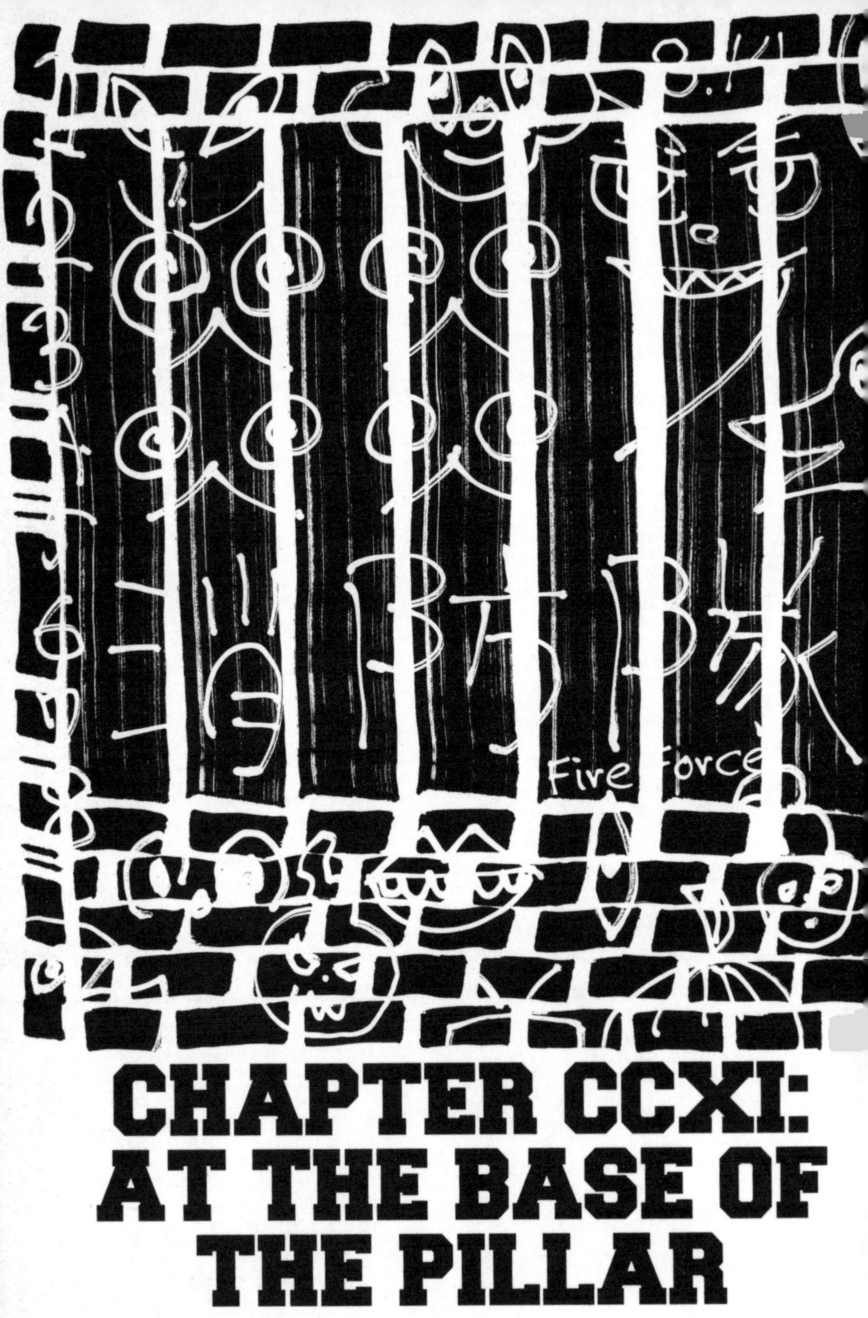
Fire Force

CHAPTER CCXI: AT THE BASE OF THE PILLAR

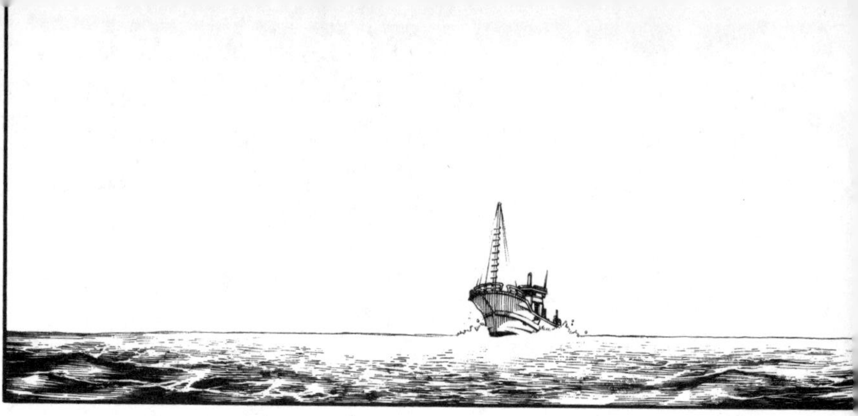

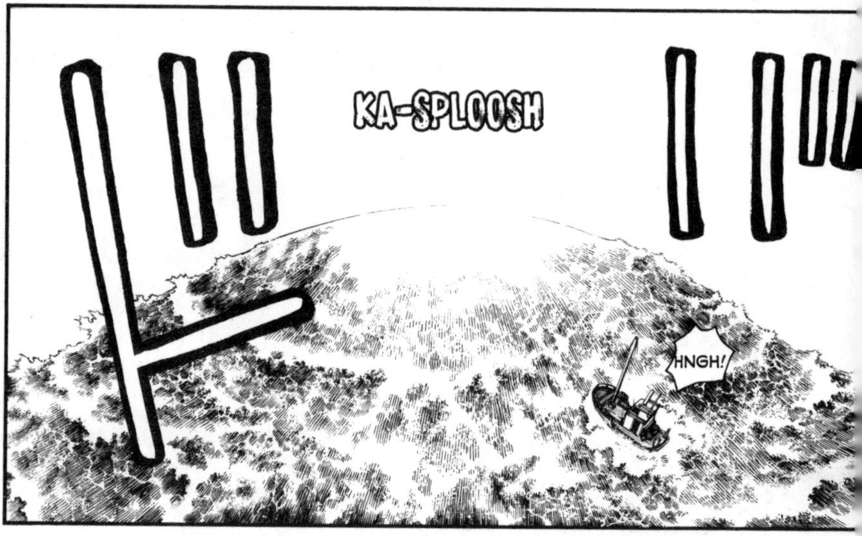
KA-SPLOOSH
HNGH!

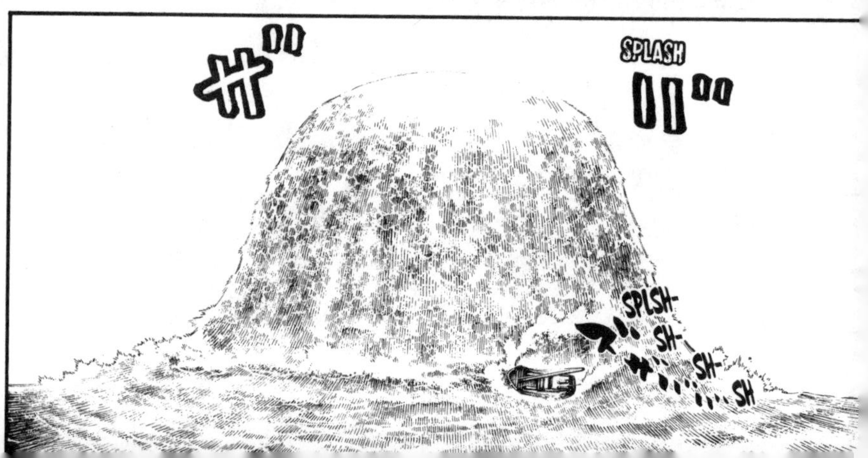
SPLASH
SPLSH- SH- SH- SH

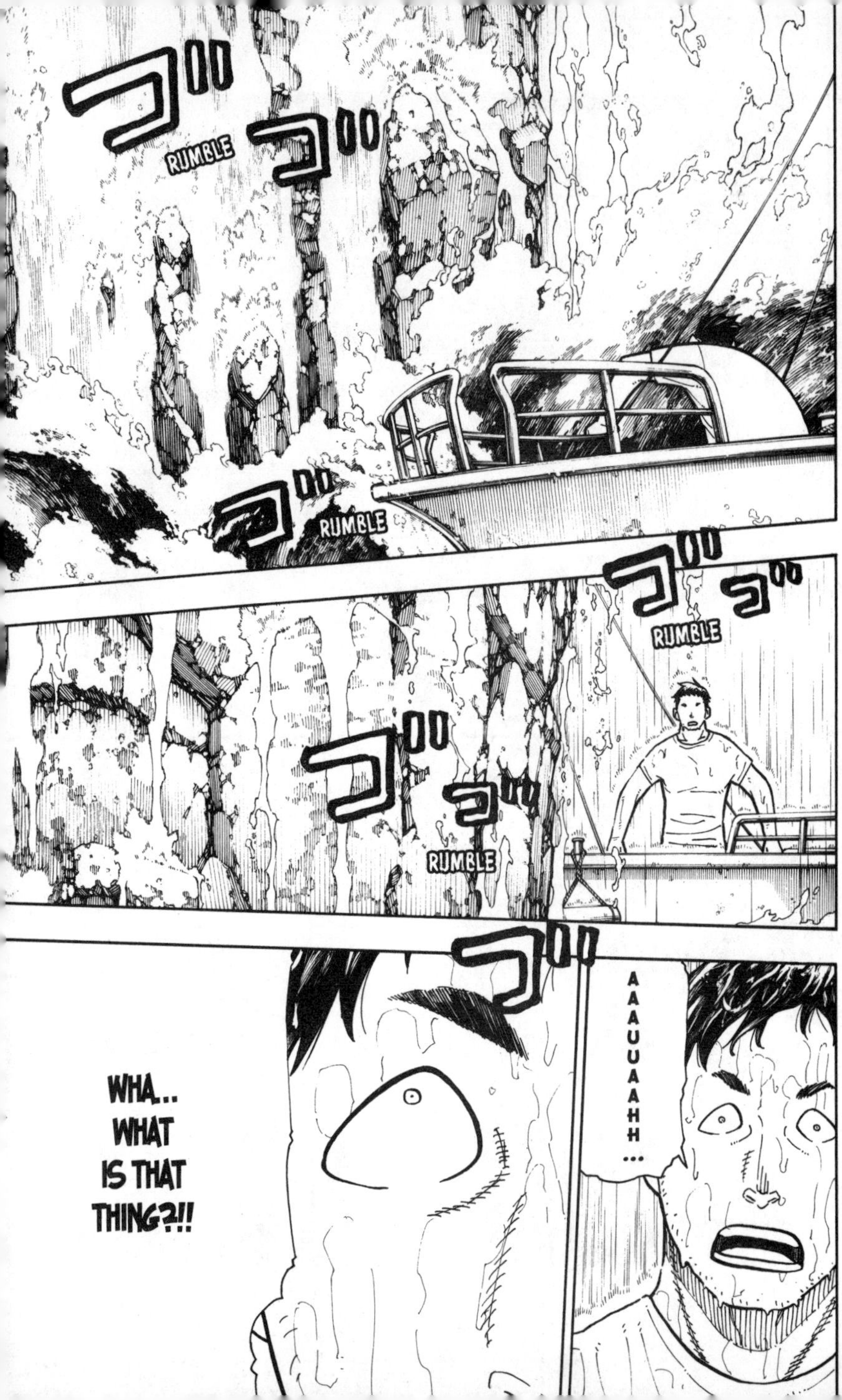
RUMBLE
RUMBLE
RUMBLE
RUMBLE
AAAUUAAHH...
WHA... WHAT IS THAT THING?!!

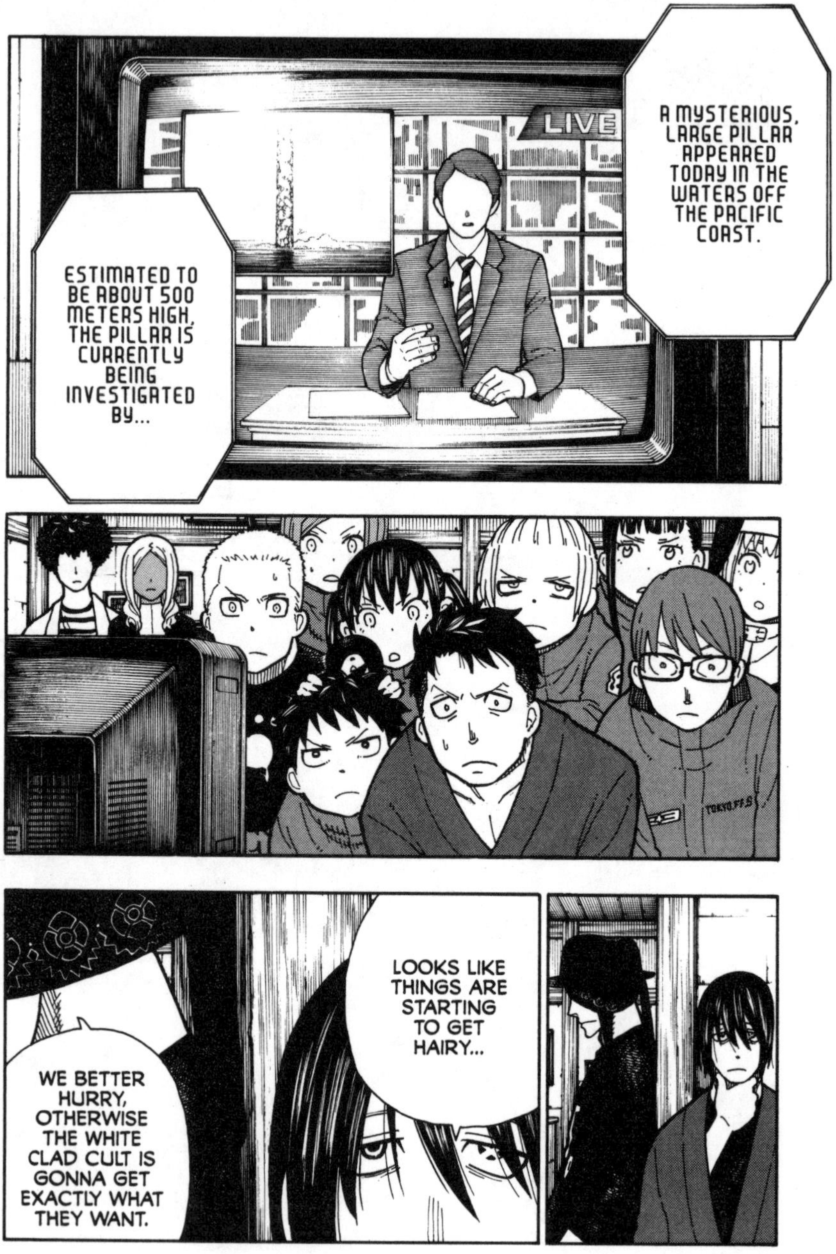
LIVE
A MYSTERIOUS, LARGE PILLAR APPEARED TODAY IN THE WATERS OFF THE PACIFIC COAST.
ESTIMATED TO BE ABOUT 500 METERS HIGH, THE PILLAR IS CURRENTLY BEING INVESTIGATED BY...
LOOKS LIKE THINGS ARE STARTING TO GET HAIRY...
WE BETTER HURRY, OTHERWISE THE WHITE CLAD CULT IS GONNA GET EXACTLY WHAT THEY WANT.

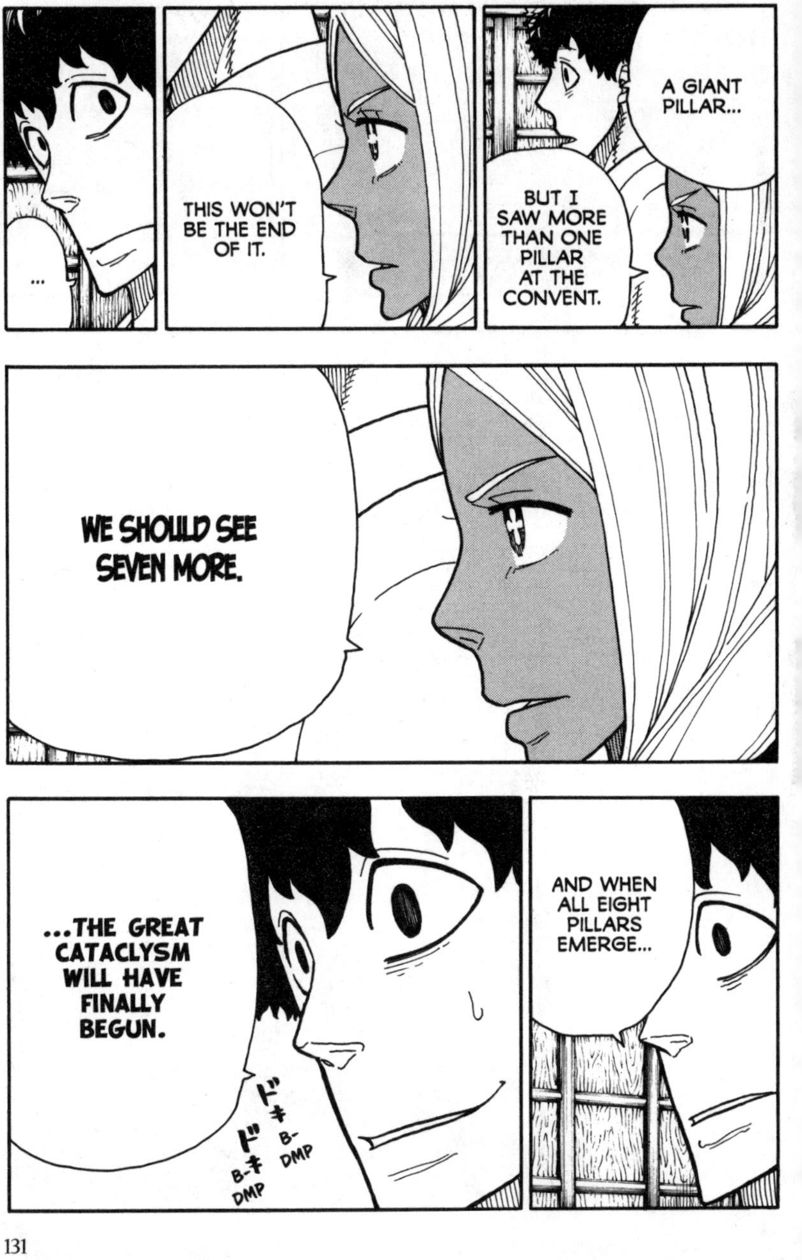
A GIANT PILLAR...
BUT I SAW MORE THAN ONE PILLAR AT THE CONVENT.
THIS WON'T BE THE END OF IT.
...
WE SHOULD SEE SEVEN MORE.
AND WHEN ALL EIGHT PILLARS EMERGE...
...THE GREAT CATACLYSM WILL HAVE FINALLY BEGUN.
ドキ B-DMP
ドキ B-DMP

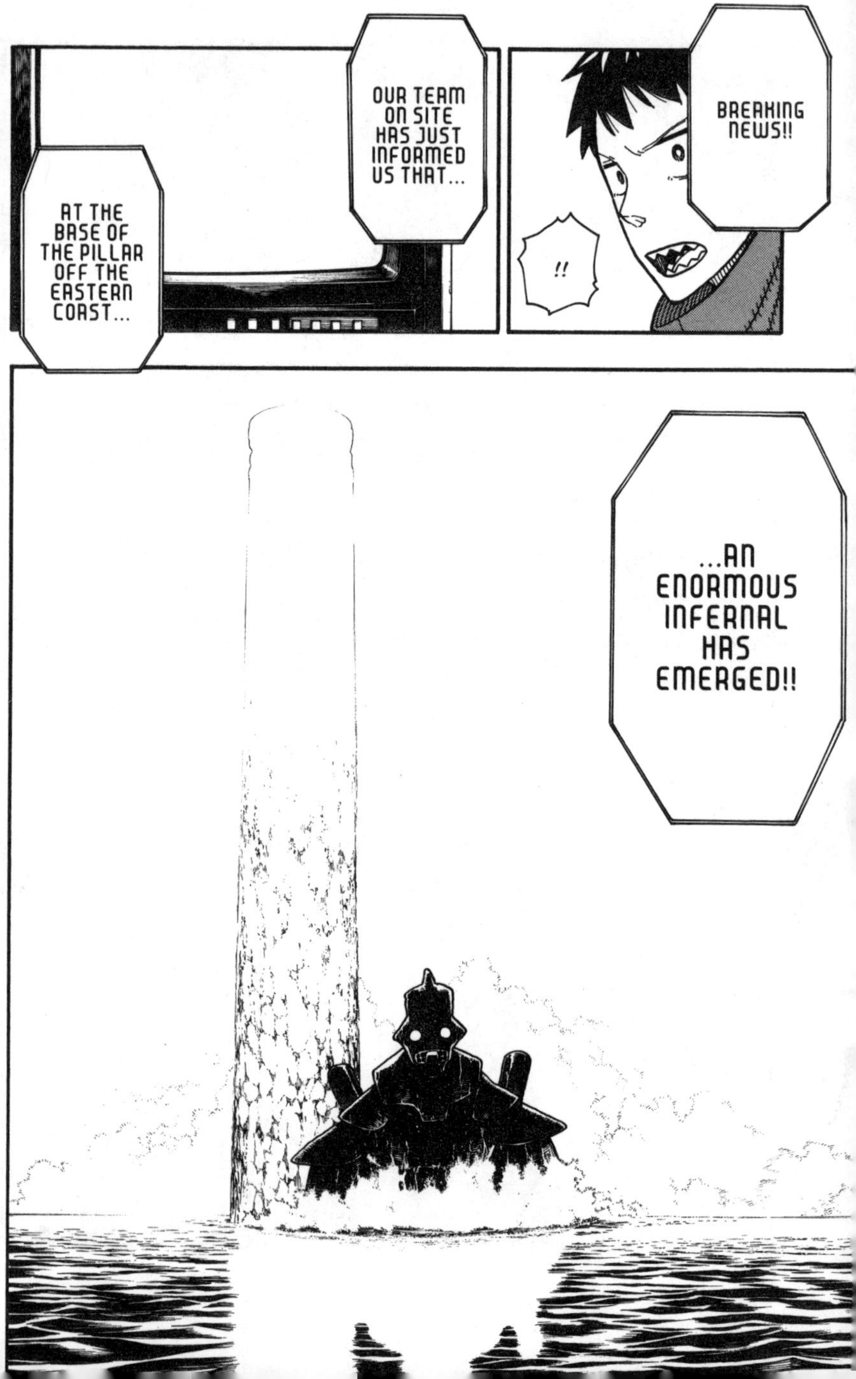
BREAKING NEWS!!
!!
OUR TEAM ON SITE HAS JUST INFORMED US THAT...
AT THE BASE OF THE PILLAR OFF THE EASTERN COAST...
...AN ENORMOUS INFERNAL HAS EMERGED!!

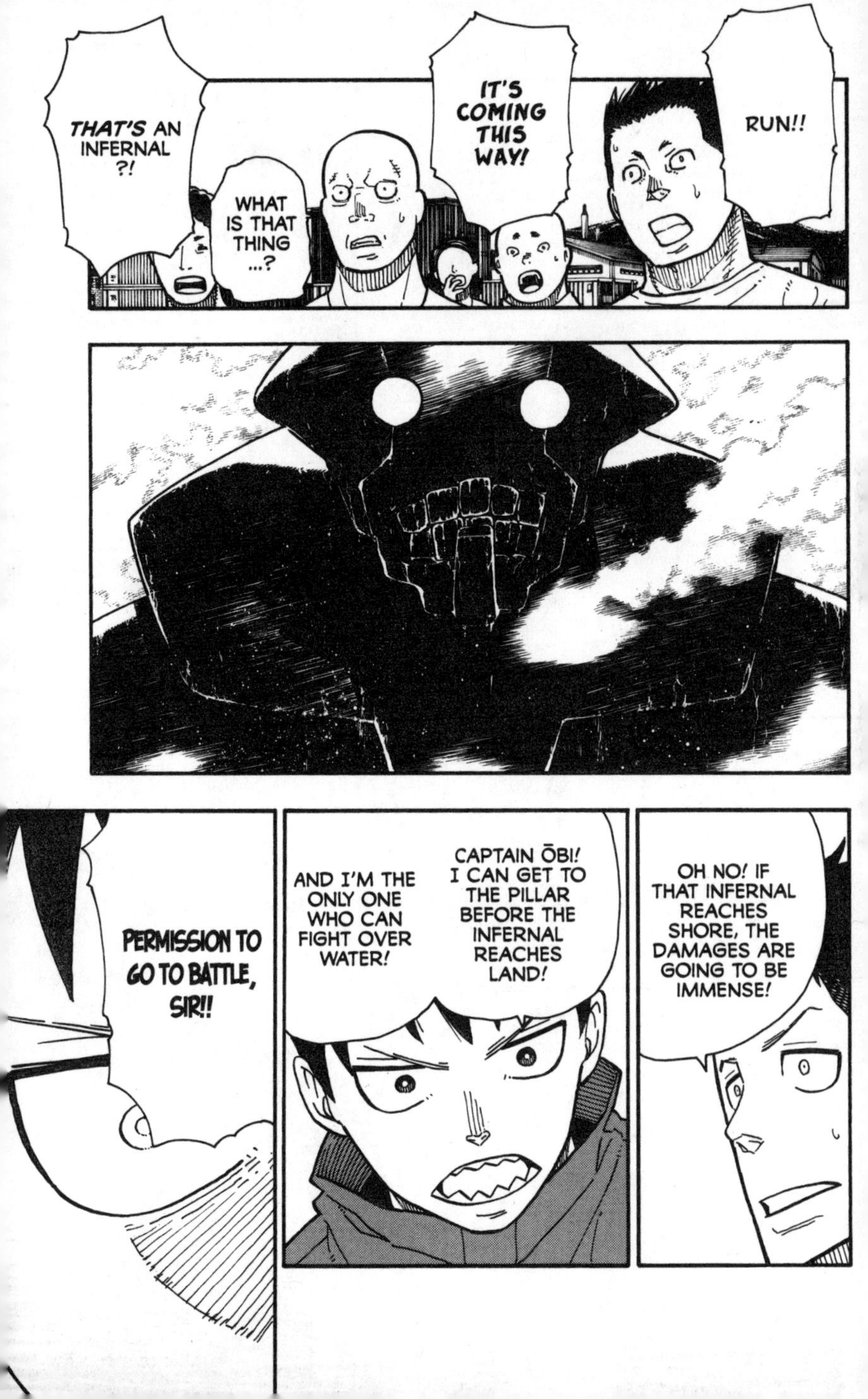
RUN!!
IT'S COMING THIS WAY!
WHAT IS THAT THING ...?
THAT'S AN INFERNAL ?!
OH NO! IF THAT INFERNAL REACHES SHORE, THE DAMAGES ARE GOING TO BE IMMENSE!
CAPTAIN ŌBI! I CAN GET TO THE PILLAR BEFORE THE INFERNAL REACHES LAND!
AND I'M THE ONLY ONE WHO CAN FIGHT OVER WATER!
PERMISSION TO GO TO BATTLE, SIR!!

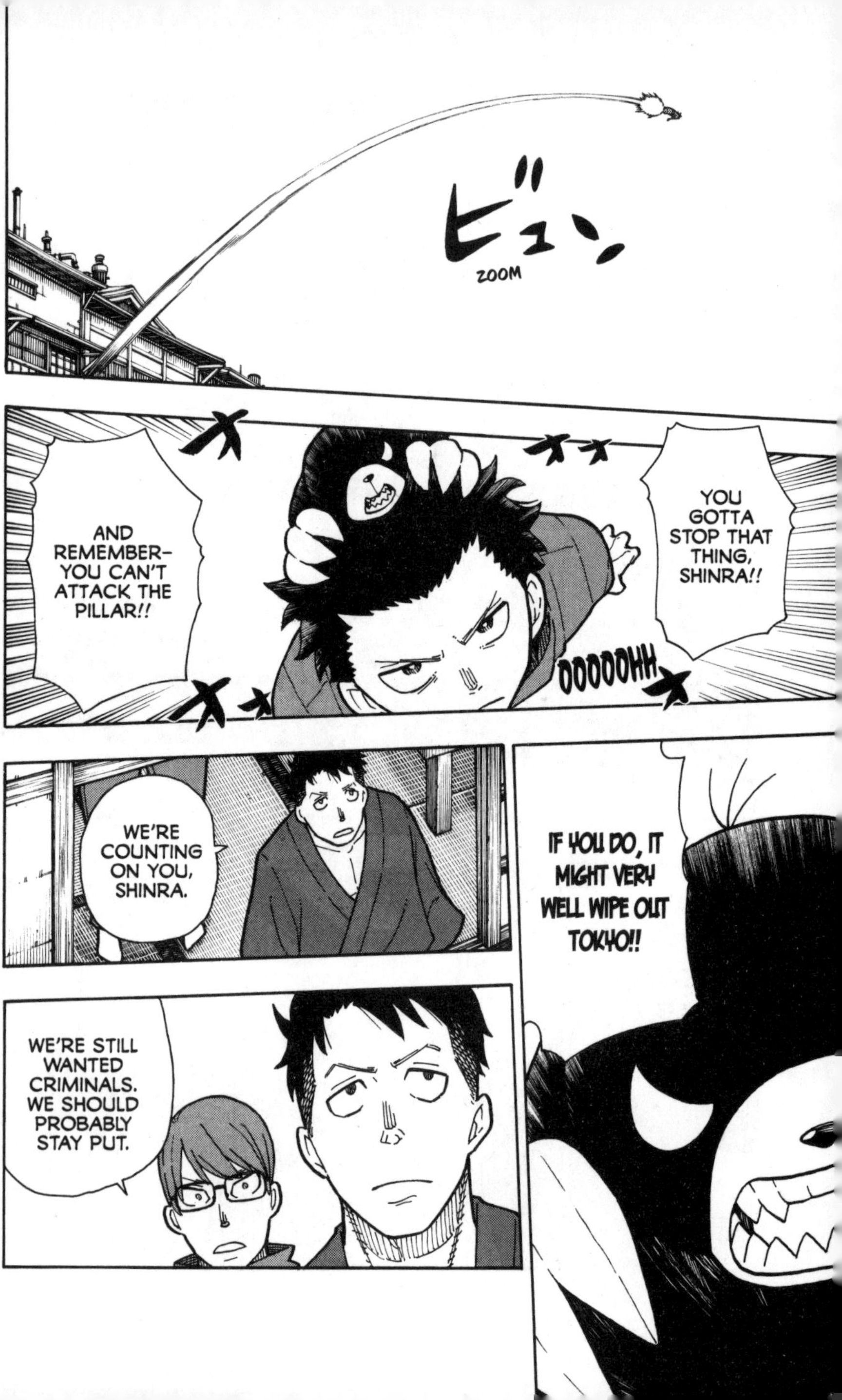
ビュン
ZOOM
YOU GOTTA STOP THAT THING, SHINRA!!
OOOOOHH
AND REMEMBER– YOU CAN'T ATTACK THE PILLAR!!
IF YOU DO, IT MIGHT VERY WELL WIPE OUT TOKYO!!
WE'RE COUNTING ON YOU, SHINRA.
WE'RE STILL WANTED CRIMINALS. WE SHOULD PROBABLY STAY PUT.

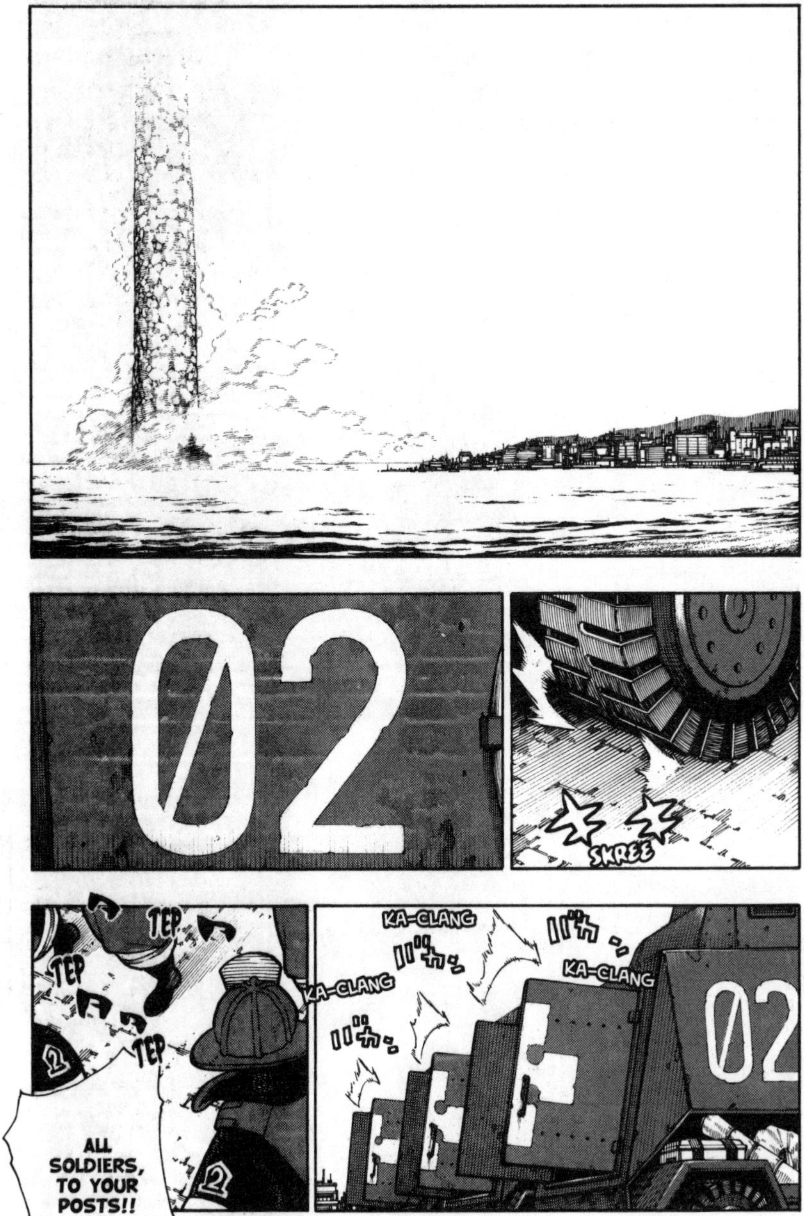
02
SKREE
KA-CLANG
KA-CLANG
02
KA-CLANG
TEP
TEP
TEP
ALL SOLDIERS, TO YOUR POSTS!!

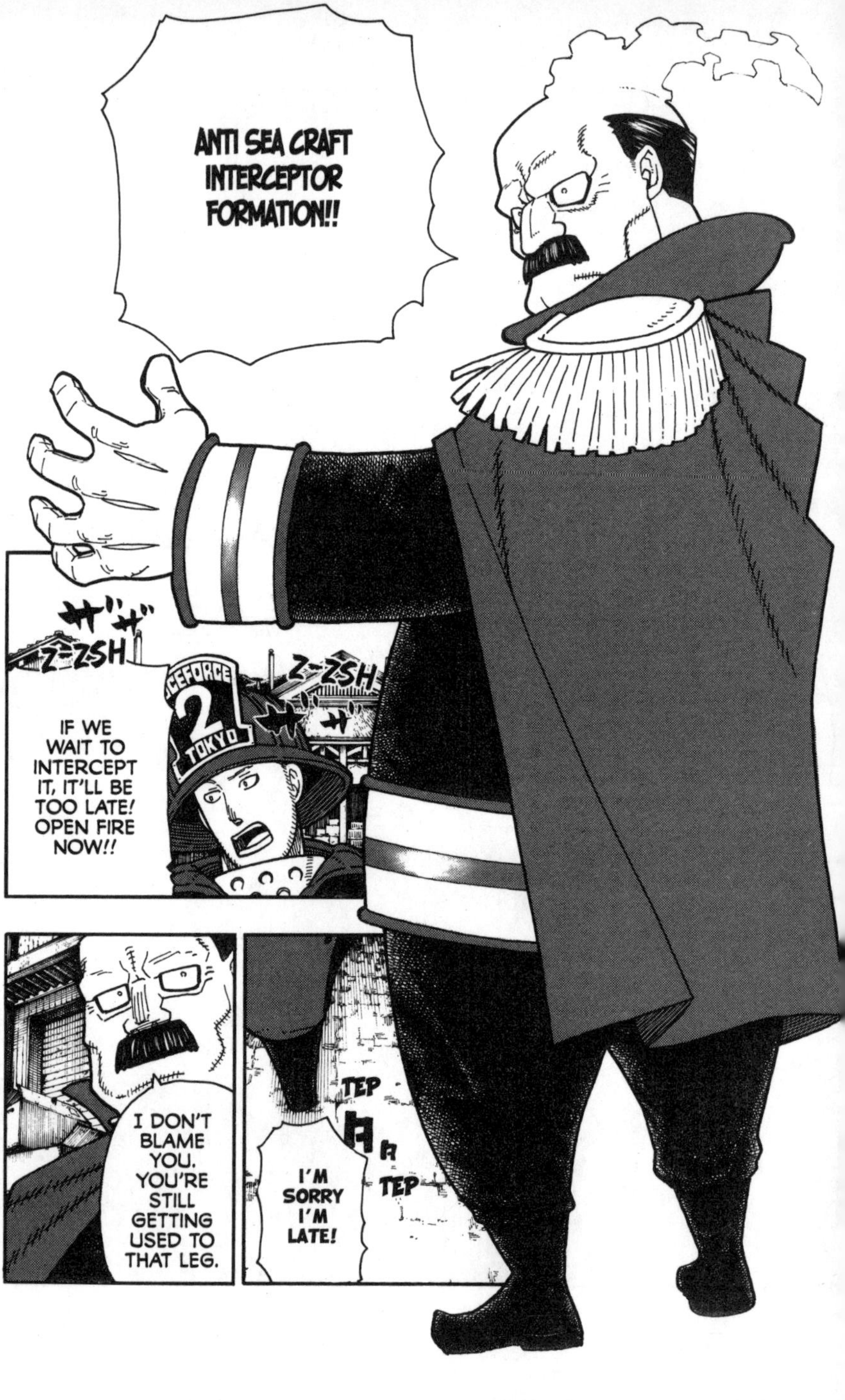
ANTI SEA CRAFT INTERCEPTOR FORMATION!!
Z-ZSH
Z-ZSH
IF WE WAIT TO INTERCEPT IT, IT'LL BE TOO LATE! OPEN FIRE NOW!!
TEP
TEP
I'M SORRY I'M LATE!
I DON'T BLAME YOU. YOU'RE STILL GETTING USED TO THAT LEG.

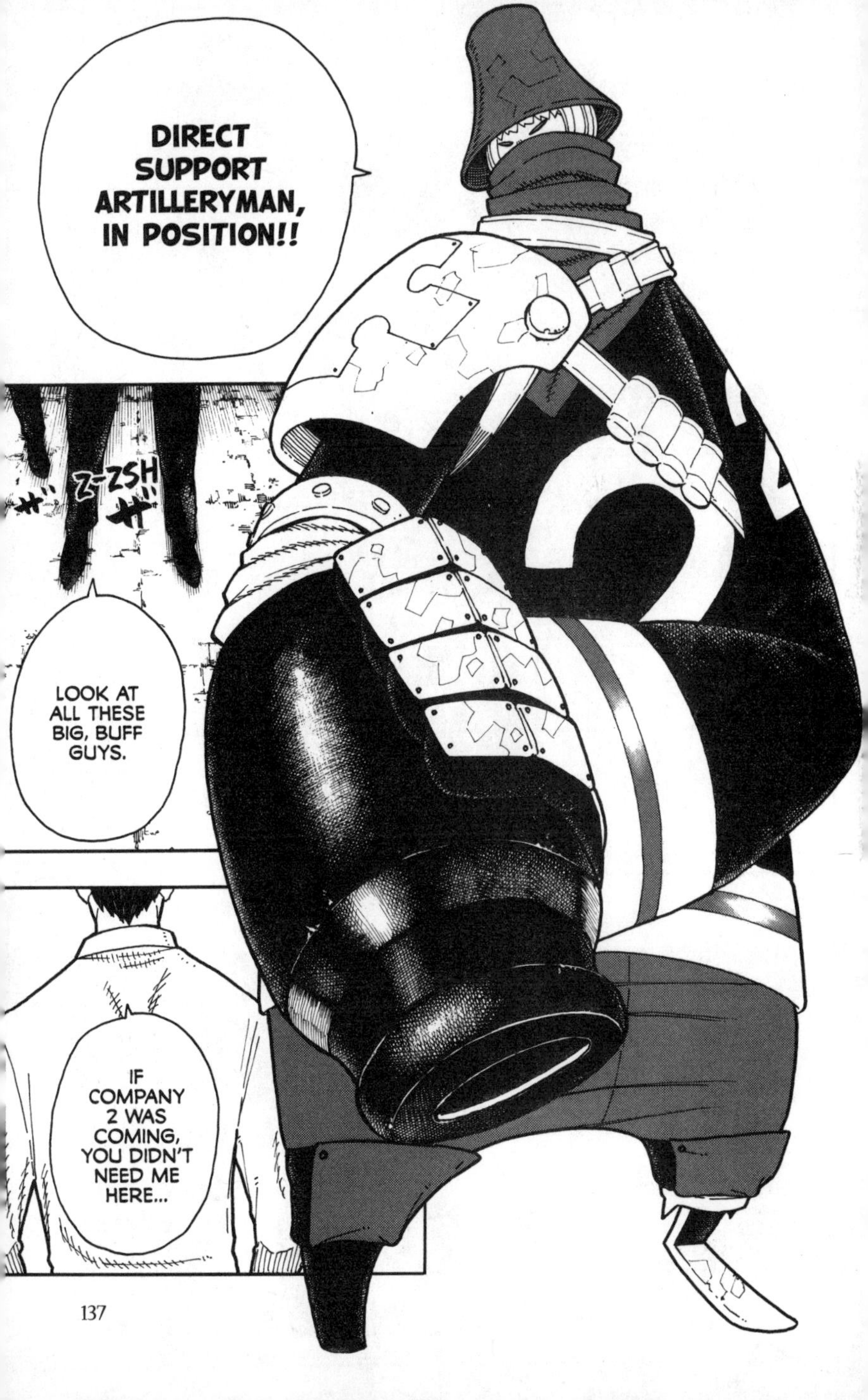
DIRECT SUPPORT ARTILLERYMAN, IN POSITION!!
Z-ZSH
ザザ
LOOK AT ALL THESE BIG, BUFF GUYS.
IF COMPANY 2 WAS COMING, YOU DIDN'T NEED ME HERE...

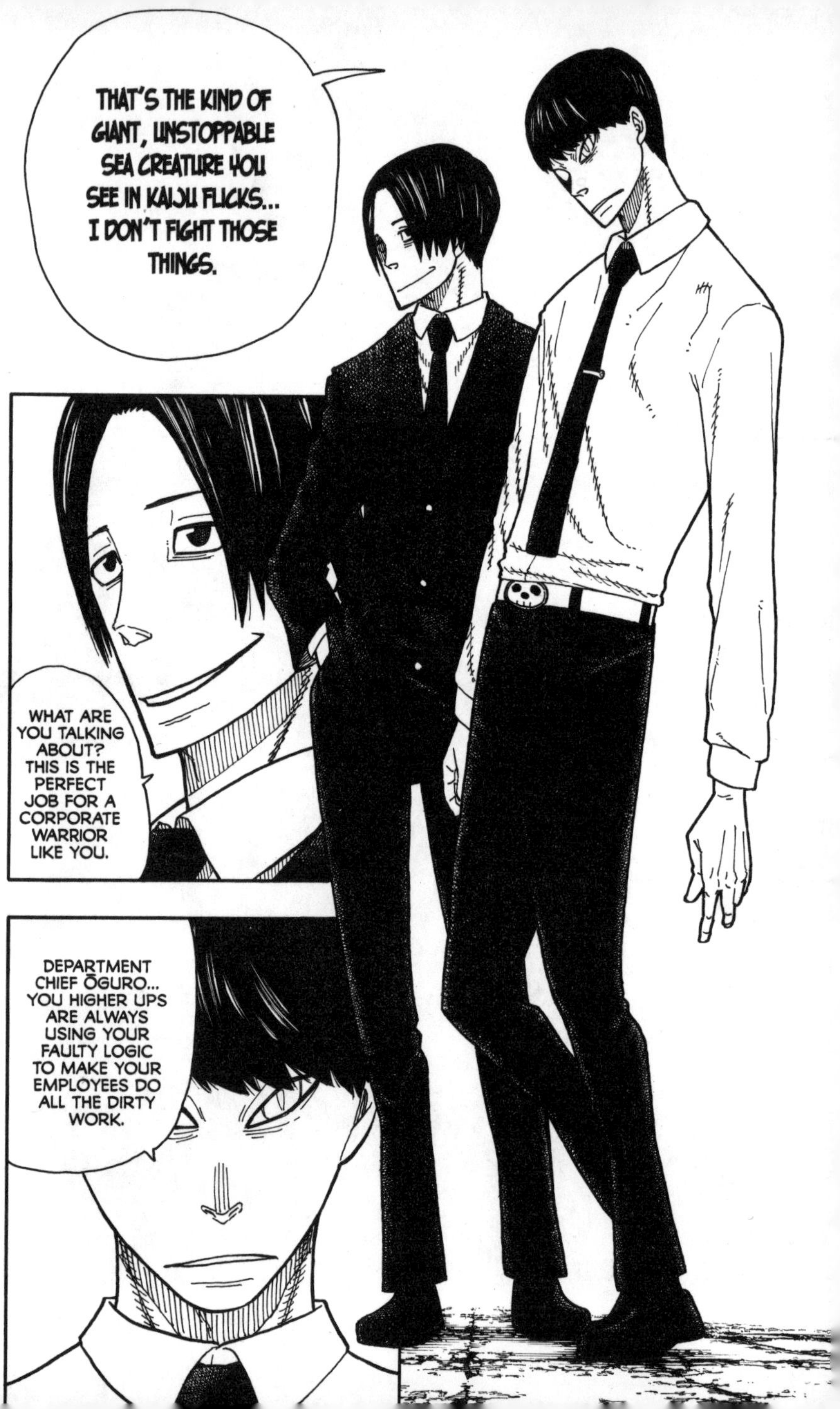
THAT'S THE KIND OF GIANT, UNSTOPPABLE SEA CREATURE YOU SEE IN KAIJU FLICKS... I DON'T FIGHT THOSE THINGS.
WHAT ARE YOU TALKING ABOUT? THIS IS THE PERFECT JOB FOR A CORPORATE WARRIOR LIKE YOU.
DEPARTMENT CHIEF ŌGURO... YOU HIGHER UPS ARE ALWAYS USING YOUR FAULTY LOGIC TO MAKE YOUR EMPLOYEES DO ALL THE DIRTY WORK.

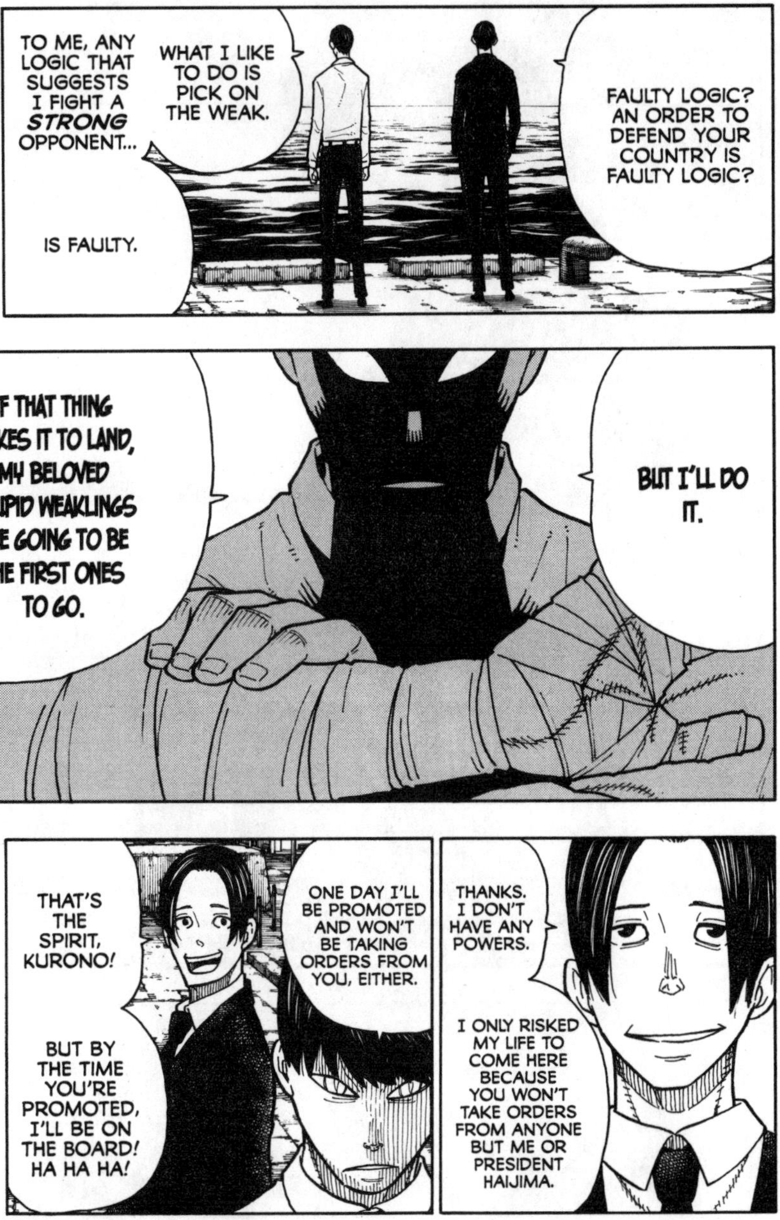
FAULTY LOGIC? AN ORDER TO DEFEND YOUR COUNTRY IS FAULTY LOGIC?
WHAT I LIKE TO DO IS PICK ON THE WEAK.
TO ME, ANY LOGIC THAT SUGGESTS I FIGHT A *STRONG* OPPONENT...
IS FAULTY.
BUT I'LL DO IT.
IF THAT THING MAKES IT TO LAND, MY BELOVED STUPID WEAKLINGS ARE GOING TO BE THE FIRST ONES TO GO.
THANKS. I DON'T HAVE ANY POWERS.
I ONLY RISKED MY LIFE TO COME HERE BECAUSE YOU WON'T TAKE ORDERS FROM ANYONE BUT ME OR PRESIDENT HAIJIMA.
ONE DAY I'LL BE PROMOTED AND WON'T BE TAKING ORDERS FROM YOU, EITHER.
THAT'S THE SPIRIT, KURONO!
BUT BY THE TIME YOU'RE PROMOTED, I'LL BE ON THE BOARD! HA HA HA!

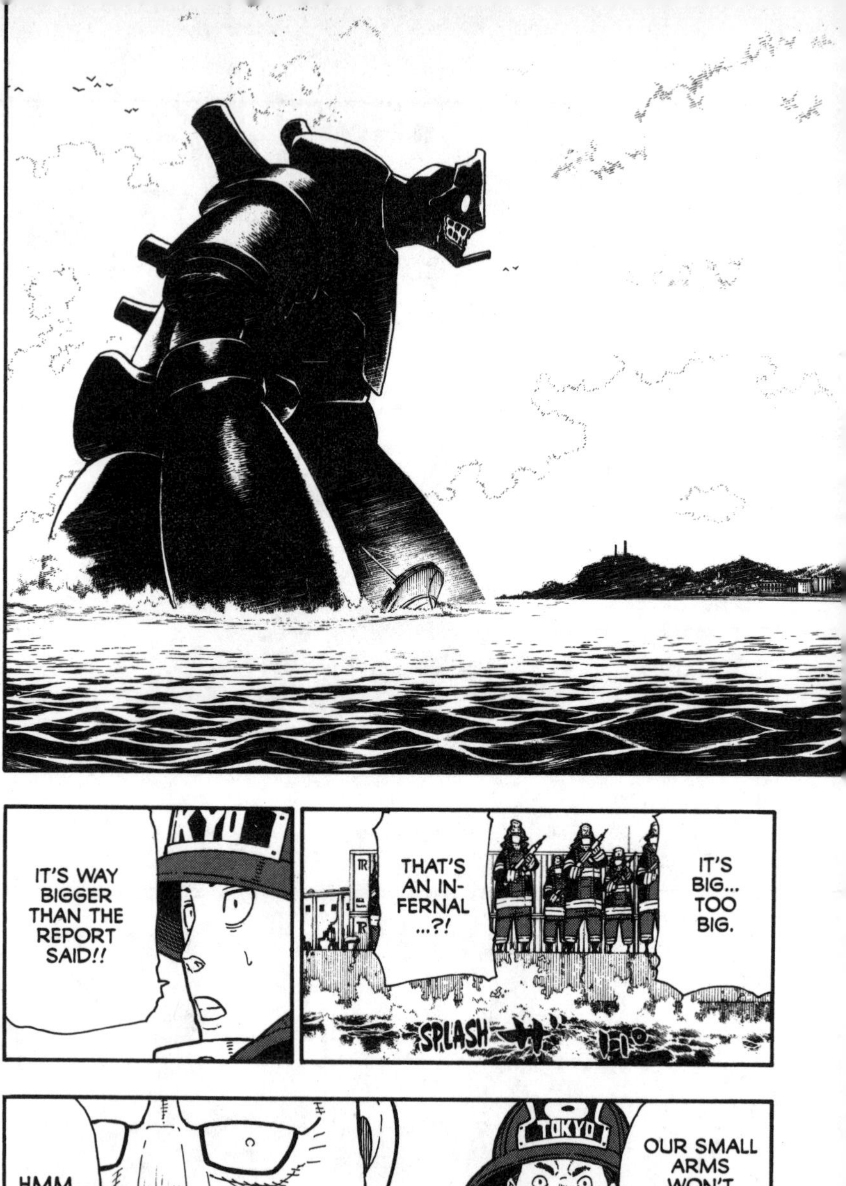
IT'S BIG... TOO BIG.
THAT'S AN IN-FERNAL ...?!
SPLASH
IT'S WAY BIGGER THAN THE REPORT SAID!!
OUR SMALL ARMS WON'T EVEN FAZE IT!!
HMM.

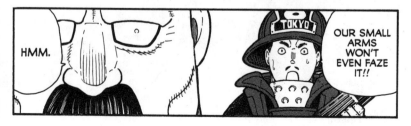

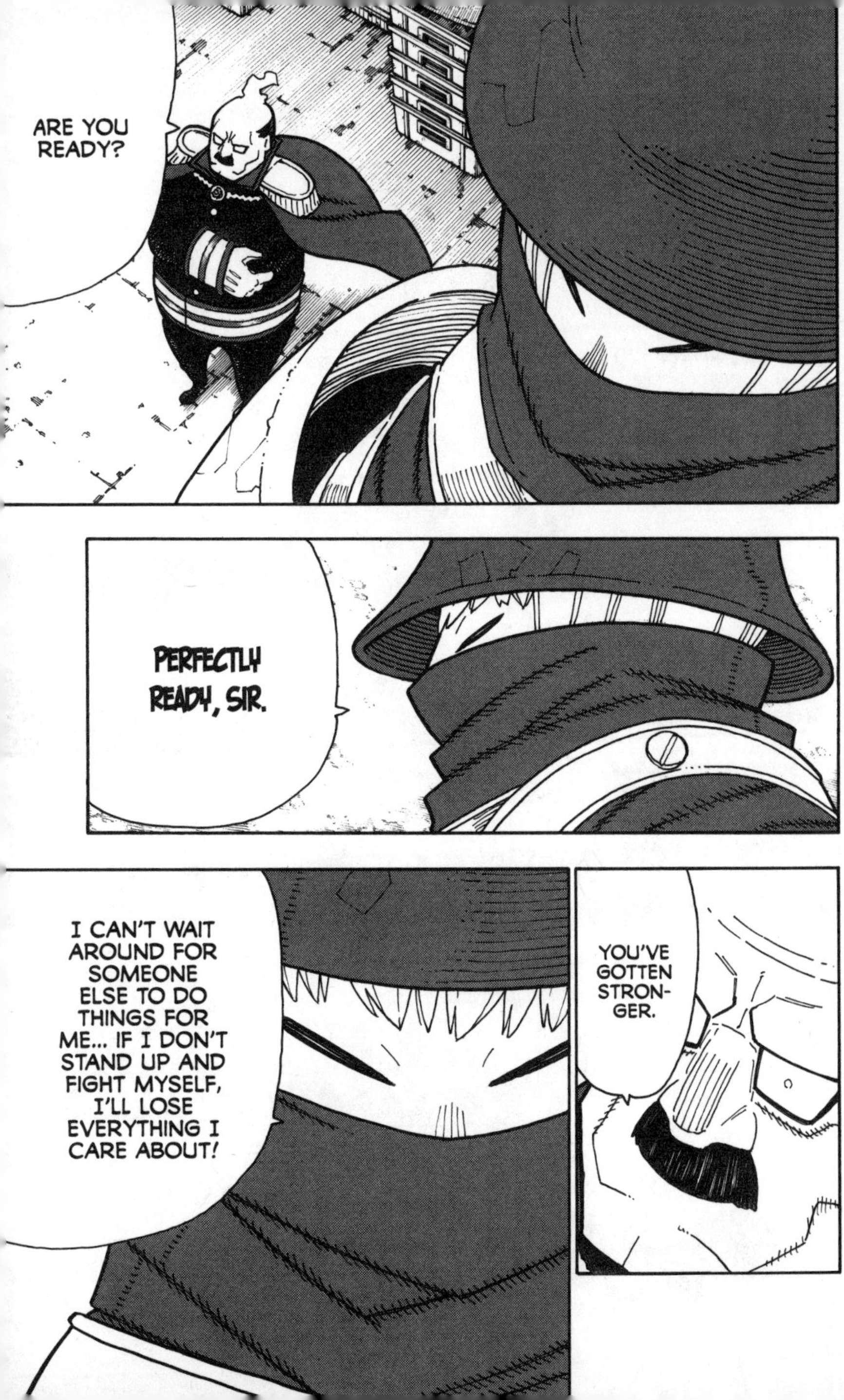
ARE YOU READY?
PERFECTLY READY, SIR.
YOU'VE GOTTEN STRONGER.
I CAN'T WAIT AROUND FOR SOMEONE ELSE TO DO THINGS FOR ME... IF I DON'T STAND UP AND FIGHT MYSELF, I'LL LOSE EVERYTHING I CARE ABOUT!

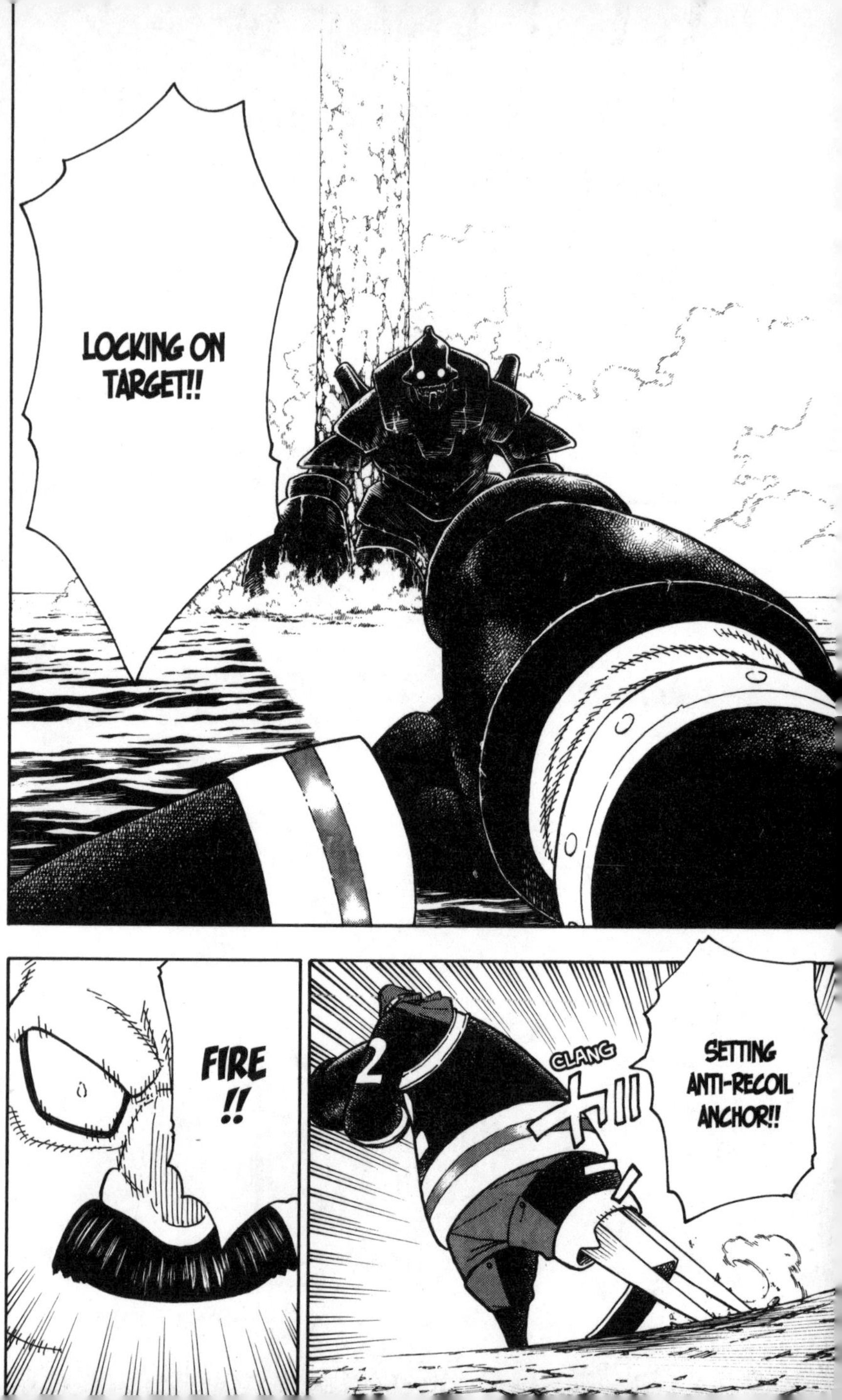
LOCKING ON TARGET!!
SETTING ANTI-RECOIL ANCHOR!!
CLANG
FIRE!!

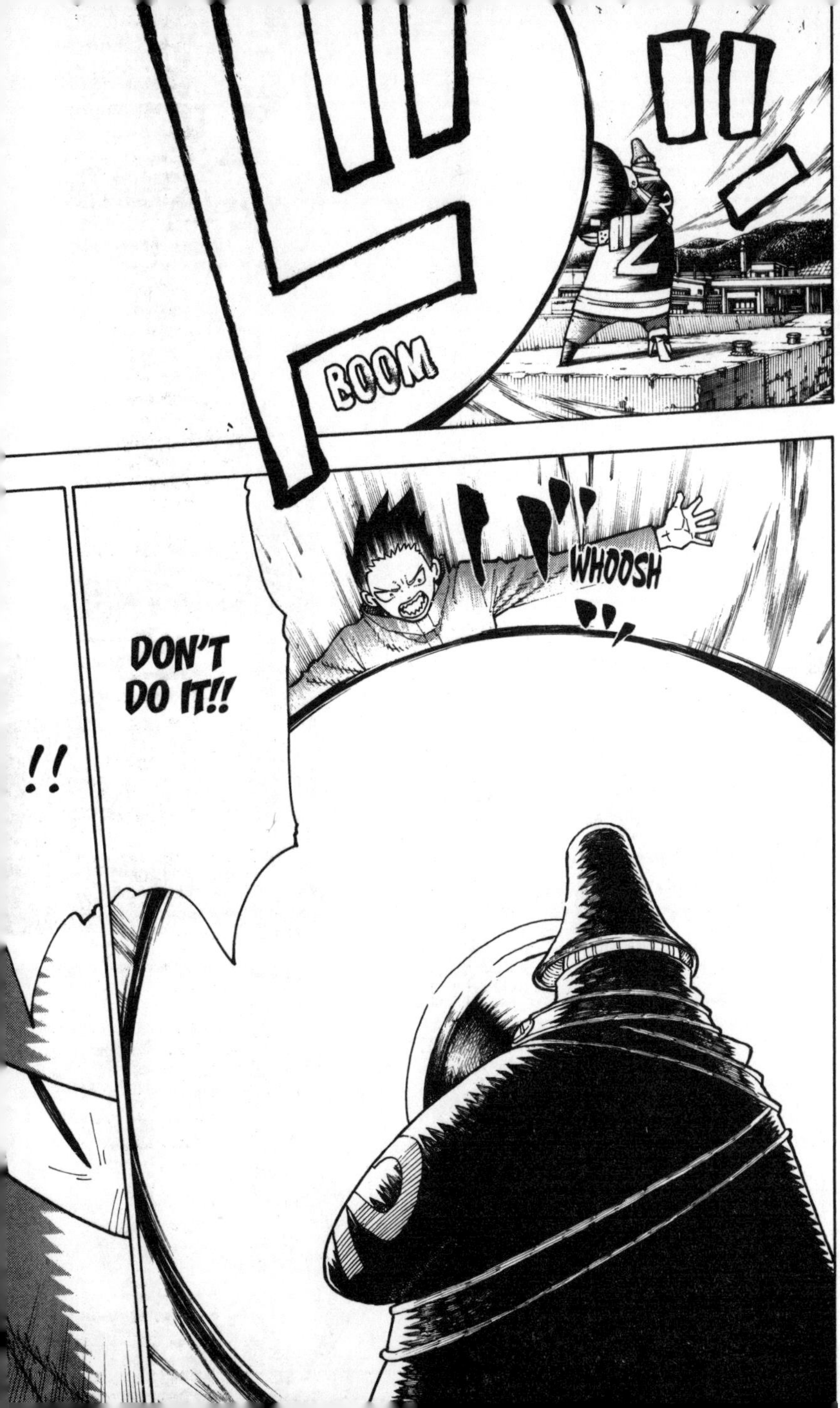
BOOM
WHOOSH
DON'T DO IT!!
!!

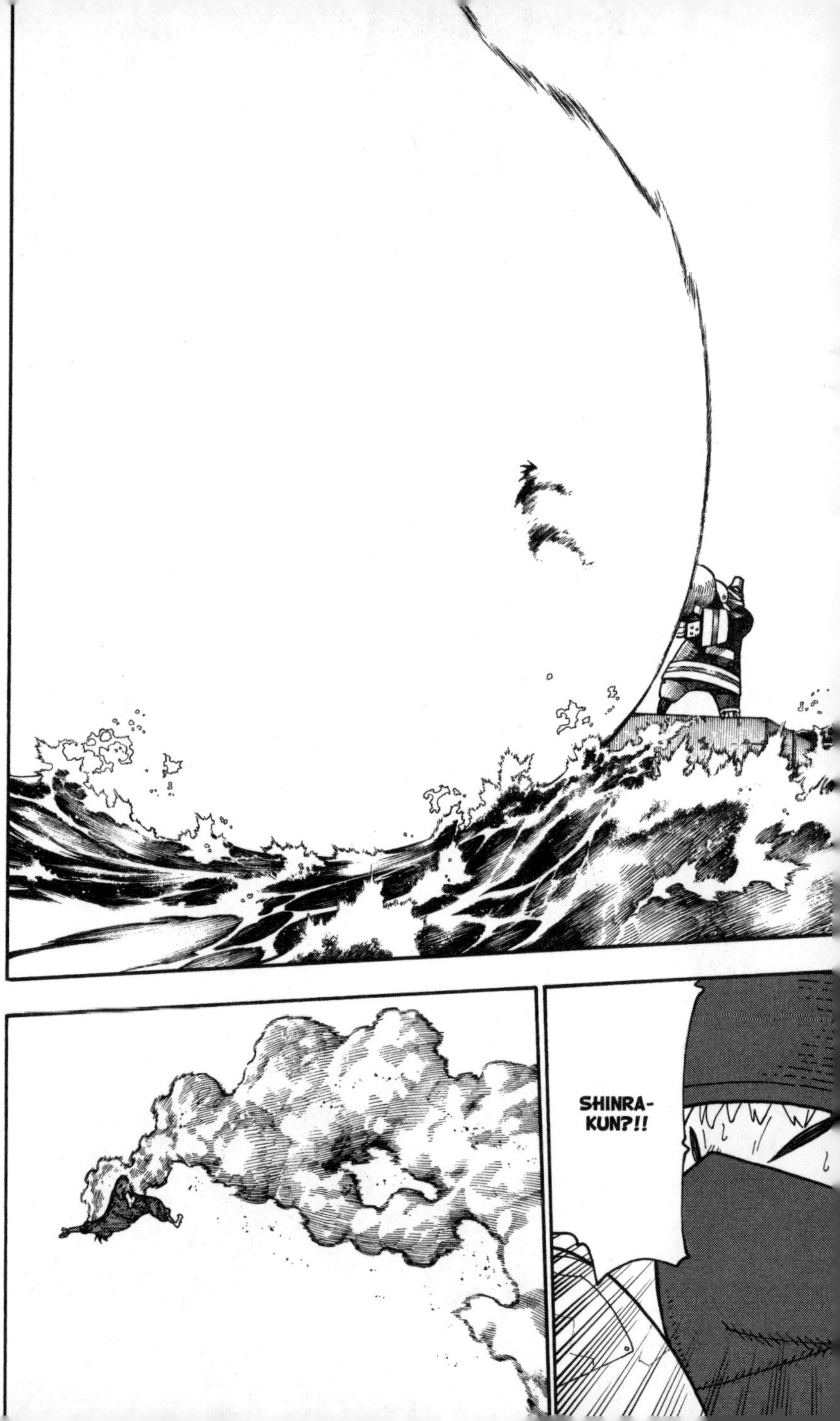
SHINRA-
KUN?!!

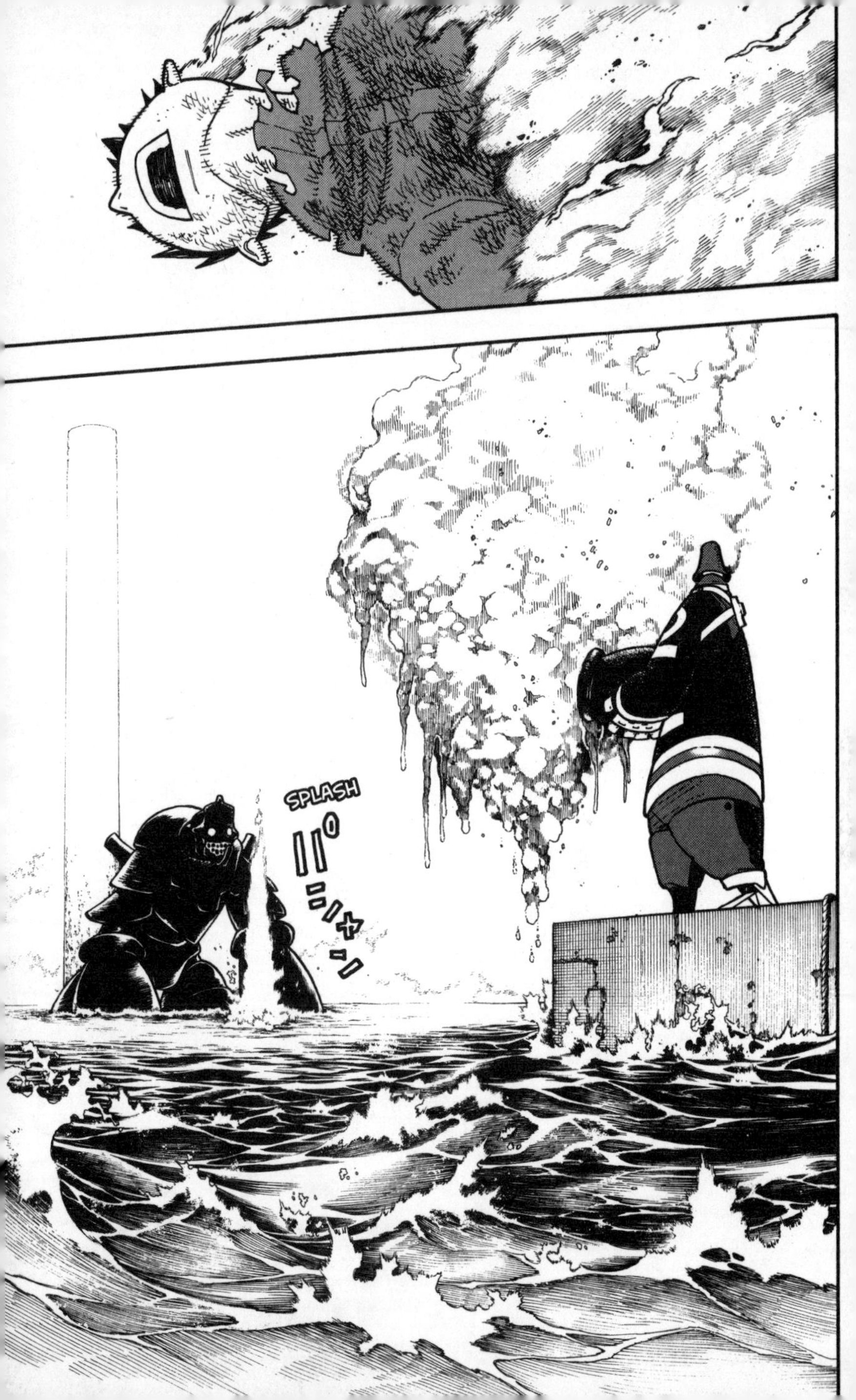
SPLASH

FIRE FORCE

CHAPTER CCXII:
COOPERATION

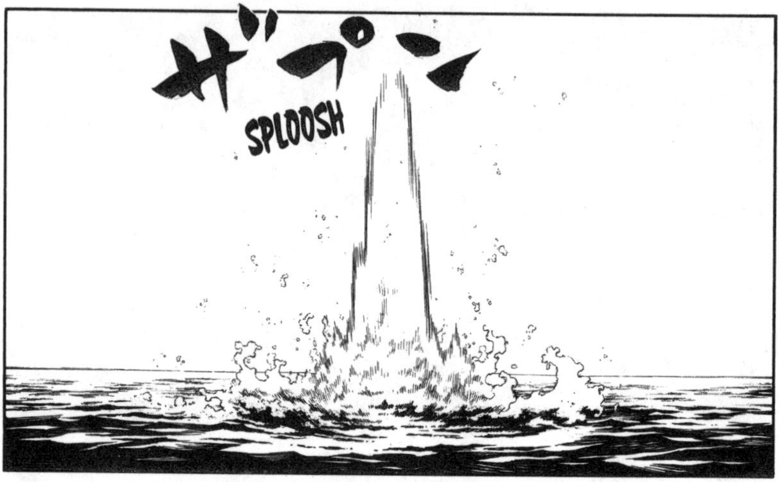
ザプーン
SPLOOSH
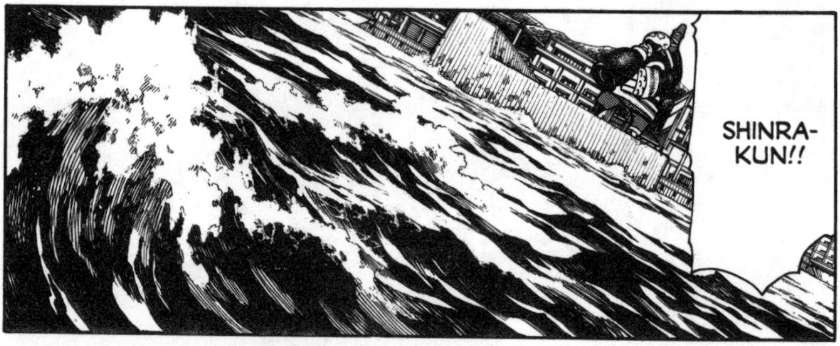
SHINRA-
KUN!!
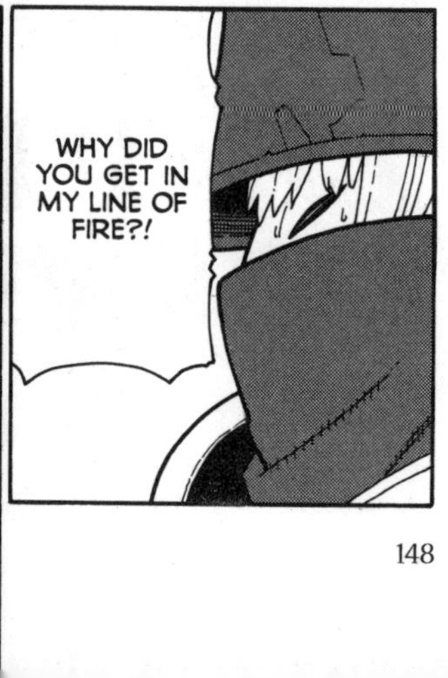
WHY DID
YOU GET IN
MY LINE OF
FIRE?!
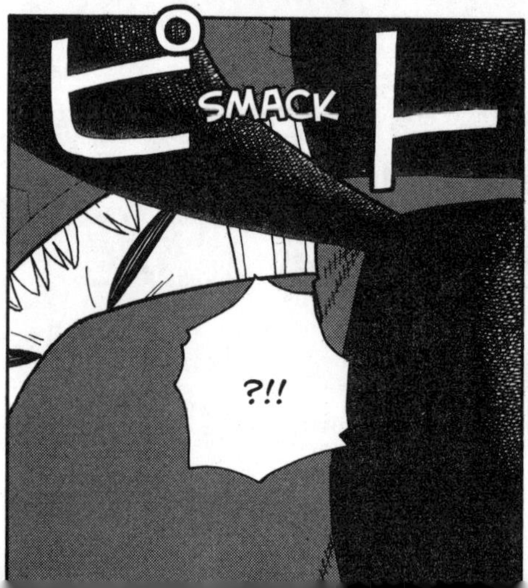
ピト
SMACK
?!!

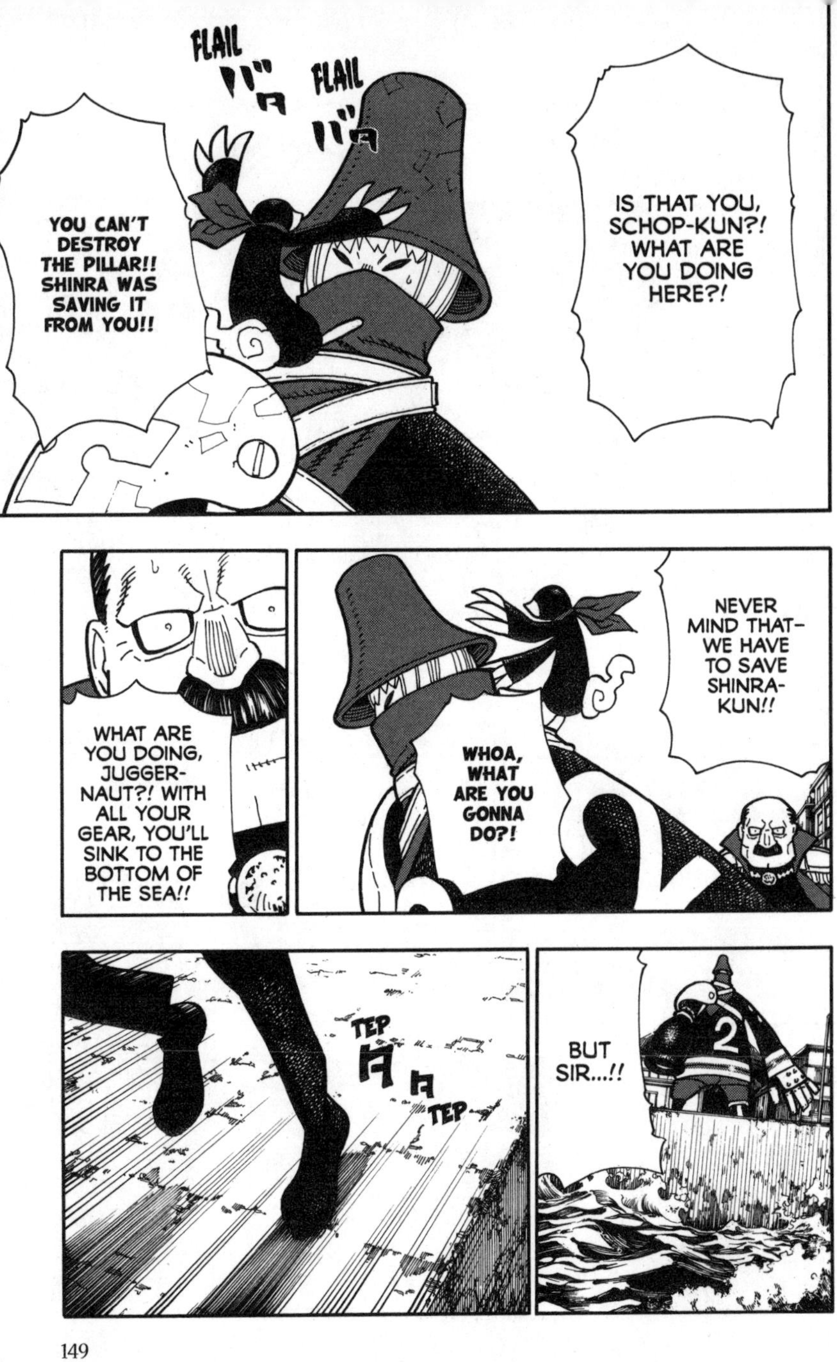
IS THAT YOU, SCHOP-KUN?! WHAT ARE YOU DOING HERE?!
FLAIL バタ
FLAIL バタ
YOU CAN'T DESTROY THE PILLAR!! SHINRA WAS SAVING IT FROM YOU!!
NEVER MIND THAT— WE HAVE TO SAVE SHINRA-KUN!!
WHOA, WHAT ARE YOU GONNA DO?!
WHAT ARE YOU DOING, JUGGERNAUT?! WITH ALL YOUR GEAR, YOU'LL SINK TO THE BOTTOM OF THE SEA!!
BUT SIR...!!
TEP タ
タ TEP

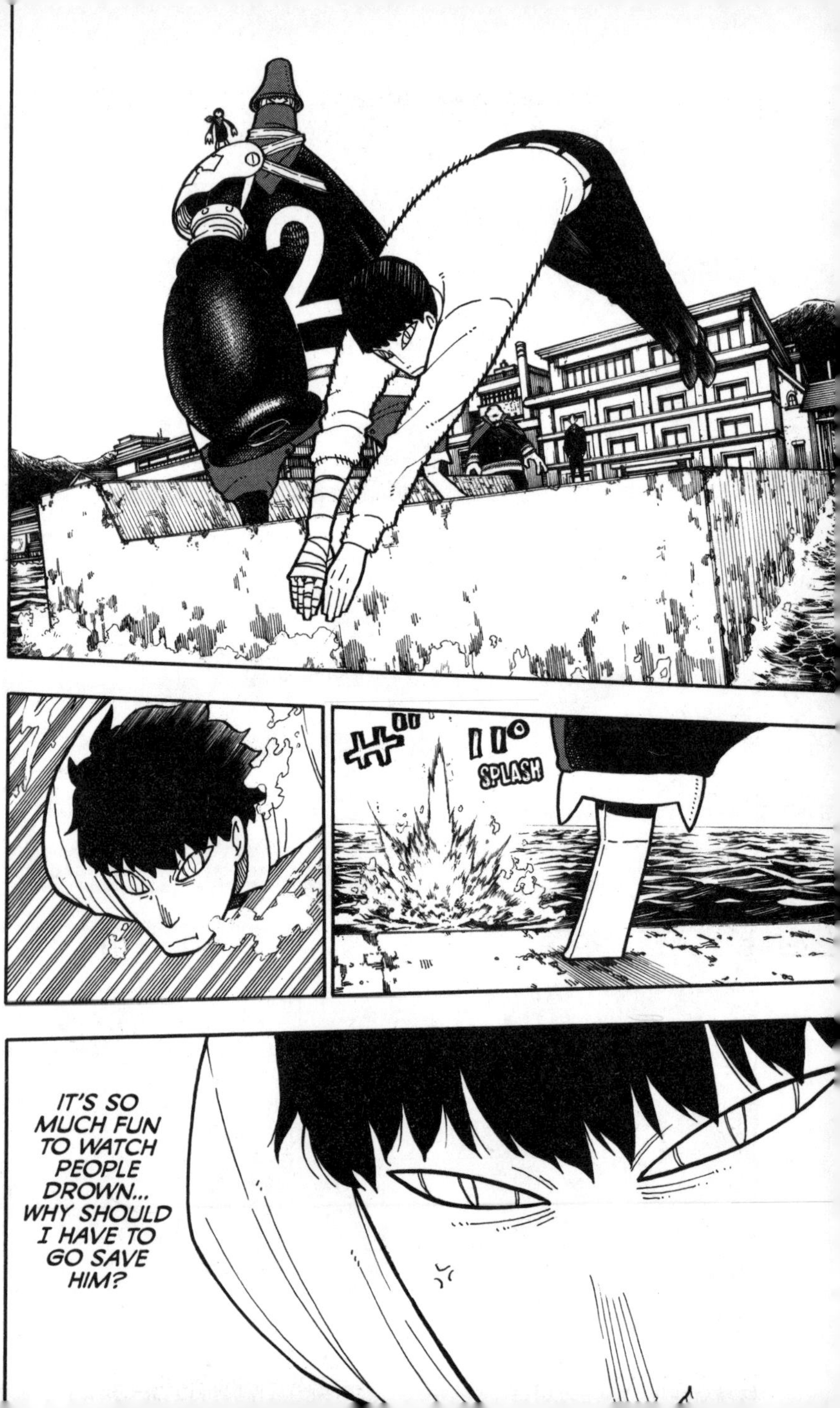
SPLASH
IT'S SO MUCH FUN TO WATCH PEOPLE DROWN... WHY SHOULD I HAVE TO GO SAVE HIM?

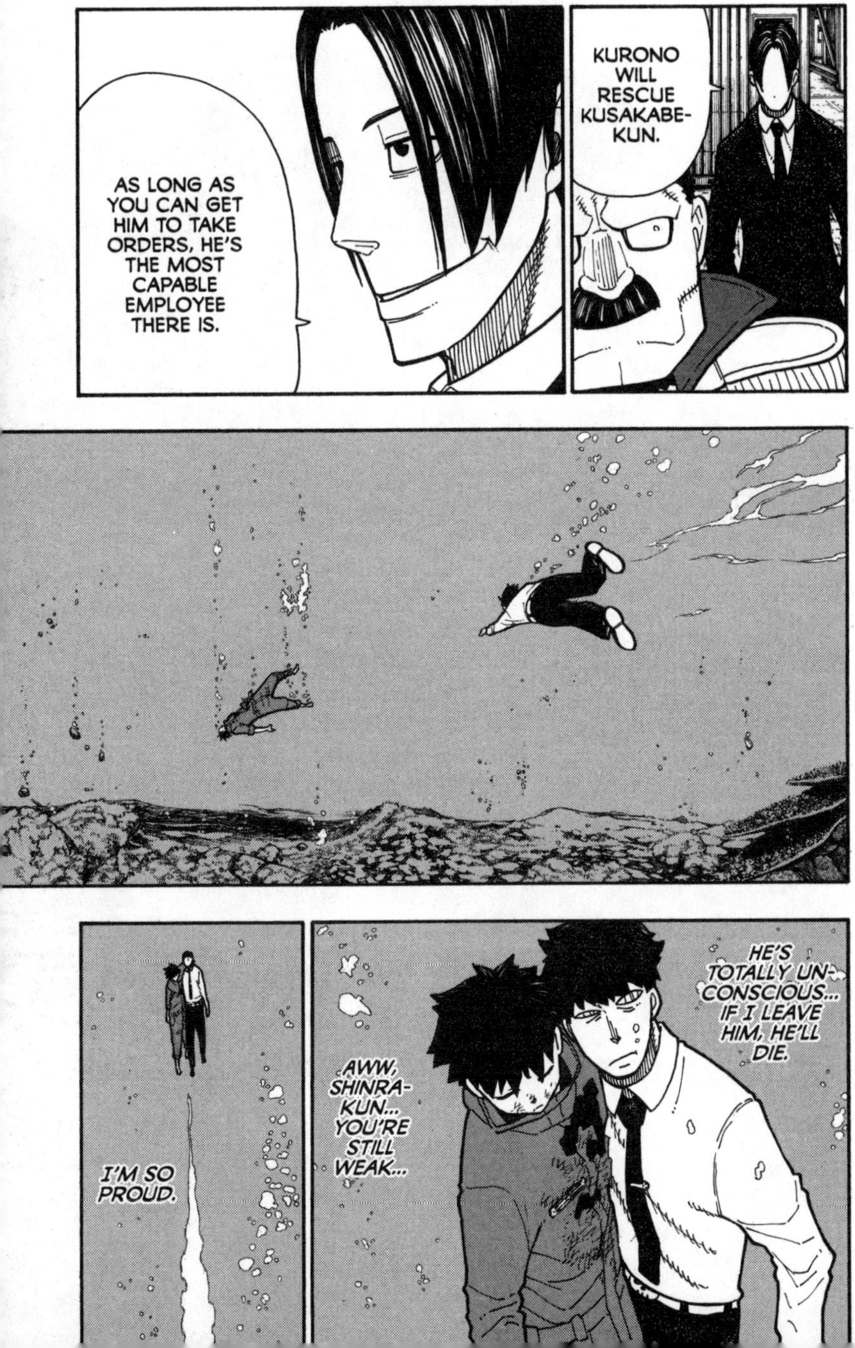
KURONO WILL RESCUE KUSAKABE-KUN.
AS LONG AS YOU CAN GET HIM TO TAKE ORDERS, HE'S THE MOST CAPABLE EMPLOYEE THERE IS.
HE'S TOTALLY UN-CONSCIOUS... IF I LEAVE HIM, HE'LL DIE.
AWW, SHINRA-KUN... YOU'RE STILL WEAK...
I'M SO PROUD.

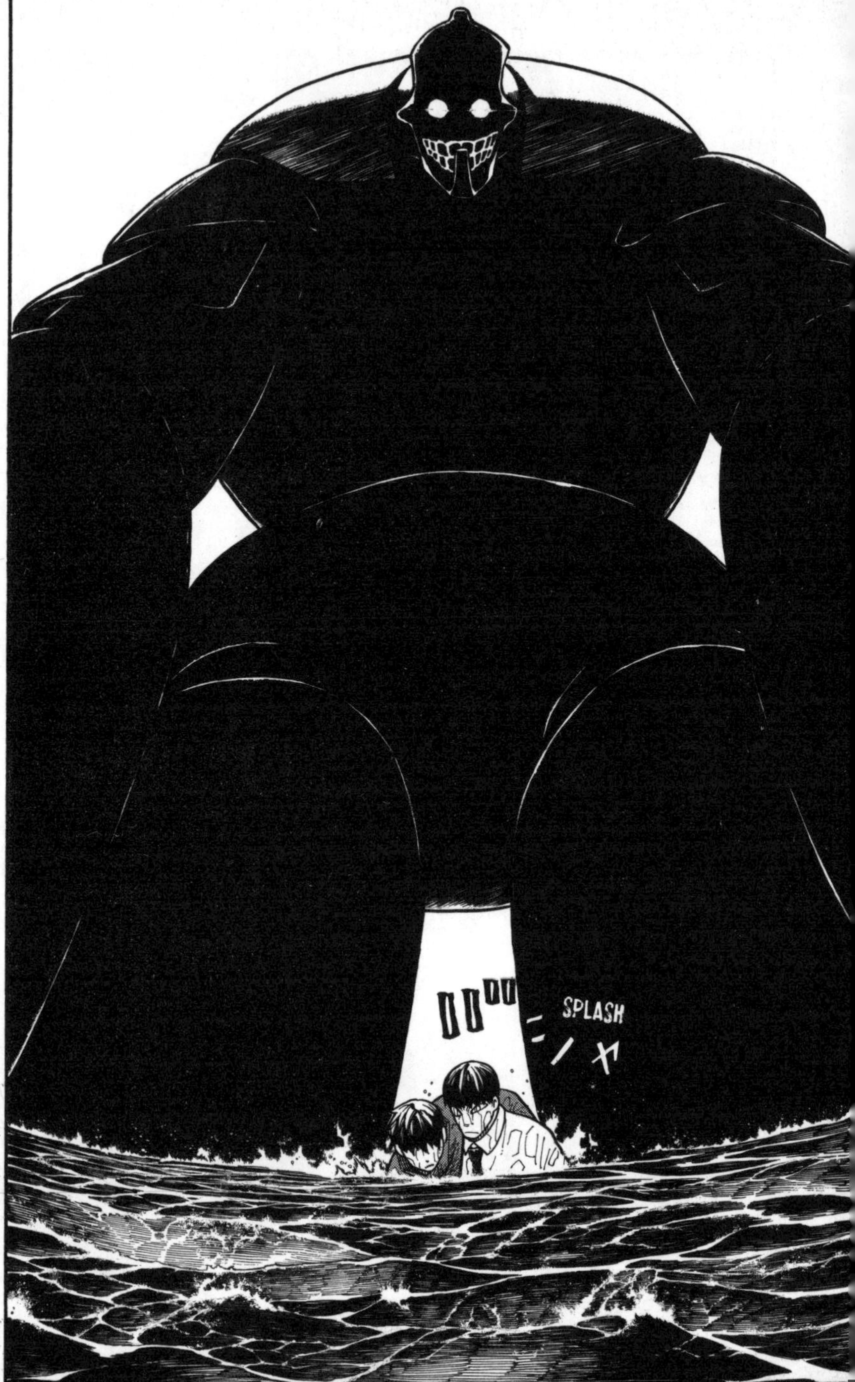
SPLASH

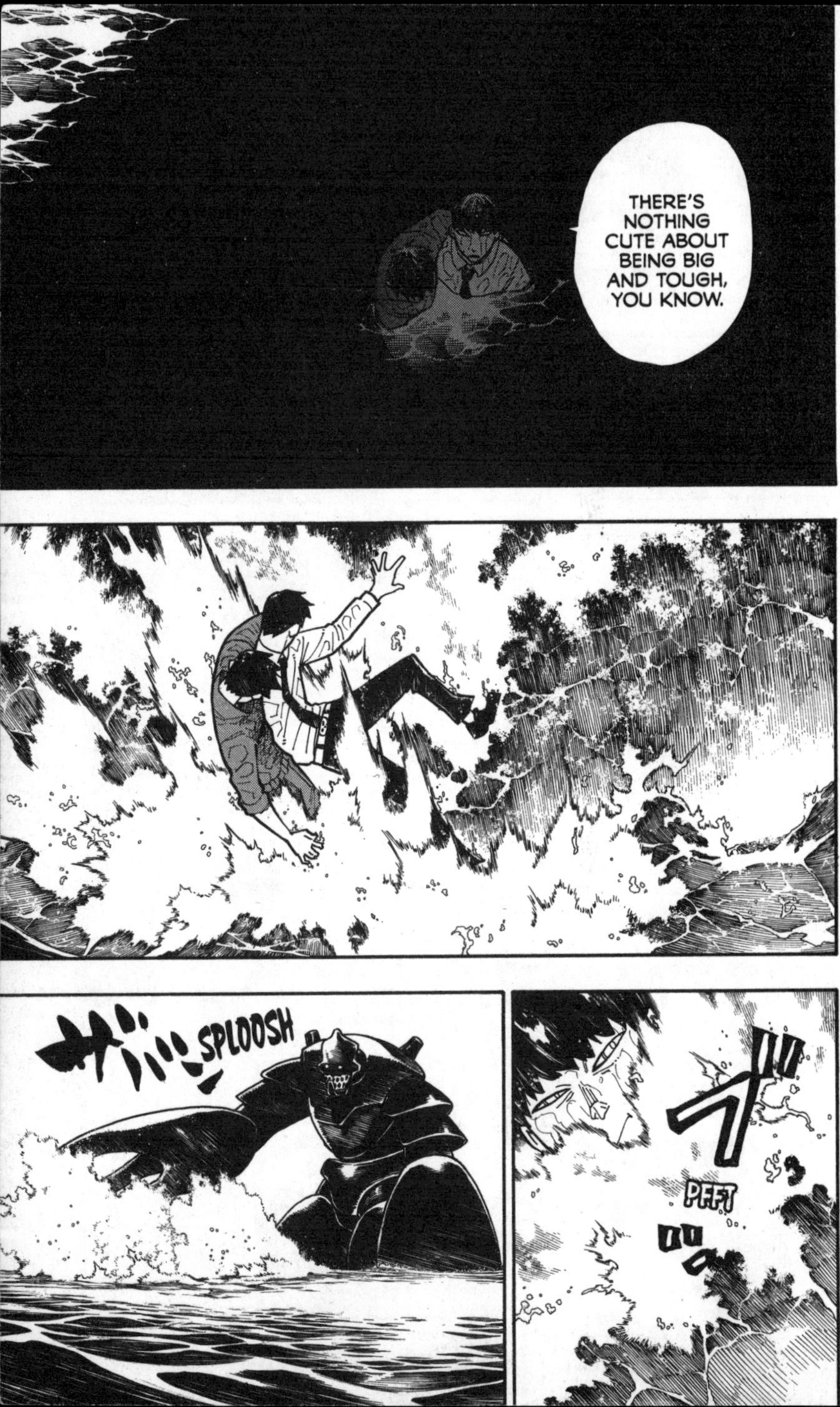
THERE'S NOTHING CUTE ABOUT BEING BIG AND TOUGH, YOU KNOW.
PFFT
SPLOOSH

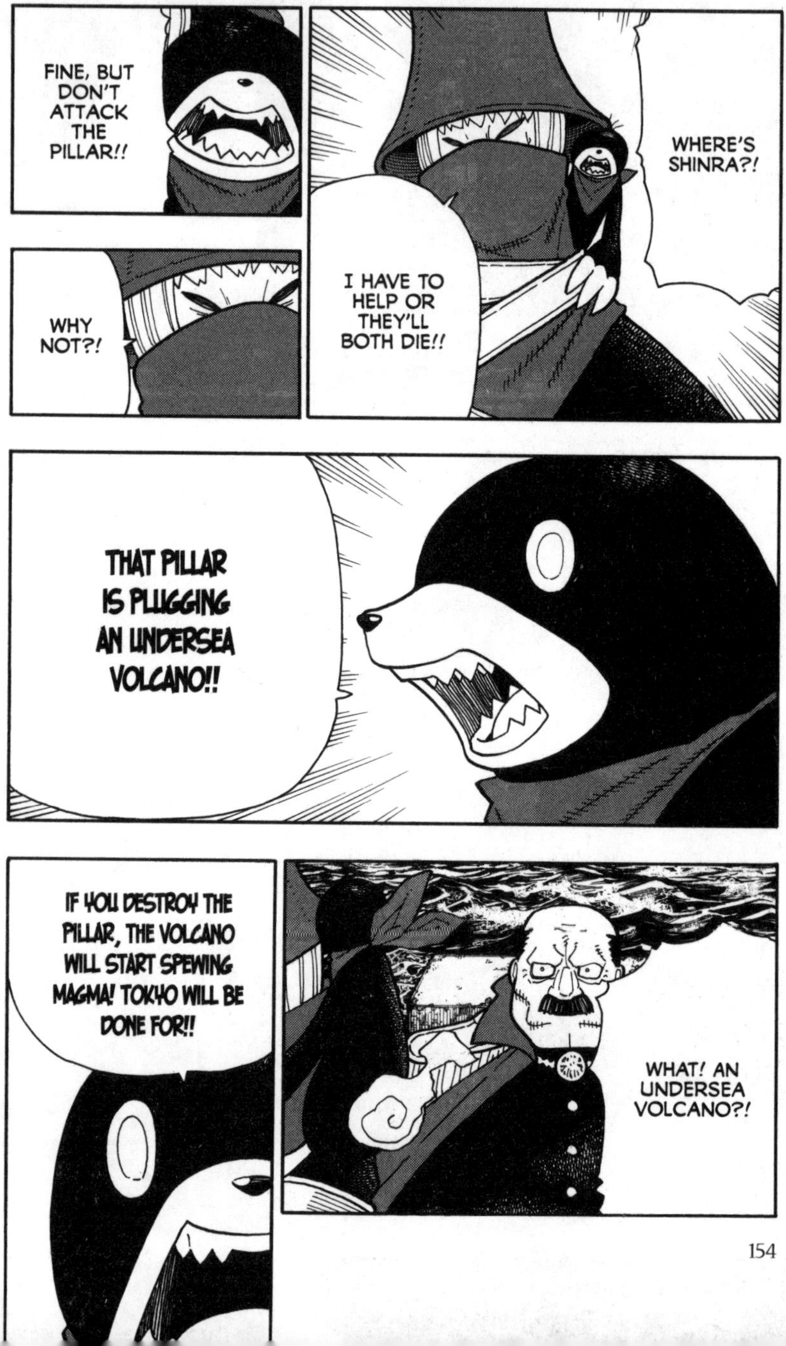
WHERE'S SHINRA?!
I HAVE TO HELP OR THEY'LL BOTH DIE!!
FINE, BUT DON'T ATTACK THE PILLAR!!
WHY NOT?!
THAT PILLAR IS PLUGGING AN UNDERSEA VOLCANO!!
WHAT! AN UNDERSEA VOLCANO?!
IF YOU DESTROY THE PILLAR, THE VOLCANO WILL START SPEWING MAGMA! TOKYO WILL BE DONE FOR!!

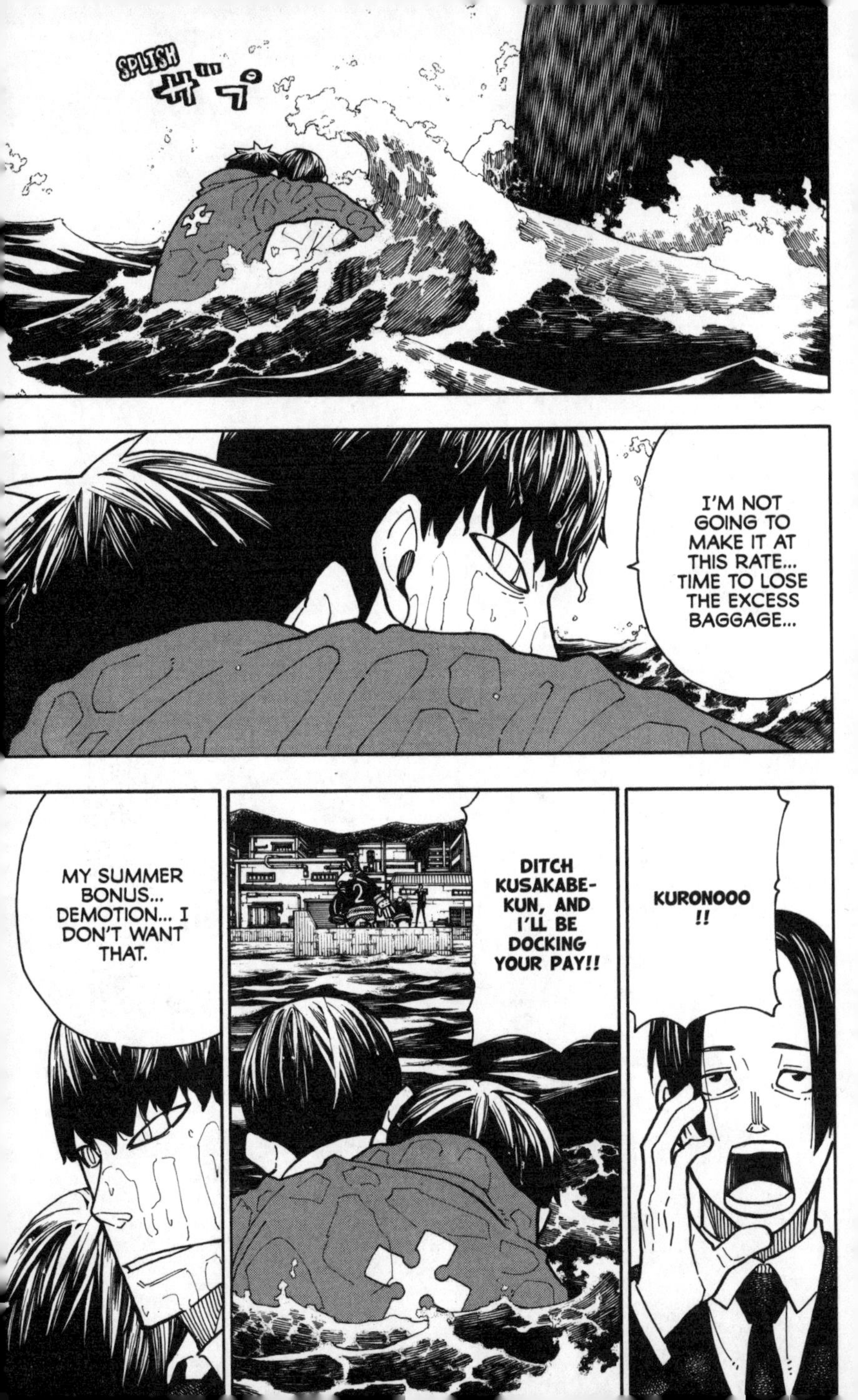
SPLISH
ザップ
I'M NOT GOING TO MAKE IT AT THIS RATE... TIME TO LOSE THE EXCESS BAGGAGE...
KURONOOO !!
DITCH KUSAKABE-KUN, AND I'LL BE DOCKING YOUR PAY!!
MY SUMMER BONUS... DEMOTION... I DON'T WANT THAT.

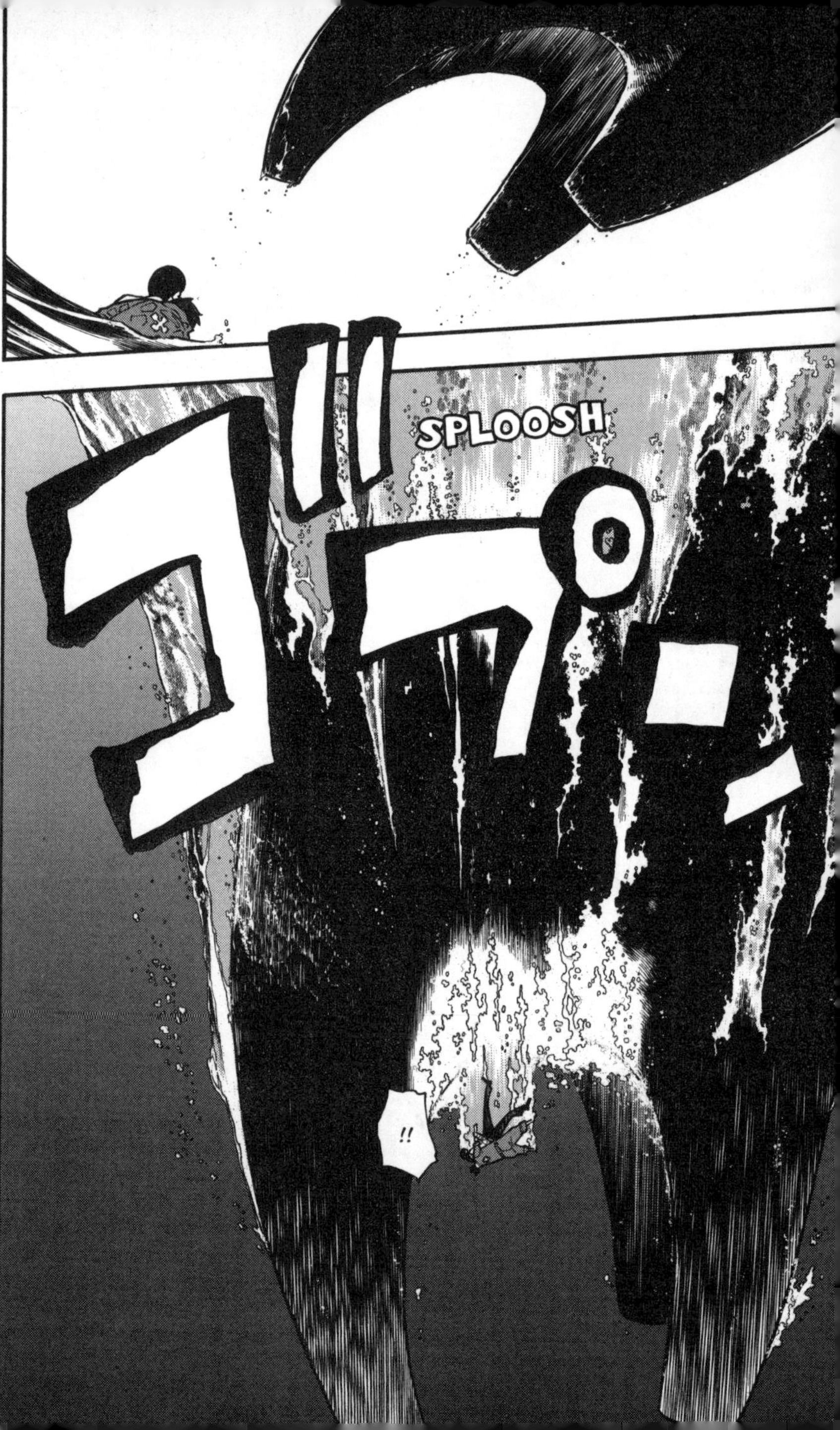
ゴプー
SPLOOSH
!!

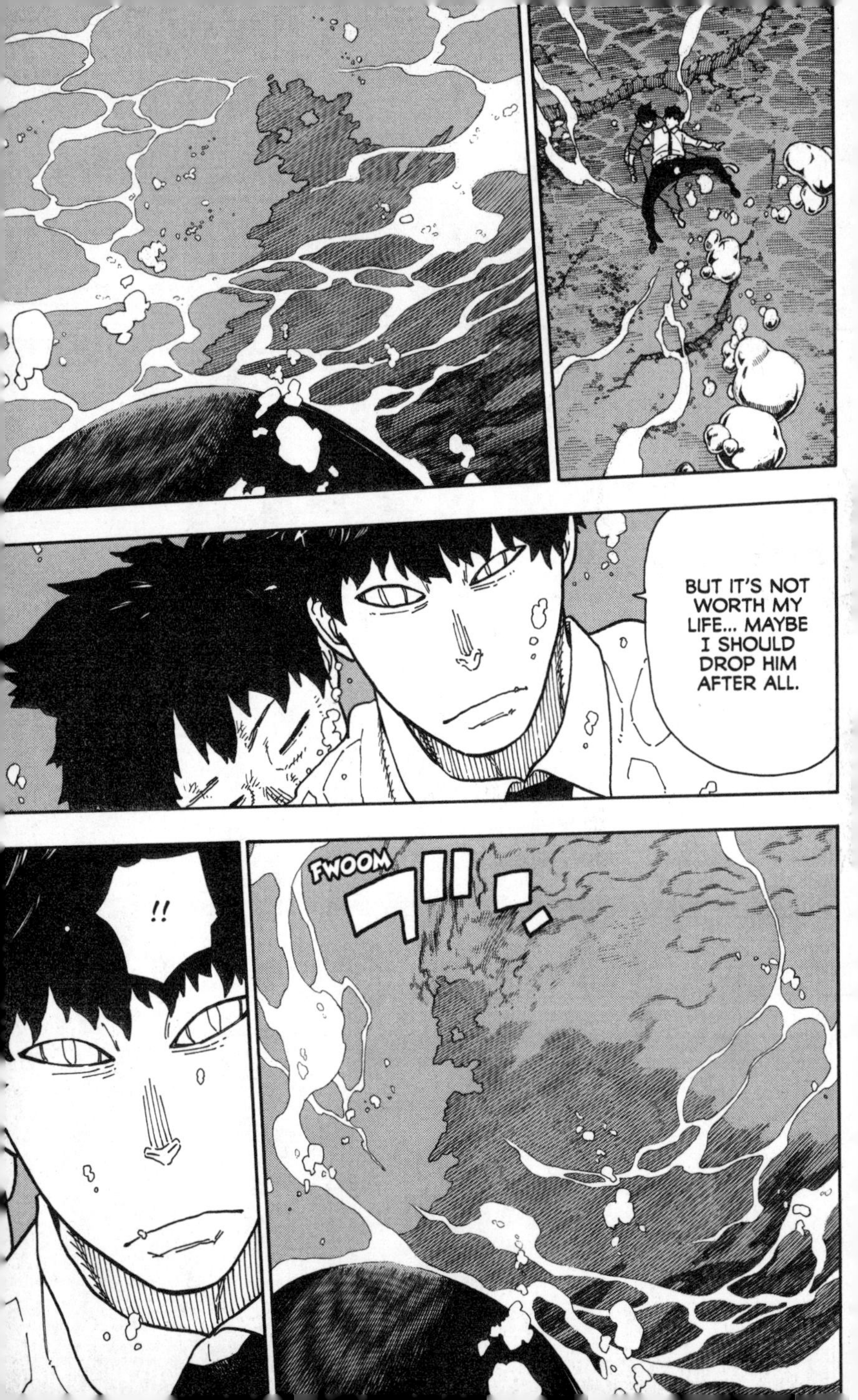
BUT IT'S NOT WORTH MY LIFE... MAYBE I SHOULD DROP HIM AFTER ALL.
FWOOM
!!

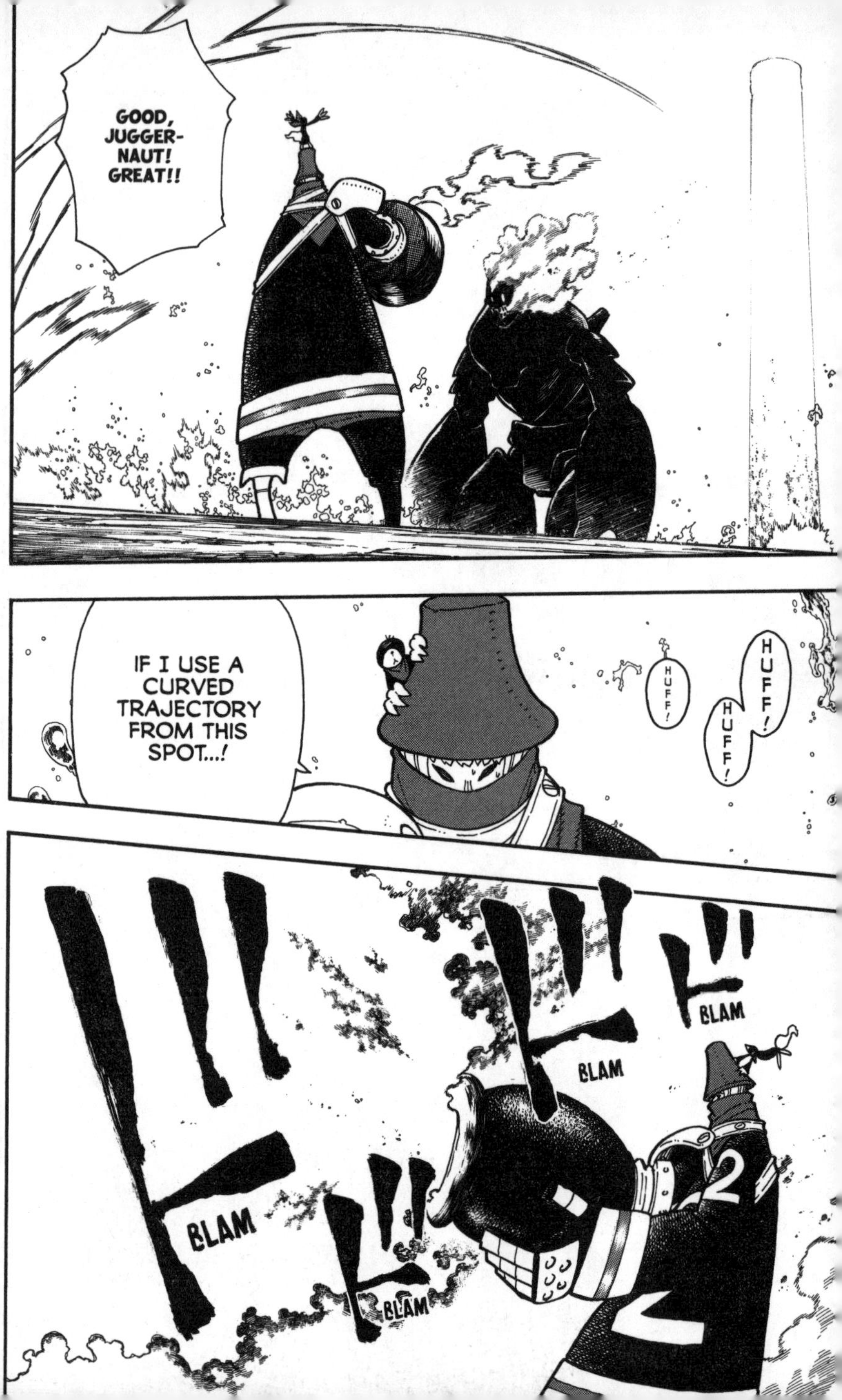
GOOD, JUGGER-NAUT! GREAT!!
HUFF! HUFF!
HUFF!
IF I USE A CURVED TRAJECTORY FROM THIS SPOT...!
BLAM
BLAM
BLAM
BLAM

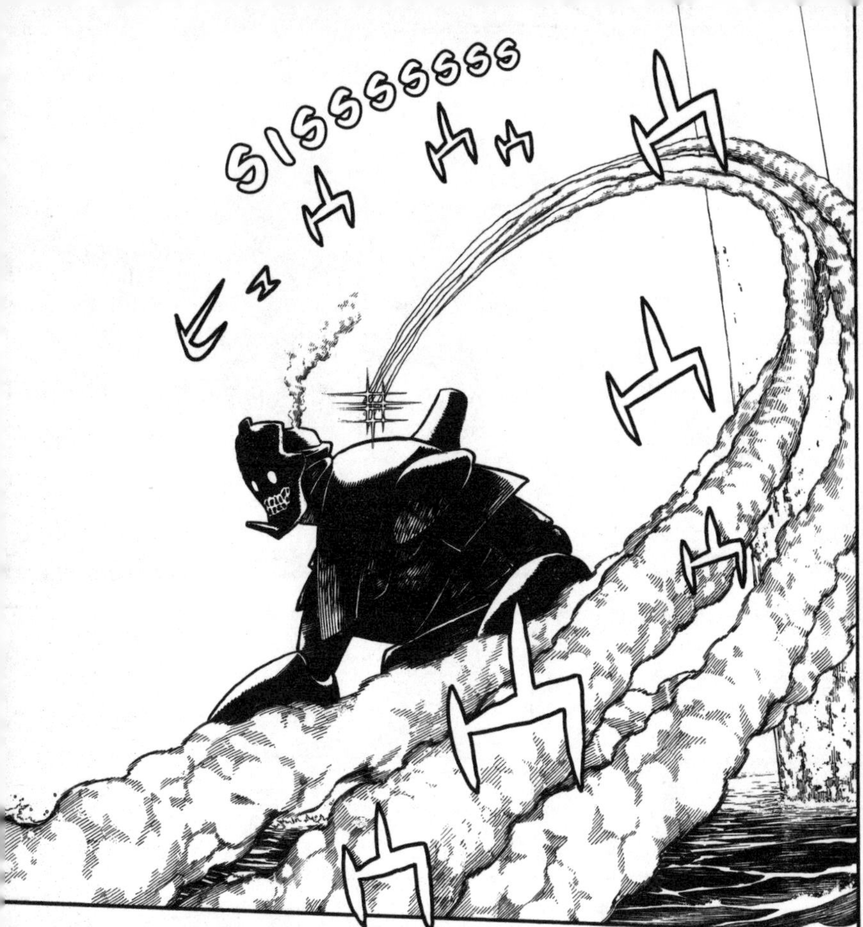
SISSSSSSS

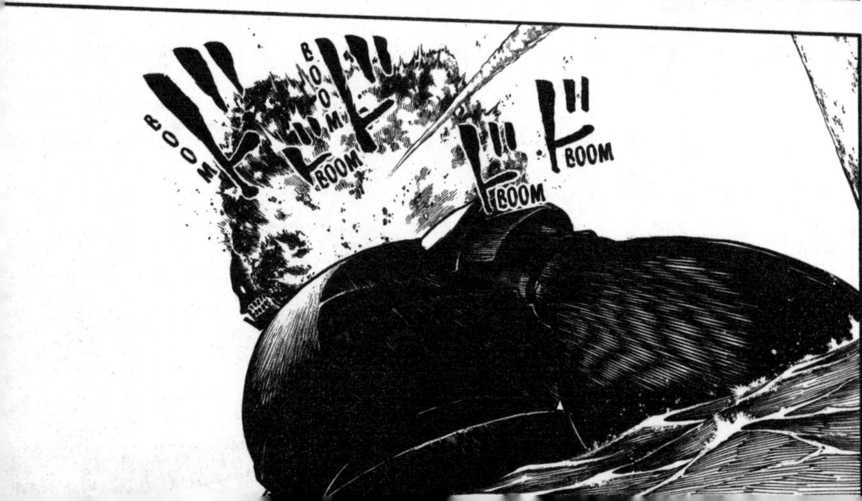
BOOM
BOOM
BOOM
BOOM
BOOM

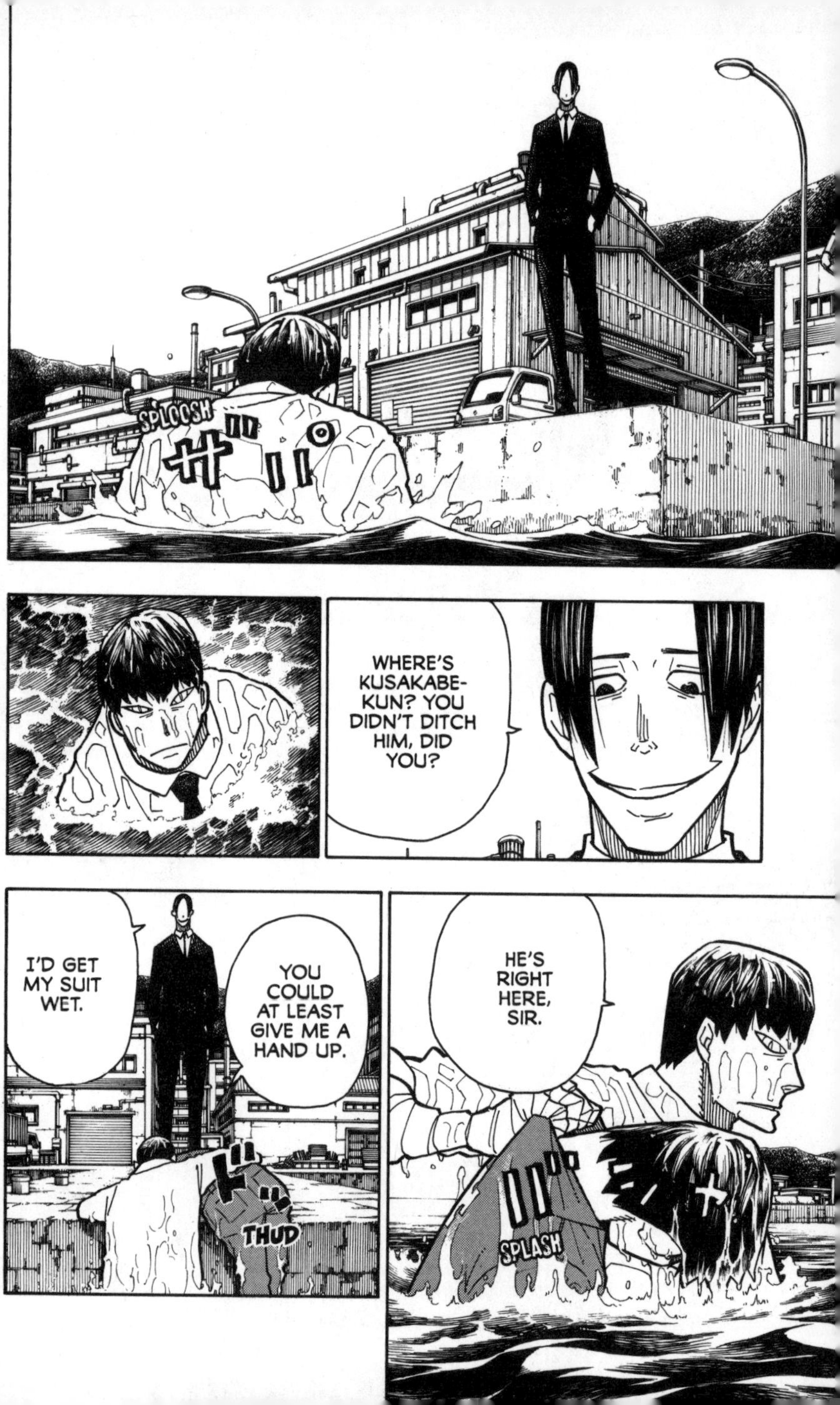
SPLOOSH
WHERE'S KUSAKABE-KUN? YOU DIDN'T DITCH HIM, DID YOU?
HE'S RIGHT HERE, SIR.
SPLASH
YOU COULD AT LEAST GIVE ME A HAND UP.
I'D GET MY SUIT WET.
THUD

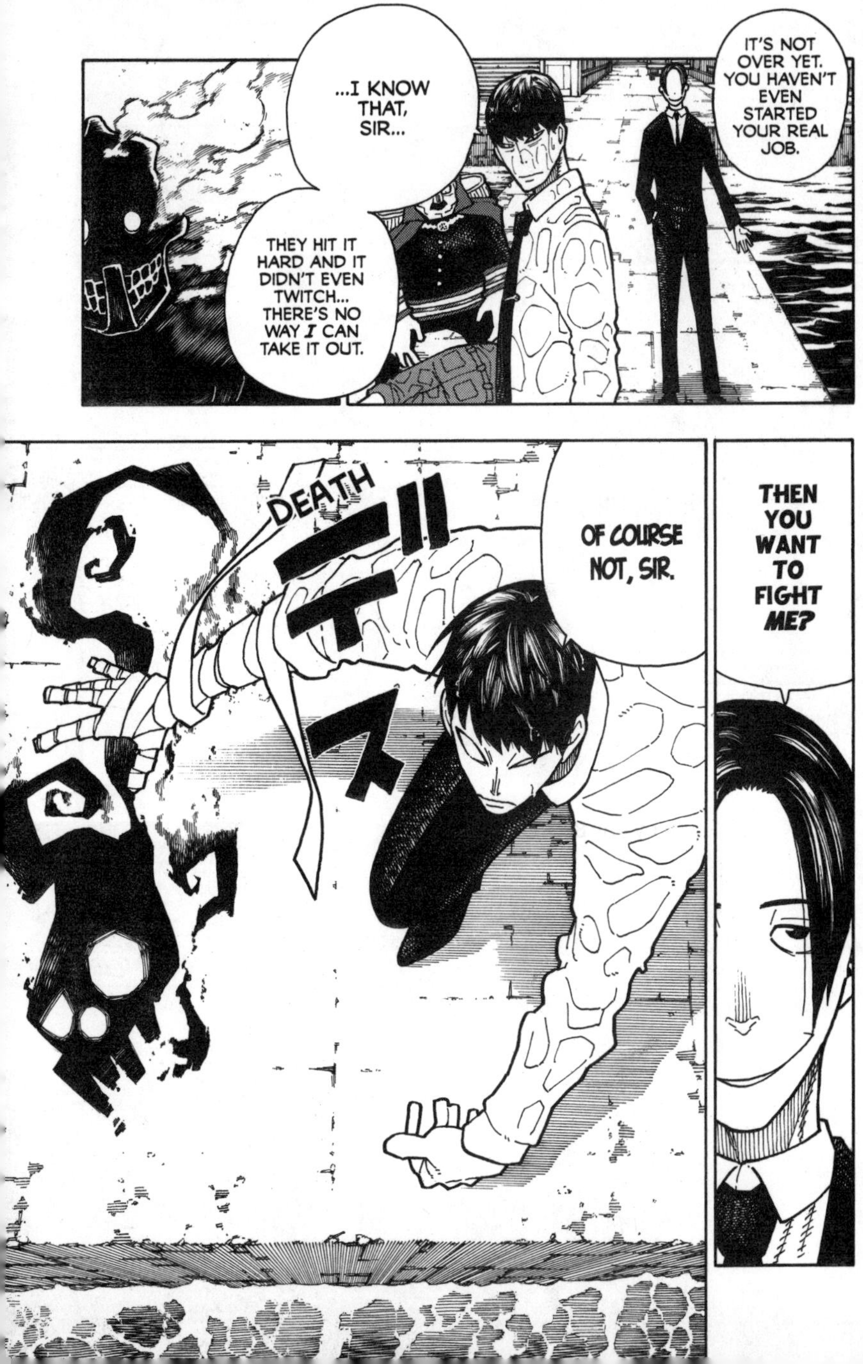
IT'S NOT OVER YET. YOU HAVEN'T EVEN STARTED YOUR REAL JOB.
...I KNOW THAT, SIR...
THEY HIT IT HARD AND IT DIDN'T EVEN TWITCH... THERE'S NO WAY *I* CAN TAKE IT OUT.
THEN YOU WANT TO FIGHT *ME?*
OF COURSE NOT, SIR.
DEATH

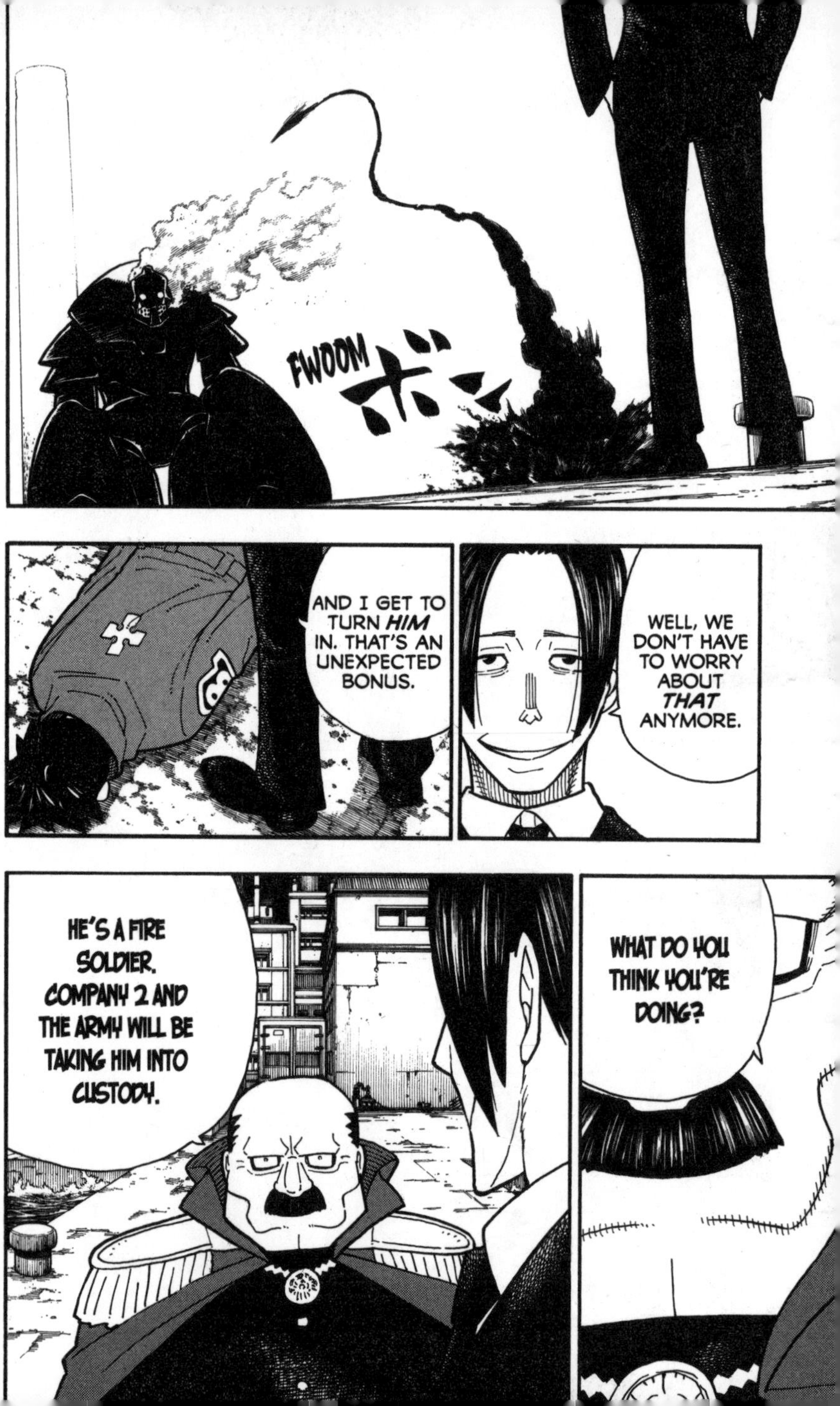
FWOOM
WELL, WE DON'T HAVE TO WORRY ABOUT *THAT* ANYMORE.
AND I GET TO TURN *HIM* IN. THAT'S AN UNEXPECTED BONUS.
WHAT DO YOU THINK YOU'RE DOING?
HE'S A FIRE SOLDIER. COMPANY 2 AND THE ARMY WILL BE TAKING HIM INTO CUSTODY.

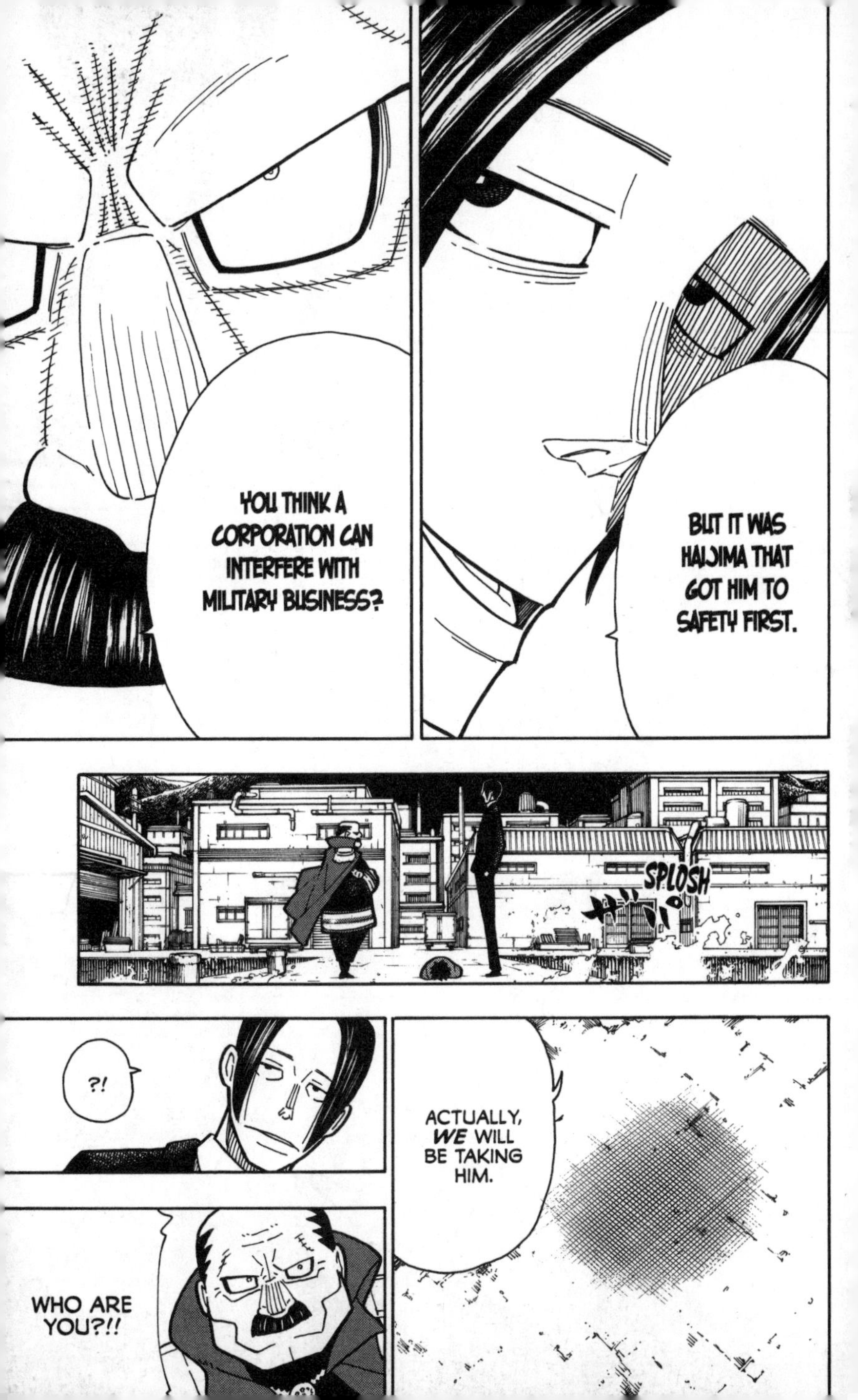
BUT IT WAS HAIJIMA THAT GOT HIM TO SAFETY FIRST.
YOU THINK A CORPORATION CAN INTERFERE WITH MILITARY BUSINESS?
SPLOSH
ACTUALLY, *WE* WILL BE TAKING HIM.
?!
WHO ARE YOU?!!

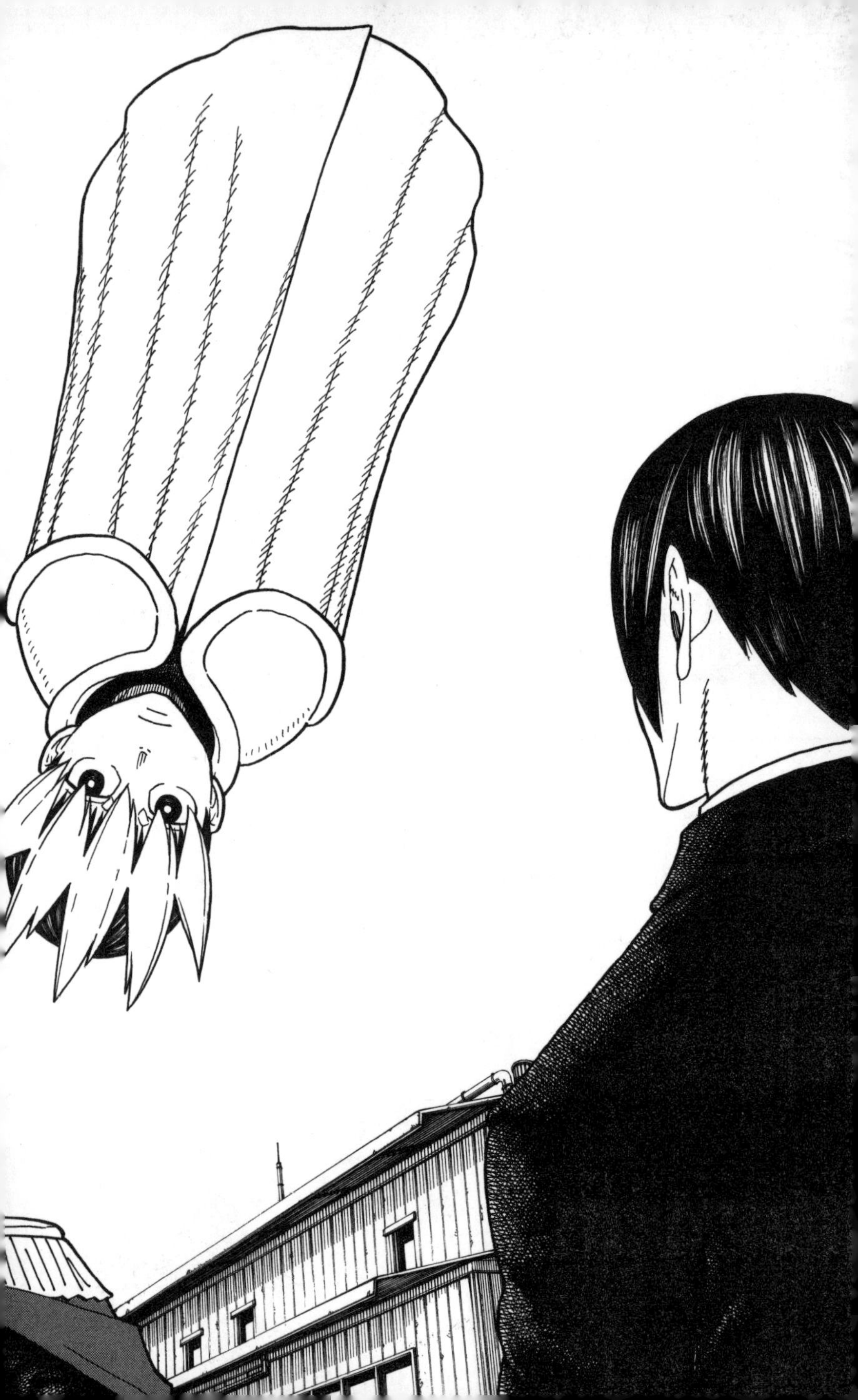

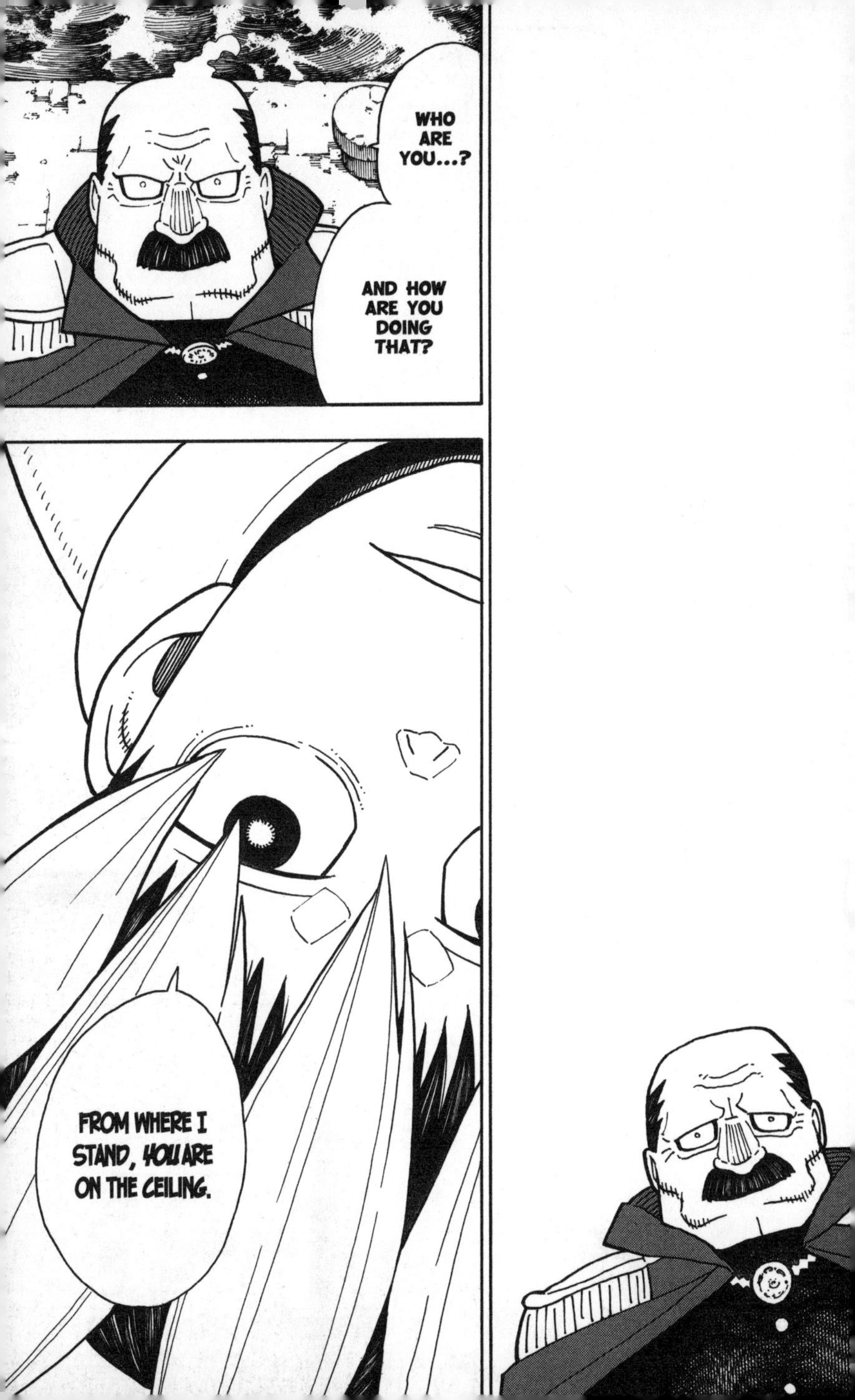
WHO ARE YOU...?
AND HOW ARE YOU DOING THAT?
FROM WHERE I STAND, YOU ARE ON THE CEILING.

FIRE FORCE

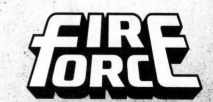

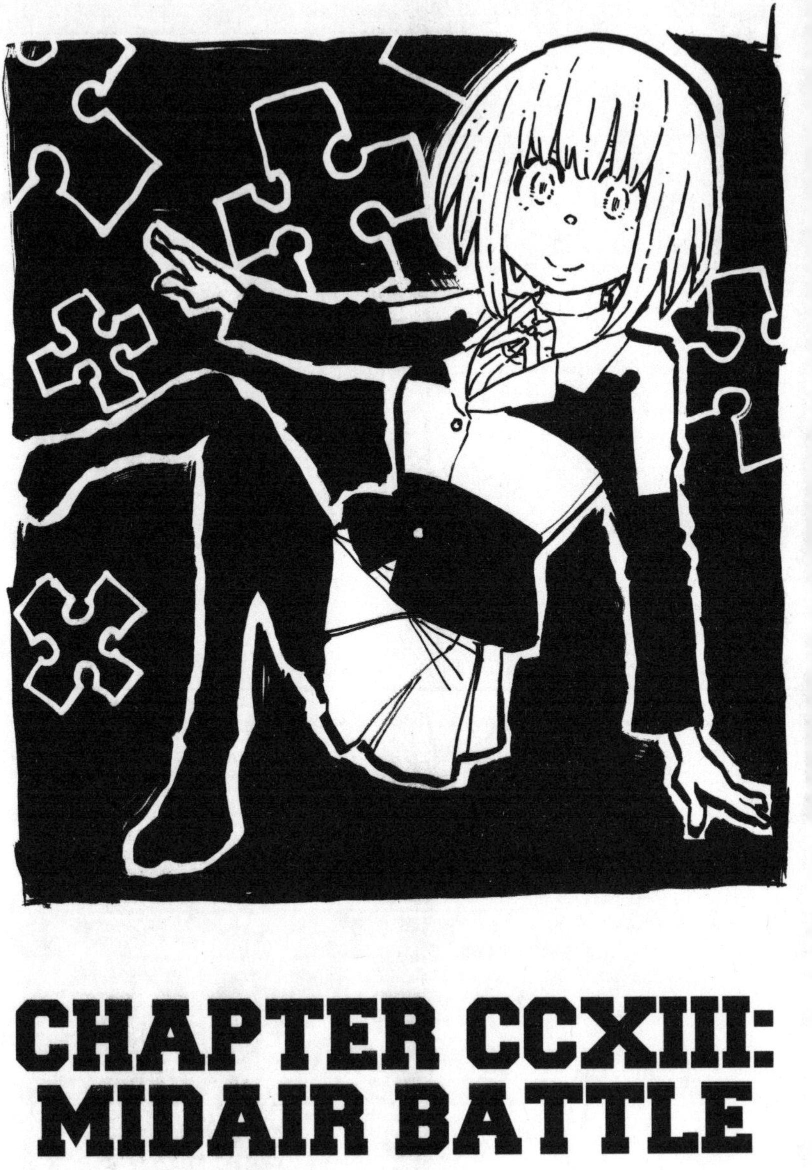

CHAPTER CCXIII: MIDAIR BATTLE

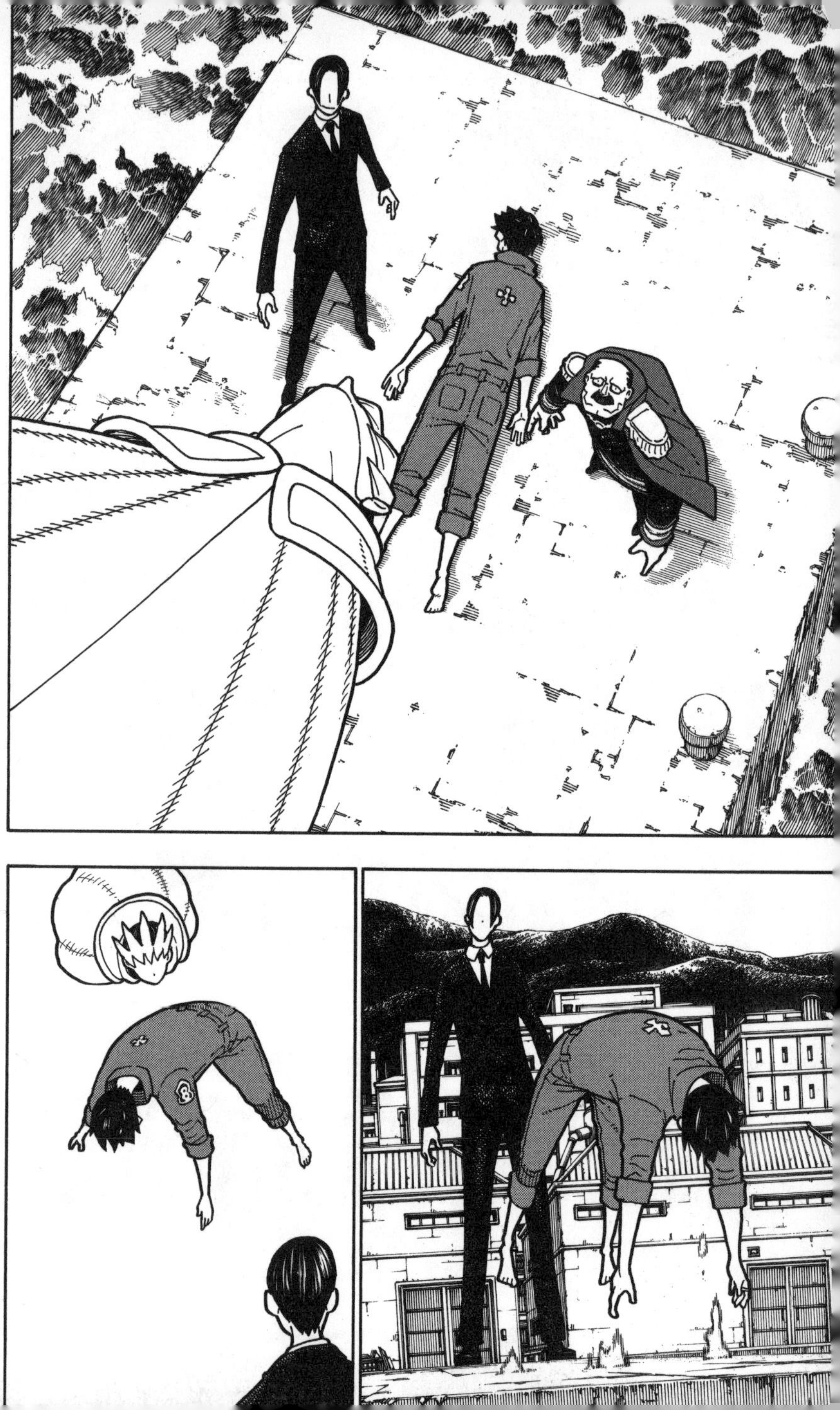

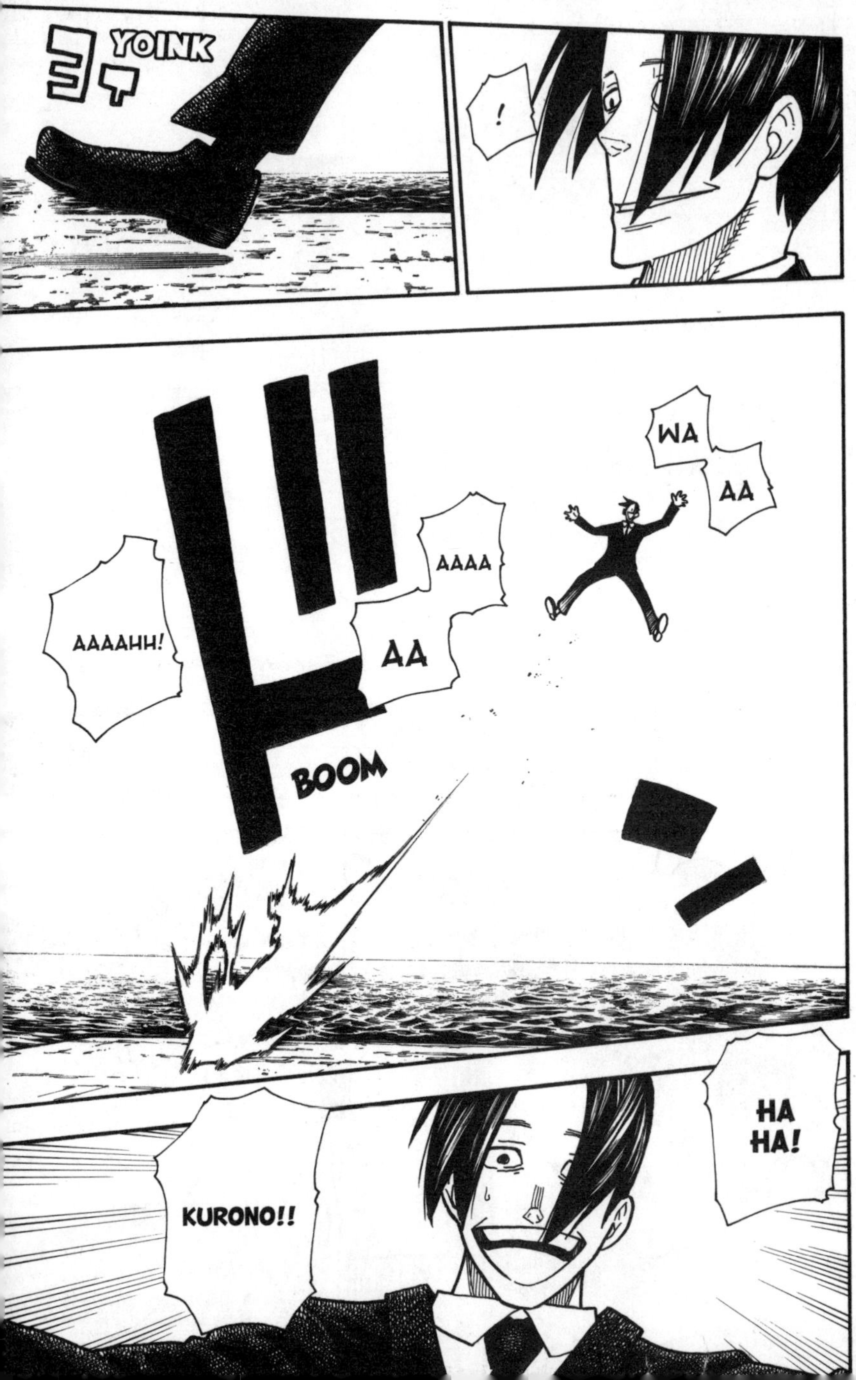
!
YOINK
WA
AA
AAAA
AA
AAAAHH!
BOOM
HA HA!
KURONO!!

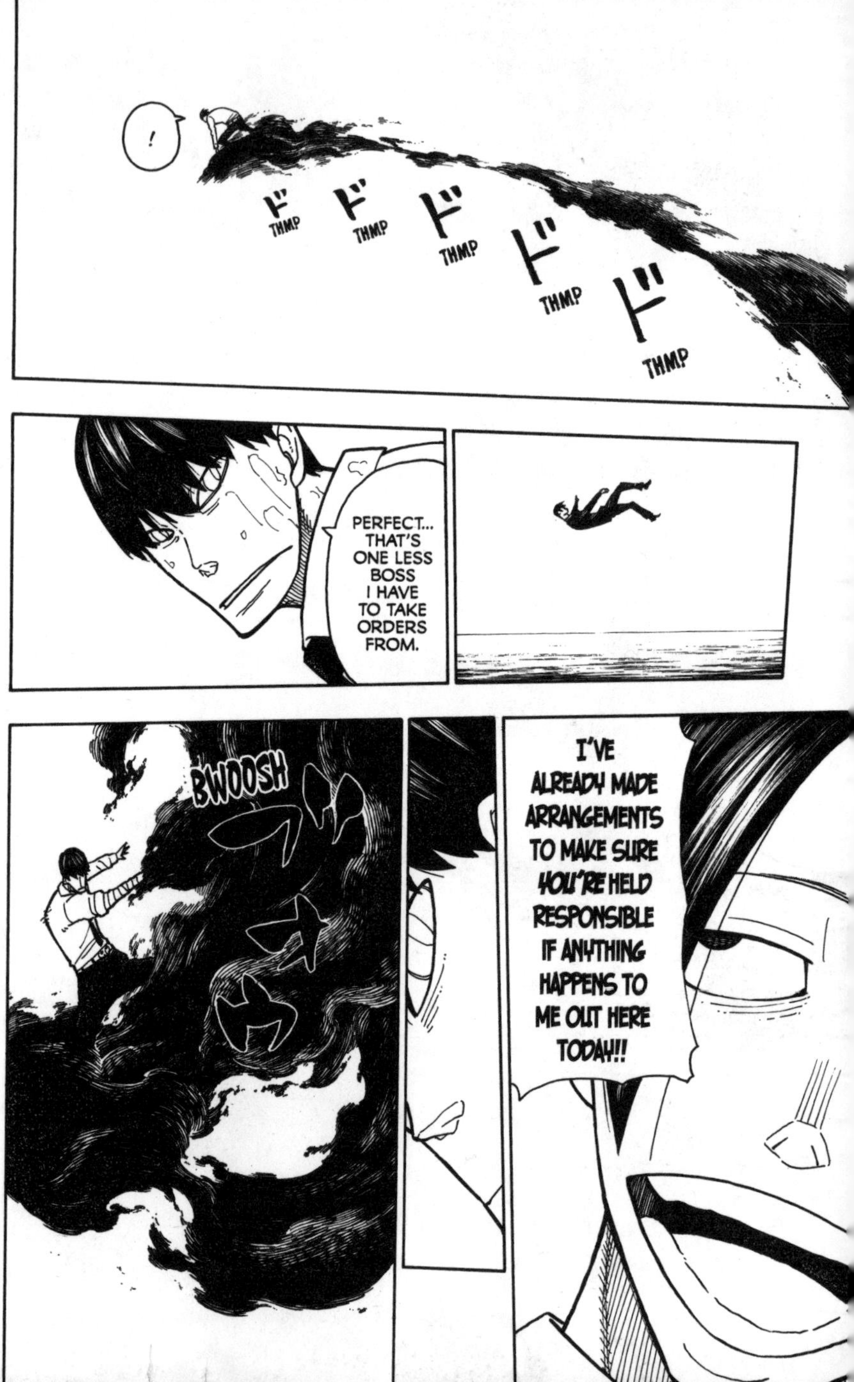
!
ド THMP
ド THMP
ド THMP
ド THMP
ド THMP
PERFECT... THAT'S ONE LESS BOSS I HAVE TO TAKE ORDERS FROM.
I'VE ALREADY MADE ARRANGEMENTS TO MAKE SURE YOU'RE HELD RESPONSIBLE IF ANYTHING HAPPENS TO ME OUT HERE TODAY!!
BWOOSH

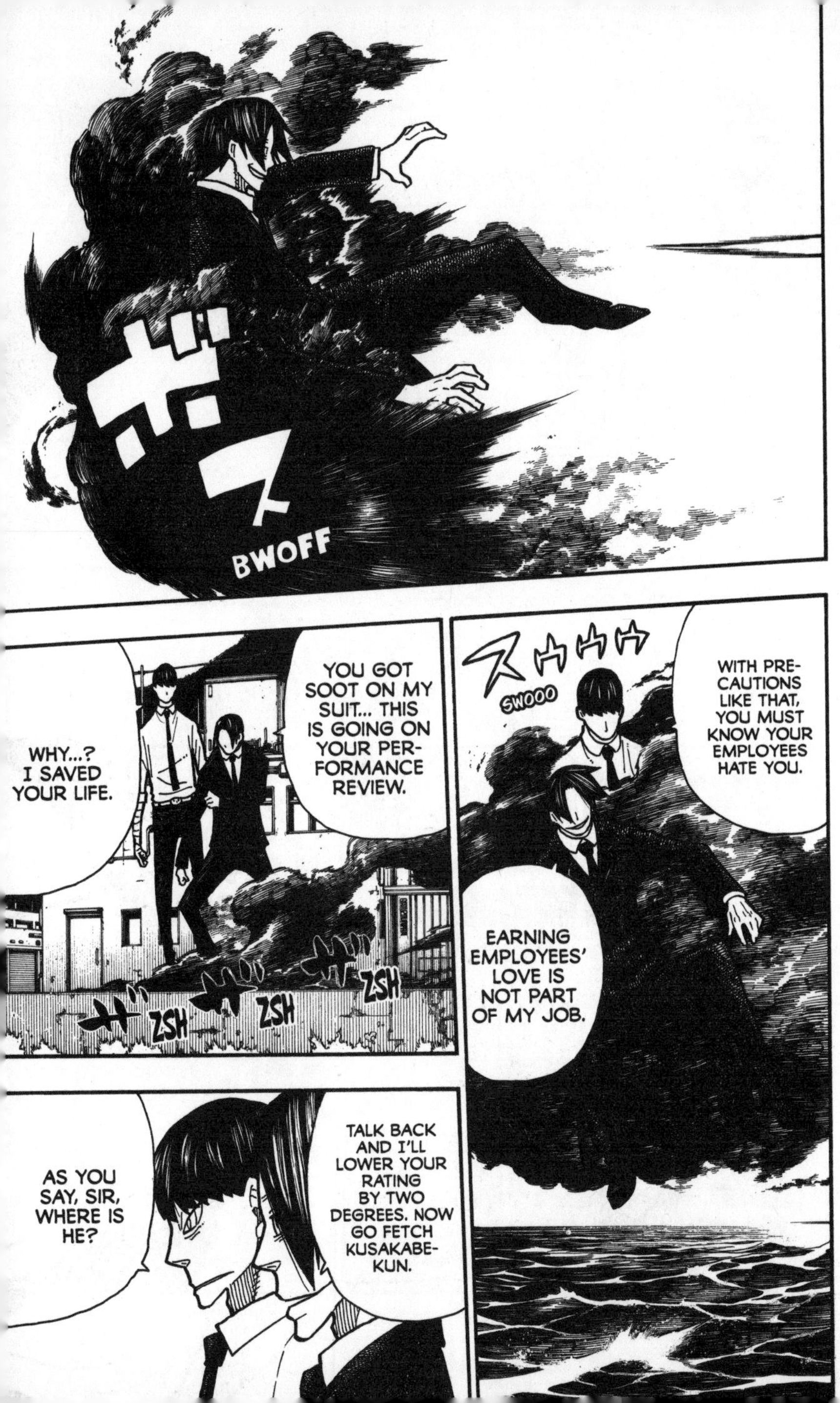
BWOFF
スゥゥゥ
SWOOO
WITH PRE-CAUTIONS LIKE THAT, YOU MUST KNOW YOUR EMPLOYEES HATE YOU.
EARNING EMPLOYEES' LOVE IS NOT PART OF MY JOB.
YOU GOT SOOT ON MY SUIT... THIS IS GOING ON YOUR PER-FORMANCE REVIEW.
WHY...? I SAVED YOUR LIFE.
ZSH
ZSH
ZSH
TALK BACK AND I'LL LOWER YOUR RATING BY TWO DEGREES. NOW GO FETCH KUSAKABE-KUN.
AS YOU SAY, SIR, WHERE IS HE?

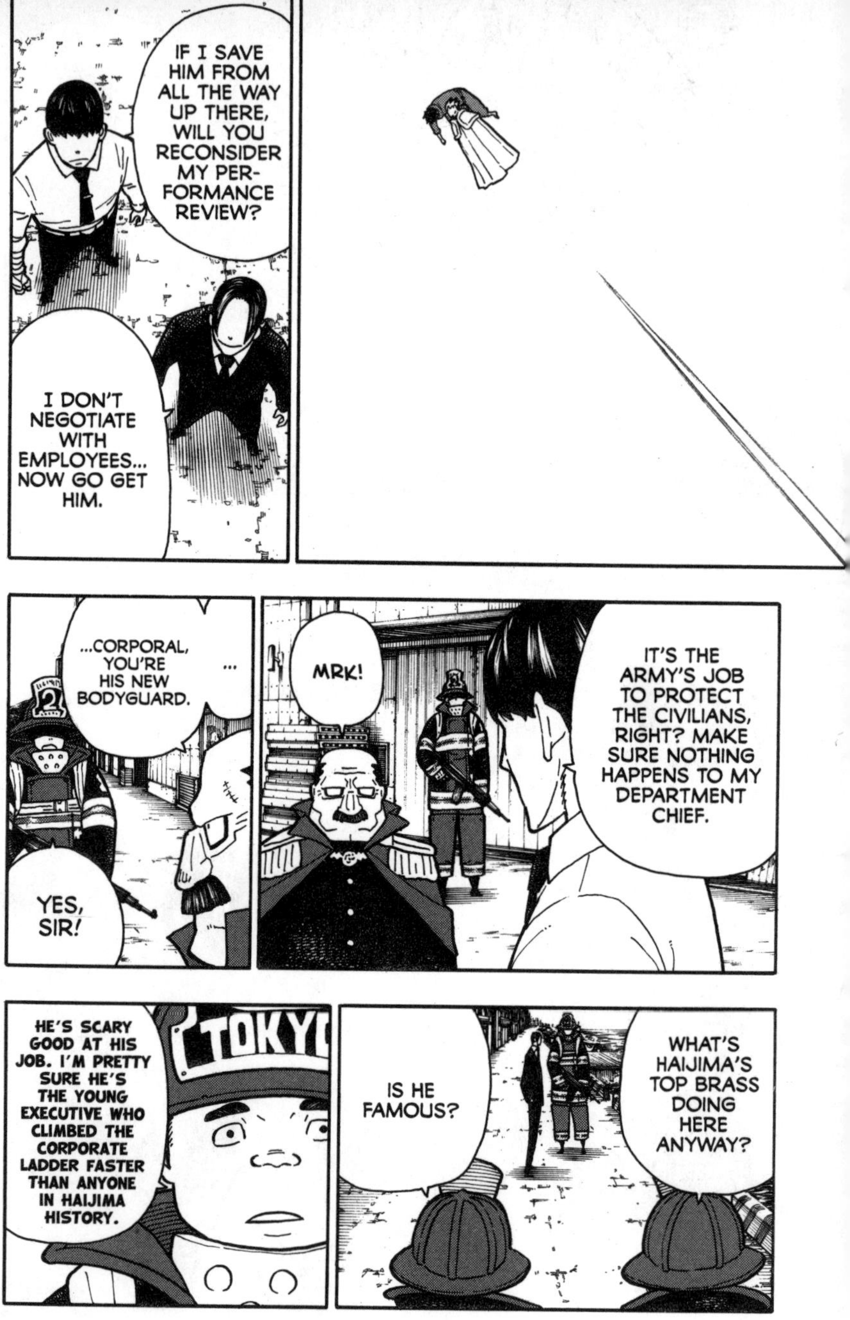
IF I SAVE HIM FROM ALL THE WAY UP THERE, WILL YOU RECONSIDER MY PER-FORMANCE REVIEW?
I DON'T NEGOTIATE WITH EMPLOYEES... NOW GO GET HIM.
IT'S THE ARMY'S JOB TO PROTECT THE CIVILIANS, RIGHT? MAKE SURE NOTHING HAPPENS TO MY DEPARTMENT CHIEF.
MRK!
...
...CORPORAL, YOU'RE HIS NEW BODYGUARD.
YES, SIR!
WHAT'S HAIJIMA'S TOP BRASS DOING HERE ANYWAY?
IS HE FAMOUS?
HE'S SCARY GOOD AT HIS JOB. I'M PRETTY SURE HE'S THE YOUNG EXECUTIVE WHO CLIMBED THE CORPORATE LADDER FASTER THAN ANYONE IN HAIJIMA HISTORY.

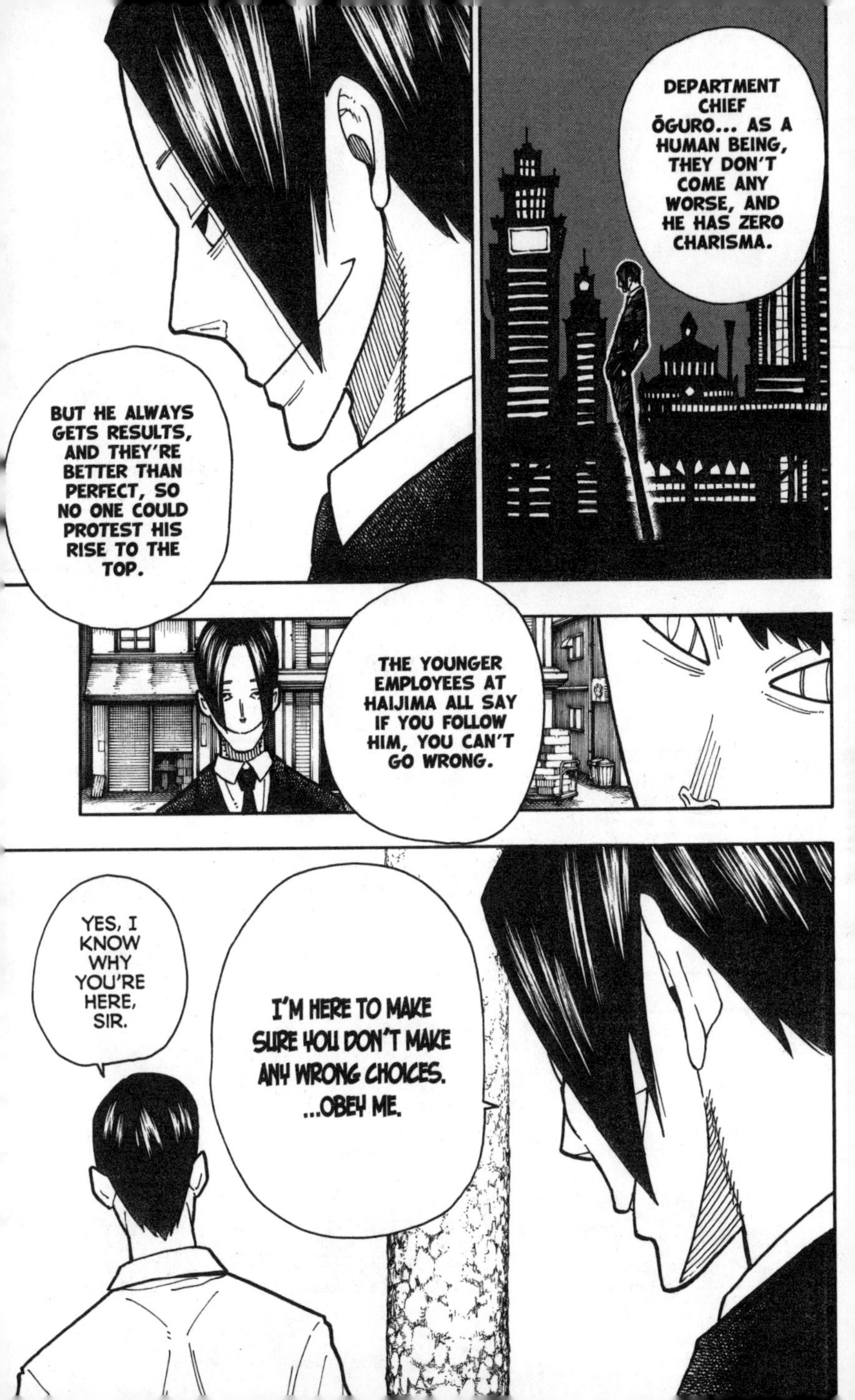
DEPARTMENT CHIEF ŌGURO... AS A HUMAN BEING, THEY DON'T COME ANY WORSE, AND HE HAS ZERO CHARISMA.
BUT HE ALWAYS GETS RESULTS, AND THEY'RE BETTER THAN PERFECT, SO NO ONE COULD PROTEST HIS RISE TO THE TOP.
THE YOUNGER EMPLOYEES AT HAIJIMA ALL SAY IF YOU FOLLOW HIM, YOU CAN'T GO WRONG.
YES, I KNOW WHY YOU'RE HERE, SIR.
I'M HERE TO MAKE SURE YOU DON'T MAKE ANY WRONG CHOICES. ...OBEY ME.

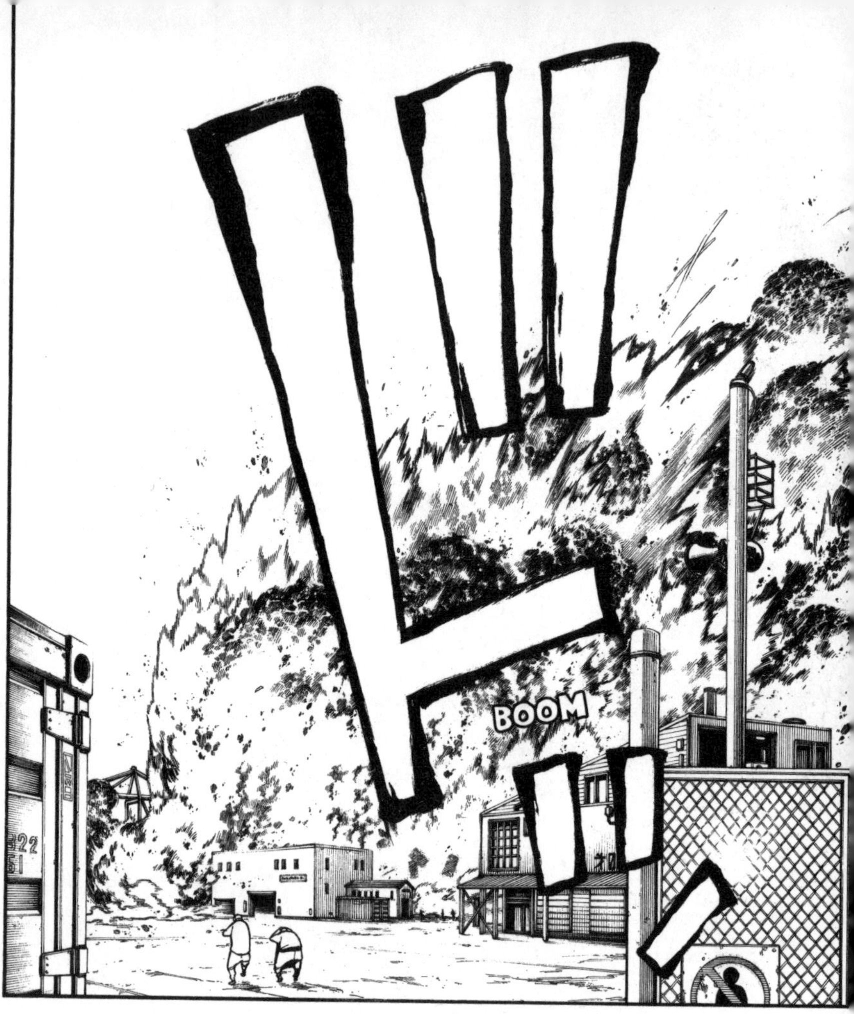
BOOM
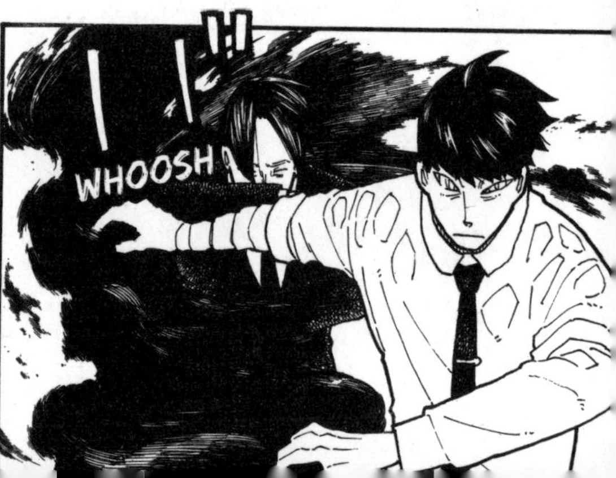
WHOOSH
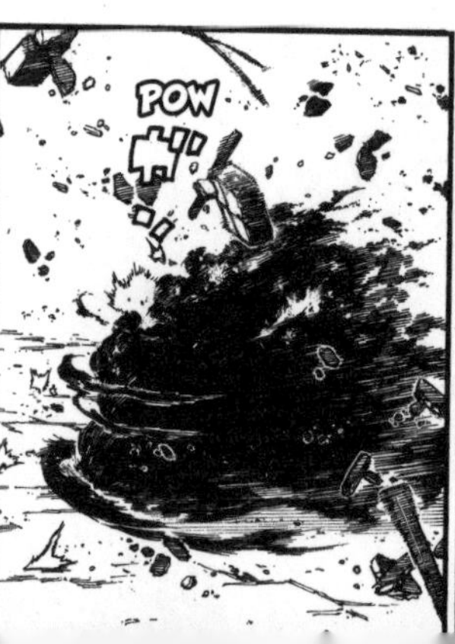
POW

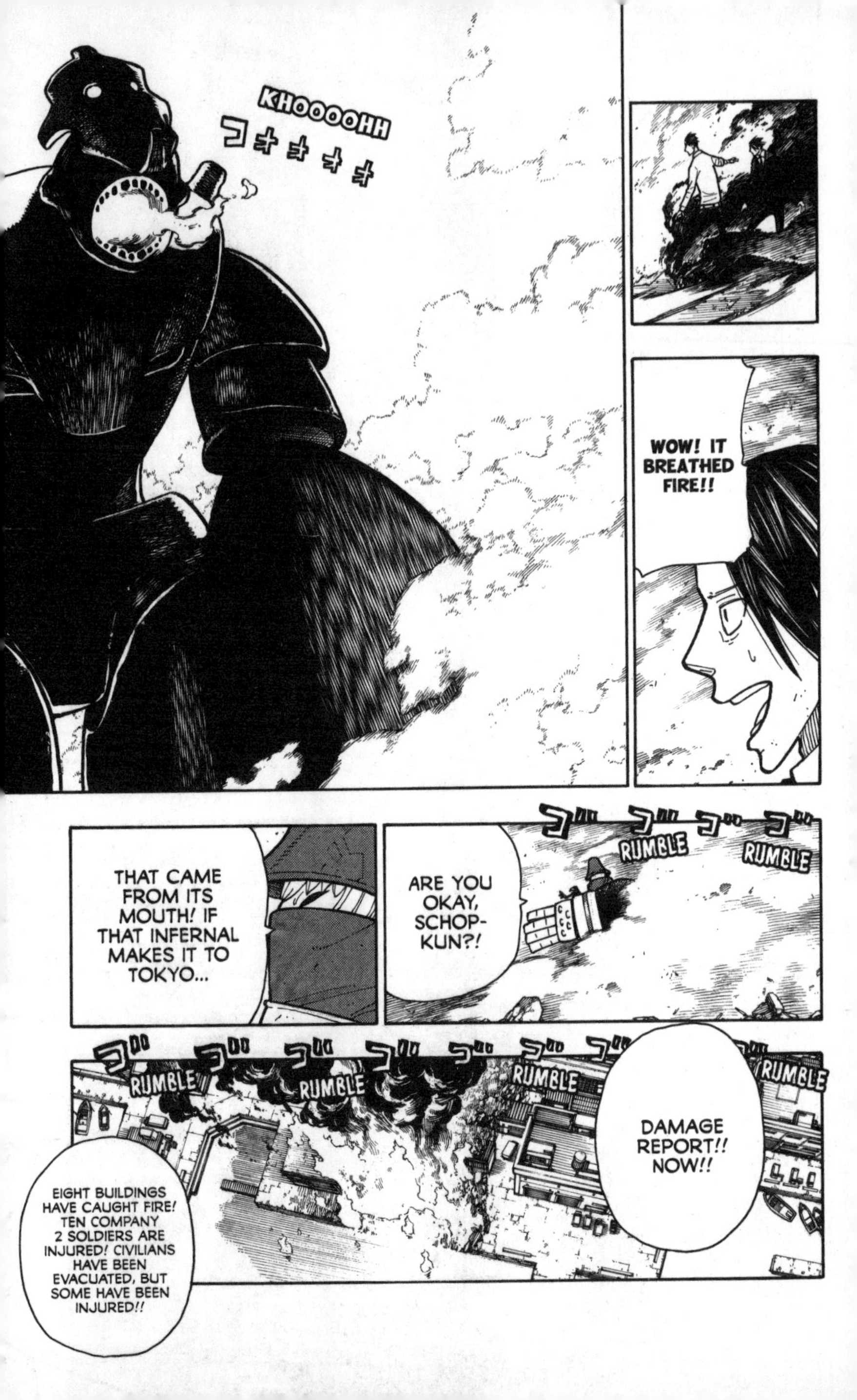
WOW! IT BREATHED FIRE!!
KHOOOOOHH
コォォォォ
RUMBLE
RUMBLE
ARE YOU OKAY, SCHOP-KUN?!
THAT CAME FROM ITS MOUTH! IF THAT INFERNAL MAKES IT TO TOKYO...
RUMBLE
DAMAGE REPORT!! NOW!!
RUMBLE
RUMBLE
RUMBLE
EIGHT BUILDINGS HAVE CAUGHT FIRE! TEN COMPANY 2 SOLDIERS ARE INJURED! CIVILIANS HAVE BEEN EVACUATED, BUT SOME HAVE BEEN INJURED!!

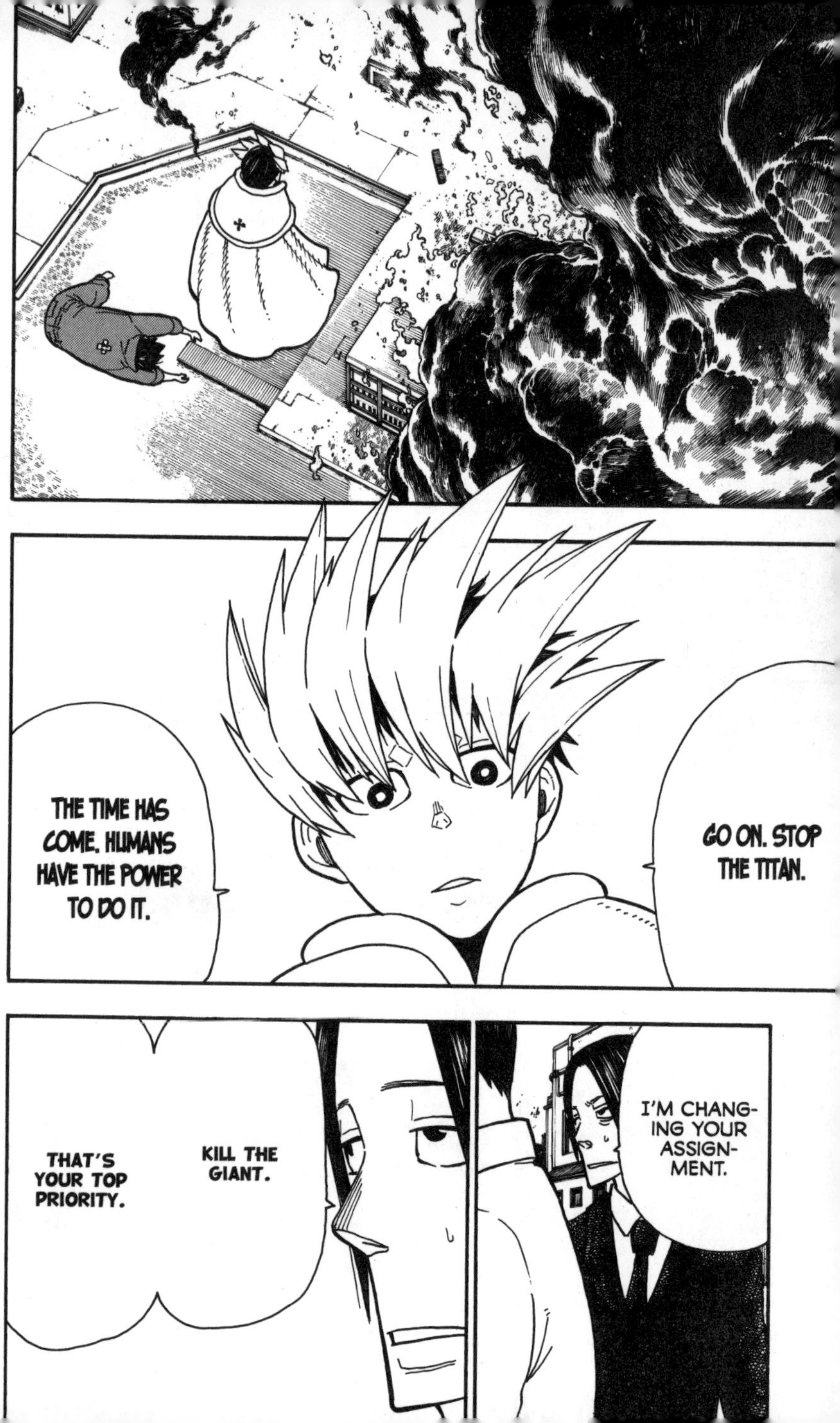
GO ON. STOP THE TITAN.
THE TIME HAS COME. HUMANS HAVE THE POWER TO DO IT.
I'M CHANGING YOUR ASSIGNMENT.
KILL THE GIANT.
THAT'S YOUR TOP PRIORITY.

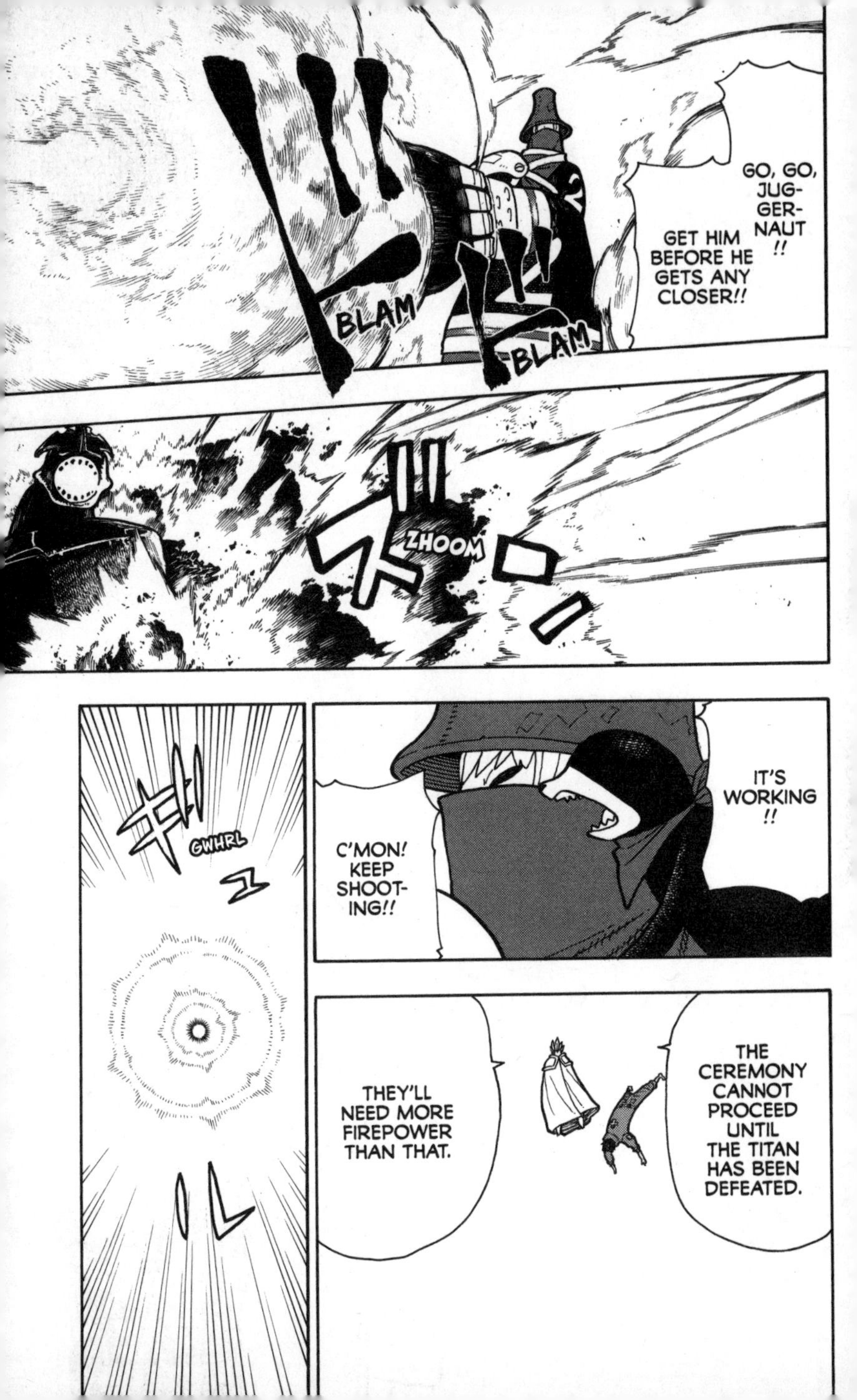
GO, GO, JUGGERNAUT!!
GET HIM BEFORE HE GETS ANY CLOSER!!
BLAM
BLAM
ZHOOM
IT'S WORKING!!
C'MON! KEEP SHOOTING!!
THE CEREMONY CANNOT PROCEED UNTIL THE TITAN HAS BEEN DEFEATED.
THEY'LL NEED MORE FIREPOWER THAN THAT.
GWHRL

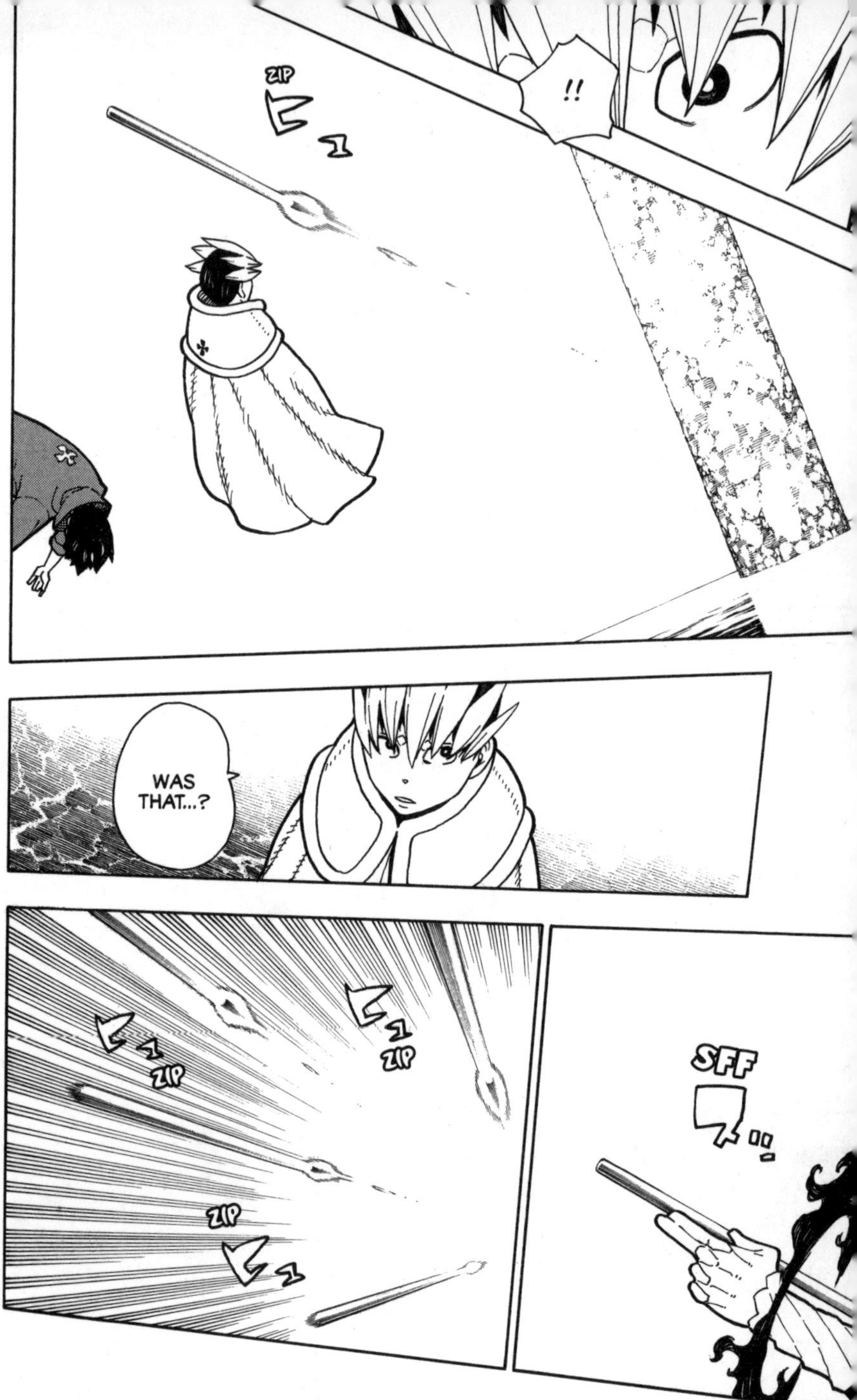
!!
ZIP
WAS THAT...?
SFF
ZIP
ZIP
ZIP

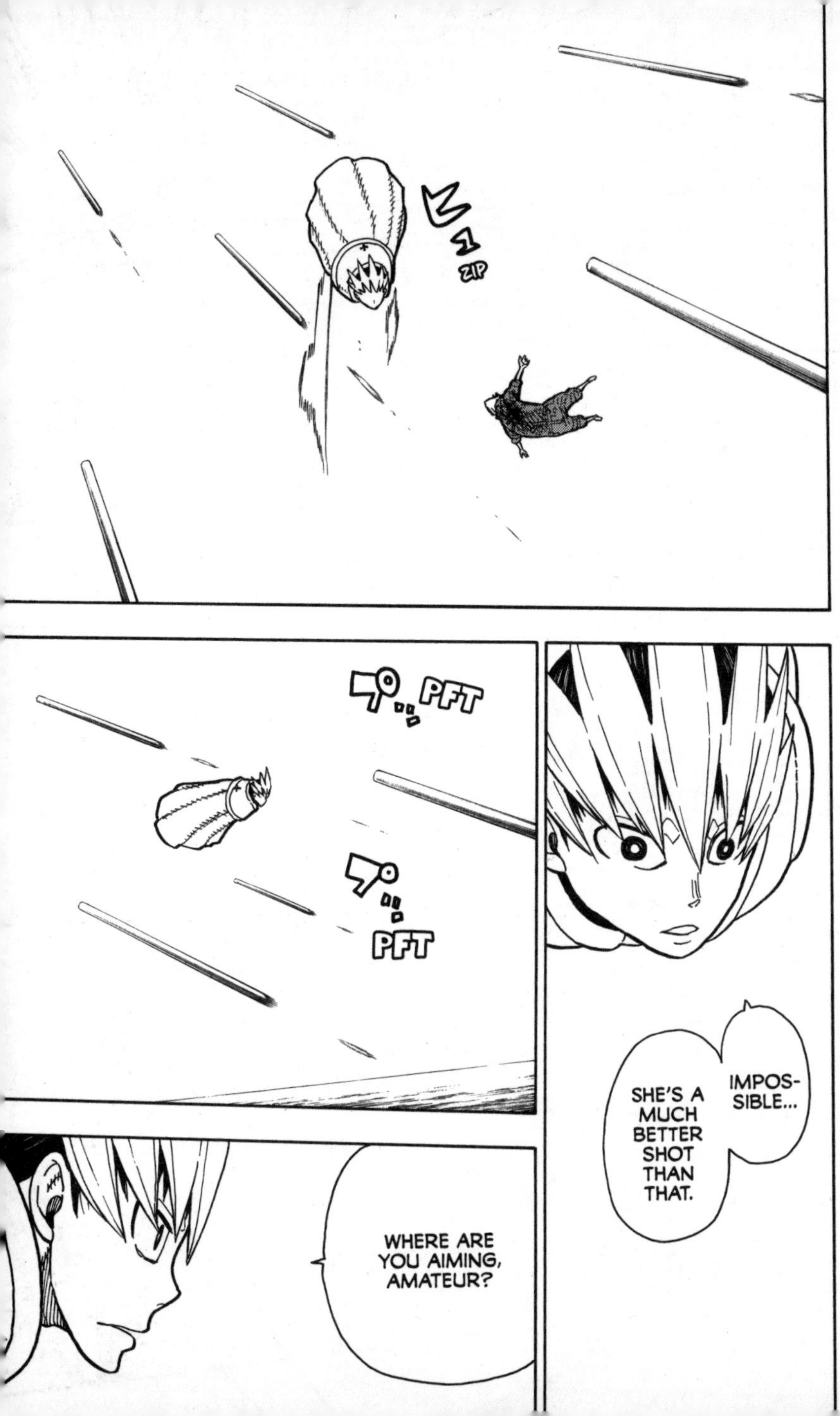
ZIP
IMPOSSIBLE...
SHE'S A MUCH BETTER SHOT THAN THAT.
PFT
PFT
WHERE ARE YOU AIMING, AMATEUR?

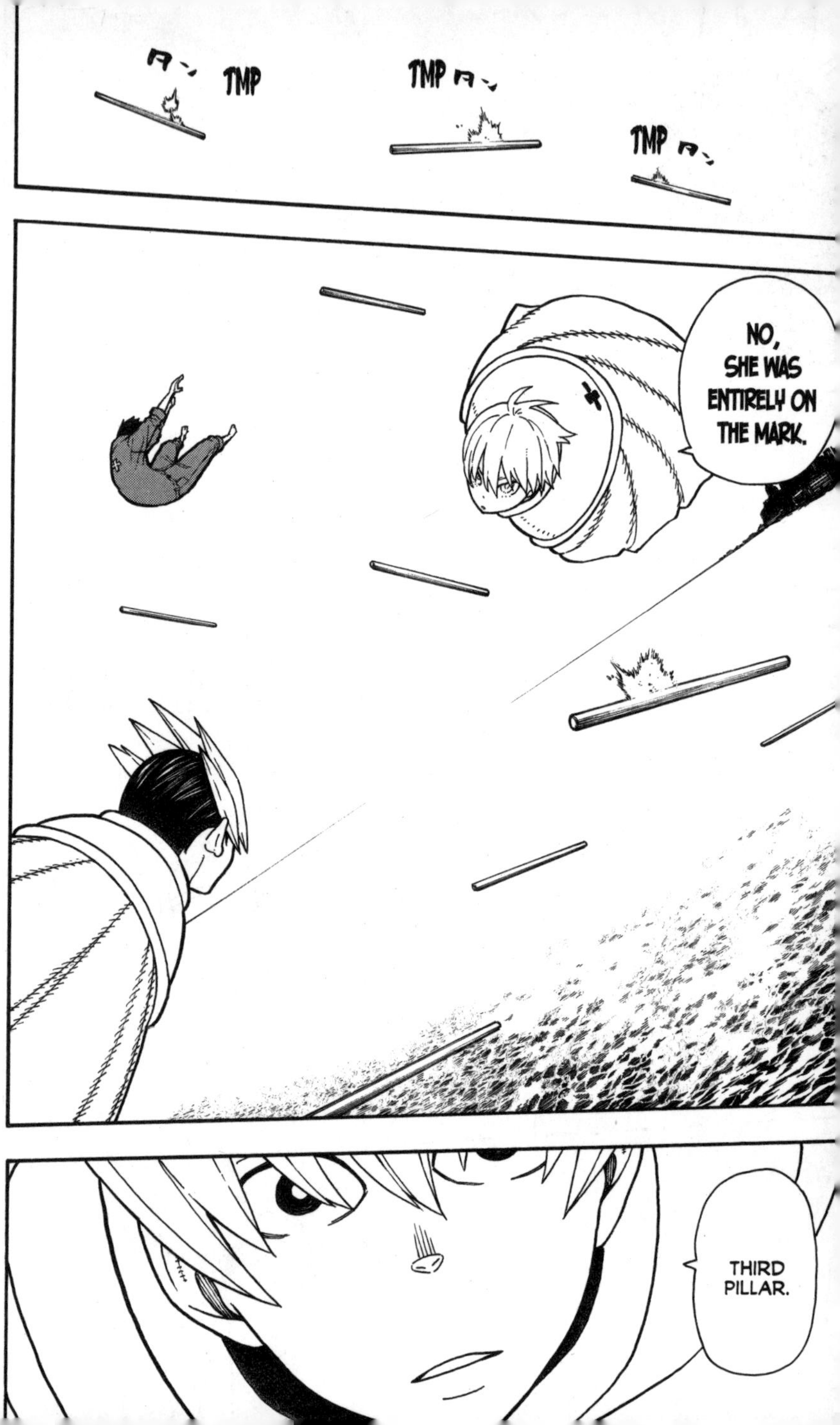
TMP タン
TMP タン
タン TMP
NO, SHE WAS ENTIRELY ON THE MARK.
THIRD PILLAR.

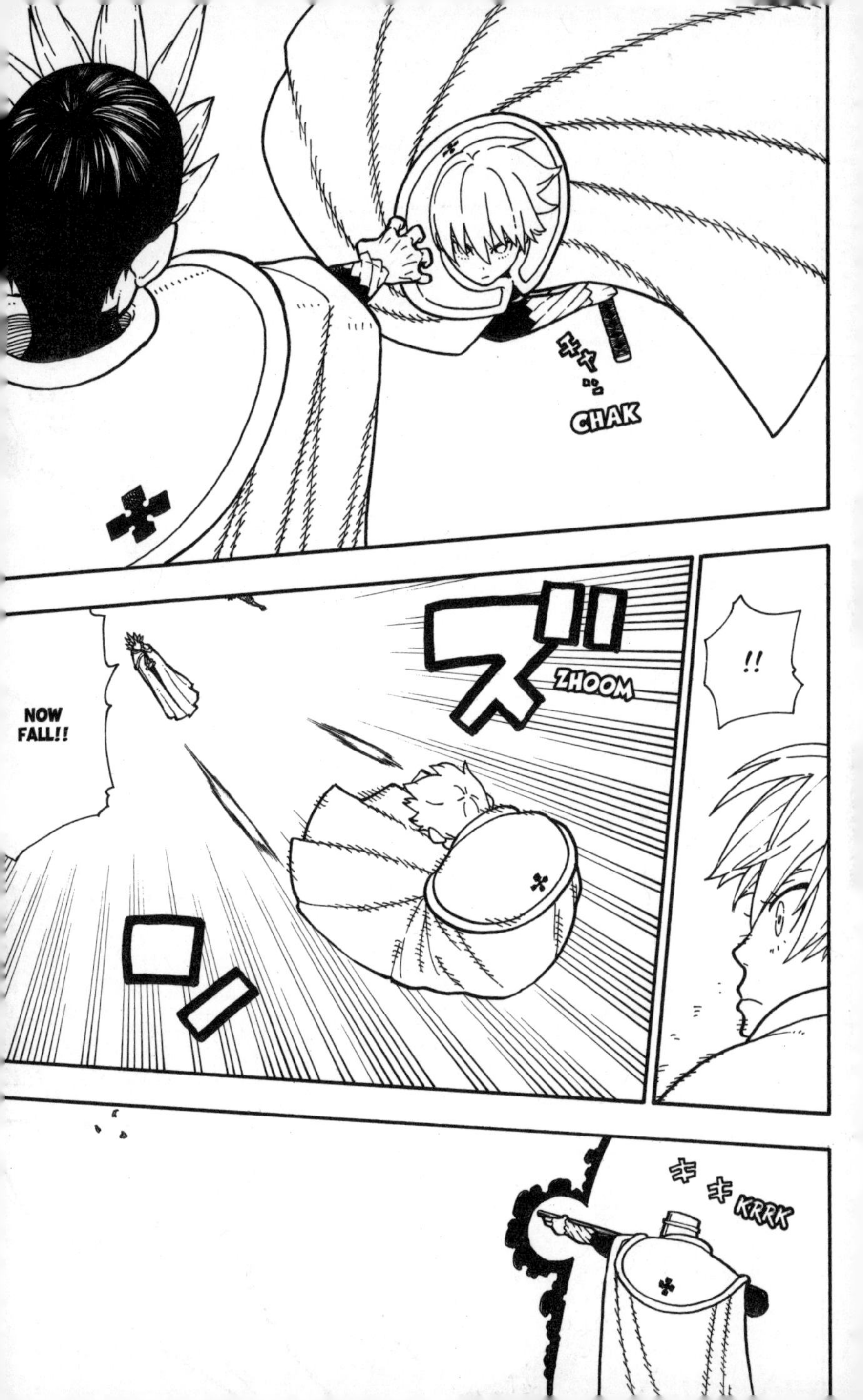
キャッ
CHAK
!!
ZHOOM
NOW FALL!!
キキ
KRRK

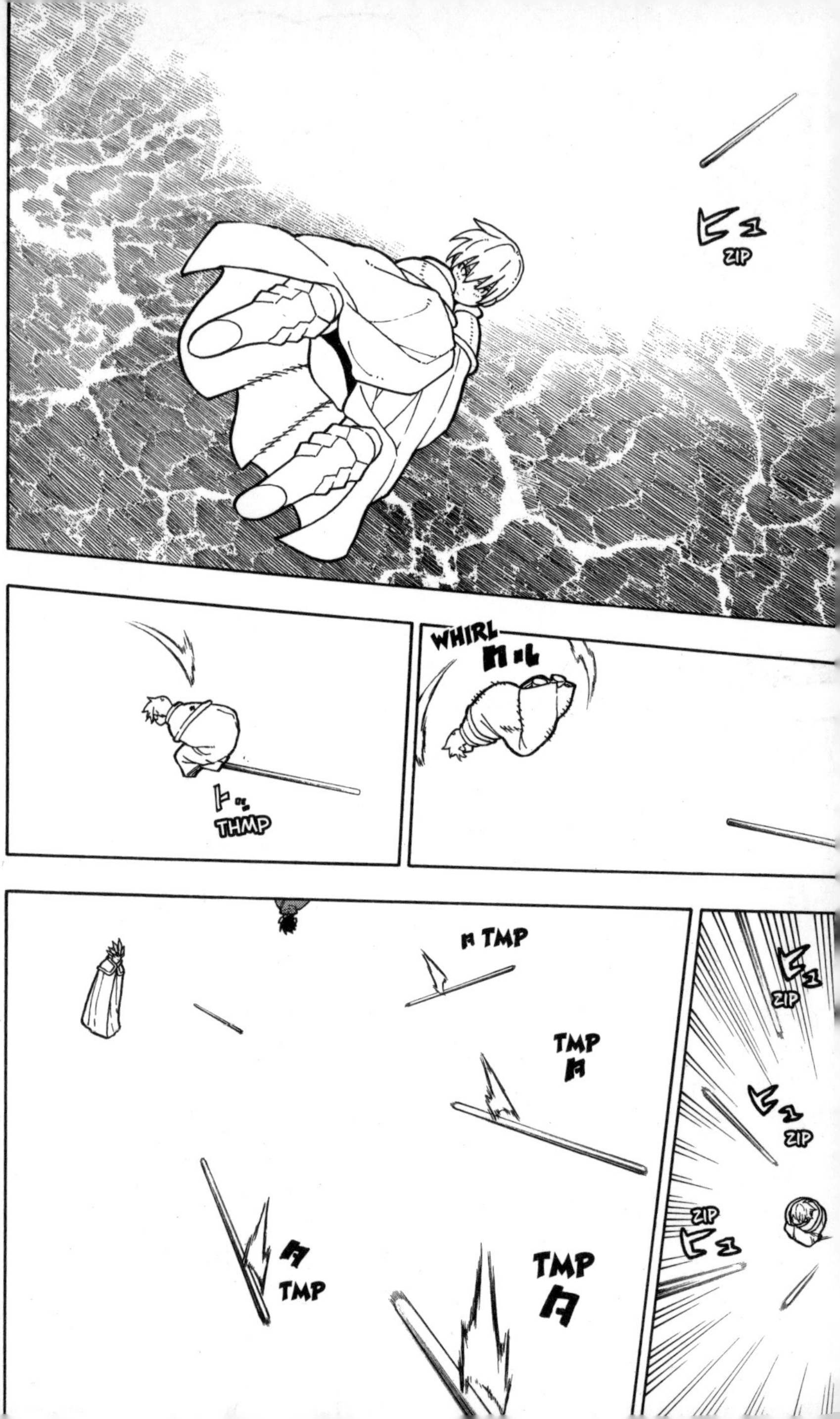
ZIP
WHIRL
THMP
ZIP
ZIP
ZIP
TMP
TMP
TMP
TMP

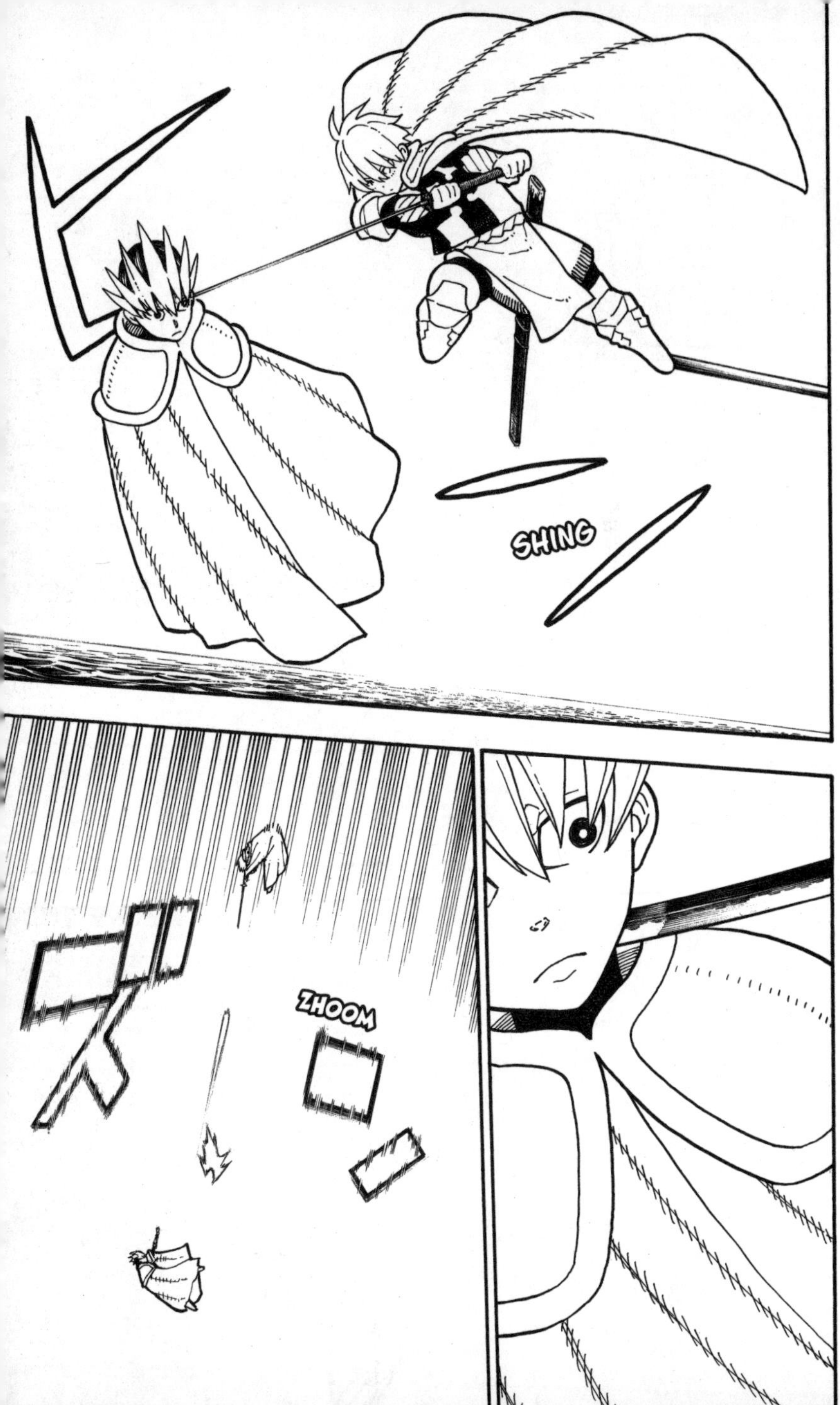
SHING
ZHOOM

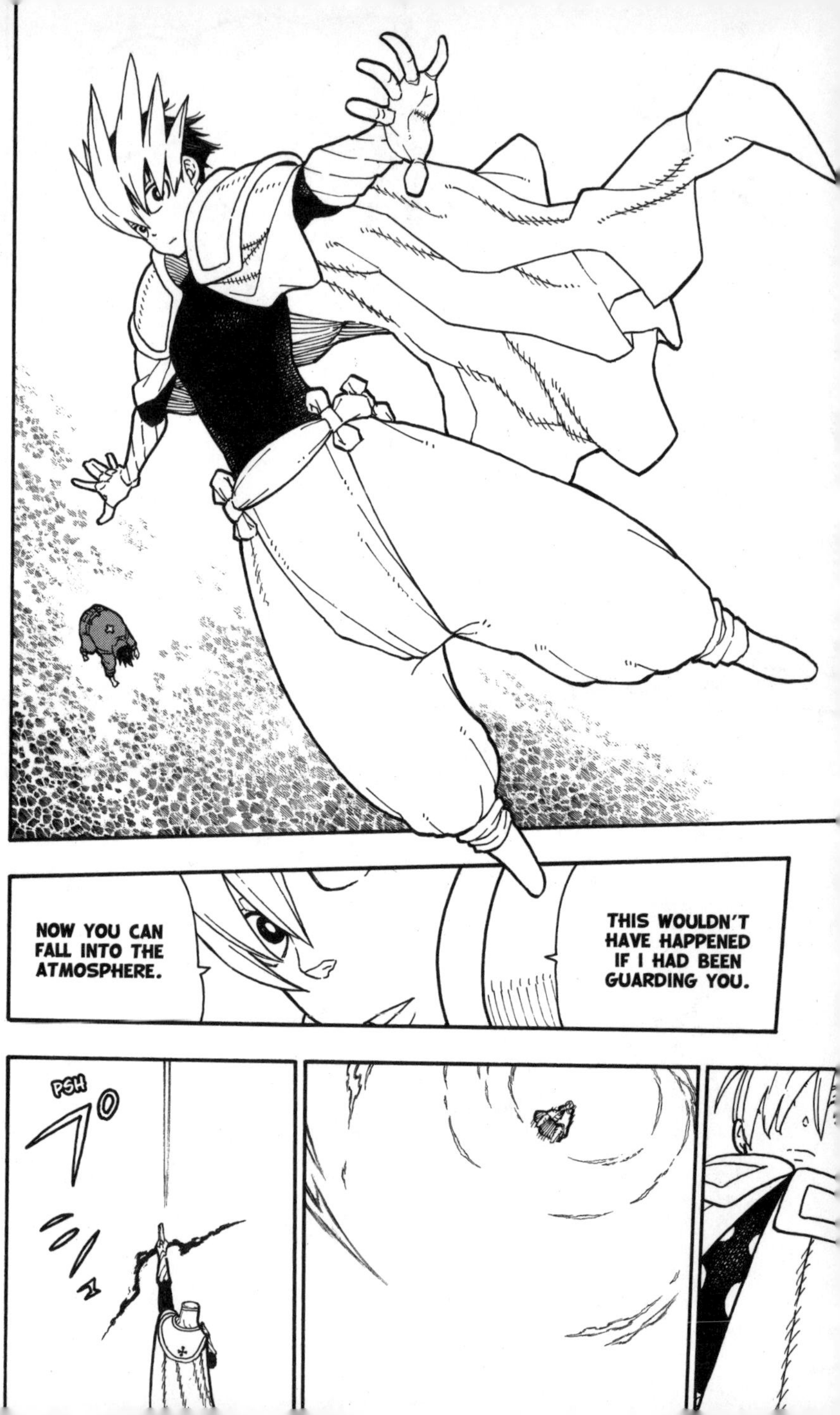
THIS WOULDN'T HAVE HAPPENED IF I HAD BEEN GUARDING YOU.
NOW YOU CAN FALL INTO THE ATMOSPHERE.
PSH

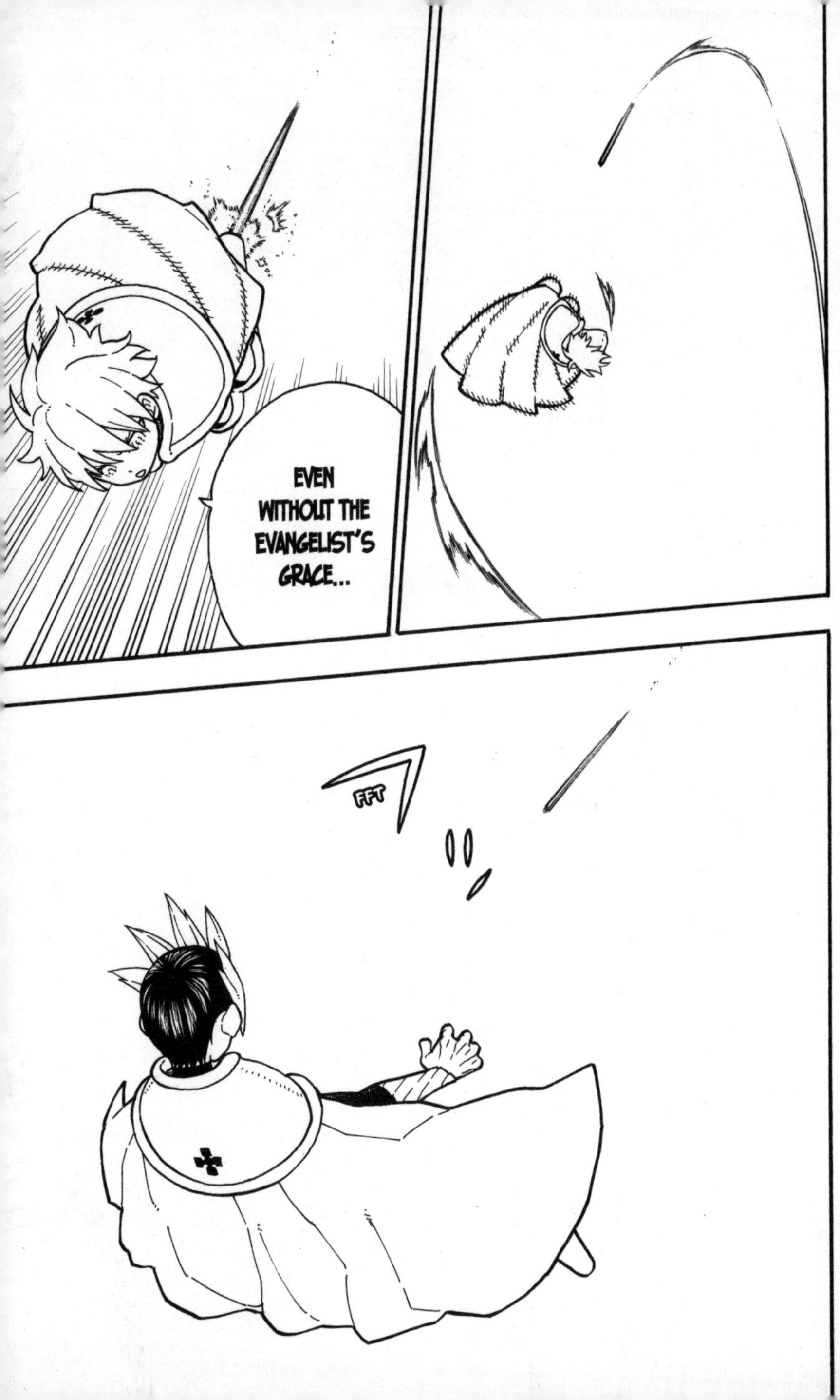
EVEN WITHOUT THE EVANGELIST'S GRACE...
FFT

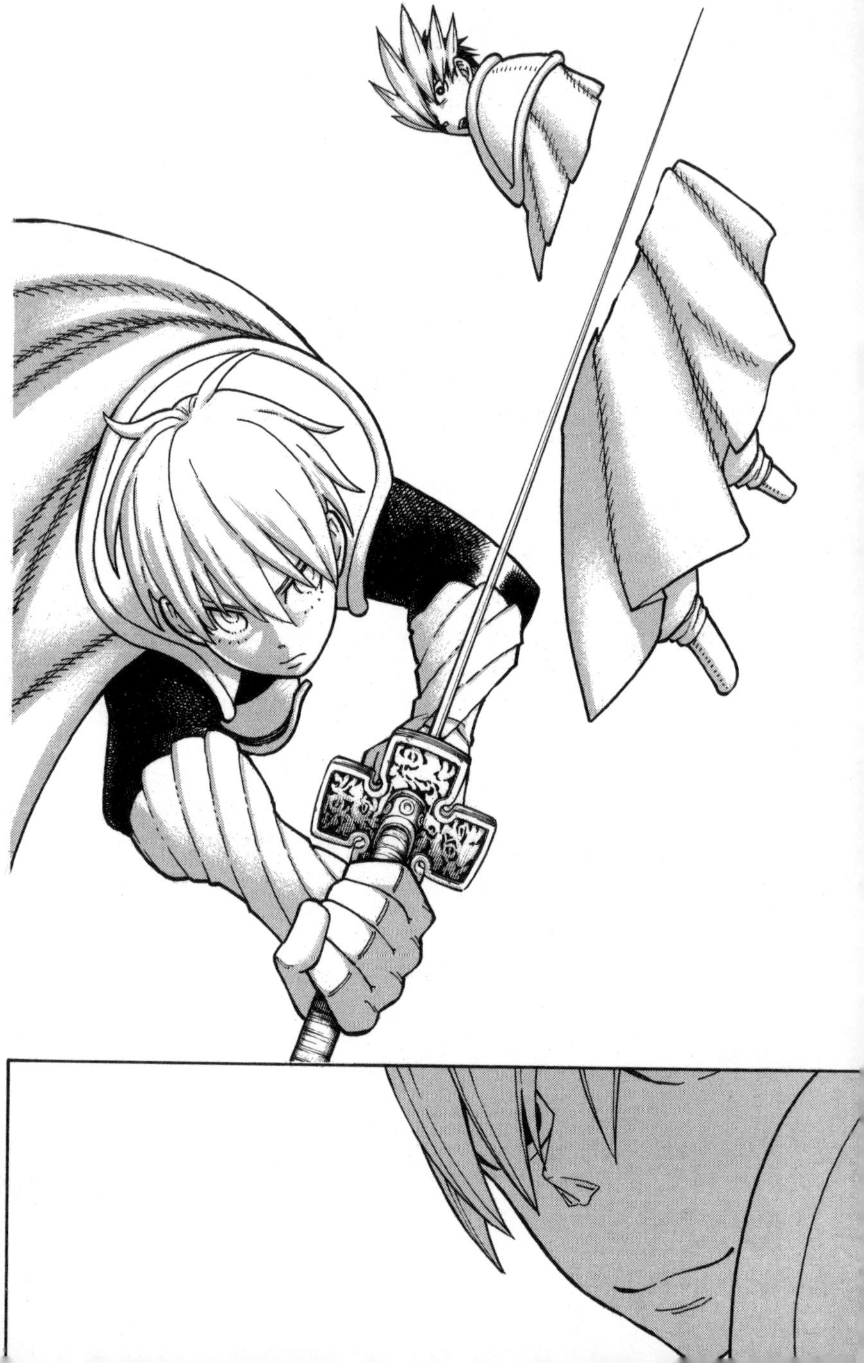

TO BE CONTINUED IN VOLUME 25!!

AFTERWORD MANGA: ATSUSHIYA

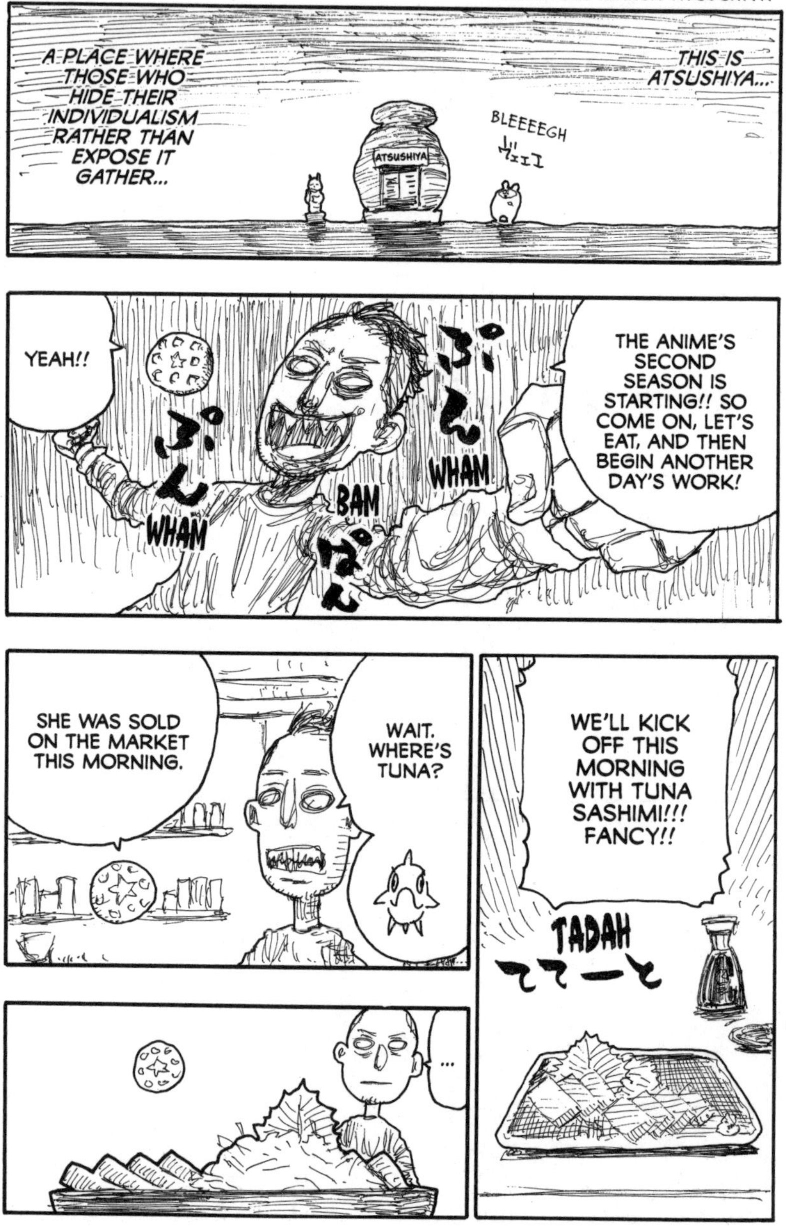
THIS IS ATSUSHIYA...
BLEEEEGH
ATSUSHIYA
A PLACE WHERE THOSE WHO HIDE THEIR INDIVIDUALISM RATHER THAN EXPOSE IT GATHER...
THE ANIME'S SECOND SEASON IS STARTING!! SO COME ON, LET'S EAT, AND THEN BEGIN ANOTHER DAY'S WORK!
WHAM
BAM
WHAM
YEAH!!
WE'LL KICK OFF THIS MORNING WITH TUNA SASHIMI!!! FANCY!!
TADAH
WAIT. WHERE'S TUNA?
SHE WAS SOLD ON THE MARKET THIS MORNING.
...

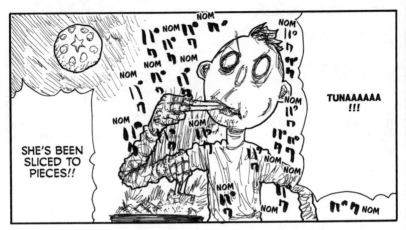

TUNAAAAAA !!!
NOM NOM NOM NOM NOM NOM NOM NOM NOM NOM NOM NOM NOM NOM
SHE'S BEEN SLICED TO PIECES!!
SO TUNA DID IT. SHE DIED.
I'VE BEEN DOING THIS BONUS MANGA SINCE *SOUL EATER,* AND TRADITIONALLY, WHEN ONE OF MY STAFF GETS A CONTRACT TO DO A SERIES, I KILL THEM OFF.
AND WE LEARN THIS ***NOW?!***
OTTER HAS A SERIES, TOO, BUT HE STILL COMES TO HELP SOMETIMES, SO HE'S A ZOMBIE.
BLEEEEEGH
IS ***THAT*** WHAT'S GOING ON!!
YOU'VE PUBLISHED MORE THAN 50 VOLUMES AND YOU FINALLY EXPLAIN THIS ***NOW***?!! WHAT'S GOING ON? ARE YOU DYING?
MAYBE I AM DYING...
EVEN IN DEATH, THE BATTLE RAGES ON.
PLEASE COME AGAIN.

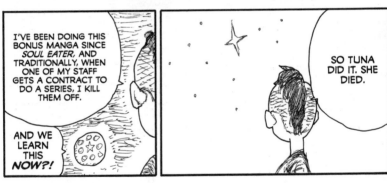

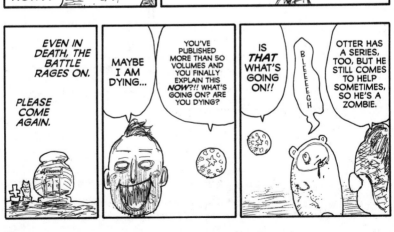

CHARACTER PROFILE

SHINRA KUSAKABE

AFFILIATION: **SPECIAL FIRE FORCE COMPANY 8**
RANK: **SECOND CLASS FIRE SOLDIER**
ABILITY: **THIRD GENERATION PYROKINETIC**
Emits fire from his feet

Height	173cm [5'8"]
Weight	67kg [148lbs.]
Age	17 years
Birthday	October 29
Sign	Scorpio
Bloodtype	AB
Nickname	The Devil's Footprints
Self-Proclaimed	Hero
Favorite Foods	Ramen Hamburgers Fried Chicken
Least Favorite Food	None
Favorite Music	Anything fast and awesome.
Favorite Animal	Leopard Anything fast
Favorite Color	Red
Favorite Type of Girl	Pretty ones
Who He Respects	Commander Ōbi His mother
Who He Has Trouble Around	Pretty girls Arthur
Who He's Afraid Of	The Lieutenant
Hobbies	Soccer Futsal
Daily Workout	Breakdancing
Dream	To become a hero
Shoe Size	27cm [10]
Eyesight	2.0 [20/10]
Favorite Subject	Math
Least Favorite Subject	Language Arts

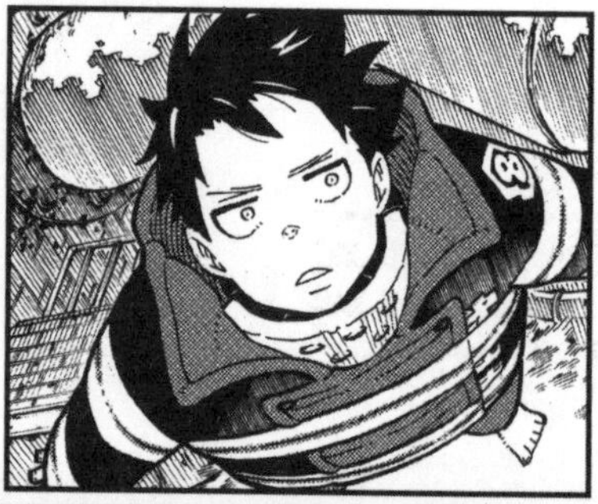

ARTHUR BOYLE

AFFILIATION: **SPECIAL FIRE FORCE COMPANY 8**
RANK: **SECOND CLASS FIRE SOLDIER**
ABILITY: **THIRD GENERATION PYROKINETIC**
Emits a blade of flame from the hilt of his sword

Height	174cm [5'8.5"]
Weight	64kg [141lbs.]
Age	17 years
Birthday	July 10
Sign	Cancer
Bloodtype	A
Nickname	Stupid
Self-Proclaimed	Knight King
Favorite Foods	Court Cuisine (has never had any) The ramen Captain Ōbi buys him
Least Favorite Food	Horse meat sashimi
Favorite Music	Court Music (has never heard any)
Favorite Animal	Horse
Favorite Color	White, Blue
Favorite Type of Girl	A girl who looks good in glass slippers and a tiara
Who He Respects	King Arthur
Who He Has Trouble Around	No one
Who He's Afraid Of	No one
Hobbies	Building model castles
Daily Workout	Sword practice
Dream	To be the Knight King
Shoe Size	26cm [9]
Eyesight	1.5 [20/12.5]
Favorite Subject	Physical Education
Least Favorite Subject	Everything taught in the classroom

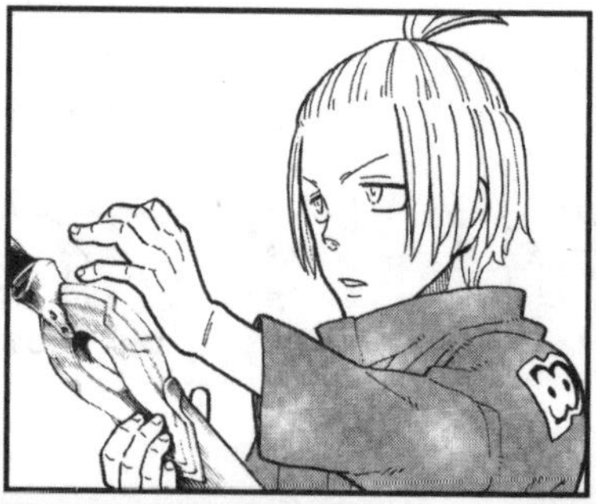

FIRE FORCE

Fire Force 24 is a work of fiction. Names, characters, places, and incidents are the products of the author's imagination or are used fictitiously. Any resemblance to actual events, locales, or persons, living or dead, is entirely coincidental.

Published in the United States by Kodansha Comics, an imprint of Kodansha USA Publishing, LLC, New York.

Publication rights for this English edition arranged through Kodansha Ltd., Tokyo.

First published in Japan in 2020 by Kodansha Ltd., Tokyo.

ISBN 978-1-64651-282-9

Printed in the United States of America.

www.kodansha.us

1st Printing
Translation: Alethea Nibley & Athena Nibley
Lettering: AndWorld Design
Editing: Ryan Holmberg
Kodansha Comics edition cover design by Phil Balsman

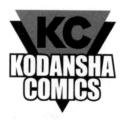

Publisher: Kiichiro Sugawara

Director of publishing services: Ben Applegate
Associate director of operations: Stephen Pakula
Publishing services managing editors: Madison Salters, Alanna Ruse
Production managers: Emi Lotto, Angela Zurlo